Drug Information for Teens

Third Edition

TEEN HEALTH SERIES

Third Edition

Drug Information for Teens

Health Tips about the Physical and Mental Effects of Substance Abuse

Including information about Alcohol, Tobacco, Marijuana, Prescription and Over-the-Counter Drugs, Club Drugs, Hallucinogens, Stimulants, Opiates, Steroids, and More

◆

Edited by Elizabeth Magill

Omnigraphics

P.O. Box 31-1640, Detroit, MI 48231

Bibliographic Note

Because this page cannot legibly accommodate all the copyright notices, the Bibliographic Note portion of the Preface constitutes an extension of the copyright notice.

Edited by Elizabeth Magill

Teen Health Series

Karen Bellenir, *Managing Editor*
David A. Cooke, MD, FACP, *Medical Consultant*
Elizabeth Collins, *Research and Permissions Coordinator*
Cherry Edwards, *Permissions Assistant*
EdIndex, Services for Publishers, *Indexers*

* * *

Omnigraphics, Inc.

Matthew P. Barbour, *Senior Vice President*
Kevin M. Hayes, *Operations Manager*

* * *

Peter E. Ruffner, *Publisher*

Copyright © 2011 Omnigraphics, Inc.

ISBN 978-0-7808-1154-6

Library of Congress Cataloging-in-Publication Data

Drug information for teens : health tips about the physical and mental effects of substance abuse including information about alcohol, tobacco, marijuana, prescription and over-the-counter drugs, club drugs, hallucinogens, stimulants, opiates, steroids, and more / edited by Elizabeth Magill. -- 3rd ed.
   p. cm. -- (Teen health series)
  Includes bibliographical references and index.
  Summary: "Provides basic consumer health information for teens on drug use, abuse, and addiction, along with facts about related health concerns, treatment, and recovery. Includes index, resource information and recommendations for further reading"--Provided by publisher.
  ISBN 978-0-7808-1154-6 (hardcover : alk. paper) 1. Teenagers--Drug use--United States. 2. Teenagers--Alcohol use--United States. 3. Teenagers--Health and hygiene--United States. 4. Drugs--Physiological effect. 5. Drug abuse--United States--Prevention. 6. Alcoholism--United States--Prevention. I. Magill, Elizabeth (Elizabeth A. H.), 1971-
  HV5824.Y68D774 2011
  613.8--dc22

                                                                        2010048932

∞

Table of Contents

Part Three: Tobacco

Part Four: Marijuana

Part Five: Abuse Of Legally Available Substances

Part Six: Abuse Of Illegal Substances

Part Seven: Other Drug-Related Health Concerns

Part Eight: Treatment For Addiction

Part Nine: If You Need More Information

Preface

About This Book

Recent scientific research shows that teenagers' brains are wired in a way that makes them prone to take risks. Because the part of the brain that is responsible for weighing consequences (the prefrontal cortex) is still developing, teenagers sometimes make choices based on their emotions or whims rather than the possible outcome of a situation. This is one reason why some teens experiment with drugs and alcohol. "Most kids don't really 'plan' to use drugs," says Professor Laurence Steinberg of Temple University, "at least not the first time. They are more likely to experiment on the spur of the moment, particularly when influenced by others [peer pressure]." Many factors can influence this impulsive decision: the desire to look cool or have fun, the desire to fit in with a particular group of people, or the desire to escape life's stressors.

Although recent studies show that overall teenage substance use is steadily declining, many teenagers still make the choice to use drugs and alcohol. A recent survey reports that in 2008, 43% of 12th graders admitted drinking an alcoholic beverage in the 30-day period prior to the survey, and 32.4% of 12th graders reported past-year marijuana use. Another survey reports that 1 in 5 teens (19%) admit to abusing a prescription medication at least once in their lives. Adolescent substance use puts teenagers at increased risk for traffic accidents, risky sexual behaviors, and violence. It can also lead to addiction—a chronic condition caused by changes in brain chemistry—which can lead to health challenges during adulthood, including infectious diseases, organ damage, and cancer.

Drug Information for Teens, Third Edition provides updated facts about drug use, abuse, and addiction. It describes the physical and psychological effects of alcohol, marijuana, prescription drugs, inhalants, club drugs, stimulants, and many other drugs and chemicals that are commonly abused. It includes information about drug-related health concerns, such as HIV infection, drug-facilitated rape, depression, and suicide. A section on substance abuse treatment describes care options and provides resources for helping yourself, a family member, or a friend recover from addiction. Resource directories provide contact information for national organizations, hotlines and helplines, and other sources of support.

How To Use This Book

This book is divided into parts and chapters. Parts focus on broad areas of interest; chapters are devoted to single topics within a part.

Part One: General Information About Addiction And Substance Abuse defines substance abuse and addiction and describes the ways in which drugs affect brain chemistry. It also includes material about the social and legal aspects of drugs, including peer pressure, statistics on teen drug use, and the Drug Enforcement Administration's Controlled Substances Act, which categorizes drugs according to their legal status, medicinal qualities, and harmful effects.

Part Two: Alcohol presents facts about alcohol use, abuse, and addiction in teens and their family members. It also discusses alcohol poisoning, statistics on alcohol consumption, and related health concerns.

Part Three: Tobacco presents facts on several forms of tobacco use, including cigarettes, cigars, pipes, smokeless tobacco, and secondhand smoke. Health risks associated with smoking are discussed, including cancer, emphysema, asthma, and bronchitis. Information on the benefits of quitting—and how to quit—is also included.

Part Four: Marijuana presents facts about the health effects of marijuana use, including respiratory disorders, anxiety and depression, and changes in brain chemistry. Information about marijuana abuse among teens and the legal debate over medical marijuana is also included.

Part Five: Abuse Of Legally Available Substances includes facts about the abuse of prescription and over-the-counter medications, including commonly abused pain relievers, sedatives, stimulants, and cold and cough medicines. Information about other legally available substances—such as inhalants, steroids and sports supplements, and caffeine—is also included.

Part Six: Abuse Of Illegal Substances offers basic information about some of the most commonly abused illegal substances, including ecstasy, ketamine, and other club drugs; LSD, PCP, and other hallucinogens; methamphetamine, cocaine, and other stimulants; and heroin and other opiates.

Part Seven: Other Drug-Related Health Concerns covers some important topics that are associated with drug use but not necessarily related to the direct effects of the substances themselves. These include stress and mental illness, drug-facilitated rape, risky sexual behavior, the spread of infectious diseases via drug paraphernalia, violence, and drugged driving.

Part Eight: Treatment For Addiction discusses the principles of treatment, the various types of treatment, and the process of recovery. It offers encouragement for teens who need to seek help themselves and provides tips for helping friends and parents who may have a substance abuse problem.

Part Nine: If You Need More Information includes a directory of national organizations able to provide drug-related information and a directory of places able to provide support services, including hotline and helpline phone numbers. A state-by-state list of referral services will help readers find local information, and a chapter of additional reading presents lists of books, magazines and journals, and web pages that can be used as a starting point for further research.

Bibliographic Note

This volume contains documents and excerpts from publications issued by the following government agencies: Centers for Disease Control and Prevention (CDC); National Cancer Institute (NCI); National Drug Intelligence Center (NDIC); National Institute on Alcohol Abuse and Alcoholism (NIAAA); National Institute on Drug Abuse (NIDA); National Institute of

Mental Health (NIMH); National Youth Anti-Drug Media Campaign; Office of National Drug Control Policy; Substance Abuse and Mental Health Services Administration (SAMHSA); U.S. Army; U.S. Department of Health and Human Services (HHS); U.S. Department of Justice; U.S. Drug Enforcement Administration (DEA); and the U.S. Food and Drug Administration (FDA).

In addition, the document contains copyrighted documents and articles produced by the following organizations: Army Times Publishing Company; Campaign for Tobacco-Free Kids; Helpguide (Center for Healthy Aging); Kaiser Family Foundation; National Campaign to Prevent Teen Pregnancy; March of Dimes; National Council on Alcoholism and Drug Dependence; Marijuana Policy Project; Nemours Foundation; Partnership for a Drug-Free America; and Scholastic.

The photograph on the front cover is from Fotosearch Stock Photography.

Full citation information is provided on the first page of each chapter. Every effort has been made to secure all necessary rights to reprint the copyrighted material. If any omissions have been made, please contact Omnigraphics to make corrections for future editions.

Acknowledgements

In addition to the organizations listed above, special thanks are due to Liz Collins, research and permissions coordinator; Cherry Edwards, permissions assistant; and Karen Bellenir, managing editor.

About the *Teen Health Series*

At the request of librarians serving today's young adults, the *Teen Health Series* was developed as a specially focused set of volumes within Omnigraphics' *Health Reference Series*. Each volume deals comprehensively with a topic selected according to the needs and interests of people in middle school and high school.

Teens seeking preventive guidance, information about disease warning signs, medical statistics, and risk factors for health problems will find answers to their questions in the *Teen Health Series*. The *Series*, however, is not intended to serve as a tool for diagnosing illness, in prescribing treatments, or as a substitute for the physician/patient relationship. All people concerned about medical symptoms or the possibility of disease are encouraged to seek professional care from an appropriate health care provider.

If there is a topic you would like to see addressed in a future volume of the *Teen Health Series*, please write to:

Editor
Teen Health Series
Omnigraphics, Inc.
P.O. Box 31-1640
Detroit, MI 48231

A Note about Spelling and Style

Teen Health Series editors use *Stedman's Medical Dictionary* as an authority for questions related to the spelling of medical terms and the *Chicago Manual of Style* for questions related to grammatical structures, punctuation, and other editorial concerns. Consistent adherence is not always possible, however, because the individual volumes within the *Series* include many documents from a wide variety of different producers and copyright holders, and the editor's primary goal is to present material from each source as accurately as is possible following the terms specified by each document's producer. This sometimes means that information in different chapters or sections may follow other guidelines and alternate spelling authorities. For example, occasionally a copyright holder may require that eponymous terms be shown in possessive forms (Crohn's disease *vs.* Crohn disease) or that British spelling norms be retained (leukaemia *vs.* leukemia).

Locating Information within the *Teen Health Series*

The *Teen Health Series* contains a wealth of information about a wide variety of medical topics. As the *Series* continues to grow in size and scope, locating the precise information needed by a specific student may become more challenging.

To address this concern, information about books within the *Teen Health Series* is included in *A Contents Guide to the Health Reference Series*. The *Contents Guide* presents an extensive list of more than 15,000 diseases, treatments, and other topics of general interest compiled from the Tables of Contents and major index headings from the books of the *Teen Health Series* and *Health Reference Series*. To access *A Contents Guide to the Health Reference Series*, visit www.healthreferenceseries.com.

Our Advisory Board

We would like to thank the following advisory board members for providing guidance to the development of this *Series*:

Dr. Lynda Baker, Associate Professor of Library and Information Science, Wayne State University, Detroit, MI

Nancy Bulgarelli, William Beaumont Hospital Library, Royal Oak, MI

Karen Imarisio, Bloomfield Township Public Library, Bloomfield Township, MI

Karen Morgan, Mardigian Library, University of Michigan-Dearborn, Dearborn, MI

Rosemary Orlando, St. Clair Shores Public Library, St. Clair Shores, MI

Medical Consultant

Medical consultation services are provided to the *Teen Health Series* editors by David A. Cooke, M.D., F.A.C.P. Dr. Cooke is a graduate of Brandeis University, and he received his M.D. degree from the University of Michigan. He completed residency training at the University of Wisconsin Hospital and Clinics. He is board-certified in internal medicine. Dr. Cooke currently works as part of the University of Michigan Health System and practices in Ann Arbor, MI. In his free time, he enjoys writing, science fiction, and spending time with his family.

Part One

General Information About Addiction And Substance Abuse

Chapter 1

The Science Of Addiction

What Brain Research Tells Us About Drug Addiction

How serious is drug addiction? According to the National Institute on Drug Abuse (NIDA), drug addiction is "a chronic, relapsing disease, characterized by compulsive drug seeking and use, and by neurochemical and molecular changes in the brain." Like other chronic diseases, drug addiction can seriously impair the functioning of the body's organs. Addiction also increases the risk of contracting other diseases, such as HIV and viral hepatitis, among those who share needles and those who engage in risky sexual behaviors stemming from drug-impaired judgment.

Drug addiction often results from drug abuse, which is the use of illegal drugs or the inappropriate use of legal drugs to produce pleasure, to alleviate stress, or to alter or avoid reality (or all three). Risk factors for addiction and protective factors against it (see Table 1.1) can be environmental as well as genetic. Scientists estimate that genetic factors, including environmental effects on these genes, account for between 40 and 60 percent of a person's vulnerability to addiction. Recent research has begun to uncover which genes make a person more vulnerable, which genes protect a person against addiction, and how one's genes and environment interact. There is also evidence that individuals with mental disorders have a much greater risk of drug abuse and addiction than the general population.

About This Chapter: This article originally appeared in a Heads Up compilation from Scholastic and the National Institute on Drug Abuse. NIH Publication No. HURN07-05SC, 2007.

What Is Addiction?

- **Addiction is a complex disease.** No single factor can predict who will become addicted to drugs. Addiction is influenced by a tangle of factors involving one's genes, environment, and age of first use.

- **Addiction is a developmental disease.** It usually begins in adolescence, even childhood, when the brain is continuing to undergo changes. The prefrontal cortex—located just behind the forehead—governs judgment and decision-making functions and is the last part of the brain to develop. This fact may help explain why teens are prone to risk-taking, and why they are also particularly vulnerable to drug abuse. It also explains why exposure to drugs during the teen years may affect the likelihood of someone becoming an addict in the future.

- **Prevention and early intervention work best in the teen years.** Because the teen brain is still developing, it may be more receptive to interventions to alter the course of addiction. Research has shown many risk factors that lead to drug abuse and addiction: mental illness, physical or sexual abuse, aggressive behavior, academic problems, poor social skills, and poor parent-child relations. This knowledge, combined with better understanding of how the teen brain works, can be applied to prevent drug abuse from starting or to intervene early to stop it when warning signs emerge.

Table 1.1. An Individual's Risk And Protective Factors For Drug Addiction

Risk Factors	Influencers	Protective Factors
Early Aggressive Behavior	Self	Self-Control
Lack of Parental Supervision	Family	Parental Monitoring
Substance Abuse	Peers	Academic Competence
Drug Availability	School	Anti-Drug Use Policies
Poverty	Community	Strong Neighborhood Attachment

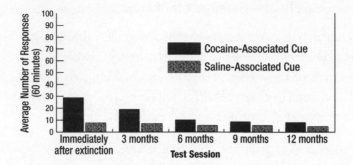

Figure 1.1. One Time Drug Use Can Set Stage For Relapse. *In this experiment, rats pressed a lever in response to a cue (white noise) that had originally indicated access to cocaine even a year after the cue stopped being associated with drug availability. This is because there is a very strong association in the brain between the drug experience and the setting of the drug experience. Even a long-dormant craving may be triggered simply by encountering people, places, and things that were present during a previous drug usage—another reason never to use drugs of abuse even once.*

Prevention Resources

- NIDA and other organizations have spearheaded a number of programs to help prevent addiction, including:

  - **Family-Based:** Teaching parents better communication skills, appropriate discipline styles, and firm and consistent rule enforcement

  - **School-Based:** Building young people's skills in the areas of peer relationships, self-control, coping, and drug refusal

  - **Community-Based:** Working with civic, religious, law enforcement, and government organizations to strengthen anti-drug norms and pro-social behaviors

- For more information on effective prevention programs, visit: www.nida.nih.gov/drugpages/prevention.html.

- For more information on healthy effects of drugs and on effective prevention and treatment approaches based on addiction research, visit NIDA at www.drugabuse.gov and www.teens.drugabuse.gov.

Latest Research: The Science Of "Dread"

New research shows that people who substantially dread an adverse experience have a different biology than those who better tolerate the experience. Dr. Gregory Berns of Emory University School of Medicine and his colleagues used MRI imaging to observe brain activity patterns in non-drug abusers who were awaiting brief electrical shocks (the adverse experience).

The subjects were given the option of a larger shock to occur in a shorter period of time, or a smaller shock after a longer period of time. The scientists noted two groups: "extreme dreaders," who could not tolerate a delay and preferred an immediate (and stronger) painful stimulus; and "mild dreaders," who could tolerate a delay for a milder shock. The findings suggest that dread derives, in part, from attention—and is not simply a fear or anxiety reaction.

Continuing to use drugs despite expecting a bad outcome is a hallmark of addiction. The results of this study form the foundation for future research to determine whether drug abusers exhibit disruption in the brain systems that process "dread"—the anticipation of unpleasant consequences.

Chapter 2

Risk Factors For Addiction

Research Shows That A Complex Set Of Biological And Environmental Risk Factors Contributes To Someone's Risk For Drug Addiction

Drug addiction is a complex disease that has serious, harmful effects on a person's health and on his or her social relationships. How does a person become addicted to drugs? The answer is not so simple—no single factor determines whether a person will become addicted to drugs. Drug addiction is defined as a treatable brain disease that makes it difficult to resist drug use. The risk factors that contribute to addiction are biological or environmental, or many different combinations of both types of factors.

Research shows that drug abuse usually begins in adolescence. There are several reasons for this. For one, the parts of the brain that control judgment, self-control, and future planning do not fully mature until young adulthood. As a result, the teen brain is wired for risk-taking and experimenting. Trying new things is part of the process of maturing and developing the brain's ability to evaluate risk and make decisions. Another important reason why drug use frequently begins in adolescence is that teens are often strongly influenced

About This Chapter: From "Do You Know Your Risk for Addiction?" which originally appeared in a Heads Up compilation from Scholastic and the National Institute on Drug Abuse. NIH Publication No. HURN09-07SC, 2009.

by their peers, who may convince them that "everybody's doing it." The good news is that teens can control factors that put them at risk of engaging in harmful behaviors, such as drug abuse. However, in order to do so, teens need to understand what those risk factors are.

Biological Factors

A person's unique biology—his or her genes, age, gender, and other factors—plays a role in his or her risk of experimenting with drugs and becoming addicted. Biological factors that can contribute to someone's risk for drug abuse and addiction include:

Genetics: You may have heard that drug and alcohol addiction can run in families. This is true, but just because someone in your family has struggled with addiction does not mean that you are destined to do the same. However, having a family member who has experienced addiction does mean that a person may be at increased risk of becoming addicted if he or she chooses to take drugs in the first place. Genes, combined with other factors, are estimated to contribute about 40 percent–60 percent of the risk for drug addiction.

Developmental Stage: Research shows that the earlier a person begins to use drugs, the greater the risk for addiction later in life. There are likely many reasons for this, but one is that the human brain undergoes dramatic changes during adolescence, which continue into early adulthood. Teens' brains are especially at risk because they are still maturing. Drugs exert long-lasting influences on a developing brain that can increase a person's vulnerability to later drug abuse and addiction.

✎ What's It Mean?

Drug Addiction: A chronic and relapsing, yet treatable, brain disease characterized by compulsive drug seeking and use, despite negative or harmful consequences. Drug addiction is considered a brain disease because drugs change the structure of the brain, as well as how the brain works. It is similar to other diseases, such as heart disease, in that it disrupts the normal, healthy functioning of the organ (the brain). Like other diseases, drug addiction can have serious harmful consequences, but it is also preventable and treatable.

Source: NIH Publication No. HURN09-07SC, 2009.

♣ It's A Fact!!
The Role Of Genes In Drug Addiction

The disease known as drug addiction shares many features with other chronic illnesses—one of which is heritability, meaning a tendency to run in families. Scientists are now studying how genes can play a role in making a person vulnerable to drug addiction, or in protecting a person against drug addiction.

While the environment a person grows up in, along with a person's behavior, influences whether he or she becomes addicted to drugs, genes play a key role as well. Scientists estimate that genetic factors account for 40 to 60 percent of a person's vulnerability to addiction.

The National Institute on Drug Abuse (NIDA) is currently supporting a major research effort to identify gene variations that make a person vulnerable to drug addiction. This effort involves studying DNA (deoxyribonucleic acid), which directs the development of every human cell (Figure 2.1). By mapping DNA sequences in drug addicts, scientists have been able to isolate gene sequences that indicate a greater risk of becoming addicted to drugs. These gene sequences contain the instructions for producing specific proteins, which perform most of a body's life functions. The way these proteins function, or don't function, can indicate how vulnerable a person is to drug addiction.

Figure 2.1. DNA: The Molecule Of Life. *A cell is the fundamental working unit of any living organism. All the instructions needed for a cell to carry out its activities are contained in the cell's DNA (deoxyribonucleic acid). These instructions are spelled out by the side-by-side arrangement of bases along a strand of DNA (for example, TTCCGGA). The specific sequences are known as genes, which contain the coded instructions on how to make proteins. All living organisms are composed largely of proteins, which perform most of a body's life functions.*

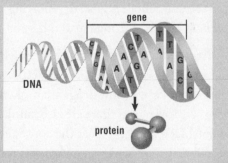

Source: Excerpted from "The Role Of Genes In Drug Addiction," which originally appeared in a Heads Up compilation from Scholastic and the National Institute on Drug Abuse. NIH Publication No. HURN07-05SC, 2007.

Sensitivity To Drugs: Have you ever noticed how some people can drink a caffeinated beverage and it has no effect on them, while others are bouncing off the walls and can't sleep? People have different sensitivities to a drug's effects—in fact, what one person likes, another may hate. These differences affect the likelihood that someone will continue to take drugs and become addicted to them.

Mental Illness: Mental disorders, such as depression, anxiety, attention deficit hyperactivity disorder (ADHD), and others, may put people at greater risk for using drugs and becoming addicted. There are many possible reasons for this increased risk for addiction. One is that some people with mental disorders take drugs because the drugs make them feel better, or they believe the drugs help them deal with their problems. Also, mental disorders affect the same brain circuits and chemicals as do drugs of abuse. The overlapping effects of a mental disorder and a drug may increase the risk for addiction.

Gender: Studies show differences in the way drugs affect male and female bodies, as well as how and why men and women use drugs. For example, women are more likely than men to become addicted to drugs designed to treat anxiety or sleeplessness, while men are more likely than women to abuse alcohol and marijuana. In the past, studies showed that, overall, there was a higher rate of drug use and addiction among men than among women. However, in recent years, this gender gap is closing—current studies show that equal numbers of male and female teens are reporting that they are using drugs. The consequences of this shifting pattern remain to be seen.

Ethnicity: Ethnicity is a factor that has both biological and environmental components. For instance, some ethnic groups show different rates of metabolism of drugs (how drugs are broken down by the body), which can affect drug sensitivity. But there are also cultural factors that influence drug use, and societal factors that impact the consequences of drug use. For example, while overall drug use by African-Americans and Hispanics is lower compared to white Americans, the consequences—such as trouble with the law or risk for disease such as HIV/AIDS—disproportionately affect minorities.

Environmental Factors

Environmental factors are related to a person's surroundings and the influences he or she lives with. Environmental factors that can contribute to someone's risk for drug abuse and addiction include:

✤ It's A Fact!!

A major finding about the genetics of drug addiction was reported in 2004 by investigators at the Howard Hughes Medical Institute at Duke University Medical Center. The researchers were able to identify a specific protein—PSD-95—that had a relationship both to drug addiction and to learning and memory. Mice that had low levels of PSD-95 took longer to learn their way around a maze, and also were much more sensitive to cocaine. The researchers concluded that mice with normal amounts of PSD-95 were more likely to learn their way around the maze and less likely to become addicted to cocaine. Because cocaine leads to sharp increases in the neurotransmitter dopamine, which is responsible for feelings of pleasure, or the high that drug users crave, PSD-95 likely is involved in other types of addiction. According to Marc G. Caron, Ph.D., an investigator who was part of the research team, PSD-95 "likely plays a role in addiction to other drugs—including nicotine, alcohol, morphine, and heroin—because they all exert effects through dopamine."

Figure 2.2. Health Or Disease?
Some variations in a cell's DNA have no negative effect and create normal-functioning proteins (Persons 1 and 2). Other variations (Person 3) can lead to low- or nonfunctioning proteins, which in turn can lead to a particular disease, or to being vulnerable to disease. By studying gene variations in the DNA of a person addicted to drugs, scientists are looking to isolate gene sequences that indicate a person's vulnerability to addiction.

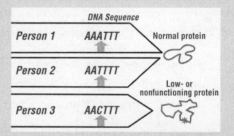

Source: Excerpted from "The Role Of Genes In Drug Addiction," which originally appeared in a Heads Up compilation from Scholastic and the National Institute on Drug Abuse. NIH Publication No. HURN07-05SC, 2007.

Home And Family: The home environment has an important impact on a person's risk for drug abuse and addiction. Teens are at greater risk if they live in chaotic homes where there is little parental or adult supervision. This type of home environment can be the result of parents or older family members who suffer from a mental disorder, engage in criminal behavior, or abuse drugs or alcohol. On the other hand, a nurturing home environment, as well as clear rules of conduct at home, can be protective factors that reduce the potential for drug abuse.

Availability Of Drugs: Research has clearly shown that the availability of drugs in a person's home, school, or community is one of the key risk factors for a person developing drug problems. For example, the abuse of prescription drugs, which has been on the rise for the last several years, is occurring at the same time as a sharp rise in medical prescriptions. This increased availability, combined with a lack of understanding about the dangers of misusing prescription drugs, affects the risk of addiction.

Social And Other Stressors: Stress, and particularly early exposure to stress, is linked to early drug use and later drug problems. For example, stressors such as physical or sexual abuse, or witnessing violence, may contribute to someone's risk of addiction. In addition, poverty is often linked to stress, and to chaotic lifestyles, which may increase the risk of drug abuse. In contrast, involvement in social networks that are supportive, and where disapproval of drug use is the norm, can protect against drug use. These groups might be sports teams, religious groups, or community groups.

Peer Influence: Associating with peers who engage in risky behaviors and who use drugs is another key risk factor, especially for teens. Choosing friends who do not use drugs can protect a person from drug abuse and addiction.

School Performance: Academic failure may be a sign that a teen is currently abusing drugs and is in need of intervention, or it may be a risk factor for later drug abuse. On the other hand, teens who are successful in school, have positive self-esteem, and develop close bonds with adults outside their families (such as teachers) are less likely to abuse drugs.

Chapter 3

How Drugs Affect The Brain

What's that gray, wrinkled blob inside your skull? It's your brain—the body's most amazing organ, a three pound factory for feelings, memories, ideas, and movement. It makes your heart beat, stores the beat to your favorite song, and prompts you to "beat it" when you sense danger. Your muscles may seem smart when you hit a home run or learn a dance step, but every instruction comes from your brain.

Your brain is always changing—and growing. New experiences create new connections between brain cells, adding to a dense web of brain tissue. There's no end to what you can learn: One brain cell, or neuron, can have thousands of connections, or synapses, with other brain cells. Messages zip from neuron to neuron, carrying information to and from your muscles and sense organs, and from brain part to brain part.

Instant Messages—IMs In Your Brain

How do brain cells get their messages across? Messages travel through brain cells, also called nerve cells or neurons, as electricity. Neurons have threadlike fibers called axons that send messages and branches called dendrites that receive them. To make messages jump from cell to cell—when your brain signals your

About This Chapter: From "Meet Your Incredible Brain," by Kathy Kukula, which origi-nally appeared in a Heads Up compilation from Scholastic and the National Institute on Drug Abuse, 2003. Despite the older date of this document, the biological information included still represents current understanding of how drugs affect the brain.

hand to scratch your head, for example—your brain creates chemicals called neurotransmitters. Whenever you think or act, axons release these chemicals. Dendrites have receptors, like custom-made garages, into which each chemical fits. A fatty white coating called myelin covers many axons; it helps messages move quickly, especially along the long axons that connect to muscles.

The Pleasure Center

If you've ever sunk a basket, held hands with someone special, or bitten into a juicy cheeseburger, you may remember the rush of pleasurable feelings those events created. These good feelings are a key to your survival—after all, if you eat well, you'll live longer, and most of us think of eating as a pleasurable experience.

Unlike remembering, say, your history homework, you remember pleasure more quickly because of a chemical called dopamine. Dopamine works in the pleasure center in the middle of your brain.

Once you've had a "feel-good" experience, your brain builds a new path, like a shortcut. That's why you'll start to feel good the next time you just pick up a basketball, smell the cheeseburger, or see your crush in the hall. Your senses send signals, and the dopamine starts flowing. You've wired your brain to repeat what brings good feelings. You smile just thinking about it!

Drugs Fool Your Brain

Different drugs act on the brain in different ways. But all drugs of abuse have one thing in common: they act on the way the brain experiences pleasure. Drugs make people "high" by invading and manipulating the brain's pleasure circuitry. They fool your brain into good feelings that are a reaction to chemicals, instead of to real experiences.

The key word is "fool." Drug abuse can damage the brain's wiring for pleasure, making it unable to function in a healthy, normal way. You can become addicted, meaning that your craving for the feeling you get from a drug will become so strong that you'll risk serious consequences to get it. And your ability to feel pleasure the old-fashioned way—the real way—may be disrupted. Good food, real accomplishments—even true love—may leave you feeling flat.

In addition to damaging the way you process pleasure, drugs can damage your brain and body in many other ways. So don't be fooled. And keep reading to learn more.

♣ It's A Fact!!
Drugs Also Change How The Teen Brain Develops

Scientists recently discovered that drugs do more than change how the limbic system works. Taken during adolescence, drugs actually change how the brain develops. "Recent animal studies provide evidence that drugs affect the developing brain differently than they do the matured brain," says Nora D. Volkow, M.D., director of the National Institute on Drug Abuse (NIDA). In studies sponsored by NIDA, scientists are learning why many adult addicts started using drugs in adolescence. For example, new studies show how vulnerable the teen brain is to nicotine, the highly addictive drug in cigarettes.

- **Here is one example.** Teen smokers are addicted more quickly than adults. Animal studies have shown that teens crave cigarettes after smoking fewer cigarettes than adults. At Duke University in Durham, North Carolina, Dr. Edward Levin and his colleagues introduced nicotine to two groups of rats equivalent in ages to adolescent and adult humans. He found that adolescent rats wanted more nicotine more quickly than adult rats. "This finding suggests that those who begin smoking during adolescence are at greater risk for increased smoking over the long term," writes Dr. Levin.

- **And…teen smokers are more likely to be addicted as adults.** At Duke University, Dr. Levin also found that, compared to rats that never had nicotine, animals that had nicotine as adolescents wanted more as adults. "Self-administration of nicotine during teenage years, when the brain is still developing, may cause some of the developmental processes to proceed inappropriately, in effect sculpting the brains of these adolescents in ways that facilitate the addiction process," writes Dr. Levin.

- **What teens do when they are teens impacts the adult body.** At the University of Miami, researchers Dr. Sari Izenwasser and Dr. Stephanie Collins found that rats that had been exposed to nicotine as adolescents were more sensitive to cocaine as adults, putting them more at risk for cocaine abuse. "This suggests that early nicotine use may create an increased risk of addiction for young people who subsequently use cocaine," writes Dr. Izenwasser.

Source: From an article, "Drug Addiction Is A Disease: Why The Teen Brain Is Vulnerable" in a Heads Up compilation from Scholastic and the National Institute on Drug Abuse, 2005.

Amazing Facts About Your Brain

- When you're born, your brain weighs about a pound. But by age six, it weighs three pounds. What happens? Learning to stand, talk, and walk creates a web of connections in your head—two pounds worth!

- Your brain weight accounts for about two percent of your body weight. But your brain uses 20 percent of your body's oxygen supply and 20 to 30 percent of your body's energy.

- Your brain has about 100 billion neurons. A typical brain cell has from 1,000 to 10,000 connections to other brain cells.

- The right side of your brain controls the left side of your body, and the left side of your brain controls the right side of your body.

- Your brain is full of nerve cells, but it has no pain receptors. Doctors can operate on your brain while you're awake—and you won't feel a thing!

- A message for action travels from your brain to your muscles as fast as 250 miles per hour.

- If you ironed out all the wrinkles in your brain, it would have an area of about two and a half square feet. It feels like soft butter.

Chapter 4

Preventing Drug Abuse

Understanding The Problem

Each year, drug abuse and addiction cost taxpayers nearly $534 billion in preventable health care, law enforcement, crime, and other costs. For the National Institute on Drug Abuse (NIDA), the key word in this assessment is "preventable." The best approach to reducing the tremendous toll substance abuse exacts from individuals, families, and communities is to prevent the damage before it occurs.

Prevention Research— Key Findings Inform Interventions

Today more than ever, science is providing us with the tools we need to better tailor our prevention efforts. Scientists are now poised to capitalize on recent advances in genetics, neuroscience, and developmental biology to create targeted science-based prevention programs that reflect the complexities underlying drug abuse and addiction. Key aspects of our approach take the following into account.

- **Addiction is a complex disease.** No single factor can predict who will become addicted to drugs. Addiction is influenced by a tangle of factors involving genes, environment, and age of first use. Recent advances in genetic research have enabled researchers to begin to uncover which

About This Chapter: From "Drug Abuse Prevention," a research update from the National Institute on Drug Abuse, March 2007.

genes make a person more vulnerable, which protect a person against addiction, and how genes and environment interact.

- **Addiction is a developmental disease.** It usually begins in adolescence or even childhood when the brain continues to undergo changes. The prefrontal cortex—located just behind the forehead—governs judgment and decision-making functions and is the last part of the brain to develop. This may help explain why teens are prone to risk-taking, are particularly vulnerable to drug abuse, and why exposure to drugs at this critical time may affect propensity for future addiction.

- **Prevention and early intervention work best.** The developmental years might also present opportunities for resiliency and for receptivity to intervention that can alter the course of addiction. We already know many of the risk factors that lead to drug abuse and addiction—mental illness, physical or sexual abuse, aggressive behavior, academic problems, poor social skills, and poor parent-child relations. This knowledge, combined with better understanding of the motivational processes at work in the young brain, can be applied to prevent drug abuse from starting or to intervene early to stop it when warning signs emerge.

NIDA Is Moving The Science Of Prevention Forward

Research has described in detail the biological variables and the social circumstances that foster or protect against drug abuse and addiction. Now NIDA has merged these historically separate fields with a new initiative that examines how neurobiology and the social environment interact to affect the likelihood of addiction. The resulting social neuroscience initiative will help us better understand how neurobiological mechanisms and responses—genetic, hormonal, and physiological—underlie, motivate, and guide social behaviors related to abuse and addiction. This perspective may help us understand adolescents' heightened sensitivity to social influences and decreased sensitivity to negative consequences, for example, which make them particularly vulnerable to drug abuse.

Prevention Works!

Over 20 years of research demonstrates that prevention interventions designed and tested to reduce risk and enhance protective factors can help children at every step along their developmental path, from early childhood into young adulthood. NIDA is actively supporting research that strives to help people across the lifespan develop and apply the skills and resources they need to stop problem behaviors before, and after, they begin.

- **Effective prevention principles can be applied.** To guide professionals in helping others, NIDA, in cooperation with prevention scientists, published *Preventing Drug Use among Children and Adolescents: A Research-Based Guide for Parents, Educators, and Community Leaders–Second Edition.* This booklet lists over 20 examples of effective research-based drug abuse prevention programs and is available free on NIDA's website.

- **Prevention programs must "speak" to their audiences**. Two highly successful school programs designed specifically for male (ATLAS) and female (ATHENA) teenage athletes address steroid abuse and other unhealthy behaviors (e.g., drinking and driving). These programs leverage the influence of coaches and peer groups to highlight proper sports nutrition, strength training, and other positive alternatives to using drugs to improve performance and build confidence. ATLAS and ATHENA have now been adopted by schools in 29 states and Puerto Rico, and endorsed by Congress as exemplary prevention programs.

- **Preventing HIV/AIDS is important.** Drug abuse and HIV/AIDS are linked epidemics. Growing recognition that HIV is transmitted not just through sharing of injection drug equipment but also through risky sexual behaviors stemming from drug-impaired judgment led NIDA to create an educational campaign to help young people learn the link between drug use, high-risk behaviors, and HIV transmission.

- **Prevention is cost-effective.** Research has demonstrated that research-based drug abuse prevention programs are cost-effective. Each dollar invested in prevention achieves a savings of up to $7 in areas such as substance abuse treatment and criminal justice system costs, not to mention their wider impact on the trajectory of young lives and their families.

Bringing Science To Communities

To promote widespread use of effective prevention programs, NIDA researchers are now studying them in communities across the United States.

Research focuses on understanding the factors that affect community willingness to adopt evidence-based programs and on developing strategies to overcome obstacles, such as organizational and financial issues. Several large-scale efforts are underway, including the Community Youth Development Study, an innovative "prevention system" that offers assessment tools and technical trainings to communities so they can more accurately identify risk and protective factors for youth drug use and related behavior problems. This system allows communities to select appropriate evidence-based prevention programs based on their particular needs.

Chapter 5

Peer Pressure: Its Influence On Teens And Decision Making

Say you're sitting around with some friends playing video games and someone mentions a particular game that happens to be one of your favorites. "Oh, that game's easy. So not worth the time," one of your friends says dismissively. The others agree. Inwardly, you know that it is a game you happen to enjoy quite a lot but, outwardly, not wanting to debate the issue, you go along with the crowd.

You have just experienced what is commonly referred to as peer pressure. It is probably more accurate to refer to this as peer influence, or social influence to adopt a particular type of behavior, dress, or attitude in order to be accepted as part of a group of your equals ("peers"). As a teen, it's likely you've experienced the effect of peer influence in a number of different areas, ranging from the clothes you wear to the music you listen to.

Peer influence is not necessarily a bad thing. We are all influenced by our peers, both negatively and positively, at any age. For teens, as school and other activities take you away from home, you may spend more time with your friends than you do with your parents and siblings. As you become more independent, your peers naturally play a greater role in your life. Sometimes, though, particularly in emotional situations, peer influence can be hard to

About This Chapter: This article originally appeared in a Heads Up compilation from Scholastic and the National Institute on Drug Abuse, August 2008.

resist—it really has become "pressure"—and you may feel compelled to do something you're uncomfortable with.

What Scientific Research Tells Us About Peer Influence

"There are two main features that seem to distinguish teenagers from adults in their decision making," says Laurence Steinberg, a researcher at Temple University in Philadelphia. "During early adolescence in particular, teenagers are drawn to the immediate rewards of a potential choice and are less attentive to the possible risks. Second, teenagers in general are still learning to control their impulses, to think ahead, and to resist pressure from others." These skills develop gradually, as a teen's ability to control his or her behavior gets better throughout adolescence.

According to Dr. B. J. Casey from the Weill Medical College of Cornell University, teens are very quick and accurate in making judgments and decisions on their own and in situations where they have time to think. However, when they have to make decisions in the heat of the moment or in social situations, their decisions are often influenced by external factors like peers. In a study funded by the National Institute on Drug Abuse (NIDA), teen volunteers played a video driving game, either alone or with friends watching. What the researchers discovered was that the number of risks teens took in the driving game more than doubled when their friends were watching as compared to when the teens played the game alone. This outcome indicates that teens may find it more difficult to control impulsive or risky behaviors when their friends are around, or in situations that are emotionally charged.

The Positive Side

While it can be hard for teens to resist peer influence sometimes, especially in the heat of the moment, it can also have a positive effect. Just as people can influence others to make negative choices, they can also influence them to make positive ones. A teen might join a volunteer project because all of his or her friends are doing it, or get good grades because the social group he or she belongs to thinks getting good grades is important. In fact, friends often encourage each other to study, try out for sports, or follow new artistic interests.

In this way, peer influence can lead teens to engage in new activities that can help build strong pathways in the brain. Neural connections that are weak or seldom used are removed during adolescence through a process called synaptic pruning, allowing the brain to redirect precious resources toward more active connections. This means that teens have the potential, through their choices and the behaviors they engage in, to shape their own brain development. Therefore, skill-building activities—such as those physical, learning, and creative endeavors that teens are often encouraged to try through positive peer influence—not only provide stimulating challenges, but can simultaneously build strong pathways in the brain.

While we are constantly influenced by those around us, ultimately the decision to act (or not to act) is up to us as individuals. So when it comes to decision making, the choice is up to you.

✔ Quick Tip
Ways To Give Drugs The Brush-Off

The Technique: A Simple No. Don't make it a big deal. Be polite.
What To Say: No, thanks.

The Technique: Tell It Like It Is. Be yourself and say it in a language that you're comfortable with.
What To Say: No, thanks. I don't drink or I don't do drugs.

The Technique: Give an Excuse. People make excuses all the time.
What To Say: I have to meet my friend. Or, I'll get kicked off the team.

The Technique: Change the Subject. This can distract people.
What To Say: No, thanks. Hey—did you see that strange outfit Mary was wearing?

The Technique: Walk Away or Leave the Situation. It's common at parties to have a brief interaction, then wander off or leave entirely.
What To Say: Say no, and then walk to another group.

The Technique: The Big Stall. This works with escalating pressure. It doesn't mean you will actually try it later.
What To Say: No, maybe later.

The Technique: The Broken Record. Give one reason, then repeat the reason, but don't get into a debate or argument—it doesn't help.
What To Say: No, thanks—it makes me sick. Repeat it if a person pressures you.

Source: From an article, "A Day In The Life Of A Teen: Decisions At Every Turn," in a Heads Up compilation by Scholastic and the National Institute on Drug Abuse, 2006.

Chapter 6

Drug Use Among U.S. Teens

Since 1975 the Monitoring the Future (MTF) survey has measured drug, alcohol, and cigarette use and related attitudes among adolescent students nationwide. Survey participants report their drug use behaviors across three time periods: lifetime, past year, and past month. For some drugs, daily use is also reported. Initially, the survey included 12th graders only, but in 1991 it was expanded to include 8th and 10th graders. The MTF survey is funded by the National Institute on Drug Abuse (NIDA) and is conducted by the University of Michigan's Institute for Social Research. The 35th annual study was conducted during 2009.

Positive Findings

Cigarette smoking is at its lowest point in the history of the survey on all measures among students in grades 8, 10, and 12. These findings are particularly noteworthy since tobacco addiction is one of the leading preventable contributors to many of our nation's health problems.

Between 2004 and 2009, a drop in past-year use of methamphetamine was reported for all grades, and lifetime use dropped significantly among 8th graders,

About This Chapter: This chapter begins with information from "NIDA InfoFacts: High School and Youth Trends," a publication of the National Institute on Drug Abuse, December 2009. Additional information from the Partnership for a Drug-Free America is cited separately within the text .

from 2.3% to 1.6%. Among 10th and 12th graders, five-year declines were reported for past-year use of amphetamines and cocaine. Among 12th graders, past-year use of cocaine decreased significantly, from 4.4% to 3.4%.

From 2004 to 2009, decreases were observed in lifetime, past-year, past-month, and binge use of alcohol across the three grades surveyed.

In 2009, 12th graders reported declines in use across several survey measures of hallucinogens. Past-year use of hallucinogens and LSD fell significantly, from 5.9% to 4.7% and from 2.7% to 1.9%, respectively; and past-year use of hallucinogens other than LSD decreased from 5.0% to 4.2% among 12th graders.

Attitudes toward substance abuse, often seen as harbingers of change in use, showed many favorable changes. Among 12th graders, perceived harmfulness of LSD, amphetamines, sedatives/barbiturates, heroin, and cocaine increased. Across the three grades, perceived availability of several drugs also decreased.

Areas Of Concern

Marijuana use across the three grades has shown a consistent decline since the mid-1990s. The trend has stalled, however, with prevalence rates remaining steady over the last five years. Past-year use was reported by 11.8% of 8th graders, 26.7% of 10th graders, and 32.8% of 12th graders. Also, perceived risk of regular use of marijuana decreased among 8th and 10th graders, although perceived availability decreased among 12th graders.

From 2008 to 2009, lifetime, past-month, and daily use of smokeless tobacco increased significantly among 10th graders.

Past-year nonmedical use of Vicodin® and OxyContin® increased during the last five years among 10th graders, and remained unchanged among 8th and 12th graders. Nearly one in 10 high school seniors reported nonmedical use of Vicodin; one in 20 reported abuse of OxyContin.

When asked how prescription narcotics were obtained for nonmedical use, 52% of 12th graders said they were given the drugs or bought them from a friend or relative. Additionally, 30% reported receiving a prescription for them, and a negligible number of 12th graders reported purchasing the narcotics over the internet.

Table 6.1. Monitoring The Future Study: Trends In Prevalence Of Various Drugs For 8th Graders, 10th Graders, And 12th Graders 2006–2009 (In Percent)*

	8th Graders				10th Graders				12th Graders			
	2006	2007	2008	2009	2006	2007	2008	2009	2006	2007	2008	2009
Any Illicit Drug Use												
Lifetime	20.9	[19.0]	19.6	**19.9**	36.1	35.6	34.1	**36.0**	48.2	46.8	47.4	**46.7**
Past Year	14.8	[13.2]	14.1	**14.5**	28.7	28.1	26.9	**29.4**	36.5	35.9	36.6	**36.5**
Past Month	8.1	7.4	7.6	**8.1**	16.8	16.9	15.8	**17.8**	21.5	21.9	22.3	**23.3**
Marijuana/Hashish												
Lifetime	15.7	14.2	14.6	**15.7**	31.8	31.0	29.9	**32.3**	42.3	41.8	42.6	**42.0**
Past Year	11.7	[10.3]	10.9	**11.8**	25.2	24.6	23.9	**26.7**	31.5	31.7	32.4	**32.8**
Past Month	6.5	5.7	5.8	**6.5**	14.2	14.2	13.8	**15.9**	18.3	18.8	19.4	**20.6**
Daily	1.0	0.8	0.9	**1.0**	2.8	2.8	2.7	**2.8**	5.0	5.1	5.4	**5.2**
Inhalants												
Lifetime	16.1	15.6	15.7	**14.9**	13.3	13.6	12.8	**12.3**	11.1	10.5	9.9	**9.5**
Past Year	9.1	8.3	8.9	**8.1**	6.5	6.6	5.9	**6.1**	4.5	3.7	3.8	**3.4**
Past Month	4.1	3.9	4.1	**3.8**	2.3	2.5	2.1	**[2.2]**	1.5	1.2	1.4	**1.2**
Hallucinogens												
Lifetime	3.4	3.1	3.3	**3.0**	6.1	6.4	5.5	**6.1**	8.3	8.4	8.7	**7.4**
Past Year	2.1	1.9	2.1	**1.9**	4.1	4.4	3.9	**4.1**	4.9	5.4	5.9	**[4.7]**
Past Month	0.9	1.0	0.9	**0.9**	1.5	1.7	1.3	**1.4**	1.5	1.7	[2.2]	**[1.6]**

Table 6.1. *Continued*

	8th Graders				10th Graders				12th Graders			
	2006	2007	2008	2009	2006	2007	2008	2009	2006	2007	2008	2009
LSD												
Lifetime	1.6	1.6	1.9	**1.7**	2.7	3.0	2.6	**3.0**	3.3	3.4	4.0	**3.1**
Past Year	0.9	1.1	1.3	**1.1**	1.7	1.9	1.8	**1.9**	1.7	2.1	2.7	**[1.9]**
Past Month	0.4	0.5	0.5	**0.5**	0.7	0.7	0.7	**0.5**	0.6	0.6	[1.1]	**[0.5]**
Cocaine												
Lifetime	3.4	3.1	3.0	**2.6**	4.8	5.3	4.5	**4.6**	8.5	7.8	7.2	**[6.0]**
Past Year	2.0	2.0	1.8	**1.6**	3.2	3.4	3.0	**2.7**	5.7	5.2	4.4	**[3.4]**
Past Month	1.0	0.9	0.8	**0.8**	1.5	1.3	1.2	**[0.9]**	2.5	[2.0]	1.9	**[1.3]**
Crack Cocaine												
Lifetime	2.3	2.1	2.0	**1.7**	2.2	2.3	2.0	**2.1**	3.5	3.2	2.8	**2.4**
Past Year	1.3	1.3	1.1	**1.1**	1.3	1.3	1.3	**1.2**	2.1	1.9	[1.6]	**1.3**
Past Month	0.6	0.6	0.5	**0.5**	0.7	[0.5]	0.5	**0.4**	0.9	0.9	0.8	**0.6**
Heroin												
Lifetime	1.4	1.3	1.4	**1.3**	1.4	1.5	[1.2]	**[1.5]**	1.4	1.5	1.3	**1.2**
Past Year	0.8	0.8	0.9	**0.7**	0.9	0.8	0.8	**0.9**	0.8	0.9	0.7	**0.7**
Past Month	0.3	0.4	0.4	**0.4**	0.5	0.4	0.4	**0.4**	0.4	0.4	0.4	**0.4**

Table 6.1. Continued

	8th Graders				10th Graders				12th Graders			
	2006	2007	2008	2009	2006	2007	2008	2009	2006	2007	2008	2009
Tranquilizers												
Lifetime	4.3	3.9	3.9	**3.9**	7.2	7.4	6.8	**7.0**	10.3	9.5	8.9	**9.3**
Past Year	2.6	2.4	2.4	**2.6**	5.2	5.3	4.6	**5.0**	6.6	6.2	6.2	**6.3**
Past Month	1.3	1.1	1.2	**1.2**	2.4	2.6	[1.9]	**2.0**	2.7	2.6	2.6	**2.7**
Alcohol												
Lifetime	40.5	38.9	38.9	**[36.6]**	61.5	61.7	[58.3]	**59.1**	72.7	72.2	71.9	**72.3**
Past Year	33.6	31.8	32.1	**30.3**	55.8	56.3	[52.5]	**52.8**	66.5	66.4	65.5	**66.2**
Past Month	17.2	15.9	15.9	**14.9**	33.8	33.4	[28.8]	**30.4**	45.3	44.4	43.1	**43.5**
Daily	0.5	0.6	0.7	**[0.5]**	1.4	1.4	[1.0]	**1.1**	3.0	3.1	2.8	**2.5**
Cigarettes (any use)												
Lifetime	24.6	[22.1]	20.5	**20.1**	36.1	34.6	[31.7]	**32.7**	47.1	46.2	44.7	**43.6**
Past Month	8.7	[7.1]	6.8	**6.5**	14.5	14.0	[12.3]	**13.1**	21.6	21.6	20.4	**20.1**
Daily	4.0	[3.0]	3.1	**2.7**	7.6	7.2	[5.9]	**6.3**	12.2	12.3	11.4	**11.2**
1/2 pack+/day	1.5	1.1	1.2	**1.0**	3.3	2.7	[2.0]	**2.4**	5.9	5.7	5.4	**5.0**
Smokeless Tobacco												
Lifetime	10.2	9.1	9.8	**9.6**	15.0	15.1	[12.2]	**[15.2]**	15.2	15.1	15.6	**16.3**
Past Month	3.7	3.2	3.5	**3.7**	5.7	6.1	5.0	**[6.5]**	6.1	6.6	6.5	**8.4**
Daily	0.7	0.8	0.8	**0.8**	1.7	1.6	1.4	**[1.9]**	2.2	2.8	2.7	**2.9**

Table 6.1. *Continued*

	8th Graders				10th Graders				12th Graders			
	2006	2007	2008	2009	2006	2007	2008	2009	2006	2007	2008	2009
Steroids												
Lifetime	1.6	1.5	1.4	1.3	1.8	1.8	1.4	1.3	2.7	2.2	2.2	2.2
Past Year	0.9	0.8	0.9	0.8	1.2	1.1	0.9	0.8	1.8	1.4	1.5	1.5
Past Month	0.5	0.4	0.5	0.4	0.6	0.5	0.5	0.5	1.1	1.0	1.0	1.0
MDMA												
Lifetime	2.5	2.3	2.4	2.2	4.5	5.2	4.3	5.5	6.5	6.5	6.2	6.5
Past Year	1.4	1.5	1.7	1.3	2.8	3.5	2.9	3.7	4.1	4.5	4.3	4.3
Past Month	0.7	0.6	0.8	0.6	1.2	1.2	1.1	1.3	1.3	1.6	1.8	1.8
Methamphetamine												
Lifetime	2.7	[1.8]	2.3	[1.6]	3.2	2.8	2.4	2.8	4.4	[3.0]	2.8	2.4
Past Year	1.8	[1.1]	1.2	1.0	1.8	1.6	1.5	1.6	2.5	[1.7]	1.2	1.2
Past Month	0.6	0.6	0.7	0.5	0.7	0.4	[0.7]	0.6	0.9	0.6	0.6	0.5
Vicodin												
Past Year	3.0	2.7	2.9	2.5	7.0	7.2	6.7	8.1	9.7	9.6	9.7	9.7
OxyContin												
Past Year	2.6	1.8	2.1	2.0	3.8	3.9	3.6	5.1	4.3	5.2	4.7	4.9
Cough Medicine (nonprescription)												
Past Year	4.2	4.0	3.6	3.8	5.3	5.4	5.3	6.0	6.9	5.8	5.5	5.9

* Data in brackets indicate a statistically significant change from the previous year.

Cause For Concern:
National Study Shows Reverse In Decade-Long Declines In Teen Abuse Of Drugs and Alcohol

More Teens Using Alcohol, Ecstasy And Marijuana Makes Early Parental Action Even More Critical

After a decade of consistent declines in teen drug abuse, a new national study released today by the Partnership for a Drug-Free America® and MetLife Foundation points to marked upswings in use of drugs that teens are likely to encounter at parties and in other social situations.

According to the 2009 Partnership Attitude Tracking Study, sponsored by MetLife Foundation, the number of teens in grades 9–12 that used alcohol in the past month has grown by 11 percent, (from 35 percent in 2008 to 39 percent in 2009), past year Ecstasy use shows a 67 percent increase (from 6 percent in 2008 to 10 percent in 2009) and past year marijuana use shows a 19 percent increase (from 32 percent in 2008 to 38 percent in 2009). The PATS data mark a reverse in the remarkable, sustained declines in several drugs of abuse among teens: methamphetamine (meth) was down by over 60 percent and past month alcohol and marijuana use had decreased a full 30 percent over the past decade from 1998–2008.

Underlying these increases are negative shifts in teen attitudes, particularly a growing belief in the benefits and acceptability of drug use and drinking. The percentage of teens agreeing that "being high feels good" increased significantly from 45 percent in 2008 to 51 percent in 2009, while those saying that "friends usually get high at parties" increased from 69 percent to 75 percent over the same time period. The Partnership/ MetLife Foundation Attitude Tracking Study (PATS) also found a significant drop in the number of teens agreeing strongly that they "don't want to hang around drug users"—from 35 percent in 2008 to 30 percent in 2009.

"These new PATS data should put all parents on notice that they have to pay closer attention to their kids' behavior—especially their social interactions—and they must take action just as soon as they think their child may be using drugs or drinking," said Steve Pasierb, president and CEO of the Partnership.

Dennis White, president and CEO of MetLife Foundation added that "the earlier parents take steps to address a child's drug or alcohol use, the greater the chance they'll be effective in preventing a serious problem. We need to be sure parents know when it's time to act, and how to act when confronted with a substance abuse situation."

Parents Not Acting Early Enough, Need To Take Immediate Action

The resurgence in teen drug and alcohol use comes at a time when pro-drug cues in popular culture—in film, television and online—abound, and when funding for federal prevention programs has been declining for several years.

This places an even greater burden on parents. Among the parents surveyed for the PATS study, 20 percent say their child (ages 10–19) has already used drugs or alcohol beyond an "experimental" level. Among parents of teens ages 14–19, that percentage jumps to 31 percent, nearly one third.

Disturbingly, among those parents of teens who have used, nearly half (47 percent) either waited to take action or took no action at all—which studies show put those children at greater risk of continued use and negative consequences.

"We're very troubled by this upswing that has implications not just for parents, who are the main focus of the Partnership's efforts, but for the country as a whole," said Partnership Chairman Patricia Russo. "The United States simply can't afford to let millions of kids struggle through their academic and professional lives hindered by substance abuse. Parents and caregivers need to play a more active role in protecting their families, trust their instincts and take immediate action as soon as they sense a problem."

Time To Act: Resource To Help Parents Take Immediate Action, Safeguarding Kids From Drugs And Alcohol

Discovering that a teen is using drugs or drinking is often a frightening experience for parents—many feel alone, ashamed, and confused about what to do next. The Partnership encourages parents of children who are using drugs or alcohol to take action as soon as they suspect or know their child is using and provides parents with free, anonymous access, to the most current, research-based information on how to help their child and their family take the next steps. Developed in collaboration with scientists from the Treatment Research Institute, Time To Act, offers step-by-step advice and compassionate guidance from substance abuse experts, family therapists, scientists and fellow parents to help guide families through the process of understanding drug and alcohol use, confronting a child, setting boundaries, and seeking outside help.

Because research tells us that kids in grades 7–12 who learn a lot about the dangers of drugs from their parents are up to 50 percent less likely to ever use, parents are encouraged to have frequent ongoing conversations with their children about the dangers of drugs and alcohol and take early action if they suspect their child is using or might have a problem. Parent visitors to drugfree.org can learn to talk with their kids about drugs and alcohol and take charge of the conversation with their kids.

No Improvement In Teen Abuse Of Rx And OTC Medicines, Cigarettes, Inhalants, Steroids, Heroin

According to the PATS survey, teen abuse of prescription (Rx) and over-the-counter (OTC) medicines has remained stable with about 1 in 5 teens in grades 9–12 (20 percent) or 3.2 million reporting abuse of a prescription medication at least once in their lives, and 1 in 7 teens (15 percent) or 2.4 million teens reporting abuse of a prescription pain reliever in the past year. Eight percent or 1.3 million teens have reported OTC cough medicine abuse in the past year.

PATS shows more than half or 56 percent of teens in grades 9–12 believe Rx drugs are easier to get than illegal drugs. Also, 62 percent believe most teens get Rx drugs from their own family's medicine cabinets and 63 percent believe Rx drugs are easy to get from their parent's medicine cabinet, up significantly from 56 percent just last year.

Teen smoking rates have remained stable with 25 percent of teens reporting smoking cigarettes in the past month. Teen inhalant use remains steady at 10 percent for past year use, yet only 66 percent of teens report that "sniffing or huffing things to get high can kill you," significantly less than the 70 percent of teens who agreed just last year. Inhalant abuse merits careful monitoring—as attitudes towards inhalant abuse weaken, abuse is more likely to increase. Steroid and heroin use among teens remains low at 5 percent for lifetime use.

The 21st annual national study of 3,287 teens in grades 9–12 and 804 parents is nationally projectable with a +/- 2.3 percent margin of error for the teen sample and +/- 3.5 percent for the parent sample. Conducted for the Partnership and MetLife Foundation by the Roper Public Affairs Division of GfK Custom Research, the 2009 PATS teen study was administered in private, public and parochial schools, while the parents study was conducted through in-home interviews by deKadt Marketing and Research, Inc. For more information or to view the full PATS Report, please visit drugfree.org.

Chapter 7

The Controlled Substances Act

Formal Scheduling

The Controlled Substances Act (CSA) places all substances which were in some manner regulated under existing federal law into one of five schedules. This placement is based upon the substance's medical use, potential for abuse, and safety or dependence liability. The Act also provides a mechanism for substances to be controlled, or added to a schedule; decontrolled, or removed from control; and rescheduled or transferred from one schedule to another. The procedure for these actions is found in Section 201 of the Act (21 U.S.C. 811).

Proceedings to add, delete, or change the schedule of a drug or other substance may be initiated by the Drug Enforcement Administration (DEA), the Department of Health and Human Services (HHS), or by petition from any interested person: the manufacturer of a drug, a medical society or association, a pharmacy association, a public interest group concerned with drug abuse, a state or local government agency, or an individual citizen. When a petition is received by the DEA, the agency begins its own investigation of the drug.

The DEA also may begin an investigation of a drug at any time based upon information received from law enforcement laboratories, state and local law enforcement and regulatory agencies, or other sources of information.

About This Chapter: Information in this chapter is excerpted from "Chapter 1: The Controlled Substances Act," *Drugs of Abuse*, the U.S. Drug Enforcement Administration, U.S. Department of Justice, 2005.

Once the DEA has collected the necessary data, the DEA Administrator, by authority of the Attorney General, requests from HHS a scientific and medical evaluation and recommendation as to whether the drug or other substance should be controlled or removed from control. This request is sent to the Assistant Secretary of Health of HHS. HHS solicits information from the Commissioner of the Food and Drug Administration (FDA), evaluations and recommendations from the National Institute on Drug Abuse, and on occasion from the scientific and medical community at large. The Assistant Secretary, by authority of the Secretary, compiles the information and transmits back to the DEA a medical and scientific evaluation regarding the drug or other substance, a recommendation as to whether the drug should be controlled, and in what schedule it should be placed.

The medical and scientific evaluations are binding on the DEA with respect to scientific and medical matters and form a part of the scheduling decision. The recommendation on the initial scheduling of a substance is binding only to the extent that if HHS recommends that the substance not be controlled, the DEA may not add it to the schedules.

Once the DEA has received the scientific and medical evaluation from HHS, the Administrator will evaluate all available data and make a final decision whether to propose that a drug or other substance should be removed or controlled and into which schedule it should be placed.

The threshold issue is whether the drug or other substance has potential for abuse. If a drug does not have a potential for abuse, it cannot be controlled.

In determining into which schedule a drug or other substance should be placed, or whether a substance should be decontrolled or rescheduled, certain factors are required to be considered. Specific findings are not required for each factor. These factors are listed in Section 201 (c), [21 U.S.C. 811 (c)] of the CSA as follows:

1. The drug's actual or relative potential for abuse.

2. Scientific evidence of the drug's pharmacological effects. The state of knowledge with respect to the effects of a specific drug is, of course, a major consideration. For example, it is vital to know whether or not a

✎ What's It Mean?

Potential For Abuse

Although the term "potential for abuse" is not defined in the CSA, there is much discussion of the term in the legislative history of the Act. The following items are indicators that a drug or other substance has a potential for abuse:

1. There is evidence that individuals are taking the drug or other substance in amounts sufficient to create a hazard to their health or to the safety of other individuals or to the community; or

2. There is significant diversion of the drug or other substance from legitimate drug channels; or

3. Individuals are taking the drug or other substance on their own initiative rather than on the basis of medical advice from a practitioner licensed by law to administer such drugs; or

4. The drug is a new drug so related in its action to a drug or other substance already listed as having a potential for abuse to make it likely that the drug will have the same potential for abuse as such drugs, thus making it reasonable to assume that there may be significant diversions from legitimate channels, significant use contrary to or without medical advice, or that it has a substantial capability of creating hazards to the health of the user or to the safety of the community. Of course, evidence of actual abuse of a substance is indicative that a drug has a potential for abuse.

drug has a hallucinogenic effect if it is to be controlled due to that effect. The best available knowledge of the pharmacological properties of a drug should be considered.

3. The state of current scientific knowledge regarding the substance. Criteria (2) and (3) are closely related. However, (2) is primarily concerned with pharmacological effects and (3) deals with all scientific knowledge with respect to the substance.

4. Its history and current pattern of abuse. To determine whether or not a drug should be controlled, it is important to know the pattern of abuse

of that substance, including the socioeconomic characteristics of the segments of the population involved in such abuse.

5. The scope, duration, and significance of abuse. In evaluating existing abuse, the DEA Administrator must know not only the pattern of abuse, but whether the abuse is widespread. In reaching a decision, the Administrator should consider the economics of regulation and enforcement attendant to such a decision. In addition, the Administrator should be aware of the social significance and impact of such a decision upon those people, especially the young that would be affected by it.

6. What, if any, risk there is to the public health. If a drug creates dangers to the public health, in addition to or because of its abuse potential, then these dangers must also be considered by the Administrator.

7. The drug's psychic or physiological dependence liability. There must be an assessment of the extent to which a drug is physically addictive or psychologically habit forming, if such information is known.

8. Whether the substance is an immediate precursor of a substance already controlled. The CSA allows inclusion of immediate precursors on this basis alone into the appropriate schedule and thus safeguards against possibilities of clandestine manufacture.

After considering the above listed factors, the Administrator must make specific findings concerning the drug or other substance. This will determine into which schedule the drug or other substance will be placed. These schedules are established by the CSA. They are as follows:

Schedule I

- The drug or other substance has a high potential for abuse.

- The drug or other substance has no currently accepted medical use in treatment in the United States.

- There is a lack of accepted safety for use of the drug or other substance under medical supervision.

- Examples of Schedule I substances include heroin, lysergic acid diethylamide (LSD), marijuana, and methaqualone.

Schedule II

- The drug or other substance has a high potential for abuse.

- The drug or other substance has a currently accepted medical use in treatment in the United States or a currently accepted medical use with severe restrictions.

- Abuse of the drug or other substance may lead to severe psychological or physical dependence.

- Examples of Schedule II substances include morphine, phencyclidine (PCP), cocaine, methadone, and methamphetamine.

Schedule III

- The drug or other substance has less potential for abuse than the drugs or other substances in Schedules I and II.

- The drug or other substance has a currently accepted medical use in treatment in the United States.

- Abuse of the drug or other substance may lead to moderate or low physical dependence or high psychological dependence.

- Anabolic steroids, codeine and hydrocodone with aspirin or Tylenol®, and some barbiturates are examples of Schedule III substances.

Schedule IV

- The drug or other substance has a low potential for abuse relative to the drugs or other substances in Schedule III.

- The drug or other substance has a currently accepted medical use in treatment in the United States.

- Abuse of the drug or other substance may lead to limited physical dependence or psychological dependence relative to the drugs or other substances in Schedule III.

- Examples of drugs included in Schedule IV are Darvon®, Talwin®, Equanil®, Valium®, and Xanax®.

Schedule V

- The drug or other substance has a low potential for abuse relative to the drugs or other substances in Schedule IV.

- The drug or other substance has a currently accepted medical use in treatment in the United States.

- Abuse of the drug or other substance may lead to limited physical dependence or psychological dependence relative to the drugs or other substances in Schedule IV.

- Cough medicines with codeine are examples of Schedule V drugs.

When the DEA Administrator has determined that a drug or other substance should be controlled, decontrolled, or rescheduled, a proposal to take action is published in the Federal Register. The proposal invites all interested persons to file comments with the DEA. Affected parties may also request a hearing with the DEA. If no hearing is requested, the DEA will evaluate all comments received and publish a final order in the Federal Register, controlling the drug as proposed or with modifications based upon the written comments filed. This order will set the effective dates for imposing the various requirements of the CSA.

If a hearing is requested, the DEA will enter into discussions with the party or parties requesting a hearing in an attempt to narrow the issue for litigation. If necessary, a hearing will then be held before an Administrative Law Judge. The judge will take evidence on factual issues and hear arguments on legal questions regarding the control of the drug. Depending on the scope and complexity of the issues, the hearing may be brief or quite extensive. The Administrative Law Judge, at the close of the hearing, prepares findings of fact and conclusions of law and a recommended decision which is submitted to the DEA Administrator. The DEA Administrator will review these documents, as well as the underlying material, and prepare his/her own findings of fact and conclusions of law (which may or may not be the same as those drafted by the Administrative Law Judge). The DEA Administrator then publishes a final order in the Federal Register either scheduling the drug or other substance or declining to do so.

Once the final order is published in the Federal Register, interested parties have 30 days to appeal to a U.S. Court of Appeals to challenge the order.

Findings of fact by the Administrator are deemed conclusive if supported by "substantial evidence." The order imposing controls is not stayed during the appeal, however, unless so ordered by the Court.

Emergency Or Temporary Scheduling

The CSA was amended by the Comprehensive Crime Control Act of 1984. This Act included a provision which allows the DEA Administrator to place a substance, on a temporary basis, into Schedule I when necessary to avoid an imminent hazard to the public safety.

This emergency scheduling authority permits the scheduling of a substance which is not currently controlled, is being abused, and is a risk to the public health while the formal rule-making procedures described in the CSA are being conducted. This emergency scheduling applies only to substances with no accepted medical use. A temporary scheduling order may be issued for one year with a possible extension of up to six months if formal scheduling procedures have been initiated. The proposal and order are published in the Federal Register as are the proposals and orders for formal scheduling.

✤ It's A Fact!!
Controlled Substance Analogues

A new class of substances was created by the Anti-Drug Abuse Act of 1986. Controlled substance analogues are substances which are not controlled substances, but may be found in the illicit traffic. They are structurally or pharmacologically similar to Schedule I or II controlled substances and have no legitimate medical use. A substance which meets the definition of a controlled substance analogue and is intended for human consumption is treated under the CSA as if it were a controlled substance in Schedule I.

International Treaty Obligations

United States treaty obligations may require that a drug or other substance be controlled under the CSA, or rescheduled if existing controls are less stringent than those required by a treaty. The procedures for these scheduling actions are found in Section 201 (d) of the Act. [21 U.S.C. 811 (d)] The United States is a party to the Single Convention on Narcotic Drugs of 1961, designed to establish effective control over international and domestic traffic in narcotics, coca leaf, cocaine, and cannabis. A second treaty, the Convention on Psychotropic Substances of 1971, which entered into force in 1976, is designed to establish comparable control over stimulants, depressants, and hallucinogens. Congress ratified this treaty in 1980.

Part Two

Alcohol

Chapter 8

Alcoholism And Alcohol Abuse

[**Editor's Note:** Alcohol consumption by teens is illegal in all 50 of the United States. And, because teens' brains and bodies are still developing, any alcohol consumption by minors can have serious consequences. Some of the text in this chapter, especially information about moderate social drinking, refers exclusively to adults. It is included for information purposes only. Teens should not drink.]

Drinking is woven into the fabric of our society—sharing a bottle of wine over a meal, going out for drinks with friends, celebrating special occasions with champagne. But because alcohol is such a common, popular element in so many activities, it can be hard to see when your drinking has crossed the line from moderate or social use to problem drinking. Alcoholism and alcohol abuse can sneak up on you, so it's important to be aware of the warning signs of a drinking problem and take steps to cut back if you recognize them. And if you or a loved one is already in the throes of an alcohol addiction, take hope. Understanding the problem is the first step to overcoming it.

About This Chapter: "Alcoholism and Alcohol Abuse: Signs, Symptoms, and Help for Drinking Problems," by Melinda Smith, M.A., Joanna Saisan, MSW, and Jeanne Segal, PhD. © 2009 Helpguide.org. All rights reserved. Reprinted with permission. Helpguide provides a detailed list of references and resources for this article, including links to related Helpguide topics and information from other websites. For a complete list of these resources, including information about the effects of alcohol abuse and support for family and friends, go to http://helpguide.org/mental/alcohol_abuse_alcoholism_signs_effects_treatment.htm.

Understanding Drinking Problems

Many people drink regularly without experiencing any harmful effects, other than perhaps a slight hangover on rare occasions. Yet millions of others suffer from alcoholism and alcohol abuse, making even an occasional drink dangerous.

Why can some people drink responsibly, while others drink to the point of losing their health, their family, or their job? There are no simple answers. Drinking problems are due to many interconnected factors, including genetics, how you were raised, your social environment, and your emotional health. People who have a family history of alcoholism or who themselves suffer from a mental health problem such as anxiety, depression, or bipolar disorder are particularly at risk, because alcohol may be used to self-medicate.

Since drinking is so common in our culture and the effects vary so widely from person to person, it's not always easy to figure out where the line is between social drinking and problem drinking. Taking an honest look at why you drink may help you figure out which side of the line you fall on. Remember, though, the bottom line is how alcohol affects you. If your drinking is causing problems in your life, you have a drinking problem.

✔ Quick Tip

What, exactly, is moderate drinking?

Moderate is probably less than you think:

For Women: No more than one drink per day

For Men: Up to two drinks a day

How much is too much?

For Women: More than seven drinks per week or three drinks per occasion

For Men: More than 14 drinks per week or four drinks per occasion

Do You Have A Drinking Problem?

You may have a drinking problem if you...

- Can never stick to "just one" drink.

- Feel guilty or ashamed about your drinking.

- Lie to others or hide your drinking habits.

- Have friends or family members who are worried about your drinking.

- Need to drink in order to relax or feel better.

- Ever "black out" or forget what you did while you were drinking.

- Regularly drink more than you intended to.

Signs And Symptoms Of Alcohol Abuse

Substance abuse experts make a distinction between alcohol abuse and alcoholism (also called alcohol dependence). Unlike alcoholics, alcohol abusers still have at least some ability to set limits on their drinking. However, their alcohol use is still self-destructive and dangerous to themselves or others.

Common signs and symptoms of alcohol abuse include:

- Repeatedly neglecting your responsibilities at home, work, or school because of your drinking. For example, performing poorly at work, flunking classes, neglecting your kids, or skipping out on commitments because you're hung over.

- Using alcohol in situations where it's physically dangerous, such as drinking and driving, operating machinery while intoxicated, or mixing alcohol with prescription medication against doctor's orders.

- Experiencing repeated legal problems on account of your drinking. For example, getting arrested for driving under the influence or drunk and disorderly conduct.

- Continuing to drink even though your alcohol use is causing problems in your relationships. Getting drunk with your buddies, for example, even though you know your wife will be very upset, or fighting with your family because they dislike how you act when you drink.

✤ It's A Fact!!
The Path From
Alcohol Abuse To Alcoholism

Not all alcohol abusers become full-blown alcoholics, but it is certainly a big risk factor. Sometimes alcoholism develops suddenly in response to a stressful change, such as a breakup, retirement, or another loss. Other times, it gradually creeps up on you as your tolerance to alcohol increases. If you're a binge drinker or you drink every day, the risks of developing alcoholism are even greater. But whether or not alcohol abuse turns into alcohol addiction, many of the problems will be the same.

Signs And Symptoms Of Alcoholism (Alcohol Dependence)

Alcoholism is the most severe form of problem drinking. Alcoholism involves all the symptoms of alcohol abuse, but it also involves another element: physical dependence on alcohol. There's a fine line between alcohol abuse and alcoholism, but if you rely on alcohol to function or feel physically compelled to drink, you've crossed it.

Tolerance: The First Major Warning Sign Of Alcoholism

Do you have to drink a lot more than you used to in order to get buzzed? Can you drink more than other people without getting drunk? These are signs of tolerance, the first warning sign of alcoholism. Tolerance means that, over time, you need more and more alcohol to feel the same effects you used to with smaller amounts.

Withdrawal: The Second Major Warning Sign Of Alcoholism

Do you need a drink to steady the shakes in the morning? Drinking to relieve or avoid withdrawal symptoms is a sign of alcoholism and a huge red flag. When you drink heavily, your body gets used to the alcohol and experiences withdrawal symptoms if it's taken away. Alcohol withdrawal symptoms include:

- Anxiety or jumpiness
- Nausea and vomiting
- Irritability
- Headache
- Shakiness or trembling
- Insomnia
- Fatigue
- Sweating
- Depression
- Loss of appetite

In severe cases, withdrawal from alcohol can also involve hallucinations, confusion, seizures, fever, and agitation. These symptoms can be dangerous, so talk to your doctor if you are a heavy drinker and want to quit.

Other Signs And Symptoms Of Alcoholism (Alcohol Dependence)

- **You've lost control over your drinking.** You often drink more alcohol than you wanted to, for longer than you intended, or despite telling yourself you wouldn't.

- **You want to quit drinking, but you can't.** You have a persistent desire to cut down or stop your alcohol use, but your efforts to quit have been unsuccessful.

- **You have given up other activities because of alcohol.** You're spending less time on activities that used to be important to you (hanging out with family and friends, going to the gym, pursuing your hobbies) because of your alcohol abuse.

- **Alcohol takes up a great deal of your energy and focus.** You spend a lot of time drinking, thinking about it, or recovering from its effects. Often, drinking is the center of your social life.

- **You drink even though you know it's causing problems.** For example, you recognize that your alcohol abuse is damaging your marriage, making your depression worse, or causing health problems, but you continue to drink anyway.

Drinking Problems And Denial

Denial is one of the biggest obstacles to getting help for alcohol abuse and alcoholism. The desire to drink is so strong that the mind finds many ways to rationalize drinking, even when the consequences are obvious. Unfortunately, denial often increases as drinking gets worse. And by keeping you from looking honestly at your behavior and its negative effects, denial also exacerbates alcohol-related problems with work, finances, and relationships. It's a vicious cycle.

If you have a drinking problem, you may deny it by:

- Drastically underestimating how much you drink
- Downplaying the negative consequences of your drinking
- Complaining that family and friends are exaggerating the problem
- Blaming your drinking or drinking-related problems on others

For example, you may blame an "unfair boss" for trouble at work or a "nagging wife" for your marital issues, rather than look at how your drinking is contributing to the problem. While work, relationship, and financial stresses happen to everyone, an overall pattern of deterioration and blaming others may be a sign of trouble.

If, once again, you find yourself rationalizing your drinking habits, lying about them, or refusing to discuss the subject, take a moment to consider why you're so defensive. If you truly believe you don't have a problem, why do you feel the need to cover up your drinking or make excuses? Is it possible that your drinking means more to you than you're ready to admit?

Five Myths About Alcoholism

Getting to the truth behind the myths that you may be using to justify your drinking is crucial to breaking down the wall of denial.

Myth #1: I can stop drinking anytime I want to. Maybe you can; more likely, you can't. Either way, it's just an excuse to keep drinking. The truth is, you don't want to stop. Telling yourself you can quit makes you feel in control, despite all evidence to the contrary and no matter the damage it's doing.

Myth #2: My drinking is my problem. I'm the one it hurts, so no one has the right to tell me to stop. It's true that the decision to quit drinking is ultimately up to you. But you are deceiving yourself if you think that your drinking hurts no one else but you. Alcoholism affects everyone around you—especially the people closest to you. Your problem is their problem.

Myth #3: I don't drink every day, so I can't be an alcoholic OR I only drink wine or beer, so I can't be an alcoholic. Alcoholism isn't defined by what you drink, when you drink it, or even, to some extent, how much you drink. If your drinking is causing problems in your life, you may be an alcoholic and you definitely have a drinking problem—whether you drink daily or only on the weekends, down shots of tequila or stick to wine, have three drinks a day or three bottles.

Myth #4: I'm not an alcoholic because I have a job and I'm doing okay. You don't have to be homeless and drinking out of a brown paper bag to be an alcoholic. Many alcoholics are able to hold down jobs, get through school, and provide for their families. Some are even able to excel. But just because you're a high-functioning alcoholic doesn't mean you're not putting yourself or others in danger. Over time, the effects will catch up with you.

Myth #5: Drinking is not a "real" addiction like drug abuse. Alcohol is a drug, and alcoholism is every bit as damaging as drug addiction. Alcohol addiction causes changes in the body and brain, and long-term alcohol abuse can have devastating effects on your health, your career, and your relationships. Alcoholics go through physical withdrawal when they stop drinking, just like drug users do when they quit.

Chapter 9

Underage Drinking Statistics

Alcohol use by persons under age 21 years is a major public health problem. Alcohol is the most commonly used and abused drug among youth in the United States, more than tobacco and illicit drugs. Although drinking by persons under the age of 21 is illegal, people aged 12 to 20 years drink 11% of all alcohol consumed in the United States. More than 90% of this alcohol is consumed in the form of binge drinks. On average, underage drinkers consume more drinks per drinking occasion than adult drinkers. In 2008, there were approximately 190,000 emergency room visits by persons under age 21 for injuries and other conditions linked to alcohol.

Drinking Levels Among Youth

The 2009 Youth Risk Behavior Survey found that among high school students, during the past 30 days the following percentages had experiences involving alcohol:

- 42% drank some amount of alcohol

- 24% binge drank

- 10% drove after drinking alcohol

- 28% rode with a driver who had been drinking alcohol

About This Chapter: Information in this chapter is from "Underage Drinking," a fact sheet from the Centers for Disease Control and Prevention, July 2010.

Other national surveys report additional facts:

- In 2008 the National Survey on Drug Use and Health reported that 28% of youth aged 12 to 20 years drink alcohol and 19% reported binge drinking.

- In 2009, the Monitoring the Future Survey reported that 37% of 8th graders and 72% of 12th graders had tried alcohol, and 15% of 8th graders and 44% of 12th graders drank during the past month.

Consequences Of Underage Drinking

Youth who drink alcohol are more likely to experience problems such as the following:

- School problems, such as higher absence and poor or failing grades

- Social problems, such as fighting and lack of participation in youth activities

- Legal problems, such as arrest for driving or physically hurting someone while drunk

- Physical problems, such as hangovers or illnesses

- Unwanted, unplanned, and unprotected sexual activity

- Disruption of normal growth and sexual development

- Physical and sexual assault

- Higher risk for suicide and homicide

- Alcohol-related car crashes and other unintentional injuries, such as burns, falls, and drowning

- Memory problems

- Abuse of other drugs

- Changes in brain development that may have life-long effects

- Death from alcohol poisoning

In general, the risk of youth experiencing these problems is greater for those who binge drink than for those who do not binge drink.

Youth who start drinking before age 15 years are five times more likely to develop alcohol dependence or abuse later in life than those who begin drinking at or after age 21 years.

Prevention Of Underage Drinking

Reducing underage drinking will require community-based efforts to monitor the activities of youth and decrease youth access to alcohol. Recent publications by the Surgeon General and the Institute of Medicine outlined many prevention strategies that will require actions on the national, state, and local levels, such as enforcement of minimum legal drinking age laws, national media campaigns targeting youth and adults, increasing alcohol excise taxes, reducing youth exposure to alcohol advertising, and development of comprehensive community-based programs. These efforts will require continued research and evaluation to determine their success and to improve their effectiveness.

Chapter 10

Recent Trends In Teen Drinking

Alcoholic beverages have been among the most widely used substances by American young people for a very long time. In 2008 the proportions of 8th, 10th, and 12th graders who admitted drinking an alcoholic beverage in the 30-day period prior to the survey were 16%, 29%, and 43%, respectively. A number of measures of alcohol use are presented in the tables at the end of this report. Here we focus on episodic heavy or "binge" drinking (i.e., five or more drinks in a row during the prior two-week interval)—the pattern of alcohol consumption that is probably of greatest concern from a public health perspective.

Trends In Use

Among 12th graders, binge drinking peaked at about the same time as overall illicit drug use, in 1979. It held steady for a few years before declining substantially from 41% in 1983 to a low of 28% in 1992 (also the low point of any illicit drug use). This was a drop of almost one third in binge drinking. Although illicit drug use rose by considerable proportions in the 1990s, binge drinking rose by only a small fraction, followed by some decline in binge drinking at all three grades. By 2008, proportional declines since recent peaks are 40%, 34%, and 22% for grades 8, 10, and 12, respectively.

About This Chapter: Information in this chapter is excerpted from Johnston, L.D., O'Malley, P.M., Bachman, J.G., and Schulenberg, J.E. (2009). *Monitoring the future national results on adolescent drug use: Overview of key findings, 2008.* (NIH Publication No. 09-7401). Bethesda, MD: National Institute on Drug Abuse. The Monitoring the Future Study has been funded under a series of investigator-initiated competing research grants from the National Institute on Drug Abuse. MTF is conducted at the University of Michigan.

It should be noted that there is no evidence of any displacement effect in the aggregate between alcohol and marijuana—a hypothesis frequently heard. The two drugs have moved much more in parallel over the years than in opposite directions.

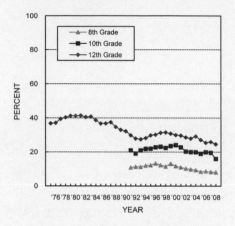 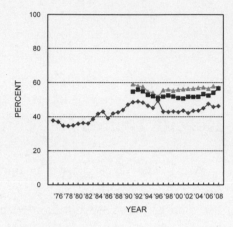

Figure 10.1. *Use: % that had five or more drinks in last two weeks. For 8th and 10th graders only: The 1991–2007 estimates for five or more drinks in a row differ slightly from some previous reports due to an error in the data editing process prior to 2008. The revised estimates average about 2% lower than previous estimates. These have been corrected here.*

Figure 10.2. *% seeing "great risk" in having five or more drinks in a row once or twice each weekend*

Perceived Risk

For most of the study, the majority of 12th graders have not viewed binge drinking on weekends as carrying a great risk. However, an increase from 36% to 49% occurred between 1982 and 1992. There then followed a decline to 43% by 1997, before it stabilized. Since 2003, perceived risk has risen some. These changes are consistent with changes in actual binge drinking. We believe that the public service advertising campaigns in the 1980s against drunk driving, as well as those that urged use of designated drivers when drinking, may have contributed to the increase in perceived risk of binge drinking. As we have published elsewhere, drunk driving by 12th graders declined during that period by an even larger proportion than binge drinking. Also, we have demonstrated that increases in the minimum drinking age during the 1980s were followed by reductions in drinking, and increases in perceived risk associated with drinking.

Disapproval

Disapproval of weekend binge drinking moved fairly parallel with perceived risk, suggesting that such drinking (and very likely the drunk driving behavior associated with it) became increasingly unacceptable in the peer group. Note that the rates of disapproval and perceived risk for binge drinking are higher in the lower grades than in 12th grade. As with perceived risk, disapproval has increased appreciably in all grades in recent years, especially in the upper grades.

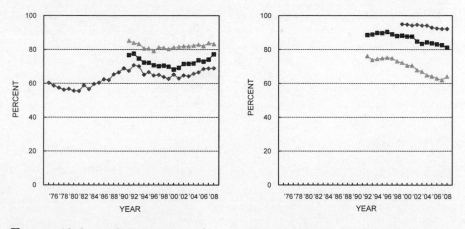

Figure 10.3. *% disapproving of having five or more drinks in a row once or twice each weekend*

Figure 10.4. *% saying "fairly easy" or "very easy" to get*

Availability

Perceived availability of alcohol, which until 1999 was asked only of 8th and 10th graders, was very high and mostly steady in the 1990s. Since 1996, however, there has been a significant decline in 8th grade (until 2008) and 10th grade. For 12th grade, availability has declined very slightly but is still at a very high level, with 92% saying that it is, or would be, fairly easy or very easy for them to get alcohol.

Chapter 11

Underage Drinking: Reasons, Risks, And Prevention

Why Do Adolescents Drink, What Are The Risks, And How Can Underage Drinking Be Prevented?

Alcohol is the drug of choice among youth. Many young people are experiencing the consequences of drinking too much, at too early an age. As a result, underage drinking is a leading public health problem in this country.

Each year, approximately 5,000 young people under the age of 21 die as a result of underage drinking; this includes about 1,900 deaths from motor vehicle crashes, 1,600 as a result of homicides, 300 from suicide, as well as hundreds from other injuries such as falls, burns, and drownings.

Yet drinking continues to be widespread among adolescents, as shown by nationwide surveys as well as studies in smaller populations. According to data from the 2005 Monitoring the Future (MTF) study, an annual survey of U.S. youth, three-fourths of 12th graders, more than two-thirds of 10th graders, and about two in every five 8th graders have consumed alcohol. And when youth drink they tend to drink intensively, often consuming four to five drinks at one

About This Chapter: Information in this chapter is from "Underage Drinking: Why Do Adolescents Drink, What Are the Risks, and How Can Underage Drinking Be Prevented?" *Alcohol Alert Number 67*, National Institute on Alcohol Abuse and Alcoholism, January 2006.

time. MTF data show that 11 percent of 8th graders, 22 percent of 10th graders, and 29 percent of 12th graders had engaged in heavy episodic (or "binge") drinking within the past two weeks. (The National Institute on Alcohol Abuse and Alcoholism [NIAAA] defines binge drinking as a pattern of drinking alcohol that brings blood alcohol concentration [BAC] to 0.08 grams percent or above. For the typical adult, this pattern corresponds to consuming five or more drinks [men], or four or more drinks [women], in about 2 hours.)

Research also shows that many adolescents start to drink at very young ages. In 2003, the average age of first use of alcohol was about 14, compared to about 17 1/2 in 1965. People who reported starting to drink before the age of 15 were four times more likely to also report meeting the criteria for alcohol dependence at some point in their lives.

Other research shows that the younger children and adolescents are when they start to drink, the more likely they will be to engage in behaviors that harm themselves and others. For example, frequent binge drinkers (nearly 1 million high school students nationwide) are more likely to engage in risky behaviors, including using other drugs such as marijuana and cocaine, having sex with six or more partners, and earning grades that are mostly Ds and Fs in school.

✤ **It's A Fact!!**
New research shows that the serious drinking problems (including what is called alcoholism) typically associated with middle age actually begin to appear much earlier, during young adulthood and even adolescence.

Why Do Some Adolescents Drink?

As children move from adolescence to young adulthood, they encounter dramatic physical, emotional, and lifestyle changes. Developmental transitions, such as puberty and increasing independence, have been associated with alcohol use. So in a sense, just being an adolescent may be a key risk factor not only for starting to drink but also for drinking dangerously.

- **Risk-Taking:** Research shows the brain keeps developing well into the twenties, during which time it continues to establish important communication connections and further refines its function. Scientists believe that this lengthy developmental period may help explain some of the behavior that is characteristic of adolescence—such as a propensity to seek out new and potentially dangerous situations. For some teens, thrill-seeking might include experimenting with alcohol. Developmental changes also offer a possible physiological explanation for why teens act so impulsively, often not recognizing that their actions—such as drinking—have consequences.

- **Expectancies:** How people view alcohol and its effects also influences their drinking behavior, including whether they begin to drink and how much. An adolescent who expects drinking to be a pleasurable experience is more likely to drink than one who does not. An important area of alcohol research is focusing on how expectancy influences drinking patterns from childhood through adolescence and into young adulthood. Beliefs about alcohol are established very early in life, even before the child begins elementary school. Before age nine, children generally view alcohol negatively and see drinking as bad, with adverse effects. By about age 13, however, their expectancies shift, becoming more positive. As would be expected, adolescents who drink the most also place the greatest emphasis on the positive and arousing effects of alcohol.

- **Sensitivity To And Tolerance Of Alcohol:** Differences between the adult brain and the brain of the maturing adolescent also may help to explain why many young drinkers are able to consume much larger amounts of alcohol than adults before experiencing the negative consequences of drinking, such as drowsiness, lack of coordination, and withdrawal/hangover effects. This unusual tolerance may help to explain the high rates of binge drinking among young adults. At the same time, adolescents appear to be particularly sensitive to the positive effects of drinking, such as feeling more at ease in social situations, and young people may drink more than adults because of these positive social experiences.

- **Personality Characteristics And Psychiatric Comorbidity:** Children who begin to drink at a very early age (before age 12) often share similar personality characteristics that may make them more likely to start drinking. Young people who are disruptive, hyperactive, and aggressive—

often referred to as having conduct problems or being antisocial—as well as those who are depressed, withdrawn, or anxious, may be at greatest risk for alcohol problems. Other behavior problems associated with alcohol use include rebelliousness, difficulty avoiding harm or harmful situations, and a host of other traits seen in young people who act out without regard for rules or the feelings of others (i.e., disinhibition).

• **Hereditary Factors:** Some of the behavioral and physiological factors that converge to increase or decrease a person's risk for alcohol problems, including tolerance to alcohol's effects, may be directly linked to genetics. For example, research shows that children of alcoholics have a distinctive brainwave pattern (called a P300 response) that could be a marker for later alcoholism risk. Other hereditary factors likely will become evident as scientists work to identify the actual genes involved in addiction. By analyzing the genetic makeup of people and families with alcohol dependence, researchers have found specific regions on chromosomes that correlate with a risk for alcoholism. Candidate genes for alcoholism risk also have been associated with those regions. The goal now is to further refine regions for which a specific gene has not yet been identified and then determine how those genes interact with other genes and gene products as well as with the environment to result in alcohol dependence. Further research also should shed light on the extent to which the same or different genes contribute to alcohol problems, both in adults and in adolescents.

• **Environmental Aspects:** Pinpointing a genetic contribution will not tell the whole story, however, as drinking behavior reflects a complex interplay between inherited and environmental factors, the implications of which are only beginning to be explored in adolescents. And what influences drinking at one age may not have the same impact at another. As Rose and colleagues show, genetic factors appear to have more influence on adolescent drinking behavior in late adolescence than in mid-adolescence. Environmental factors, such as the influence of parents and peers, also play a role in alcohol use. For example, parents who drink more and who view drinking favorably may have children who drink more, and an adolescent girl with an older or adult boyfriend is more likely to use alcohol and other drugs and to engage in delinquent

✤ It's A Fact!!
Children Of Alcoholics

Being a child of an alcoholic or having several alcoholic family members places a person at greater risk for alcohol problems. Children of alcoholics (COAs) are between four and 10 times more likely to become alcoholics themselves than are children who have no close relatives with alcoholism. COAs also are more likely to begin drinking at a young age and to progress to drinking problems more quickly.

Research shows that COAs may have subtle brain differences which could be markers for developing later alcohol problems. For example, using high-tech brain-imaging techniques, scientists have found that COAs have a distinctive feature in one brainwave pattern (called a P300 response) that could be a marker for later alcoholism risk. Researchers also are investigating other brainwave differences in COAs that may be present long before they begin to drink, including brainwave activity recorded during sleep as well as changes in brain structure and function.

Some studies suggest that these brain differences may be particularly evident in people who also have certain behavioral traits, such as signs of conduct disorder, antisocial personality disorder, sensation-seeking, or poor impulse control. Studying how the brain's structure and function translates to behavior will help researchers to better understand how pre-drinking risk factors shape later alcohol use. For example, does a person who is depressed drink to alleviate his or her depression, or does drinking lead to changes in his brain that result in feelings of depression?

behaviors. Researchers are examining other environmental influences as well, such as the impact of the media. Today alcohol is widely available and aggressively promoted through television, radio, billboards, and the Internet. Researchers are studying how young people react to these advertisements. In a study of third, sixth, and ninth graders, those who found alcohol ads desirable were more likely to view drinking positively and to want to purchase products with alcohol logos. Research is mixed, however, on whether these positive views of alcohol actually lead to underage drinking.

What Are The Health Risks?

Whatever it is that leads adolescents to begin drinking, once they start they face a number of potential health risks. Although the severe health problems associated with harmful alcohol use are not as common in adolescents as they are in adults, studies show that young people who drink heavily may put themselves at risk for a range of potential health problems.

- **Brain Effects:** Scientists currently are examining just how alcohol affects the developing brain, but it's a difficult task. Subtle changes in the brain may be difficult to detect but still have a significant impact on long-term thinking and memory skills. Add to this the fact that adolescent brains are still maturing, and the study of alcohol's effects becomes even more complex. Research has shown that animals fed alcohol during this critical developmental stage continue to show long-lasting impairment from alcohol as they age. It's simply not known how alcohol will affect the long-term memory and learning skills of people who began drinking heavily as adolescents.

- **Liver Effects:** Elevated liver enzymes, indicating some degree of liver damage, have been found in some adolescents who drink alcohol. Young drinkers who are overweight or obese showed elevated liver enzymes even with only moderate levels of drinking.

- **Growth And Endocrine Effects:** In both males and females, puberty is a period associated with marked hormonal changes, including increases in the sex hormones, estrogen and testosterone. These hormones, in turn, increase production of other hormones and growth factors, which are vital for normal organ development. Drinking alcohol during this period of rapid growth and development (i.e., prior to or during puberty) may upset the critical hormonal balance necessary for normal development of organs, muscles, and bones. Studies in animals also show that consuming alcohol during puberty adversely affects the maturation of the reproductive system.

Treatment: An Unmet Need

A major unmet need exists in the treatment of alcohol use disorders. In 2002, 1.4 million youth met the criteria for alcohol abuse or dependence, but only 227,000 actually received any treatment for these problems. Moreover, much of the treatment available today does not address the specific needs of adolescents. For example, most young people prefer easy access to treatment, with strategies tailored to their age group, and treatments that do not remove them from their home or academic settings. Youth perceive traditional services (e.g., alcoholism treatment programs, Alcoholics Anonymous) as less helpful than brief interventions tailored to their concerns. Consequently, alternative formats, attention to developmental transitions, and social marketing are needed to better address alcohol problems that emerge during adolescence.

Adolescent Treatment Interventions: Complex interventions have been developed and tested in adolescents referred for treatment of alcohol and other drug disorders. Many of these patients are likely to have more than one substance use disorder (e.g., alcohol and marijuana) and to have other psychiatric disorders as well (e.g., depression, anxiety, or conduct disorder). Brief interventions are, as a rule, delivered to adolescents in general medical settings (e.g., primary care clinics, emergency rooms) or in school-based settings. These settings offer an excellent opportunity for intervening with adolescents to address their drinking before they progress to serious alcohol use disorders and to prevent the development of alcohol-related problems.

Preventing Underage Drinking Within A Developmental Framework

Complex behaviors, such as the decision to begin drinking or to continue using alcohol, are the result of a dynamic interplay between genes and environment. For example, biological and physiological changes that occur during adolescence may promote risk-taking behavior, leading to early experimentation with alcohol. This behavior then shapes the child's environment, as he or she chooses friends and situations that support further drinking. Continued drinking may lead to physiological reactions, such as depression or anxiety disorders, triggering even greater alcohol use or dependence. In this way, youthful patterns of alcohol use can mark the start of a developmental pathway that may lead to abuse and dependence. Then again, not all young people who travel this pathway experience the same outcomes.

Perhaps the best way to understand and prevent underage alcohol use is to view drinking as it relates to development. This "whole system" approach to underage drinking takes into account a particular adolescent's unique risk and protective factors—from genetics and personality characteristics to social and environmental factors. Viewed in this way, development includes not only the adolescent's inherent risk and resilience but also the current conditions that help to shape his or her behavior.

Children mature at different rates. Developmental research takes this into account, recognizing that during adolescence there are periods of rapid growth and reorganization, alternating with periods of slower growth and integration of body systems. Periods of rapid transitions, when social or cultural factors most strongly influence the biology and behavior of the adolescent, may be the best time to target delivery of interventions. Interventions that focus on these critical development periods could alter the life course of the child, perhaps placing him or her on a path to avoid problems with alcohol.

To date, researchers have been unable to identify a single track that predicts the course of alcohol use for all or even most young people. Instead, findings provide strong evidence for wide developmental variation in drinking patterns within this special population.

> ### ✦ It's A Fact!!
> ### Who Drinks?
>
> Rates of drinking and alcohol-related problems are highest among White and American Indian or Alaska Native youth, followed by Hispanic youth, African Americans, and Asians. Prevalence rates of drinking for boys and girls are similar in the younger age groups; among older adolescents, however, more boys than girls engage in frequent and heavy drinking and boys show higher rates of drinking problems.

Interventions For Preventing Underage Drinking

Intervention approaches typically fall into two distinct categories: environmental-level interventions, which seek to reduce opportunities for underage drinking, increase penalties for violating minimum legal drinking age (MLDA) and other alcohol use laws, and reduce community tolerance for alcohol use by youth; and individual-level interventions, which seek to change knowledge, expectancies, attitudes, intentions, motivation, and skills so that youth are better able to resist the pro-drinking influences and opportunities that surround them. Environmental approaches include:

- **Raising The Price Of Alcohol:** A substantial body of research has shown that higher prices or taxes on alcoholic beverages are associated with lower levels of alcohol consumption and alcohol-related problems, especially in young people.

- **Increasing The Minimum Legal Drinking Age:** Today all states have set the minimum legal drinking age at 21. Increasing the age at which people can legally purchase and drink alcohol has been the most successful intervention to date in reducing drinking and alcohol-related crashes among people under age 21. The National Highway Traffic Safety Administration (NHTSA) estimates that a legal drinking age of 21 saves 700 to 1,000 lives annually. Since 1976, these laws have prevented more than 21,000 traffic deaths. Just how much the legal drinking age relates to drinking-related crashes is shown by a recent study in New Zealand. Six years ago that country lowered its minimum legal drinking age to 18. Since then, alcohol-related crashes have risen 12 percent among 18- to 19-year-olds and 14 percent among 15- to 17-year-olds. Clearly a higher minimum drinking age can help to reduce crashes and save lives, especially in very young drivers.

- **Enacting Zero-Tolerance Laws:** All states have zero-tolerance laws that make it illegal for people under age 21 to drive after any drinking. When the first eight states to adopt zero-tolerance laws were compared with nearby states without such laws, the zero-tolerance states showed a 21-percent greater decline in the proportion of single-vehicle night-time fatal crashes involving drivers under 21, the type of crash most likely to involve alcohol.

- **Stepping Up Enforcement Of Laws:** Despite their demonstrated benefits, legal drinking age and zero-tolerance laws generally have not been vigorously enforced. Alcohol purchase laws aimed at sellers and buyers also can be effective, but resources must be made available for enforcing these laws.

Individual-focused interventions include:

- **School-Based Prevention Programs:** The first school-based prevention programs were primarily informational and often used scare tactics; it was assumed that if youth understood the dangers of alcohol use, they would choose not to drink. These programs were ineffective. Today, better programs are available and often have a number of elements in common: They follow social influence models and include setting norms, addressing social pressures to drink, and teaching resistance skills. These programs also offer interactive and developmentally appropriate information, include peer-led components, and provide teacher training.

- **Family-Based Prevention Programs:** Parents' ability to influence whether their children drink is well documented and is consistent across racial/ethnic groups. Setting clear rules against drinking, consistently enforcing those rules, and monitoring the child's behavior all help to reduce the likelihood of underage drinking. The Iowa Strengthening Families Program (ISFP), delivered when students were in grade six, is a program that has shown long-lasting preventive effects on alcohol use.

Selected Programs Showing Promise

Environmental interventions are among the recommendations included in the recent National Research Council (NRC) and Institute of Medicine (IOM) report on underage drinking. These interventions are intended to reduce commercial and social availability of alcohol and/or reduce driving while intoxicated. They use a variety of strategies, including server training and compliance checks in places that sell alcohol; deterring adults from purchasing alcohol for minors or providing alcohol to minors; restricting drinking in public places and preventing underage drinking parties; enforcing penalties for the use of false IDs, driving while intoxicated, and violating zero-tolerance laws; and raising public awareness of policies and sanctions.

The following community trials show how environmental strategies can be useful in reducing underage drinking and related problems.

- **The Massachusetts Saving Lives Program:** This intervention was designed to reduce alcohol-impaired driving and related traffic deaths. Strategies included the use of drunk-driving checkpoints, speeding and drunk-driving awareness days, speed-watch telephone hotlines, high school peer-led education, and college prevention programs. The five-year program decreased fatal crashes, particularly alcohol-related fatal crashes involving drivers ages 15–25, and reduced the proportion of

16- to 19-year-olds who reported driving after drinking, in comparison with the rest of Massachusetts. It also made teens more aware of penalties for drunk driving and for speeding.

- **The Community Prevention Trial Program:** This program was designed to reduce alcohol-involved injuries and death. One component sought to reduce alcohol sales to minors by enforcing underage sales laws; training sales clerks, owners, and managers to prevent sales of alcohol to minors; and using the media to raise community awareness of underage drinking. Sales to apparent minors (people of legal drinking age who appear younger than age 21) were significantly reduced in the intervention communities compared with control sites.

- **Communities Mobilizing For Change On Alcohol:** This intervention, designed to reduce the accessibility of alcoholic beverages to people under age 21, centered on policy changes among local institutions to make underage drinking less acceptable within the community. Alcohol sales to minors were reduced: 18- to 20-year-olds were less likely to try to purchase alcohol or provide it to younger teens, and the number of DUI [driving under the influence] arrests declined among 18- to 20-year-olds.

- **Multi-Component Comprehensive Interventions:** Perhaps the strongest approach for preventing underage drinking involves the coordinated effort of all the elements that influence a child's life—including family, schools, and community. Ideally, intervention programs also should integrate treatment for youth who are alcohol dependent. Project Northland is an example of a comprehensive program that has been extensively evaluated.

Project Northland was tested in 22 school districts in northeastern Minnesota. The intervention included (1) school curricula, (2) peer leadership, (3) parental involvement programs, and (4) community-wide task force activities to address larger community norms and alcohol availability. It targeted adolescents in grades six through 12.

Intervention and comparison communities differed significantly in "tendency to use alcohol," a composite measure that combined items about intentions to use alcohol and actual use, as well as in the likelihood of drinking "five or more in a row." Underage drinking was less prevalent in the intervention communities during phase one; higher during the interim period (suggesting a "catch-up" effect while intervention activities were minimal); and again lower during phase two, when intervention activities resumed.

Project Northland has been designated a model program by the Substance Abuse and Mental Health Services Administration (SAMHSA), and its materials have been adapted for a general audience. It now is being replicated in ethnically diverse urban neighborhoods.

☞ Remember!!

Today, alcohol is widely available and aggressively promoted throughout society. And alcohol use continues to be regarded, by many people, as a normal part of growing up. Yet underage drinking is dangerous, not only for the drinker but also for society, as evident by the number of alcohol-involved motor vehicle crashes, homicides, suicides, and other injuries. People who begin drinking early in life run the risk of developing serious alcohol problems, including alcoholism, later in life. They also are at greater risk for a variety of adverse consequences, including risky sexual activity and poor performance in school. Identifying adolescents at greatest risk can help stop problems before they develop. And innovative, comprehensive approaches to prevention, such as Project Northland, are showing success in reducing experimentation with alcohol as well as the problems that accompany alcohol use by young people.

Chapter 12

Drinking Too Fast Can Kill You

Hundreds of people die each year from acute alcohol intoxication, more commonly known as alcohol poisoning. Caused by drinking too much alcohol too fast, it often occurs on college campuses or wherever heavy drinking takes place. Two cases of alcohol poisoning, at the Massachusetts Institute of Technology and Louisiana State University, that received national attention were both linked to fraternity pledging.

Acute Intoxication

If people knew more about alcohol poisoning, it could be avoided.

Alcohol poisoning, like other drug overdoses, can occur after the ingestion of a large amount of any alcoholic beverage, including beer, wine or distilled spirits (so-called "hard liquor"). But inexperienced drinkers, or those sensitive to alcohol, may become acutely intoxicated and suffer serious consequences after drinking smaller amounts. Because of differences in body chemistry, women can overdose after drinking lesser amounts than men.

Here's what happens. Alcohol (a depressant drug), once ingested, works to slow down some of the body's functions including heart rate, blood pressure,

About This Chapter: Information in this chapter is from "Drinking Too Fast Can Kill You," © National Council on Alcoholism and Drug Dependence (www.ncadd.org). Reprinted with permission.

and breathing. When the vital centers have been depressed enough by alcohol, unconsciousness occurs. Further, the amount of alcohol that it takes to produce unconsciousness is dangerously close to a fatal dose. People who survive alcohol poisoning sometimes suffer irreversible brain damage.

Many students are surprised to learn that death can occur from acute intoxication. Most think the worst that can happen is they'll pass out and have a hangover the next day.

Knowing the signs and symptoms of acute alcohol intoxication and the proper action to take can help you avoid a tragedy.

A Dead Giveaway

Binge drinking (drinking five or more drinks in a row on a single occasion) is a common phenomenon on college campuses. As a result, you may come into contact with a person who is experiencing a life-threatening acute alcohol intoxication episode.

But how can you tell if someone is about to become a victim of alcohol poisoning? And if they are, what can you do to help?

Alcohol Poisoning: A Medical Emergency

Signs and symptoms:

- Unconsciousness or semi-consciousness.
- Slow respirations (breaths) of eight or less per minute, or lapses between respirations of more than eight seconds.
- Cold, clammy, pale, or bluish skin.

In the event of alcohol poisoning, these signs and symptoms will most likely be accompanied by a strong odor of alcohol. While these are obvious signs of alcohol poisoning, the list is certainly not all inclusive.

Appropriate action:

- If you encounter a person who exhibits one or more of the signs and symptoms, do what you would do in any medical emergency: call 911 immediately.

- While waiting for 911 emergency transport, gently turn the intoxicated person on his/her side and maintain that position by placing a pillow in the small of the person's back. This is important to prevent aspiration (choking) should the person vomit. Stay with the person until medical help arrives.

Sleeping It Off?

A more difficult situation occurs when an intoxicated person appears to be "sleeping it off." It is important to understand that even though a person may be semi-conscious, alcohol already in the stomach may continue to enter the bloodstream and circulate throughout the body. The person's life still may be in danger.

If you should encounter such a situation, place the person on his/her side, help him/her maintain that position, and watch closely for signs of alcohol poisoning. If any signs appear, call 911.

If you are having difficulty in determining whether an individual is acutely intoxicated, contact a health professional immediately—you cannot afford to guess.

You Also Need To Know

- Purchase and public possession of alcohol by persons under the age of 21 is illegal in all 50 states.

- Standard servings of beer (12 oz.), wine (5 oz.) and distilled spirits (1.5 oz, 80 proof) all contain the same amount of alcohol.

- Any net health benefits associated with alcohol consumption don't begin until middle age and occur only with moderate drinking (defined by the federal government as not more than two drinks per day for men and not more than one for women).

- Although certain groups of people are at higher risk for becoming alcoholic, anyone who drinks can develop the disease.

- The most significant predictor of alcohol problems is the quantity and frequency of an individual's drinking.

- Some people should not drink alcoholic beverages at all, including women who are trying to conceive or are pregnant; individuals using prescription and over-the-counter medications; individuals who plan to drive or take part in activities that require attention or skill; and individuals of any age who cannot restrict their drinking to moderate levels.

Chapter 13

Binge Drinking

Chet has known Dave since they were in elementary school together, but lately their friendship has been strained. Dave's drinking on weekends has turned him into a completely different person. Dave used to get good grades and play sports, but since he started drinking he hasn't been finishing assignments and he has quit the soccer team.

When Chet saw Dave pound five beers in 30 minutes at two different parties, he realized how serious Dave's problem was.

What Is Binge Drinking?

Binge drinking used to mean drinking heavily over several days. Now, however, the term refers to the heavy consumption of alcohol over a short period of time (just as binge eating means a specific period of uncontrolled overeating).

Today the generally accepted definition of binge drinking in the United States is the consumption of five or more drinks in a row by men—or four or more drinks in a row by women—at least once in the previous 2 weeks. Heavy binge drinking includes three or more such episodes in 2 weeks.

Why Do People Binge Drink?

Liquor stores, bars, and alcoholic beverage companies make drinking seem attractive and fun. It's easy for a high school student to get caught up in a social scene with lots of peer pressure. Inevitably, one of the biggest areas of peer pressure is drinking.

Other reasons why people drink include:

- They're curious—they want to know what it's like to drink alcohol.
- They believe that it will make them feel good, not realizing it could just as easily make them sick and hung-over.
- They may look at alcohol as a way to reduce stress, even though it can end up creating more stress.
- They want to feel older.

What Are the Risks Of Binge Drinking?

Many people don't think about the negative side of drinking. Although they think about the possibility of getting drunk, they may not give much consideration to being hung-over or throwing up.

You may know from experience that excessive drinking can lead to difficulty concentrating, memory lapses, mood changes, and other problems that affect your day-to-day life. But binge drinking carries more serious and longer-lasting risks as well.

Alcohol Poisoning

Alcohol poisoning is the most life-threatening consequence of binge drinking. When someone drinks too much and gets alcohol poisoning, it affects the body's involuntary reflexes—including breathing and the gag reflex. If the gag reflex isn't working properly, a person can choke to death on his or her vomit.

Other signs someone may have alcohol poisoning include:

- extreme confusion
- inability to be awakened
- vomiting

- seizures
- slow or irregular breathing
- low body temperature
- bluish or pale skin

If you think someone has alcohol poisoning, call 911 immediately.

Impaired Judgment

Binge drinking impairs judgment, so drinkers are more likely to take risks they might not take when they're sober. They may drive drunk and injure themselves or others. Driving isn't the only motor skill that's impaired, though. Walking is also more difficult while intoxicated. In 2000, roughly one third of pedestrians 16 and older who were killed in traffic accidents were intoxicated.

People who are drunk also take other risks they might not normally take when they're sober. For example, people who have impaired judgment may have unprotected sex, putting them at greater risk of a sexually transmitted disease (STD) or unplanned pregnancy.

✤ It's A Fact!!
Drinkers At Greater Risk Of Injury

According to a 2006 Australian study, people who drink are four times more likely than nondrinkers to suffer physical injuries such as falls. And binge drinkers are at an even greater risk of injury.

Physical Health

Studies show that people who binge-drink throughout high school are more likely to be overweight and have high blood pressure by the time they are 24. Just one regular beer contains about 150 calories, which adds up to a lot of calories if someone drinks four or five beers a night.

Mental Health

Binge drinkers have a harder time in school and they're more likely to drop out. Drinking disrupts sleep patterns, which can make it harder to stay awake and concentrate during the day. This can lead to struggles with studying and poor academic performance.

People who binge-drink may find that their friends drift away—which is what happened with Chet and Dave. Drinking can affect personality; people might become angry or moody while drinking, for example.

Alcoholism

Some studies have shown that people who binge-drink heavily—those who have three or more episodes of binge drinking in 2 weeks—have some of the symptoms of alcoholism.

Getting Help

If you think you or a friend have a binge-drinking problem, get help as soon as possible. The best approach is to talk to an adult you trust—if you can't approach your parents, talk to your doctor, school counselor, clergy member, aunt, or uncle.

It can be hard for some people to talk to adults about these issues, so an alternative could be a trusted friend or older sibling who is easy to talk to. Drinking too much can be the result of social pressures, and sometimes it helps to know there are others who have gone through the same thing.

If you're worried, don't hesitate to ask someone for help. A supportive friend or adult could help you to avoid pressure situations, stop drinking, or find counseling.

❖ It's A Fact!!
Binge Drinking Affects Nondrinkers Too

Nondrinkers may be killed or injured by drunk drivers or by the aggressive actions of someone who has been drinking heavily. Nondrinkers may also find it hard to stay connected to friends or significant others who binge-drink because of the changes in that person's behavior.

Chapter 14

Questions And Answers About Alcoholism

The National Institute on Alcohol Abuse and Alcoholism (NIAAA) routinely receives a variety of questions about alcohol. We would like to share the following frequently asked questions and their answers.

It is important to understand that these answers are not meant to provide specific medical advice, but to provide information to better understand the health consequences of alcohol abuse and dependence (alcoholism). Please consult your physician or other health care provider if you or a loved one has an alcohol problem.

What is alcoholism?

Alcoholism, also known as alcohol dependence, is a disease that includes the following four symptoms:

- **Craving:** A strong need, or urge, to drink.

- **Loss Of Control:** Not being able to stop drinking once drinking has begun.

- **Physical Dependence:** Withdrawal symptoms, such as nausea, sweating, shakiness, and anxiety after stopping drinking.

- **Tolerance:** The need to drink greater amounts of alcohol to get "high."

About This Chapter: Information in this chapter is from "FAQs for the General Public," National Institute on Alcohol Abuse and Alcoholism, February 2007.

For clinical and research purposes, formal diagnostic criteria for alcoholism also have been developed. Such criteria are included in the *Diagnostic and Statistical Manual of Mental Disorders, Fourth Edition*, published by the American Psychiatric Association, as well as in the *International Classification Diseases*, published by the World Health Organization.

Is alcoholism a disease?

Yes, alcoholism is a disease. The craving that an alcoholic feels for alcohol can be as strong as the need for food or water. An alcoholic will continue to drink despite serious family, health, or legal problems.

Like many other diseases, alcoholism is chronic, meaning that it lasts a person's lifetime, it usually follows a predictable course, and it has symptoms. The risk for developing alcoholism is influenced both by a person's genes and by his or her lifestyle.

Is alcoholism inherited?

Research shows that the risk for developing alcoholism does indeed run in families. The genes a person inherits partially explain this pattern, but lifestyle is also a factor. Currently, researchers are working to discover the actual genes that put people at risk for alcoholism. Your friends, the amount of stress in your life, and how readily available alcohol is also are factors that may increase your risk for alcoholism.

☞ Remember!!

Risk is not destiny. Just because alcoholism tends to run in families doesn't mean that a child of an alcoholic parent will automatically become an alcoholic too. Some people develop alcoholism even though no one in their family has a drinking problem. By the same token, not all children of alcoholic families get into trouble with alcohol. Knowing you are at risk is important, though, because then you can take steps to protect yourself from developing problems with alcohol.

Can alcoholism be cured?

No, alcoholism cannot be cured at this time. Even if an alcoholic hasn't been drinking for a long time, he or she can still suffer a relapse. Not drinking is the safest course for most people with alcoholism.

Can alcoholism be treated?

Yes, alcoholism can be treated. Alcoholism treatment programs use both counseling and medications to help a person stop drinking. Treatment has helped many people stop drinking and rebuild their lives.

Which medications treat alcoholism?

Three oral medications—disulfiram (Antabuse®), naltrexone (Depade®, ReVia®), and acamprosate (Campral®)—are currently approved to treat alcohol dependence. In addition, an injectable, long-acting form of naltrexone (Vivitrol®) is available. These medications have been shown to help people with dependence reduce their drinking, avoid relapse to heavy drinking, and achieve and maintain abstinence. Naltrexone acts in the brain to reduce craving for alcohol after someone has stopped drinking. Acamprosate is thought to work by reducing symptoms that follow lengthy abstinence, such as anxiety and insomnia. Disulfiram discourages drinking by making the person taking it feel sick after drinking alcohol.

Other types of drugs are available to help manage symptoms of withdrawal (such as shakiness, nausea, and sweating) if they occur after someone with alcohol dependence stops drinking.

Although medications are available to help treat alcoholism, there is no "magic bullet." In other words, no single medication is available that works in every case and/or in every person. Developing new and more effective medications to treat alcoholism remains a high priority for researchers.

Does alcoholism treatment work?

Alcoholism treatment works for many people. But like other chronic illnesses, such as diabetes, high blood pressure, and asthma, there are varying levels of success when it comes to treatment. Some people stop drinking and remain sober. Others have long periods of sobriety with bouts of relapse. And still others cannot stop drinking for any length of time. With treatment, one thing is clear, however: the longer a person abstains from alcohol, the more likely he or she will be able to stay sober.

Do you have to be an alcoholic to experience problems?

No. Alcoholism is only one type of an alcohol problem. Alcohol abuse can be just as harmful. A person can abuse alcohol without actually being an alcoholic—that is, he or she may drink too much and too often but still not be dependent on alcohol. Some of the problems linked to alcohol abuse include not being able to meet work, school, or family responsibilities, drunk-driving arrests and car crashes, and drinking-related medical conditions. Under some circumstances, even social or moderate drinking is dangerous—for example, when driving, during pregnancy, or when taking certain medications.

✔ Quick Tip

How can you tell if someone has a problem?

Answering the following four questions can help you find out if you or a loved one has a drinking problem:

1. Have you ever felt you should cut down on your drinking?

2. Have people annoyed you by criticizing your drinking?

3. Have you ever felt bad or guilty about your drinking?

4. Have you ever had a drink first thing in the morning to steady your nerves or to get rid of a hangover?

One "yes" answer suggests a possible alcohol problem. More than one "yes" answer means it is highly likely that a problem exists. If you think that you or someone you know might have an alcohol problem, it is important to see a doctor or other health care provider right away. They can help you determine if a drinking problem exists and plan the best course of action.

Are specific groups of people more likely to have problems?

Alcohol abuse and alcoholism cut across gender, race, and nationality. In the United States, 17.6 million people—about 1 in every 12 adults—abuse alcohol or are alcohol dependent. In general, more men than women are alcohol dependent or have alcohol problems. And alcohol problems are highest among young adults ages 18-29 and lowest among adults ages 65 and older. We also know that people who start drinking at an early age—for example, at age 14 or younger—are at much higher risk of developing alcohol problems at some point in their lives compared to someone who starts drinking at age 21 or after.

Can a problem drinker simply cut down?

It depends. If that person has been diagnosed as an alcoholic, the answer is "no." Alcoholics who try to cut down on drinking rarely succeed. Cutting out alcohol—that is, abstaining—is usually the best course for recovery. People who are not alcohol dependent but who have experienced alcohol-related problems may be able to limit the amount they drink. If they can't stay within those limits, they need to stop drinking altogether.

If an alcoholic is unwilling to get help, what can you do about it?

This can be a challenge. An alcoholic can't be forced to get help except under certain circumstances, such as a traffic violation or arrest that results in court-ordered treatment. But you don't have to wait for someone to "hit rock bottom" to act. Many alcoholism treatment specialists suggest the following steps to help an alcoholic get treatment:

1. **Stop all "cover ups."** Family members often make excuses to others or try to protect the alcoholic from the results of his or her drinking. It is important to stop covering for the alcoholic so that he or she experiences the full consequences of drinking.

2. **Time your intervention.** The best time to talk to the drinker is shortly after an alcohol-related problem has occurred—like a serious family argument or an accident. Choose a time when he or she is sober, both of you are fairly calm, and you have a chance to talk in private.

3. **Be specific.** Tell the family member that you are worried about his or her drinking. Use examples of the ways in which the drinking has caused problems, including the most recent incident.

4. **State the results.** Explain to the drinker what you will do if he or she doesn't go for help—not to punish the drinker, but to protect yourself from his or her problems. What you say may range from refusing to go with the person to any social activity where alcohol will be served to moving out of the house. Do not make any threats you are not prepared to carry out.

5. **Get help.** Gather information in advance about treatment options in your community. If the person is willing to get help, call immediately for an appointment with a treatment counselor. Offer to go with the family member on the first visit to a treatment program and/or an Alcoholics Anonymous meeting.

6. **Call on a friend.** If the family member still refuses to get help, ask a friend to talk with him or her using the steps just described. A friend who is a recovering alcoholic may be particularly persuasive, but any person who is caring and nonjudgmental may help. The intervention of more than one person, more than one time, is often necessary to coax an alcoholic to seek help.

7. **Find strength in numbers.** With the help of a health care professional, some families join with other relatives and friends to confront an alcoholic as a group. This approach should only be tried under the guidance of a health care professional who is experienced in this kind of group intervention.

8. **Get support.** It is important to remember that you are not alone. Support groups offered in most communities include Al-Anon, which holds regular meetings for spouses and other significant adults in an alcoholic's life, and Alateen, which is geared to children of alcoholics. These groups help family members understand that they are not responsible for an alcoholic's drinking and that they need to take steps to take care of themselves, regardless of whether the alcoholic family member chooses to get help.

What is a safe level of drinking?

For most adults, moderate alcohol use—up to two drinks per day for men and one drink per day for women and older people—causes few if any problems. (One drink equals one 12-ounce bottle of beer or wine cooler, one 5-ounce glass of wine, or 1.5 ounces of 80-proof distilled spirits.)

Certain people should not drink at all, however:

- Women who are pregnant or trying to become pregnant
- People who plan to drive or engage in other activities that require alertness and skill (such as driving a car)
- People taking certain over-the-counter or prescription medications
- People with medical conditions that can be made worse by drinking
- Recovering alcoholics
- People younger than age 21

Is it safe to drink during pregnancy?

No, alcohol can harm the baby of a mother who drinks during pregnancy. Although the highest risk is to babies whose mothers drink heavily, it is not clear yet whether there is any completely safe level of alcohol during pregnancy. For this reason, the U.S. Surgeon General released advisories in 1981 and again in 2005 urging women who are pregnant or may become pregnant to abstain from alcohol (http://www.lhvpn.net/hhspress.html). The damage caused by prenatal alcohol includes a range of physical, behavioral, and learning problems in babies. Babies most severely affected have what is called Fetal Alcohol Syndrome (FAS). These babies may have abnormal facial features and severe learning disabilities. Babies can also be born with mild disabilities without the facial changes typical of FAS.

Does alcohol affect older people differently?

Alcohol's effects do vary with age. Slower reaction times, problems with hearing and seeing, and a lower tolerance to alcohol's effects put older people at higher risk for falls, car crashes, and other types of injuries that may result from drinking.

Older people also tend to take more medicines than younger people. Mixing alcohol with over-the-counter or prescription medications can be very dangerous, even fatal. In addition, alcohol can make many of the medical conditions common in older people, including high blood pressure and ulcers, more serious. Physical changes associated with aging can make older people feel "high" even after drinking only small amounts of alcohol. So even if there is no medical reason to avoid alcohol, older men and women should limit themselves to one drink per day.

Does alcohol affect women differently?

Yes, alcohol affects women differently than men. Women become more impaired than men do after drinking the same amount of alcohol, even when differences in body weight are taken into account. This is because women's bodies have less water than men's bodies. Because alcohol mixes with body water, a given amount of alcohol becomes more highly concentrated in a woman's body than in a man's. In other words, it would be like dropping the same amount of alcohol into a much smaller pail of water. That is why the recommended drinking limit for women is lower than for men.

In addition, chronic alcohol abuse takes a heavier physical toll on women than on men. Alcohol dependence and related medical problems, such as brain, heart, and liver damage, progress more rapidly in women than in men.

When taking medications, must you stop drinking?

Possibly. More than 150 medications interact harmfully with alcohol. These interactions may result in increased risk of illness, injury, and even death. Alcohol's effects are heightened by medicines that depress the central nervous system, such as sleeping pills, antihistamines, antidepressants, anti-anxiety drugs, and some painkillers. In addition, medicines for certain disorders, including diabetes, high blood pressure, and heart disease, can have harmful interactions with alcohol. If you are taking any over-the-counter or prescription medications, ask your doctor or pharmacist if you can safely drink alcohol.

Chapter 15

Alcohol Use And Health Risks

There are approximately 79,000 deaths attributable to excessive alcohol use each year in the United States. This makes excessive alcohol use the third leading lifestyle-related cause of death for the nation. Additionally, excessive alcohol use is responsible for 2.3 million years of potential life lost (YPLL) annually, or an average of about 30 years of potential life lost for each death. In the single year 2005, there were over 1.6 million hospitalizations and over 4 million emergency room visits for alcohol-related conditions.

The Standard Measure Of Alcohol

In the United States, a standard drink is any drink that contains 0.6 ounces (13.7 grams or 1.2 tablespoons) of pure alcohol. Generally, this amount of pure alcohol is found in drinks of the following sizes:

- 12 ounces of regular beer or wine cooler

- 8 ounces of malt liquor

- 5 ounces of wine

- 1.5 ounces of 80-proof distilled spirits or liquor (e.g., gin, rum, vodka, whiskey)

About This Chapter: Information in this chapter is from "Alcohol Use and Health," a fact sheet from the Centers for Disease Control and Prevention (CDC), July 2010.

Definitions Of Patterns Of Drinking Alcohol

Binge Drinking

- For women, four or more drinks during a single occasion
- For men, five or more drinks during a single occasion

Heavy Drinking

- For women, more than one drink per day on average
- For men, more than two drinks per day on average

Excessive drinking includes heavy drinking, binge drinking, or both.

Most people who binge drink are not alcoholics or alcohol dependent.

✤ It's A Fact!!

According to the *Dietary Guidelines for Americans*, adults who drink alcoholic beverages, should do so in moderation, which is defined as no more than one drink per day for women and no more than two drinks per day for men. However, there are some persons who should not drink any alcohol, including those in the following groups:

- Pregnant or trying to become pregnant
- Taking prescription or over-the-counter medications that may cause harmful reactions when mixed with alcohol
- Younger than age 21
- Recovering from alcoholism or are unable to control the amount they drink
- Suffering from a medical condition that may be worsened by alcohol
- Driving, planning to drive, or participating in other activities requiring skill, coordination, and alertness

Immediate Health Risks

Excessive alcohol use has immediate effects that increase the risk of many harmful health conditions. These immediate effects are most often the result of binge drinking and include the following:

- Unintentional injuries, including traffic injuries, falls, drownings, burns and unintentional firearm injuries.

- Violence, including intimate partner violence and child maltreatment. About 35% of victims report that offenders are under the influence of alcohol. Alcohol use is also associated with two out of three incidents of intimate partner violence. Studies have also shown that alcohol is a leading factor in child maltreatment and neglect cases, and is the most frequent substance abused among these parents.

- Risky sexual behaviors, including unprotected sex, sex with multiple partners, and increased risk of sexual assault. These behaviors can result in unintended pregnancy or sexually transmitted diseases.

- Miscarriage and stillbirth among pregnant women, and a combination of physical and mental birth defects among children that last throughout life.

- Alcohol poisoning, a medical emergency that results from high blood alcohol levels that suppress the central nervous system and can cause loss of consciousness, low blood pressure and body temperature, coma, respiratory depression, or death.

Long-Term Health Risks

Over time, excessive alcohol use can lead to the development of chronic diseases, neurological impairments and social problems. These include but are not limited to the following effects:

- Neurological problems, including dementia, stroke and neuropathy
- Cardiovascular problems, including myocardial infarction, cardiomyopathy, atrial fibrillation and hypertension
- Psychiatric problems, including depression, anxiety, and suicide

- Social problems, including unemployment, lost productivity, and family problems

- Cancer of the mouth, throat, esophagus, liver, colon, and breast. In general, the risk of cancer increases with increasing amounts of alcohol.

- Liver diseases, including:

  - Alcoholic hepatitis

  - Cirrhosis, which is among the 15 leading causes of all deaths in the United States

  - Among persons with Hepatitis C virus, worsening of liver function and interference with medications used to treat this condition

- Other gastrointestinal problems, including pancreatitis and gastritis

Chapter 16

A Family History Of Alcoholism

If you are among the millions of people in this country who have a parent, grandparent, or other close relative with alcoholism, you may have wondered what your family's history of alcoholism means for you. Are problems with alcohol a part of your future? Is your risk for becoming an alcoholic greater than for people who do not have a family history of alcoholism? If so, what can you do to lower your risk?

Many scientific studies, including research conducted among twins and children of alcoholics, have shown that genetic factors influence alcoholism. These findings show that children of alcoholics are about four times more likely than the general population to develop alcohol problems. Children of alcoholics also have a higher risk for many other behavioral and emotional problems. But alcoholism is not determined only by the genes you inherit from your parents. In fact, more than one half of all children of alcoholics do not become alcoholic. Research shows that many factors influence your risk of developing alcoholism. Some factors raise the risk while others lower it. Genes are not the only things children inherit from their parents. How parents act and how they treat each other and their children has an influence on children growing up in the family. These aspects of family life also affect the risk for alcoholism.

About This Chapter: Information in this chapter is from "A Family History of Alcoholism: Are You at Risk?" a publication of the National Institute on Alcohol Abuse and Alcoholism. NIH Publication No. 03–5340, September 2005.

The good news is that many children of alcoholics from even the most troubled families do not develop drinking problems. Just as a family history of alcoholism does not guarantee that you will become an alcoholic, neither does growing up in a very troubled household with alcoholic parents. Just because alcoholism tends to run in families does not mean that a child of an alcoholic parent will automatically become an alcoholic too. The risk is higher but it does not have to happen. If you are worried that your family's history of alcohol problems or your troubled family life puts you at risk for becoming alcoholic, here is some common-sense advice to help you:

- **Avoid underage drinking.** First, underage drinking is illegal. Second, research shows that the risk for alcoholism is higher among people who begin to drink at an early age, perhaps as a result of both environmental and genetic factors.

- **Drink moderately as an adult.** Even if they do not have a family history of alcoholism, adults who choose to drink alcohol should do so in moderation—no more than one drink a day for most women, and no more than two drinks a day for most men, according to guidelines from the U.S. Department of Agriculture and the U.S. Department of Health and Human Services. Some people should not drink at all, including women who are pregnant or who are trying to become pregnant, recovering alcoholics, people who plan to drive or engage in other activities that require attention or skill, people taking certain medications, and people with certain medical conditions.

✤ It's A Fact!!

Researchers believe a person's risk increases if he or she is in a family with the following difficulties:

- An alcoholic parent is depressed or has other psychological problems
- Both parents abuse alcohol and other drugs
- The parents' alcohol abuse is severe
- Conflicts lead to aggression and violence in the family

People with a family history of alcoholism, who have a higher risk for becoming dependent on alcohol, should approach moderate drinking carefully. Maintaining moderate drinking habits may be harder for them than for people without a family history of drinking problems. Once a person moves from moderate to heavier drinking, the risks of social problems (for example, drinking and driving, violence, and trauma) and medical problems (for example, liver disease, brain damage, and cancer) increase greatly.

- **Talk to a health care professional.** Discuss your concerns with a doctor, nurse, nurse practitioner, or other health care provider. They can recommend groups or organizations that could help you avoid alcohol problems. If you are an adult who already has begun to drink, a health care professional can assess your drinking habits to see if you need to cut back on your drinking and advise you about how to do that.

Chapter 17

Coping With An Alcoholic Parent

Anthony is in bed when he hears the front door slam. He covers his head with his pillow so he doesn't have to listen to the sound of his parents arguing. Anthony knows that his mother has been drinking again. He starts worrying about getting to school on time and realizes he will probably have to help get his younger sister ready too.

Why Do People Drink Too Much?

Lots of people live with a parent or caregiver who is an alcoholic or who drinks too much. Alcoholism has been around for centuries, yet no one has discovered an easy way to prevent it.

Alcohol can affect people's health and also how they act. People who are drunk might be more aggressive or have mood swings. They may act in a way that is embarrassing to them or other people.

Alcoholism is a disease. Like any disease, it needs to be treated. Without professional help, a person with alcoholism will probably continue to drink and may even become worse over time.

About This Chapter: "Coping with an Alcoholic Parent," February 2010, reprinted with permission from www.kidshealth.org. Copyright © 2010 The Nemours Foundation. This information was provided by KidsHealth, one of the largest resources online for medically reviewed health information written for parents, kids, and teens. For more articles like this one, visit www.KidsHealth.org, or www.TeensHealth.org.

Diseases like alcoholism are no one's fault. Some people are more susceptible to wanting to drink too much. Scientists think it has to do with genetics, as well as things like family history, and life events.

Sometimes what starts as a bad habit can become a very big problem. For example, people may drink to cope with problems like boredom, stress, or money troubles. Maybe there's an illness in the family, or parents are having marriage problems.

No matter what anyone says, people don't drink because of someone else's behavior. So if you live with someone who has a drinking problem, don't blame yourself.

♣ **It's A Fact!!**
Problem Drinker Or Social Drinker?

Many people like to have a glass of wine, beer, or other alcohol, but they're not alcoholics. They're in control. They can stop after one or two glasses, and they usually drink in social situations or at specific times, like dinner. But when someone drinks so much that it changes their behavior and makes them unpredictable, mean, or embarrassing, it's a problem.

How Does Alcoholism Affect Families?

If you live with a parent who drinks, you may feel embarrassed, angry, sad, hurt, or any number of emotions. You may feel helpless: When parents promise to stop drinking, for example, it can end in frustration when they don't keep their promises.

Problem drinking can change how families function. A parent may have trouble keeping a job and problems paying the bills. Older kids may have to take care of younger siblings.

Some parents with alcohol problems might mistreat or abuse their children emotionally or physically. Others may neglect their kids by not providing sufficient care and guidance. Parents with alcohol problems might also use other drugs.

Despite what happens, most children of alcoholics love their parents and worry about something bad happening to them. Kids who live with problem drinkers often try all kinds of ways to prevent them from drinking. But, just as family members don't cause the addiction, they can't stop it either.

The person with the drinking problem has to take charge. Someone who has a bad habit or an addiction to alcohol needs to get help from a treatment center.

Alcoholism affects family members just as much as it affects the person drinking. Because of this, there are lots of support groups to help children of alcoholics cope with the problem.

What If A Parent Doesn't See A Problem?

Drinking too much can be a problem that nobody likes to talk about. In fact, lots of parents may become enraged at the slightest suggestion that they are drinking too much.

Sometimes, parents deny that they have a problem. A person in denial refuses to believe the truth about a situation. So problem drinkers may try to blame someone else because it is easier than taking responsibility for their own drinking.

Some parents make their families feel bad by saying stuff like, "You're driving me crazy!" or "I can't take this anymore." That can be harmful, especially to kids: Most young children don't know that the problem has nothing to do with their actions and that it's all in the drinker's mind.

Some parents do acknowledge their drinking, but deny that it's a problem. They may say stuff like, "I can stop anytime I want to," "Everyone drinks to unwind sometimes," or "My drinking is not a problem."

Lots of people fall into the trap of thinking that a parent's drinking is only temporary. They tell themselves that, when a particular problem is over, like having a rough time at work, the drinking will stop. But even if a parent who drinks too much has other problems, drinking is a separate problem. And that problem won't go away unless the drinker gets help.

Why Do I Feel So Bad?

If you're like most teens, your life is probably filled with emotional ups and downs, regardless of what's happening at home. Add a parent with a drinking problem to the mix, and it can all seem like too much.

There are many reasons why a parent's drinking can contribute to feelings of anger, frustration, disappointment, sadness, embarrassment, worry, loneliness, and helplessness. For example:

- **You might be subjected to a parent's changing moods.** People who drink can behave unpredictably. Kids who grow up around them may spend a lot of energy trying to figure out a parent's mood or guess what that parent wants. One day you might walk on eggshells to avoid an outburst because the dishes aren't done or the lawn isn't mowed. The next day, you may find yourself comforting a parent who promises that things will be better.

- **It may be hard to do things with friends or other people.** For some people, it feels like too much trouble to have a friend over or do the things that everyone else does. You just never know how your parent will act. Will your mom or dad show up drunk for school events or drive you (and your friends) home drunk?

- **You might be stressed or worried.** It can be scary to listen to adults in the house yell, fight, or break things by accident. Worrying about a parent just adds to all the other emotions you may be feeling. Are you lying awake waiting for mom or dad to get home safely? Do you feel it's not fair that you have to be the grown up and take care of things around the house? These are all normal reactions.

Although each family is different, people who grow up with alcoholic parents often feel alone, unloved, depressed, or burdened by the secret life they lead at home.

You know it's not possible to cause or stop the behavior of an alcoholic. So what can you do to feel better (or help a friend feel better)?

What Can I Do?

Acknowledge the problem. Many kids of parents who drink too much try to protect their parents or hide the problem. Admitting that your parent has a problem—even if he or she won't—is the first step in taking control. Start by talking to a friend, teacher, counselor, or coach. If you can't face telling someone you know, call an organization like Al-Anon/Alateen (they have a 24-hour hotline at 1-800-344-2666) or go online for help.

✔ Quick Tip

Get Help

You're not betraying your parent by seeking help. Keeping "the secret" is part of the disease of alcoholism—and it allows the problem to get worse. Getting help is a healthy step in dealing with the problems a parent's drinking create. In fact, taking care of yourself is what your parents would want you to do, especially if they have trouble doing it every day because of their drinking.

Be informed. Being aware of how your parent's drinking affects you can help put things in perspective. For example, some teens who live with alcoholic adults become afraid to speak out or show any normal anger or emotion because they worry it may trigger a parent's drinking. Remind yourself that you are not responsible for your parent drinking too much, and that you cannot cause it or stop it.

Be aware of your emotions. When you feel things like anger or resentment, try to identify those feelings. Talk to a close friend or write down how you are feeling. Recognizing how a parent's problem drinking makes you feel can help you from burying your feelings and pretending that everything's OK.

Learn healthy coping strategies. When we grow up around people who turn to alcohol or other unhealthy ways of dealing with problems, they become our example. Watching new role models can help people learn healthy coping mechanisms and ways of making good decisions.

Coaches, aunts, uncles, parents of friends, or teachers all have to deal with things like frustration or disappointment. Watch how they do it. School counselors can be a great resource here. Next time you have a problem, ask someone you trust for help.

Find support. It's good to share your feelings with a friend, but it's equally important to talk to an adult you trust. A school counselor, favorite teacher, or coach may be able to help. Some teens turn to their school D.A.R.E. (Drug and Alcohol Resistance Education) officer. Others prefer to talk to a family member or parents of a close friend.

Because alcoholism is such a widespread problem, several organizations offer confidential support groups and meetings for people living with alcoholics. Alateen is a group specifically geared to young people living with adults who have drinking problems. Alateen can also help teens whose parents may already be in treatment or recovery. The group Alcoholics Anonymous (AA) also offers resources for people living with alcoholics.

Find a safe environment. Do you find yourself avoiding your house as much as possible? Are you thinking about running away? If you feel that the situation at home is becoming dangerous, you can call the National Domestic Violence Hotline at (800) 799-SAFE. And don't hesitate to dial 911 if you think you or another family member is in immediate danger.

Stop the cycle. Teenage children of alcoholics are at higher risk of becoming alcoholics themselves. Scientists think this is because of genetics and the environment that kids grow up in. For example, people might learn to drink as a way to avoid fear, boredom, anxiety, sadness, or other unpleasant feelings. Understanding that there could be a problem and finding adults and peers to help you can be the most important thing you do to reduce the risk of problem drinking.

Alcoholism is a disease. You can show your love and support, but you won't be able to stop someone from drinking. Talking about the problem, finding support, and choosing healthy ways to cope are choices you can make to feel more in control of the situation. Above all, don't give up!

Part Three

Tobacco

Chapter 18

Tobacco Addiction

What is tobacco addiction?

When people are addicted, they have a compulsive need to seek out and use a substance, even when they understand the harm it can cause. Tobacco products—cigarettes, cigars or pipes, and smokeless tobacco—all can lead to addiction. Everyone knows that smoking is bad for you, and most people that do it want to quit. In fact, nearly 35 million people make a serious attempt to quit each year. Unfortunately, most who try to quit on their own relapse—often within a week.

Is nicotine addictive?

Yes. It is actually the nicotine in tobacco that is addictive. Each cigarette contains about 10 milligrams of nicotine. Because the smoker inhales only some of the smoke from a cigarette, and not all of each puff is absorbed in the lungs, a smoker gets about 1 to 2 milligrams of the drug from each cigarette. Although that may not seem like much, it is enough to make someone addicted.

Is nicotine the only harmful part of tobacco?

No. Nicotine is only one of more than 4,000 chemicals, many of which are poisonous, found in the smoke from tobacco products. Smokeless tobacco products also contain many toxins as well as high levels of nicotine. Many of these

About This Chapter: Information in this chapter is from "Tobacco Addiction," NIDA for Teens, National Institute on Drug Abuse, a component of the United States Department of Health and Human Services, 2009.

other ingredients are things we would never consider putting in our bodies, like tar, carbon monoxide, acetaldehyde, and nitrosamines. Tar causes lung cancer, emphysema, and bronchial diseases. Carbon monoxide causes heart problems, which is one reason why smokers are at high risk for heart disease.

How is tobacco used?

Tobacco can be smoked in cigarettes, cigars, or pipes. It can be chewed or, if powdered, sniffed. "Bidis" are an alternative cigarette. They come originally from India and are hand-rolled. In the U.S., bidis are popular with teens because they come in colorful packages with flavor choices. Some teens think that bidis are less harmful than regular cigarettes, but in fact they have more nicotine, which may make people smoke more, giving bidis the potential to be even more harmful than cigarettes. Hookah—or water pipe smoking—practiced for centuries in other countries, has recently become popular among teens as well. Hookah tobacco comes in many flavors, and the pipe is typically passed around in groups. Although many hookah smokers think it is less harmful than smoking cigarettes, water pipe smoking still delivers the addictive drug nicotine and is at least as toxic as cigarette smoking.

What are the common street names?

You might hear cigarettes referred to as "smokes," "cigs," or "butts." Smokeless tobacco is often called "chew," "dip," "spit tobacco," "snus," or "snuff." People may refer to hookah smoking as "narghile," "argileh," "shisha," "hubble-bubble," or "goza."

How many teens use it?

First, the good news: Smoking is at historically low levels among 8th, 10th, and 12th graders, according to the Monitoring the Future Survey from the National Institute on Drug Abuse (NIDA). That said, in 2009, 20.1% of 12th graders, 13.1% of 10th graders, and 6.5% of 8th graders still reported smoking in the month prior to the survey.

Use of smokeless tobacco had been showing a decline over the past decade—until 2009, that is. According to the survey, current use of smokeless tobacco among 8th graders was 3.7% and 6.5% for 10th graders. Among 12th graders, 8.4% reported using smokeless tobacco in the last month, a number not seen since 1999.

✤ It's A Fact!!

As if cigarettes aren't bad enough, there are other hazardous tobacco products. Because of how they look or smell or how they're used, some people might think they're not as addictive or harmful as cigarettes. But here's the truth:

- **Chewing Tobacco:** Spit, snuff, dip, smokeless. The amount of nicotine in one pinch of dip can be five times as high as in a cigarette. Plus, dip comes with its own health risks. From the toxins in the juice created, chewers can develop painful lesions on their tongue, as well as cancer of the esophagus, pharynx, larynx, and stomach. Perhaps worst of all are cancers of the mouth and tongue, which often require surgery to remove parts of a user's face. These cancers from chewing tobacco often occur earlier, rather than later, in a user's life.

- **Cigars:** Cigars are puffed and not inhaled, but the smoke still gets into the lungs and does just as much damage as cigarettes, and cigar smokers risk the same oral cancer and other irritation problems as people who chew tobacco. Also, a cigar delivers nicotine. In fact, it delivers about four times as much nicotine as a cigarette.

- **Bidis:** These hand-rolled cigarettes from India (pronounced "beedees") are often packaged in cinnamon, orange, and chocolate flavors to appeal to kids. But don't let the taste fool you. Bidis are generally unfiltered and can have 28 percent higher nicotine concentration levels than cigarettes.

Source: From "By Any Other Name," an article in a Heads Up compilation by Scholastic and the National Institute on Drug Abuse. Published 2003. Despite the older date of this document, the information about tobacco products is still relevant to today's readers.

How does tobacco deliver its effects?

With each puff of a cigarette, a smoker pulls nicotine and other harmful substances into the lungs, where it is absorbed into the blood. It takes just eight seconds for nicotine to hit the brain. Nicotine happens to be shaped like the natural brain chemical acetylcholine. Acetylcholine is one of many chemicals called neurotransmitters that carry messages between brain cells. Neurons (brain cells) have specialized proteins called receptors, into which specific neurotransmitters can fit, like a key fitting into a lock. Nicotine locks into acetylcholine receptors, rapidly causing changes in the brain and body. For instance, nicotine increases blood pressure, heart rate, and respiration (breathing).

Nicotine also attaches to cholinergic receptors on neurons that release a neurotransmitter called dopamine. Dopamine is released normally when you experience something pleasurable like good food, surfing, or the company of people you love. But smoking cigarettes causes neurons to release excess dopamine, which is responsible for the feelings of pleasure experienced by the smoker. However, this effect wears off rapidly, causing smokers to get the urge to light up again for another dose of the drug.

Nicotine may be the primary addictive component in tobacco but it's not the only ingredient that is biologically important. Using advanced neuroimaging technology, scientists have found that smokers have a significant reduction in the levels of an enzyme called monoamine oxidase (MAO) in the brain and throughout the body. This enzyme is responsible for the breakdown of dopamine, other neurotransmitters involved in mood regulation, and in a variety of bodily functions. Having lower amounts of MAO in the brain may lead to higher dopamine levels and be another reason that smokers continue to smoke—to sustain the pleasurable feelings that high dopamine levels create.

Also, researchers have recently shown in animals that acetaldehyde, another chemical constituent of tobacco smoke, dramatically increases the rewarding properties of nicotine—particularly in adolescent animals—which may be one reason why teens are more vulnerable to becoming addicted to tobacco than adults.

What happens when someone uses tobacco for long periods of time?

Long-term use of nicotine frequently leads to addiction. Research is just beginning to document all of the changes in the brain that accompany nicotine addiction. The behavioral consequences of these changes are well documented, however.

The way that nicotine is absorbed and metabolized by the body enhances its addictive potential. Each inhalation brings a rapid distribution of nicotine to the brain—peaking within 10 seconds and then disappearing quickly, along

♣ It's A Fact!!

Cigarette smoke contains more than 4,000 chemicals, including toxins like ammonia. But the chief culprit in cigarettes is nicotine, a powerfully addictive drug.

With every puff of a cigarette, nicotine alters how your brain functions. Like cocaine and heroin, nicotine stimulates the release of a molecule called dopamine, located in parts of the brain that are involved in addictive behaviors. Although a user does not get the high from cigarettes that one might get from drugs like cocaine and heroin, make no mistake: nicotine affects your brain.

Nicotine "primes" the brain for addiction. You can begin to crave cigarettes more than anything else. "Smoking becomes your sole focus," says Dr. Cindy Miner, the Chief of NIDA's Science Policy Branch. "Nothing else is as pleasurable as it used to be." Indeed, your brain becomes so used to the presence of nicotine that, when you try to quit, it rebels and craves more.

But addiction may be just the tip of the iceberg when it comes to risks from smoking. When you inhale, cigarette smoke and the chemicals it carries are absorbed by the lungs and quickly move into the bloodstream, where they circulate through your heart to your brain and the rest of your body. Your lungs fill with chemical deposits. "You're taking tar into your lungs and there's no way to clear out all that debris," says Miner. "Suddenly you find that you are gasping for breath on the soccer field."

Research suggests that nicotine is even more harmful to the developing heart, lungs, and brains of teens. "The younger you start, the more likely you will get hooked," Miner says. "The younger you get hooked, the more cigarettes you will smoke. And the more cigarettes you smoke— Well, we know where that leads."

Source: From "Cigarettes: How They Hook and Hurt," an article in a Heads Up compilation by Scholastic and the National Institute on Drug Abuse. Published 2003. Despite the older date of this document, the information about tobacco products is still relevant to today's readers.

with the associated pleasurable feelings. Over the course of the day, tolerance develops—meaning that higher (or more frequent) doses are required to produce the same initial effects. Some of this tolerance is lost overnight, and smokers often report that the first cigarette of the day is the strongest or the "best."

When people quit smoking, they usually experience withdrawal symptoms, which often drive them back to tobacco use. Nicotine withdrawal symptoms include irritability, cognitive and attention deficits, sleep disturbances, increased appetite, and craving. Craving—an intense urge for nicotine that can persist for six months or longer—is an important but poorly understood component of the nicotine withdrawal syndrome. Some people describe it as a major stumbling block to quitting.

Withdrawal symptoms usually peak within the first few days and may subside within a few weeks. The withdrawal syndrome is related to the pharmacological effects of nicotine, but many behavioral factors also affect the severity and persistence of withdrawal symptoms. For example, the cues associated with smoking—the end of a meal, the sight or smell of a cigarette, the ritual of obtaining, handling, lighting, and smoking the cigarette, the people you hung out with when you smoked, and alcohol use—all can be powerful triggers of craving that can last or re-emerge months or even years after smoking has ceased. While nicotine gum and patches may stop the pharmacological aspects of withdrawal, cravings often persist.

What are other adverse health effects?

Tobacco abuse harms every organ in the body. It has been conclusively linked to leukemia, cataracts, and pneumonia, and accounts for about one-third of all cancer deaths. The overall rates of death from cancer are twice as high among smokers as nonsmokers, with heavy smokers having rates that are four times greater than those of nonsmokers. And, you guessed it—foremost among the cancers caused by tobacco use is lung cancer. In fact, cigarette smoking has been linked to about 90 percent of all lung cancer cases, the number-one cancer killer of both men and women. Tobacco abuse is also associated with cancers of the mouth, pharynx, larynx, esophagus, stomach, pancreas, cervix, kidney, ureter, and bladder.

Smokers also lose some of their sense of smell and taste, don't have the same stamina for exercise and sports they once did, and may smell of smoke. After smoking for a long time, smokers find that their skin ages faster and their teeth discolor or turn brown.

It's not just the smokers who are affected. Nonsmokers are exposed to "secondhand smoke," which comes from both the smoke that a smoker exhales and from the smoke floating from the end of a cigarette, cigar, or pipe. Inhaling secondhand smoke increases a person's risk of developing heart disease by 25 to 30 percent and lung cancer by 20 to 30 percent. In fact, secondhand smoke is estimated to contribute to as many as 40,000 deaths related to heart disease and about 3,000 lung cancer deaths per year among nonsmokers. Secondhand smoke also causes respiratory problems in nonsmokers, like coughing, phlegm, and reduced lung function. Children exposed to secondhand smoke are at an increased risk for sudden infant death syndrome, acute respiratory infections, ear problems, and more severe asthma. And, believe it or not, dropped cigarettes are the leading cause of residential fire fatalities, leading to more than 1,000 such deaths each year.

Each year, almost half a million Americans die from tobacco use. One of every six deaths in the United States is a result of tobacco use, making tobacco more lethal than all other addictive drugs combined.

Smoking and pregnancy: What are the risks?

In the United States between 2007 and 2008, 20.6% of teens ages 15 to 17 smoked cigarettes during their pregnancies. Carbon monoxide and nicotine from tobacco smoke may interfere with fetal oxygen supply—and because nicotine readily crosses the placenta, it can reach concentrations in the fetus that are much higher than maternal levels. Nicotine concentrates in fetal blood, amniotic fluid, and breast milk, exposing both fetuses and infants to toxic effects. These factors can have severe consequences for the fetuses and infants of smoking mothers, including increased risk for stillbirth, infant mortality, sudden infant death syndrome, preterm birth, and respiratory problems. In addition, smoking more than a pack a day during pregnancy nearly doubles the risk that the affected child will become addicted to tobacco if that child starts smoking.

How is tobacco addiction treated?

The good news is that treatments for tobacco addiction do work. Although some smokers can quit without help, many people need help. Behavioral treatment programs help smokers learn about and change their behaviors using self-help materials, counselor-staffed telephone "quitlines," and individual therapy. Over-the-counter medications, such as the nicotine patch, gum, inhalers, and lozenges, replace nicotine and relieve the symptoms of withdrawal. It is important to know that nicotine replacement medicines can be safely used as a medication when taken properly. They have lower overall nicotine levels than tobacco and they have little abuse potential since they do not produce the pleasurable effects of tobacco products. They also don't contain the carcinogens and gases found in tobacco smoke, making them a good treatment approach for quitting.

There are also prescription medications now available for smoking cessation, such as bupropion (Zyban®) and varenicline tartrate (Chantix®), that have been shown to help people quit. But research shows that the most effective way to quit smoking is to use both medications and behavioral treatment programs.

The bottom line: People who quit smoking can have immediate health benefits. Believe it or not, within 24 hours of quitting, a person's blood pressure decreases and they have less of a chance of having a heart attack. Over the long haul, quitting means less chance of stroke, lung and other cancers, and coronary heart disease, and more chance for a long and healthy life.

Chapter 19

Child And Teen Tobacco Use

Smoking And Kids

- Each day, more than 3,500 kids in the United States try their first cigarette; and each day about 1,000 other kids under 18 years of age become new regular, daily smokers. That's 350,000 new underage daily smokers in this country each year.

- The addiction rate for smoking is higher than the addiction rates for marijuana, alcohol, or cocaine; and symptoms of serious nicotine addiction often occur only weeks or even just days after youth "experimentation" with smoking first begins.

- 90 percent of all adult smokers begin while in their teens, or earlier, and two-thirds become regular, daily smokers before they reach the age of 19.

- 20.1 percent of high school students are current smokers by the time they leave high school.

- 20 percent of all high school students (9-12 grades) are current smokers, including 18.7 percent of females and 21.3 percent of males. White high school students have the highest smoking rate (23.2 percent) compared to Hispanics (16.7 percent), and African-Americans (11.6 percent).

About This Chapter: This chapter includes "Smoking and Kids," © 2009, and "Smokeless Tobacco and Kids," © 2008, both reprinted with permission from the Campaign for Tobacco-Free Kids. To view the complete documents including references, visit www.tobaccofreekids.org.

- Roughly one-third of all youth smokers will eventually die prematurely from smoking-caused disease.

- Smoking can also seriously harm kids while they are still young. Besides the immediate bad breath, irritated eyes and throat, and increased heartbeat and blood pressure, near-term harms from youth smoking include respiratory problems, reduced immune function, increased illness, tooth decay, gum disease, and pre-cancerous gene mutations.

- Smoking during youth is also associated with an increased likelihood of using illegal drugs.

- The cigarette companies spend more than $12.5 billion each year to promote their deadly products—that's more than $34 million spent every day to market cigarettes, and much of that marketing directly reaches and influences kids.

- Kids are more susceptible to cigarette advertising and marketing than adults. 81.3 percent of youth smokers (12–17) prefer Marlboro, Camel, and Newport, three heavily advertised brands, while only 54.1 percent of smokers over age 26 prefer these brands. For example, between 1989 and 1993, spending on the Joe Camel ad campaign jumped from $27 million to $43 million, which prompted a 50 percent increase in Camel's share of the youth market but had no impact at all on its adult market share. Additionally, a survey released in March 2008 showed that kids were almost twice as likely as adults to recall tobacco advertising.

- A *Journal of the National Cancer Institute* study found that teens were more likely to be influenced to smoke by cigarette marketing than by peer pressure. Similarly, a *Journal of the American Medical Association* study found that as much as a third of underage experimentation with smoking was attributable to tobacco company marketing efforts.

Smokeless Tobacco And Kids

Since 1970, smokeless, or spit, tobacco has gone from a product used primarily by older men to one used predominantly by young men and boys. This trend has occurred as smokeless tobacco promotions have increased dramatically and a new generation of smokeless tobacco products has hit the market.

Far from being a "safe" alternative to cigarette smoking, smokeless tobacco use increases the risk of developing many health problems. Furthermore, evidence shows that adolescent boys who use smokeless tobacco products have a higher risk of becoming cigarette smokers within four years.

In 1970, men 65 and older were almost six times as likely as those aged 18 to 24 to use spit tobacco regularly (12.7 vs. 2.2 percent). By 1991, however, young men were 50 percent more likely than the oldest men to be regular users. (8.4 vs. 5.6 percent). This pattern holds especially true for moist snuff, the most popular type of smokeless tobacco. From 1970 to 1991, the regular use of moist snuff by 18 to 24 year old men increased almost ten-fold, from less than one percent to 6.2 percent. Conversely, use among men 65 and older decreased by almost half, from four percent to 2.2 percent. Among all high school seniors who have ever used spit tobacco, almost three-fourths began by the ninth grade.

Despite some recent declines in youth spit tobacco use, 13.4 percent of U.S. high school boys and 2.3 percent of high school girls currently use smokeless tobacco products. In some states, smokeless tobacco use among high school boys is particularly high, including Kentucky (26.7 percent), Montana (20.3 percent), Oklahoma (24.8 percent), Tennessee (22.8 percent), West Virginia (27.0 percent), and Wyoming (21.3 percent).

The U.S. Smokeless Tobacco Company (UST) is the biggest smokeless tobacco company in the U.S. and controls two-thirds of the moist snuff tobacco market (with leading premium brands Skoal and Copenhagen). Reynolds-American Tobacco Company recently acquired the second largest smokeless tobacco company in the U.S., Conwood Smokeless Tobacco Company (makers of Grizzly and Kodiak), which has nearly one-fourth share of the moist snuff market, and other cigarette companies have also started test marketing their own smokeless tobacco products.

Marketing Smokeless Tobacco To Kids

According to internal company documents, UST developed a strategy for hooking new spit-tobacco users, meaning kids, some time ago. As one document states:

New users of smokeless tobacco—attracted to the product for a variety of reasons— are most likely to begin with products that are milder tasting, more flavored, and/or easier to control in the mouth. After a period of time, there is a natural progression of product switching to brands that are more full-bodied, less flavored, have more concentrated 'tobacco taste' than the entry brand.

Following this strategy, between 1983 to 1984, UST introduced Skoal Bandits and Skoal Long Cut, designed to "graduate" new users from beginner strength to stronger, more potent products. A 1985 internal UST newsletter indicates the company's desire to appeal to youth: "Skoal Bandits is the introductory product, and then we look towards establishing a normal graduation process." In 1993, cherry flavoring was added to UST's Skoal Long Cut, another starter product. A former UST sales representative revealed that "Cherry Skoal is for somebody who likes the taste of candy, if you know what I'm saying." According to UST's 2005 Annual Report, flavored products (that now include flavors such as apple, peach, vanilla, berry blend, and citrus blend) account for more than 11 percent of all moist snuff sales. UST launched "new and improved" Skoal Bandits in August 2006.

✎ **What's It Mean?**

Types Of Spit Tobacco

- Oral (moist) snuff is a finely cut, processed tobacco, which the user places between the cheek and gum, that releases nicotine which, in turn, is absorbed by the membranes of the mouth.

- Looseleaf chewing tobacco is stripped and processed cigar-type tobacco leaves that are loosely packed to form small strips, often sold in a foil-lined pouch and usually treated with sugar or licorice.

- Plug chewing tobacco consists of small, oblong blocks of semi-soft chewing tobacco that often contain sweeteners and other flavoring agents.

- Nasal snuff is a fine tobacco powder that is sniffed into the nostrils. Flavorings may be added during fermentation, and perfumes may be added after grinding.

Source: © 2008 Campaign for Tobacco-Free Kids.

Smokeless tobacco products have been marketed to youth through a number of channels, including sporting events like auto racing and rodeos that are widely attended by kids. Although the state tobacco settlement agreements have limited UST's ability to continue to do brand-name sponsorships of events and teams, UST continues to be a promotional sponsor of both professional motorsports and rodeo and bull riding. As the general manager of the College Finals said, "U.S. Tobacco is the oldest and best friend college rodeo ever had." Some cities, including Boulder and Greeley, CO, have prohibited free tobacco product giveaways, making it more difficult for UST to lure new users at these events.

Back in 1999, UST ran a full-color advertising insert for its Rooster brand smokeless tobacco in San Diego State University's college paper, the Daily Aztec. The ad offered a sweepstakes for an all expenses paid trip to the Playboy mansion and, in direct violation of California law, included a $1.00 coupon. State enforcement efforts related to the ad forced UST to pay a fine of $150,000 and pay for a parallel ad insert opposing smokeless tobacco use.

Continuing its efforts to lure and maintain young users, in 2001, UST ran a magazine ad for its Rooster brand in Rolling Stone with the phrase, "Cock-A-Doodle Freakin' Do." After UST received criticism for the ad's blatant appeal to youth, it promised not to use those ads anymore. But less than a year later, ads for Rooster appeared in Sports Illustrated, bearing the same image as before, but with the phrases, "Where's The Chicks?," and "Birds of a Feather Party Together."

From 1998 to 2005 (the most recent year for which data are available), the total advertising and marketing expenditures of the top-five smokeless tobacco companies in the U.S. (Conwood Company, National Tobacco Company, Swedish Match North America, Inc., Swisher International, and UST) increased by 72.4 percent. In 2005, these smokeless tobacco companies spent more than $250.7 million to advertise and market their products. Some of these funds pay for smokeless tobacco ads in magazines with high youth readership, such as Sports Illustrated and Rolling Stone. In fact, despite the restrictions placed on youth advertising by the Smokeless Tobacco Master Settlement Agreement, UST has continued to advertise in youth-oriented magazines. From 1997 to 2001, UST's expenditures in youth magazines increased 161 percent, from $3.6 million to $9.4 million.

Given the track record of UST and its marketing behavior aimed at kids and adolescents, of equal or greater concern is the recent entry of Reynolds-American—labeled as a "serial violator" of the Master Settlement Agreement by the U.S. Department of Justice—into the smokeless tobacco market with its purchase of Conwood. For instance, in 2006, the California Supreme Court ruled that R.J. Reynolds had violated state's ban on free distribution of cigarettes at events attended by minors on six separate occasions.

Other notable smokeless tobacco products that have been launched in the last several years include UST's product Revel. UST test marketed Revel as a way to consume tobacco in places or situations when smoking is not allowed or is not socially acceptable. Star Scientific's Ariva tobacco lozenges and Stonewall Hard Snuff, both dissolvable tobacco tablets, are meant to replace cigarettes in situations where smokers cannot smoke. The website states, "Dissolvable tobacco has no boundaries, there are no locations or situations where you cannot use it and nobody can tell you're using it." In an agreement with Star Scientific and just prior to its merger with R.J. Reynolds, Brown & Williamson briefly test marketed Interval tobacco tabs, which were similar to the Star Scientific products.

Seeing the downward trend in smoking rates and the increasing popularity of smokeless tobacco products, cigarette companies have released their own smokeless tobacco products that draw on the brand names of their popular cigarettes to attract new users. R.J. Reynolds's Camel Snus, Philip Morris USA's Marlboro Snus, Liggett Group's Grand Prix Snus, and Lorillard's Triumph Snus have been released into test market within the last year. Snus are small, teabag-like pouches containing tobacco and other flavorings that users place between their upper gum and lip. Because these products do not require spitting, their use can be easily concealed. One high school student admitted using Camel Snus during class, saying, "It's easy, it's super-discreet… and none of the teachers will ever know what I'm doing."

These new products concern public health organizations because they may lure even more kids into smokeless tobacco use and addiction—because of their novelty, the misconception that they are a "safe" form of tobacco use, and they can be consumed much less conspicuously than either cigarettes or existing spit tobacco products at home, in school, and in other locations. Furthermore, cigarette smokers who might ultimately quit because of the social stigma associated with smoking, the inconvenience caused by smoking restrictions at work and elsewhere, or a desire to protect their family and friends from secondhand smoke may instead switch to smokeless tobacco products.

♣ **It's A Fact!!**
Spit Tobacco And Other Drugs

High school students who use spit tobacco 20 to 30 days per month are nearly four times more likely to currently use marijuana than nonusers, almost three times more likely to ever use cocaine, and nearly three times more likely to ever use inhalants to get high. In addition, heavy users of smokeless or spit tobacco are almost 16 times more likely than nonusers are to currently consume alcohol, as well.

Source: © 2008 Campaign for Tobacco-Free Kids.

Harms From Smokeless Tobacco Use

Smokeless tobacco use can lead to oral cancer, gum disease, and nicotine addiction; and it increases the risk of cardiovascular disease, including heart attacks. More specifically:

- Smokeless tobacco causes leukoplakia, a disease of the mouth characterized by white patches and oral lesions on the cheeks, gums, and/or tongue. Leukoplakia, which can lead to oral cancer, occurs in more than half of all users in the first three years of use. Studies have found that 60 to 78 percent of spit tobacco users have oral lesions.

- Constant exposure to tobacco juice causes cancer of the esophagus, pharynx, larynx, stomach and pancreas. Smokeless tobacco users are at heightened risk for oral cancer compared to non-users and these cancers can form within five years of regular use.

- A 2008 study from the WHO International Agency for Research on Cancer concluded that smokeless tobacco users have an 80 percent higher risk of developing oral cancer and a 60 percent higher risk of developing pancreatic and esophageal cancer.

- Smokeless tobacco contains nitrosamines—proven and potent carcinogens. A study by the American Health Foundation for the Commonwealth of Massachusetts found that the level of cancer causing tobacco specific nitrosamines (TSNAs) in U.S. oral moist snuff brands were significantly higher than comparable Swedish Match brands. These data suggest that it is possible for smokeless tobacco companies to produce oral snuff with significantly lower TSNA levels.

- Chewing tobacco has been linked to dental caries. A study by the National Institutes of Health and the Centers for Disease Control and Prevention found chewing tobacco users were four times more likely than non-users to have decayed dental root surfaces. Spit tobacco also causes gum disease (gingivitis), which can lead to bone and tooth loss.

- A study in the *American Journal of Preventive Medicine* found that "snuff use may be a gateway form of nicotine dosing among males in the United States that may lead to subsequent cigarette smoking." Further, the study found that "the prevalence of smoking was substantially higher among men who had quit using snuff than among those who had never used snuff, suggesting that more than 40% of men who had been snuff users continued or initiated smoking."

Despite all the evidence of the harms of smokeless tobacco, in April 1999, a spokesperson for UST, quoted in the *Providence Journal*, claimed that it has not been "scientifically established" that smokeless tobacco is "a cause of oral cancer." The Rhode Island Attorney General subsequently filed a legal action against UST for violating the multi-state settlement agreement's provisions prohibiting false statements about the health effects of tobacco products. As a result, UST was required to formally acknowledge that the Surgeon General and other public health authorities have concluded that smokeless tobacco is addictive and can cause oral cancer and to pay $15,000 to the Attorney General's office for efforts to prevent Rhode Island youths from using tobacco.

Chapter 20

Smoking's Immediate Effects On The Body

Many teenagers and adults think that there are no effects of smoking on their bodies until they reach middle age. Smoking-caused lung cancer, other cancers, heart disease, and stroke typically do not occur until years after a person's first cigarette. However, there are many serious harms from smoking that occur much sooner. In fact, smoking has numerous immediate health effects on the brain and on the respiratory, cardiovascular, gastrointestinal, immune and metabolic systems. While these immediate effects do not all produce noticeable symptoms, most begin to damage the body with the first cigarette—sometimes irreversibly— and rapidly produce serious medical conditions and health consequences.

Rapid Addiction From Early Smoking

Many teenagers and younger children inaccurately believe that experimenting with smoking or even casual use will not lead to any serious dependency. In fact, the latest research shows that serious symptoms of addiction—such as having strong urges to smoke, feeling anxious or irritable, or having unsuccessfully tried to not smoke—can appear among youths within weeks or only days after occasional smoking first begins. The average smoker tries their first cigarette at age 12 and may be a regular smoker by age 14.

About This Chapter: "Smoking's Immediate Effects on the Body," reprinted with permission from the Campaign for Tobacco-Free Kids, © 2009. To view the complete document including references, visit www.tobaccofreekids.org.

❖ It's A Fact!!

Every day, more than 3,500 kids try their first cigarette and about 1,000 other kids under 18 years of age become new regular, daily smokers. Almost 90% of youths that smoke regularly report seriously strong cravings, and more than 70% of adolescent smokers have already tried and failed to quit smoking.

Source: © 2009 Campaign for Tobacco-Free Kids.

Immediate And Rapid Effects On The Brain

Part of the addictive power of nicotine comes from its direct effect on the brain. In addition to the well-understood chemical dependency, cigarette smokers also show evidence of a higher rate of behavioral problems and suffer the following immediate effects:

- **Increases Stress:** Contrary to popular belief, smoking does not relieve stress. Studies have shown that on average, smokers have higher levels of stress than non-smokers. The feelings of relaxation that smokers experience while they are smoking are actually a return to the normal unstressed state that non-smokers experience all of the time.

- **Alters Brain Chemistry:** When compared to non-smokers, smokers brain cells—specifically brain cell receptors—have been shown to have fewer dopamine receptors. Brain cell receptors are molecules that sit on the outside of the cell interacting with the molecules that fit into the receptor, much like a lock and key. Receptors (locks) are important because they guard and mediate the functions of the cell. For instance when the right molecule (key) comes along it unlocks the receptor, setting off a chain of events to perform a specific cell function. Specific receptors mediate different cell activities.

Smokers have fewer dopamine receptors, a specific cell receptor found in the brain that is believed to play a role in addiction. Dopamine is normally released naturally while engaging in certain behaviors like eating, drinking, and copulation. The release of dopamine is believed to give one a sense of reward. One of the leading hypotheses regarding the mechanism of addiction theorizes that nicotine exposure initially increases dopamine transmission, but subsequently decreases dopamine receptor function and number. The initial increase in dopamine activity from nicotine results initially in pleasant feelings for the smoker, but the subsequent decrease in dopamine leaves the smoker craving more cigarettes.

New animal studies have shown that brain chemistry and receptors may be altered early in the smoking process. Habitual smoking may continue to change brain chemistry, including decreasing dopamine receptors and thus yielding a more intense craving and risk of addiction. These brain chemistry changes may be permanent. In addition, because the role played by receptors in other cognitive functions, such as memory and intelligence, is unknown, how cigarette smoking affects other brain functions by altering brain chemistry is unknown.

Immediate And Rapid Effects On The Respiratory System

The respiratory system includes the passages from the nose and sinuses down into the smallest airways of the lungs. Because all of these spaces are in direct communication with one another, they can all be affected by tobacco smoke simultaneously.

- **Bronchospasm:** This term refers to "airway irritability" or the abnormal tightening of the airways of the lungs. Bronchospasm makes airways smaller and leads to wheezing similar to that experienced by someone with asthma during an asthma attack. While smokers may not have asthma, they are susceptible to this type of reaction to tobacco smoke. An asthmatic that starts smoking can severely worsen his/her condition. Bronchospasm makes breathing more difficult, as the body tries to get more air into irritated lungs.

- **Increases Phlegm Production:** The lungs produce mucus to trap chemical and toxic substances. Small "finger like" hairs, called cilia, coat the lung's airways and move rhythmically to clear this mucus from the lungs. Combined with coughing, this is usually an effective method of clearing the lungs of harmful substances. Tobacco smoke paralyzes these hairs, allowing mucus to collect in the lungs of the smoker. Cigarette smoke also promotes goblet cell growth resulting in an increase in mucus. More mucus is made with each breath of irritating tobacco and the smoker cannot easily clear the increased mucus.

- **Persistent Cough:** Coughing is the body's natural response to clear irritants from the lungs. Without the help of cilia (above), a smoker is faced with the difficult task of clearing increased amounts of phlegm with cough alone. A persistent cough, while irritating, is the smoker's only defense against the harmful products of tobacco smoke. A smoker will likely have a persistent, annoying cough from the time they start smoking. A smoker who is not coughing is probably not doing an effective job of clearing his/her lungs of the harmful irritants found in tobacco smoke.

- **Decreases Physical Performance:** When the body is stressed or very active (for example, running, swimming, playing competitive sports), it requires that more oxygen be delivered to active muscles. The combination of bronchospasm and increased phlegm production result in airway obstruction and decreased lung function, leading to poor physical performance. In addition, smoking has been shown to stunt lung development in adolescent girls, limiting adult breathing capacity. Smoking not only limits one's current state of fitness, but can also restrict future physical potential.

Immediate And Rapid Effects On The Cardiovascular System

The cardiovascular system includes the heart and all of the blood vessels that carry blood to and from the organs. Blood vessels include arteries, veins, and capillaries, which are all connected and work in unison with the lungs to deliver oxygen to the brain, heart, and other vital organs.

- **Adverse Lipid Profile:** Lipids, a form of fat, are a source of energy for the body. Most people use this fat in its good form, called high-density lipoproteins, or HDLs. Some forms of fat, such as low-density lipoproteins (LDLs, triglycerides and cholesterol) can be harmful to the body. These harmful forms have their greatest effects on blood vessels.

If produced in excess or accumulated over time, they can stick to blood vessel walls and cause narrowing. Such narrowing can impair blood flow to the heart, brain and other organs, causing them to fail. Most bodies have a balance of good and bad fats. However, that is not the case for smokers. Nicotine increases the amount of bad fats (LDL, triglycerides, cholesterol) circulating in the blood vessels and decreases the amount of good fat (HDL) available. These silent effects begin immediately and greatly increase the risk for heart disease and stroke. In fact, smoking one to five cigarettes per day presents a significant risk for a heart attack.

- **Atherosclerosis:** Atherosclerosis is a process in which fat and cholesterol form "plaques" and stick to the walls of an artery. These plaques reduce the blood's flow through the artery. While this process starts at a very young age (Some children younger than one year of age already show some of the changes that lead to plaque formation.) there are several factors that can accelerate atherosclerosis. Nicotine and other toxic substances from tobacco smoke are absorbed through the lungs into the blood stream and are circulated throughout the body. These substances damage the blood vessel walls, which allow plaques to form at a faster rate than they would in a non-smoker. In this way, smoking increases the risk of heart disease by hastening atherosclerosis. In addition, a recent study in Japan showed a measurable decrease in the elasticity of the coronary arteries of non-smokers after just 30 minutes of exposure to second hand smoke.

- **Thrombosis:** Thrombosis is a process that results in the formation of a clot inside a blood vessel. Normally, clots form inside blood vessels to stop bleeding, when vessels have been injured. However, components of tobacco smoke result in dangerously increased rates of clot formation. Smokers have elevated levels of thrombin, an enzyme that causes the blood to clot, after fasting, as well as a spike immediately after smoking. This process may result in blockage of blood vessels, stopping blood flow to vital organs. In addition, thrombosis especially occurs around sites of plaque formation (above). Because of this abnormal tendency to clot, smokers with less severe heart disease, have more heart attacks than nonsmokers. In addition, sudden death is four times more likely to occur in young male cigarette smokers than in nonsmokers.

- **Constricts Blood Vessels:** It has been shown that smoking, even light smoking, causes the body's blood vessels to constrict (vasoconstriction). Smoking does this by decreasing the nitric oxide (NO2), which dilates blood vessels, and increasing the endothelin-1 (ET-1), which causes constriction of blood vessels. The net effect is constriction of blood vessels right after smoking and transient reduction in blood supply. Vasoconstriction may have immediate complications for certain persons, particularly individuals whose blood vessels are already narrowed by plaques (atherosclerosis), or partial blood clots, or individuals who are in a hyper-coagulable state (i.e., have sickle cell disease). These individuals will be at increased risk of stroke or heart attack.

♣ **It's A Fact!!**
Why Secondhand Smoke Is Dangerous

More than 126 million nonsmoking Americans are regularly exposed to secondhand smoke—at home, at work, and in indoor public spaces. Secondhand smoke is the smoke from the burning end of a cigarette and the smoke breathed out by smokers. Cigarette smoke contains thousands of dangerous chemicals that endanger the health of smokers and nonsmokers.

The U.S. Surgeon General's report on secondhand smoke warned in 2006, "There is no risk-free level of exposure to secondhand smoke." A research project highlighted in the Surgeon General's report was conducted in 2001 by Dr. Ryo Otsuka and other scientists in Osaka, Japan. They looked at what happened to healthy young adults, both smokers and nonsmokers, who were exposed to secondhand smoke for 30 minutes. The researchers measured changes in blood flow through the subjects' hearts before and after they spent 30 minutes in a hospital smoking lounge.

The researchers found that even a brief 30-minute exposure to secondhand smoke had a harmful effect on the blood vessels of the nonsmokers. Blood vessels are lined by a cell layer known as the endothelium. The endothelium plays a critical role in controlling blood flow. In nonsmokers the effects of 30 minutes of exposure to secondhand smoke significantly reduced the velocity of blood flow to the heart. In smokers, the blood flow velocity was already low and did not change significantly.

Based on this study and on other research, the 2006 Surgeon General's report described smoking as "the single greatest avoidable cause of disease and death." Major conclusions of the report included:

- **Increases Heart Rate:** Heart rate is a measure of how fast your heart is pumping blood around your body. Young adult smokers have a resting heart rate of two to three beats per minute faster than the resting heart rate of young adult nonsmokers. Nicotine consumption increases a resting heart rate, as soon as 30 minutes after puffing; and the higher the nicotine consumption (through deep inhalation or increased number of cigarettes) the higher the heart rate. Smokers' hearts have to work harder than nonsmokers' hearts. A heart that is working harder is a heart that can tire-out faster and may result in an early heart attack or stroke.

- Many millions of Americans, both children and adults, are still exposed to secondhand smoke in their homes and workplaces despite substantial progress in tobacco control.

- Secondhand smoke exposure causes disease and premature death in children and adults who do not smoke.

- Children exposed to secondhand smoke are at an increased risk for sudden infant death syndrome (SIDS), acute respiratory infections, ear problems, and more severe asthma. Smoking by parents causes respiratory symptoms and slows lung growth in their children.

- Exposure of adults to secondhand smoke has immediate adverse effects on the cardiovascular system and causes coronary heart disease and lung cancer.

- The scientific evidence indicates that there is no risk-free level of exposure to secondhand smoke.

- Eliminating smoking in indoor spaces fully protects nonsmokers from exposure to secondhand smoke. Separating smokers from nonsmokers, cleaning the air, and ventilating buildings cannot eliminate exposures of nonsmokers to secondhand smoke.

Source: This article originally appeared in a Heads Up compilation from Scholastic and the National Institute on Drug Abuse, NIH Publication No. HURN07-05SC, 2007.

- **Increases Blood Pressure:** Blood pressure is a measure of tension upon the walls of arteries by blood. It is reported as a fraction, systolic over diastolic pressure. Systolic blood pressure is the highest arterial pressure reached during contraction of the heart. Diastolic blood pressure is the lowest pressure, found during the heart's relaxation phase. Nicotine consumption increases blood pressure. Older male smokers have been found to have higher systolic blood pressure than nonsmoking men do. Higher blood pressure requires that the heart pump harder in order to overcome the opposing pressure in the arteries. This increased work, much like that related to increased heart rate, can wear out a heart faster. The higher pressure can also cause organ damage where blood is filtered, such as in the kidneys.

Immediate And Rapid Effects On The Gastrointestinal System

The gastrointestinal system is responsible for digesting food, absorbing nutrients, and dispensing of waste products. It includes the mouth, esophagus, stomach, small and large intestines, and the anus. These continuous parts are all easily affected by tobacco smoke.

- **Gastroesophageal Reflux Disease:** This disease includes symptoms of heartburn and acid regurgitation from the stomach. Normally the body prevents these occurrences by secreting a base to counteract digestive acids and by keeping the pathway between the esophagus (the tube between the mouth and stomach) and stomach tightly closed; except when the stomach is accepting food from above. The base smokers' bodies secrete is less neutralizing than nonsmokers and thus allows digestive acids a longer period of time to irritate the esophagus. Smokers also have an intermittent loosening of the muscle separating the esophagus and stomach, increasing the chance of stomach acid rising up to damage the esophagus. These immediate changes in base secretion and esophagus/stomach communication cause painful heartburn and result in an increased risk of long-term inflammation and dysfunction of the esophagus and stomach. Smoking also increases reflux of stomach contents into the esophagus and pharynx. Occurring regularly over time, this reflux may cause ulcerations of the lower esophagus, called Barrett's esophagus, to develop. Barrett's esophagus may develop into esophageal cancer, which has a poor prognosis in most patients.

- **Peptic Ulcer Disease:** Peptic ulcers are self-digested holes extending into the muscular layers of the esophagus, stomach, and a portion of the small intestine. These ulcers form when excess acid is produced or when the protective inner layer of these structures is injured. Mucus is produced in the stomach to provide a protective barrier between stomach acid and cells of the stomach. Unlike in the lungs where mucus production is stimulated by cigarette smoke, mucous production in the stomach is inhibited. Peptic ulcers usually result from a failure of wound-healing due to outside factors, including tobacco smoke. Cigarette smoking increases acid exposure of the esophagus and stomach, while limiting neutralizing base production (above). Smoking also decreases blood flow to the inner layer of the esophagus, stomach and small intestine. In these ways, cigarette smoking immediately hinders gastrointestinal wound healing, which has been shown to result in peptic ulcer formation, when not treated. Peptic ulcers are terribly painful and treatment involves the long-term use of medications. Complications of peptic ulcers often require hospitalization and may be fatal secondary to excessive blood loss.

- **Periodontal Diseases:** These occur when groups of bacteria are able to form colonies that cause infections and diseases of the mouth. Smoking quickly changes the blood supply, immune response, and healing mechanisms of the mouth, resulting in the rapid initiation and progression of infections. In this way, smoking makes the mouth more vulnerable to infections and allows the infections to become more severe. The bacterial plaques of smoking also cause gum inflammation and tooth decay. In addition, smoking increases tooth and bone loss and hastens deep gum pocket formation.

- **Halitosis:** This is a fancy word for bad breath. Everybody knows that smoking makes individuals and everything around them smell bad. Bad breath, smelly hair and clothes, and yellow teeth are among the most immediate and unattractive effects of smoking.

Immediate And Rapid Effects On The Immune System

The immune system is the body's major defense against the outside world. It is a complicated system that involves several different types of cells that attack and destroy foreign substances. It begins in the parts of the body, which are in direct contact with the environment, such as the skin, ears, nose, mouth, stomach, and lungs. When these barriers become compromised, there are serious health consequences. Tobacco smoke weakens the immune system in a number of ways.

- **Otitis Media:** This is inflammation of the middle ear. The middle ear is the space immediately behind the eardrum. It turns received vibrations into sound. The middle ear is very vulnerable to infection. Children exposed to environmental tobacco smoke (ETS) have more ear infections than those not exposed. Tobacco smoke disrupts the normal clearing mechanism of the ear canal, facilitating infectious organism entry into the body. The resulting middle ear infection can be very painful, as pressure and fluid build up in the ear. Continued exposure to tobacco smoke may result in persistent middle ear infections and eventually, hearing loss.

- **Sinusitis:** Sinusitis is sinus inflammation. Sinuses are spaces in the skull that are in direct communication with the nose and mouth. They are important for warming and moisturizing inhaled air. The lining of the sinuses consists of the same finger-like hairs found in the lungs. These hairs clear mucus and foreign substances and are therefore critical in preventing mucus buildup and subsequent infection. Cigarette smoke slows or stops the movement of these hairs, resulting in inflammation and infection. Sinusitis can cause headaches, facial pain, tenderness, and swelling. It can also cause fever, cough, runny nose, sore throat, bad breath, and a decreased sense of smell. Sinusitis is more serious and requires a longer course of medical treatment than the common cold. Long-term smoke exposure can result in more frequent episodes and chronic cases of sinusitis; and the rate of sinusitis among smokers is high.

- **Rhinitis:** This is an inflammation of the inner lining of the nasal passages and results in symptoms of sneezing, congestion, runny nose, and itchy eyes, ears, and nose. Similar to symptoms of the common cold, rhinitis may begin immediately in the regular smoker. Smoking causes rhinitis by damaging the same clearing mechanism involved in sinusitis (above). Rhinitis can cause sleep disturbances, activity limitations, irritability, moodiness, and decreased school performance. Smoking causes immediate and long-lasting rhinitis.

- **Pneumonia:** Pneumonia is an inflammation of the lining of the lungs. This inflammation causes fluid to accumulate deep in the lung, making it an ideal region for bacterial growth. Pneumonia results in a persistent cough and difficulty breathing. A serious case of pneumonia often requires hospitalization. Smoking increases the body's susceptibility to the most common bacterial causes of pneumonia and is therefore a risk factor for pneumonia, regardless of age. Pneumonia, if left untreated, can lead to pus pocket formation, lung collapse, blood infection, and severe chest pain.

Immediate And Rapid Effects On The Metabolic System

Your metabolic system includes a complicated group of processes that break down foods and medicines into their components. Proteins, called enzymes, are responsible for this breakdown. The metabolic system involves many organs, especially those of the gastrointestinal tract.

- **Scurvy And Other Micronutrient Disorders:** Micronutrients are dietary components necessary to maintain good health. These include vitamins, minerals, enzymes (above) and other elements that are critical to normal function. They must be consumed and absorbed in sufficient quantities to meet the body's needs. The daily requirement of these micronutrients changes naturally with age and can also be affected by environmental factors, including tobacco smoke. Smoking interferes with the absorption of a number of micronutrients, especially vitamins C, E, and folic acid that can result in deficiencies of these vitamins. A deficiency in Vitamin C can lead to scurvy which is a disease characterized by weakness, depression, inflamed gums, poor wound healing, and uncontrolled bleeding. Vitamin E deficiency may cause blood breakdown, eye disease, and irreversible nerve problems of the hands, feet, and spinal cord. Folic acid deficiency may result in long-lasting anemia, diarrhea, and tongue swelling.

- **Oxidative Damage:** Oxidants are active particles that are byproducts of normal chemical processes that are constantly underway inside the body. Their formation is called oxidation. These particles are usually found and destroyed by antioxidants, including vitamins A, C, and E. The balance of oxidation and anti-oxidation is critical to health. When oxidation overwhelms anti-oxidation, harmful consequences occur. Oxidants directly damage cells and change genetic material, likely contributing to the development of cancer, heart disease, and cataracts. Oxidants also speed up blood vessel damage due to atherosclerosis (above) which is a known risk factor for heart disease. Because smoking increases the number of circulating oxidants, it also increases the consumption of existing antioxidants. This increase in antioxidant consumption reduces the levels of antioxidants such as alpha-tocopherol, the active form of vitamin E. Smoking immediately causes oxidant stress in blood while the antioxidant potential is reduced because of this stress. This dangerous imbalance cannot be neutralized and results in immediate cell, gene, and blood vessel damage. In addition, a National Cancer Institute study found that beta-carotene supplements, which contain precursors of vitamin A, modestly increase the incidence of lung cancer and overall mortality in cigarette smokers.

Immediate And Rapid Effects On Drug Interactions

Drug breakdown, or metabolism, is important to drug effectiveness and safety. Medicines are naturally broken down into their components by enzymes. Factors that affect drug metabolism affect drug function. Factors that speed up drug metabolism decrease drug exposure time and reduce the circulating concentrations of the drug, which compromises the effectiveness of the prescription. Conversely, factors that slow down drug metabolism increase the circulating time and concentration of the drug, allowing the drug to be present at harmful levels. Tobacco smoke interferes with many medications by both of these mechanisms. For example, the components of tobacco smoke hasten the breakdown of some blood-thinners, antidepressants, and anti-seizure medications; and tobacco smoke also decreases the effectiveness of certain sedatives, painkillers, heart, ulcer, and asthma medicines.

Especially Vulnerable Populations

- **Asthmatics:** Mainstream or environmental tobacco smoke (ETS) exacerbates asthma symptoms in known asthmatics. In addition, some studies have shown a link between ETS in childhood and a higher prevalence of asthma in adulthood.

- **Infants And Children:** Infants and children exposed to environmental tobacco smoke (ETS) are at increased risk for death and disease. Mothers who smoke during pregnancy are known to have low birth-weight babies. In breastfeeding women who smoke, there is a decrease in maternal milk production and less weight gain in the exposed infant. In addition, infants whose mothers smoke have an increased risk of sudden infant death syndrome (SIDS), and their overall perinatal mortality rate is 25–56% higher than those infants of mothers who choose not to smoke. Children exposed to ETS are at increased risk of many infections, most commonly middle ear and respiratory infections, and thus require more doctor visits and hospital stays.

- **Sickle Cell Patients:** Patients with sickle cell anemia who smoke are known to have increased incidence of acute chest syndrome. Acute chest syndrome is a condition that presents with severe chest pain, and is a life-threatening emergency.

☞ **Remember!!**

While some of these effects are wholly or partially reversible upon quitting smoking, research has shown that many are not. Quitting smoking provides enormous health benefits, but some smoking-caused damage simply cannot be reversed. Moreover, many of the effects outlined here can cause considerable harm to kids and others soon after they begin smoking and well before they become long-term smokers.

Source: © 2009 Campaign for Tobacco-Free Kids.

Chapter 21

Health Harms From Smoking And Other Tobacco Use

Tobacco use kills more than 400,000 people each year in the United States, or more than the total number killed by AIDS, alcohol, motor vehicles, homicide, illegal drugs, and suicide combined. Among current smokers 57 percent of all male deaths and nearly 50 percent of all deaths in women are attributed to smoking. Even if the number of smoking related deaths were cut in half, smoking would still kill more people than all of these other causes.

In 1964, the Surgeon General first documented the harmful effects of smoking in *Smoking and Health: Report of the Advisory Committee of the Surgeon General of the Public Health Service*, which summarized the state of the science knowledge regarding tobacco use at that time. Research conducted since then has firmly established that smoking and other forms of tobacco consumption cause an enormous amount of health problems and related death and suffering. Today, smoking is the leading preventable cause of death in the United States. Despite the numerous reports of the Surgeon General and the National Institute for Health on the risks of smoking, 46 million Americans still smoke; and approximately half of all continuing smokers will die prematurely as a result of their habit.

Smoking-Caused Cancer: Smoking is responsible for 87 percent of lung cancer deaths (90 percent in men, 80 percent in women). Over 125,000 men and women die of smoking caused lung cancer each year. Compared to nonsmokers, men who smoke are about 23 times more likely to develop lung cancer and women who smoke are about 13 times more likely. Beyond just lung cancer, thirty percent of all cancer deaths are due to smoking. Smoking is a known cause of cancer of the lung, larynx, oral cavity, bladder, pancreas, uterus, cervix, kidney, stomach, and esophagus.

Smoking-Caused Respiratory Diseases: Twenty-three percent of smoking-attributable deaths, or more than 100,000 smoking deaths per year, involve respiratory diseases. Smoking is a known cause of most cases of chronic obstructive pulmonary disease (COPD) which includes emphysema and chronic bronchitis. Smoking is accountable for more than 90 percent of all COPD deaths. Male and female smokers increase their risk of death from bronchitis and emphysema by 10 times.

Smoking-Caused Heart Disease And Heart Attacks: Cancer and respiratory disease are not the only health risks associated with smoking. More men and women in the United States have died from cardiovascular disease attributed to smoking than cancer. Twenty-one percent of all coronary heart disease deaths in the United States each year are attributable to smoking. This risk is strongly dose-related. Smoking triples the risk of dying from heart disease among middle-aged men and women. Cardiovascular smoking deaths are also due to hypertension and stroke. The risk of ischemic stroke is nearly doubled by smoking. Smoking accounted for 18 percent of all stroke deaths. Both active and passive smoking are associated with an increase in the progression of atherosclerosis. More than 128,000 Americans die from smoking related cardiovascular diseases.

Other Direct Health Harms From Smoking: Heart disease, cancer and respiratory diseases are just a few of the physical and medical problems associated with smoking. Smoking may reduce fertility and lead to impotence among men. Cigarette smoking increases both the risk and the severity of rheumatoid arthritis. Hearing loss and vision problems, including cataracts, have been linked to smoking. Chronic coughing, increased phlegm, emphysema and bronchitis have been well-established products of smoking for decades; and smokers are also more susceptible to influenza and more likely to experience severe symptoms when they get the flu. While many smokers believe that smoking relieves stress, it is actually a major cause. Smoking only appears to reduce stress because it lessens the irritability and tension caused by the underlying nicotine addiction.

Harm Caused By Smokeless Tobacco Use: The Surgeon General has determined that the use of oral snuff can lead to oral cancer, gum disease, and nicotine addiction, and increases the risk of cardiovascular disease, including heart attack. Constant exposure to tobacco juice causes cancer of the esophagus, pharynx, larynx, stomach and pancreas. Smokeless tobacco users are at a heightened risk for oral cancer compared to non-users and these cancers can form within five years of regular use. New studies have found that the levels of the carcinogenic NNK in smokeless tobacco products were comparable to those cigarettes and using Swedish snus can heighten one's risk for pancreatic cancer. A 2008 study from the WHO International Agency for Research on Cancer concluded that smokeless tobacco users have an 80 percent higher risk of developing oral cancer and a 60 percent higher risk of developing pancreatic and esophageal cancer. Spit tobacco causes leukoplakia, a disease of the mouth characterized by white patches and oral lesions on the cheeks, gums, and/or tongue. Leukoplakia, which can lead to oral cancer, occurs in more than half of all users in the first three years of use. Studies have found that 60 to 78 percent of smokeless tobacco users have oral lesions. Gum disease (gingivitis) is also caused by spit tobacco. Spit tobacco has also been linked to dental caries. A study by the National Institutes of Health and the Centers for Disease Control and Prevention found chewing tobacco users were four times more likely than non-users to have decayed dental root surfaces.

Harms From Pregnant Smokers Or Exposure To Secondhand Smoke: Even more disturbing is the impact of smoking on pregnant women. Research studies have found that smoking and exposure to secondhand smoke among pregnant women is a major cause of spontaneous abortions, stillbirths, and sudden infant death syndrome (SIDS) after birth. According to a meta-analysis of published studies, tobacco use is responsible each year for 19,000 to 141,000 spontaneous abortions, 1,900 to 4,800 infant deaths caused by prenatal or pre-birth disorders, and 1,200 to 2,200 deaths from SIDS. A more recent

✤ It's A Fact!!
FDA Warns Of Health Risks Posed By E-Cigarettes

The Food and Drug Administration (FDA) has joined other health experts to warn consumers about potential health risks associated with electronic cigarettes.

Also known as "e-cigarettes," electronic cigarettes are battery-operated devices designed to look like and to be used in the same manner as conventional cigarettes.

Sold online and in many shopping malls, the devices generally contain cartridges filled with nicotine, flavor, and other chemicals. They turn nicotine, which is highly addictive, and other chemicals into a vapor that is inhaled by the user.

"The FDA is concerned about the safety of these products and how they are marketed to the public," says Margaret A. Hamburg, M.D., commissioner of food and drugs.

The agency is concerned about the following:

- E-cigarettes can increase nicotine addiction among young people and may lead kids to try other tobacco products, including conventional cigarettes, which are known to cause disease and lead to premature death.

- The products may contain ingredients that are known to be toxic to humans.

- Because clinical studies about the safety and efficacy of these products for their intended use have not been submitted to FDA, consumers currently have no way of knowing 1) whether e-cigarettes are safe for their intended use, or 2) about what types or concentrations of potentially harmful chemicals or what dose of nicotine they are inhaling when they use these products.

The potential health risks posed by the use of e-cigarettes were addressed in a July 22, 2009, phone conference between Joshua M. Sharfstein, M.D., principal deputy commissioner of food and drugs; Jonathan Winickoff, M.D., chair of the American Academy of Pediatrics Tobacco Consortium; Jonathan Samet, M.D., director of the University of Southern California's Institute for Global Health; and Matthew T. McKenna, M.D., director of the Office on Smoking and Health at the national Centers for Disease Control and Prevention.

Conference participants stressed the importance of parents being aware of the health and marketing concerns associated with e-cigarettes. It was stated that parents may want to tell their children and teenagers that these products are not safe to use.

Of particular concern to parents is that e-cigarettes are sold without any legal age restrictions, and are available in different flavors (such as chocolate, strawberry and mint) which may appeal to young people.

In addition, the devices do not contain any health warnings comparable to FDA-approved nicotine replacement products or conventional cigarettes.

During the phone conference, which was shared with the news media, FDA announced findings from a laboratory analysis that indicates that electronic cigarettes expose users to harmful chemical ingredients.

FDA's Division of Pharmaceutical Analysis—part of the agency's Center for Drug Evaluation and Research—analyzed the ingredients in a small sample of cartridges from two leading brands of e-cigarette samples.

One sample was found to contain diethylene glycol, a toxic chemical used in antifreeze. Several other samples were found to contain carcinogens, including nitrosamines.

Agency Actions

FDA has been examining and detaining shipments of e-cigarettes at the border and has found that the products it has examined thus far meet the definition of a combination drug device product under the Federal Food, Drug, and Cosmetic Act. The agency has been challenged regarding its jurisdiction over certain e-cigarettes in a case currently pending in federal district court.

FDA is planning additional activities to address its concerns about electronic cigarettes.

Meanwhile, health care professionals and consumers may report serious adverse events or product quality problems with the use of e-cigarettes to FDA through the MedWatch3 program, either online or by phone at 800-FDA-1088.

Source: Consumer Update, U.S. Food and Drug Administration (http://www.fda.gov), July 23, 2009.

comprehensive study found that parental smoking causes 2,800 deaths at birth and 2,000 deaths from SIDS. Children exposed to secondhand smoke before and after birth are at a great risk of abnormal blood pressure, cleft pallets and lips, childhood leukemia, attention deficit disorder, childhood wheezing and respiratory disorders.

Other Secondhand Smoke Harms: Secondhand smoke is the combination of "mainstream smoke (exhaled by a smoker) and side-stream smoke (from the burning end of the cigarette). Secondhand smoke is also referred to as environmental tobacco smoke, passive smoke, or involuntary tobacco smoke. It is a complex mixture of over 4,000 chemicals that are produced by the burning materials of a cigarette. Secondhand smoke exposure is causally associated with several different health risks in both children and adults. Children exposed to secondhand smoke are at a higher risk of sudden infant death syndrome (SIDS), acute lower respiratory tract infections, asthma induction and exacerbation, chronic respiratory symptoms, middle ear infections. In adults, secondhand smoke exposure increase the risk of lung cancer, nasal sinus cancer, heart disease mortality, acute and chronic coronary heart disease morbidity eye and nasal irritation. A 1997 analysis of 37 epidemiological studies of lung cancer and ETS found that lifelong nonsmokers living with smokers had, on average, a 24 percent higher chance of contracting lung cancer than those living with nonsmokers, and that those exposed to the heaviest smokers for the longest time had the highest risks. Subsequent research studies have made similar findings. Secondhand smoke is listed as a carcinogen in the U.S. Public Health Services' *Ninth Report on Carcinogens*, as recommended by a scientific advisory panel of the National Toxicology Program that unanimously affirmed the findings of two other scientific groups that secondhand smoke is a carcinogen and should be included in the report.

Immediate And Short-Term Harms From Smoking: While most of the major health harms from smoking, such as lung cancer and heart disease, typically appear after years of tobacco use, many health problems can appear almost immediately, even among otherwise young and healthy kids. For example cigarette smoking immediately increases heart rate and blood pressure, and the resting heart rates of young adult smokers are two to three beats per minute faster than nonsmokers. In addition, high school seniors who are regular smokers and began smoking by grade nine are 2.4 times more likely than their nonsmoking peers to report poorer overall health. High school seniors who smoke are 2.4 to 2.7 times more likely to report cough with phlegm or blood, shortness of breath when not exercising, and wheezing or gasping. Teens who smoke are also three times more likely than nonsmokers to use alcohol, eight times more likely to use marijuana, and 22 times more likely to use cocaine.

Tobacco Use And Appearance: Concern about body weight and appearance are just a few reasons that smokers begin. Most adolescents believe that smoking controls body weight and many times women report that they smoke to keep their weight down. While smoking cessation has been shown to result in weight gain among both men and women, initiation of smoking does not appear to be associated with weight loss. Among women, the average weight of current smokers is only modestly lower than that of never or long-term former smokers. Smoking has also been linked with facial wrinkling. Smokers were significantly more likely than nonsmokers to be evaluated with having prominent wrinkling.

Smoking Addiction Starts Early: The peak years for first trying to smoke appear to be in the sixth and seventh grades, or between the ages of 11 and 12, with a considerable number starting even earlier. Within weeks or just days of first starting to smoke occasionally, young smokers show numerous signs of addiction, such as feeling anxious or irritable and having strong urges to smoke; and more than a third of all kids who ever try smoking a cigarette will become regular, daily smokers before they even leave high school. Addiction rates for experimenters who become habitual users for smoking are higher than addiction rates for marijuana, alcohol, or even cocaine. Every day more than 3,500 kids under 18 try smoking for the first time, and another 1,000 kids who have already experimented with cigarettes become new regular daily smokers. Overall, more than 80 percent of all adult smokers first become regular smokers before the age of 18 and more than 90 percent do so before leaving their teens.

Quitting Is Difficult, But Not Impossible: Although half of all Americans who have ever smoked have quit, and most current smokers want to stop, an established addiction to nicotine is difficult to escape. Of the more than one million smokers who quit each year, 75 to 80 percent relapse within six months. To quit, smokers must not only overcome their physiological dependence on nicotine but also cut their strong psychological and social ties to smoking or otherwise using tobacco. The three most effective components of smoking cessation treatment are pharmacological treatments (such as nicotine gum and patches), clinician-provided social support and advice, and skills training regarding techniques to achieve and maintain abstinence. Another treatment approach combines nicotine replace, counseling and use of anti depressants like bupropion. In general, more inclusive treatments are more effective in producing long-term abstinence from tobacco, and combined therapies raise the absolute percentage of smokers who remain abstinent.

Health Benefits From Quitting: There are substantial and immediate health benefits from quitting smoking. A 2007 study in the *New England Journal of Medicine* found that 11.7 percent of the decrease in coronary heart disease deaths between 1980 and 2000 were avoided or postponed by quitting smoking. Upon quitting, former smokers' blood circulation immediately increases, their blood pressure and heart rate quickly return to normal, and the carbon monoxide and oxygen levels in the blood soon return to normal. Within a few days of quitting, a person's breathing becomes easier and their sense of smell and taste improve. One year after quitting, a person's additional risk of heart disease is reduced by half, and after 15 years, this risk equals that of a person who never smoked. Five to 15 years after quitting, the risk of stroke for an ex-smoker equals that of a person who never smoked. Within 10 years of quitting a former smoker's risk of developing lung cancer is 30 to 50 percent below that of a person who continues to smoke. The risk of developing cancers of the mouth, throat and esophagus lessen significantly after five years of quitting. Persons aged 60 to 64 years of age who quit smoking are 10 percent less likely to die during the next 15 years than regular smokers are. The benefit is even greater for individuals who quit smoking before the age of 50. Their risk of dying in the next 15 years is half that of a person who smokes.

Chapter 22

Facts About Smoking Cessation

Nicotine Dependence

Nicotine is the psychoactive drug in tobacco products that produces dependence. Most smokers are dependent on nicotine. Nicotine dependence is the most common form of chemical dependence in the United States. Research suggests that nicotine is as addictive as heroin, cocaine, or alcohol.

Quitting tobacco use is difficult and may require multiple attempts; users often relapse because of withdrawal symptoms. The following are examples of nicotine withdrawal symptoms: irritability, anxiety, difficulty concentrating, and increased appetite.

Tobacco dependence is a chronic condition that often requires repeated intervention.

Health Benefits Of Cessation

Breaking free from nicotine dependence is not the only reason to quit smoking. Cigarette smoke contains at least 250 chemicals known to be toxic

About This Chapter: Information in this chapter is from "Smoking Cessation," Centers for Disease Control and Prevention, Office on Smoking and Health, September 2009.

or carcinogenic (i.e., cause cancer). Cigarette smoke can cause serious health problems, numerous diseases, and death.

Fortunately, people who stop smoking greatly reduce their risk of disease and premature death. Benefits are greater for people who stop at earlier ages, but cessation is beneficial at all ages.

- Smoking cessation lowers the risk for lung and other types of cancer. The risk for developing cancer declines with the number of years of smoking cessation.

✔ Quick Tip
Smoke-Free Facts And Healthy Solutions

Smoke-Free Fact: When people quit smoking, they tend to eat more, have more cravings for sugary/junk foods, and drink more alcohol than before they quit.

Healthy Solution: Practice healthy eating. Healthy eating is easier than you think! You don't need to buy special foods or go on a strict diet. Small changes like these can make a big difference:

- At mealtimes, fix your plate with bigger servings of fruits/vegetables and smaller servings of starches (such as potatoes, pasta, and rice) and meat.

- Instead of "heaping" food onto your plate, start out with less. If it turns out to be too little, you can always go back for more.

- If snacking helps to curb the cravings, snack on fruits and veggies instead of candy and chips. Try some frozen grapes or crunchy carrot and celery sticks.

- Stick to non-alcoholic drinks. Alcohol can cause weight gain. Also, when you drink alcohol, you may do things that you wouldn't have done while sober. For example, you may decide to "pig out" or have "just one cigarette."

Smoke-Free Fact: When you were smoking, the nicotine in each cigarette gave your body a little burst of energy. Your body used this energy to help burn off the food you ate. While your body adjusts to being nicotine-free, there may not be as much energy available to burn off the food that you eat.

- Risk for coronary heart disease, stroke, and peripheral vascular disease is reduced after smoking cessation. Coronary heart disease risk is substantially reduced within one to two years of cessation.

- Smoking cessation reduces respiratory symptoms, such as coughing, wheezing, and shortness of breath. The rate of decline in lung function is slower among persons who quit smoking.

- Smoking cessation reduces the risk of developing chronic obstructive pulmonary disease (COPD), one of the leading causes of death in the U.S.

Healthy Solution: Exercise! A 10-minute exercise session is a much healthier way to get the same burst of energy that you used to get from a cigarette! Fitting exercise into your daily routine is possible! In fact, it doesn't have to take up much time or be very tough to improve your health. Here are some tips to help you get going:

- Plan to exercise 3 times a day, for about 10 minutes at a time.

- Don't overdo it! During exercise, you should feel warm and slightly out of breath. Anything more and you are working too hard.

- Get friends, family members, and pets to join you. Play a game of chase with the kids/grandkids or take the dog out for a brisk walk.

- Make "exercise appointments" for the times when you crave cigarettes the most. Schedule 10 minutes of housework first thing in the morning, or a 10-minute walk after a meal.

- Exercise is a great way to manage unexpected cravings too! The next time you feel the urge for a cigarette, do something active until the craving passes.

Learning these new habits may take some practice. But the more you practice, the healthier you will become. And remember, even if you gain a little weight as a result of becoming smoke-free, you are still much healthier than when you were smoking!

Source: From "Weight Management: Smoke-Free Facts and Healthy Solutions," Smokefree Women (smokefree.women.gov), a website created by the Tobacco Control Research Branch, Behavioral Research Program, Division of Cancer Control and Population Sciences of the National Cancer Institute. 2009.

- Women who stop smoking during their reproductive years reduce their risk for infertility. Women who stop smoking during pregnancy also reduce their risk of having a low birth weight baby.

Methods To Quit Smoking

Effective treatments that can increase the chances of successful cessation include the following:

- Brief clinical interventions (i.e., when a doctor takes 10 minutes or less to deliver advice and assistance about quitting)
- Counseling (e.g., individual, group, or telephone counseling)
- Behavioral cessation therapies (e.g., training in problem solving)
- Treatments with more person-to-person contact and intensity (e.g., more time with counselors)

Cessation medications found to be effective for treating tobacco dependence include the following:

- Over-the-counter and prescription nicotine replacement products (e.g., nicotine gum, inhaler, nasal spray, lozenge, or patch)
- Prescription non-nicotine medications, such as bupropion SR (Zyban) and varenicline tartrate (Chantix)

The combination of medication and counseling is more effective for smoking cessation than either medication or counseling alone.

Helpful Cessation Resources

Cessation Services

- Quitline Services: 800-QUIT-NOW is a free telephone support service that can help individuals who want to stop smoking or using tobacco.
- CDC's How to Quit web pages (www.cdc.gov/tobacco/quit_smoking/how_to_quit/index.htm) provide a variety of cessation tips, tools, and resources.
- Smokefree.gov is a website dedicated to helping smokers quit.

Chapter 23

How Can I Quit Smoking?

First, congratulate yourself. Just reading this article is a huge step toward becoming tobacco free. Many people don't quit smoking because they think it's too hard to do. They think they'll quit someday.

It's true, for most people quitting isn't easy. After all, the nicotine in cigarettes is a powerfully addictive drug. But with the right approach, you can overcome the cravings.

The Difficulty In Kicking The Habit

Smokers may have started smoking because their friends did or because it seemed cool. But they keep on smoking because they became addicted to nicotine, one of the chemicals in cigarettes and smokeless tobacco.

Nicotine is both a stimulant and a depressant. That means it increases the heart rate at first and makes people feel more alert (like caffeine, another stimulant). Then it causes depression and fatigue. The depression and fatigue—and the drug withdrawal from nicotine—make people crave another cigarette to perk up again. According to many experts, the nicotine in tobacco is as addictive as cocaine or heroin.

"How Can I Quit Smoking?" September 2009, reprinted with permission from www .kidshealth.org. Copyright © 2009 The Nemours Foundation. This information was provided by KidsHealth, one of the largest resources online for medically reviewed health information written for parents, kids, and teens. For more articles like this one, visit www.Kids Health.org, or www.TeensHealth.org.

But don't be discouraged; millions of Americans have permanently quit smoking. These strategies can help you quit, too:

Put it in writing. People who want to make a change often are more successful when they put it in writing. So write down all the reasons why you want to quit smoking, such as the money you will save or the stamina you'll gain for playing sports. Keep that list where you can see it, and add to it as you think of new reasons.

Get support. People whose friends and family help them quit are much more likely to succeed. If you don't want to tell your parents or family that you smoke, make sure your friends know, and consider confiding in a counselor or other adult you trust. And if you're having a hard time finding people to support you (if, say, all your friends smoke and none of them is interested in quitting), you might consider joining a support group, either in person or online.

More Strategies That Work

Set a quit date. Pick a day that you'll stop smoking. Tell your friends (and your family, if they know you smoke) that you're going to quit smoking on that day. Just think of that day as a dividing line between the smoking you and the new and improved nonsmoker you'll become. Mark it on your calendar.

> **❖ It's A Fact!!**
> **Trying To Quit?**
> You'll be in good company. Fewer teens are smoking. Only 23% of U.S. high school students said they smoked in 2005, compared with 35% in 1999.

Throw away your cigarettes—*all* of your cigarettes. People can't stop smoking with cigarettes still around to tempt them. Even toss out that emergency pack you have stashed in the secret pocket of your backpack. Get rid of your ashtrays and lighters, too.

Wash all your clothes. Get rid of the smell of cigarettes as much as you can by washing all your clothes and having your coats or sweaters dry-cleaned. If you smoked in your car, clean that out, too.

Think about your triggers. You're probably aware of the situations when you tend to smoke, such as after meals, when you're at your best friend's house, while drinking coffee, or as you're driving. These situations are your triggers for smoking—it feels automatic to have a cigarette when you're in them. Once you've figured out your triggers, try these tips:

- **Avoid these situations.** For example, if you smoke when you drive, get a ride to school, walk, or take the bus for a few weeks. If you normally smoke after meals, make it a point to do something else after you eat, like read or call a friend.

- **Change the place.** If you and your friends usually smoke in restaurants or get takeout and eat in the car, suggest that you sit in the no-smoking section the next time you go out to eat.

- **Substitute something else for cigarettes.** It can be hard to get used to not holding something and having something in your mouth. If you have this problem, stock up on carrot sticks, sugar-free gum, mints, toothpicks, or even lollipops.

Physical And Mental Effects

Expect some physical symptoms. If you smoke regularly, you're probably physically addicted to nicotine and your body may experience some symptoms of withdrawal when you quit. These may include:

- headaches or stomachaches

- crabbiness, jumpiness, or depression

- lack of energy

- dry mouth or sore throat

- desire to pig out

Luckily, the symptoms of nicotine withdrawal will pass—so be patient. Try not to give in and sneak a smoke because you'll just have to deal with the symptoms longer.

Keep yourself busy. Many people find it's best to quit on a Monday, when they have school or work to keep them busy. The more distracted you are, the less likely you'll be to crave cigarettes. Staying active is also a good way to make sure you keep your weight down and your energy up, even as you're experiencing the symptoms of nicotine withdrawal.

Quit gradually. Some people find that gradually decreasing the number of cigarettes they smoke each day is an effective way to quit. However, this strategy doesn't work for everyone—you may find you have to stop completely at once. This is known as "cold turkey."

Use a nicotine replacement if you need to. If you find that none of these strategies is working, you might talk to your doctor about treatments. Using a nicotine replacement, such as gum, patches, inhalers, or nasal sprays, can be very helpful. Sprays and inhalers are available by prescription only, and it's important to see your doctor before buying the patch and gum over the counter. That way, your doctor can help you find the solution that will work best for you. For example, the patch requires the least effort on your part, but it doesn't offer the almost instantaneous nicotine kick that gum does.

Slip-Ups Happen

If you slip up, don't give up! Major changes sometimes have false starts. If you're like many people, you may quit successfully for weeks or even months and then suddenly have a craving that's so strong you feel like you have to give in. Or maybe you accidentally find yourself in one of your trigger situations and give in to temptation.

If you slip up, it doesn't mean you've failed, it just means you're human. Here are some ways to get back on track:

- **Think about your slip as one mistake.** Take notice of when and why it happened and move on.

- **Did you become a heavy smoker after one cigarette?** We didn't think so—it happened more gradually, over time. Keep in mind that one cigarette didn't make you a smoker to start with, so smoking one cigarette (or even two or three) after you've quit doesn't make you a smoker again.

- **Remind yourself why you've quit and how well you've done**—or have someone in your support group, family, or friends do this for you.

- **Reward yourself.** As you already know, quitting smoking isn't easy. Give yourself a well-deserved reward! Set aside the money you usually spend on cigarettes. When you've stayed tobacco free for a week, two weeks, or a month, buy yourself a treat like a new CD, book, movie, or some clothes. And every smoke-free year, celebrate again. You earned it.

Part Four

Marijuana

Chapter 24

What Is Marijuana?

Marijuana is a mixture of the dried and shredded leaves, stems, seeds, and flowers of the cannabis sativa plant. The mixture can be green, brown, or gray.

A bunch of leaves seem harmless, right? But think again. Marijuana has a chemical in it called delta-9-tetrahydrocannabinol, better known as THC. A lot of other chemicals are found in marijuana, too—about 400 of them, many of which could affect your health. But THC is the main psychoactive (i.e., mind altering) ingredient. In fact, marijuana's strength or potency is related to the amount of THC it contains. The THC content of marijuana has been increasing since the 1970s. For the year 2007, estimates from confiscated marijuana indicated that it contains almost 10 percent THC on average.

What Are The Common Street Names?

There are many slang terms for marijuana that vary from city to city and from neighborhood to neighborhood. Some common names are: "pot," "grass," "herb," "weed," "Mary Jane," "reefer," "skunk," "boom," "gangster," "kif," "chronic," and "ganja."

About This Chapter: Information in this chapter is from "Marijuana," NIDA for Teens, National Institute on Drug Abuse, a component of the United States Department of Health and Human Services, 2009.

How Is It Used?

Marijuana is used in many ways. The most common method is smoking loose marijuana rolled into a cigarette called a "joint" or "nail." Sometimes marijuana is smoked through a water pipe called a "bong." Others smoke "blunts"—cigars hollowed out and filled with the drug. And some users brew it as tea or mix it with food.

How Many Teens Use Marijuana?

Some people mistakenly believe that "everybody's doing it" and use that as an excuse to start using marijuana themselves. Well, they need to check the facts, because that's just not true. According to a 2009 survey called Monitoring the Future, about 7% of 8th graders, 16% of 10th graders, and 21% of 12th graders had used marijuana in the month before the survey. In fact, marijuana use declined from the late 1990s through 2007, with a decrease in past-year use of more than 20% in all three grades combined from 2000 to 2007. Unfortunately, this trend appears to be slowing, and marijuana use remains at unacceptably high levels, as the most commonly used illegal drug.

What Are The Short-Term Effects Of Marijuana Use?

For some people, smoking marijuana makes them feel good. Within minutes of inhaling, a user begins to feel "high," or filled with pleasant sensations. THC triggers brain cells to release the chemical dopamine. Dopamine creates good feelings—for a short time. But that's just one effect…

Imagine this: You're in a ball game, playing out in left field. An easy fly ball comes your way, and you're psyched. When that ball lands in your glove your team will win, and you'll be a hero. But, you're a little off. The ball grazes your glove and hits dirt. So much for your dreams of glory.

Such loss of coordination can be caused by smoking marijuana. And that's just one of its many negative effects. Marijuana affects memory, judgment, and perception. Under the influence of marijuana, you could fail to remember things you just learned, watch your grade point average drop, or crash a car.

Also, since marijuana can affect judgment and decision making, using it can cause you to do things you might not do when you are thinking straight—such as risky sexual behavior, which can result in exposure to sexually transmitted diseases, like HIV, the virus that causes AIDS; or getting in a car with someone who's been drinking or is high on marijuana.

It's also difficult to know how marijuana will affect a specific person at any given time, because its effects vary based on individual factors: a person's genetics, whether they've used marijuana or any other drugs before, how much marijuana is taken, and its potency. Effects can also be unpredictable when marijuana is used in combination with other drugs.

THC Impacts Brain Functioning

THC is up to no good in the brain. THC finds brain cells, or neurons, with specific kinds of receptors called cannabinoid receptors and binds to them.

Certain parts of the brain have high concentrations of cannabinoid receptors. These areas are the hippocampus, the cerebellum, the basal ganglia, and the cerebral cortex. The functions that these brain areas control are the ones most affected by marijuana.

For example, THC interferes with learning and memory because the hippocampus—a part of the brain with a funny name and a big job—plays a critical role in certain types of learning. Disrupting its normal functioning can lead to problems studying, learning new things, and recalling recent events. The difficulty can be a lot more serious than forgetting if you took out the trash this morning, which happens to everyone once in a while.

Do these effects persist? We don't know for sure, but as adolescents your brains are still developing. So is it really worth the risk?

Smoking Marijuana Can Make Driving Dangerous

The cerebellum is the section of our brain that controls balance and coordination. When THC affects the cerebellum's function, it makes scoring a goal in soccer or hitting a home run pretty tough. THC also affects the basal ganglia, another part of the brain that's involved in movement control.

These THC effects can cause disaster on the road. Research shows that drivers on marijuana have slower reaction times, impaired judgment, and problems responding to signals and sounds. Studies conducted in a number of localities have found that approximately 4 to 14 percent of drivers who sustained injury or death in traffic accidents tested positive for delta-9-tetrahydrocannabinol (THC), the active ingredient in marijuana.

Marijuana Use Increases Heart Rate

Within a few minutes after inhaling marijuana smoke, an individual's heart begins beating more rapidly, the bronchial passages relax and become enlarged, and blood vessels in the eyes expand, making the eyes look red. The heart rate, normally 70 to 80 beats per minute, may increase by 20 to 50 beats per minute or, in some cases, even double. This effect can be greater if other drugs are taken with marijuana.

What Are the Long-Term Health Effects Of Marijuana Use?

The list of negative effects that can arise from using marijuana goes on and on. Here are a few examples:

The Brain

When people smoke marijuana for years they can suffer some pretty negative consequences. For example, because marijuana affects brain function, your ability to do complex tasks could be compromised, as well as your pursuit of academic, athletic, or other life goals that require you to be 100 percent focused and alert. In fact, long-term users self-report less life satisfaction, poorer education and job achievement, and more interpersonal and mental health problems compared to nonusers.

Marijuana also may affect your mental health. Studies show that early use may increase your risk of developing psychosis [a severe mental disorder in which there is a loss of contact with reality, including false ideas about what is happening (delusions) and seeing or hearing things that aren't there (hallucinations)], particularly if you carry a genetic vulnerability to the disease. Also, rates of marijuana use are often higher in people with symptoms of depression or anxiety—but it is very difficult to determine which came first, so we don't yet know whether they are causally related.

Lungs And Airways

People who abuse marijuana are at risk of injuring their lungs through exposure to respiratory irritants and carcinogens found in marijuana smoke. The smoke from marijuana contains some of the same chemicals found in tobacco smoke; plus, marijuana users tend to inhale more deeply and hold their breath longer, so more smoke enters the lungs. Not surprisingly, marijuana smokers have some of the same breathing problems as tobacco smokers—they are more susceptible to chest colds, coughs, and bronchitis than nonsmokers. And, even though we don't know yet whether or how marijuana use affects the risk for lung and other cancers—why take the risk?

Addiction

Many people don't think of marijuana as addictive—they are wrong. In 2007, the majority of youth (aged 17 or younger) entering drug abuse treatment reported marijuana as their primary drug abused. Marijuana increases dopamine, which creates the good feelings or "high" associated with its use. A user may feel the urge to smoke marijuana again, and again, and again to re-create that experience. Repeated use could lead to addiction—a disease where people continue to do something, even when they are aware of the severe negative consequences at the personal, social, academic, and professional levels.

Marijuana users may also experience a withdrawal syndrome when they stop using the drug. It is similar to what happens to tobacco smokers when they quit—people report being irritable, having sleep problems, and weight loss—effects which can last for several days to a few weeks after drug use is stopped. Relapse is common during this period, as users also crave the drug to relieve these symptoms.

What About Medical Marijuana?

Under U.S. law since 1970, marijuana has been a Schedule I controlled substance. This means that the drug has no approved medical use. However, there are medications containing synthetic THC, the main active ingredient in marijuana, that are used to treat nausea in cancer patients undergoing chemotherapy, and to stimulate appetite in patients with wasting syndrome—severe, involuntary weight loss—due to AIDS.

♣ It's A Fact!!
Does marijuana use lead to the use of other drugs?

While most marijuana smokers do not go on to use other drugs, long-term studies of high school students show that few young people use other illegal drugs without first trying marijuana. For example, the risk of using cocaine is much greater for those who have tried marijuana than for those who have never tried it. Using marijuana puts children and teens in contact with people who are users and sellers of other drugs. So, a marijuana user is more likely to be exposed to and urged to try other drugs. The effects of marijuana on the brain of adolescents—still a work in progress—may also affect their likelihood of using other drugs as they get older. Animal studies suggest this to be true, but it is not yet demonstrated in people.

Since the discovery of the cannabinoid system—receptors in the body that bind THC, and chemicals that act as these receptors—scientists are actively looking for ways to make use of this system for medical purposes. Several highly promising compounds are already being tested for the treatment of obesity, pain, and other disorders. However, it is unlikely that smoked marijuana will be developed as a medication, both because of its negative health effects on the lungs and the numerous other ingredients in the marijuana plant that may be harmful to a person's health.

Chapter 25

Marijuana Abuse Among U.S. Teens

How Widespread Is Marijuana Abuse?

National Survey On Drug Use And Health (NSDUH)

According to the National Survey on Drug Use and Health, in 2007, 14.4 million Americans aged 12 or older used marijuana at least once in the month prior to being surveyed, which is similar to the 2006 rate. About 6,000 people a day in 2007 used marijuana for the first time—2.1 million Americans. Of these, 62.2% were under age 18.

Monitoring The Future Survey

The Monitoring the Future survey indicates that marijuana use among 8th, 10th, and 12th graders—which has shown a consistent decline since the mid-1990s—appears to have leveled off, with 10.9% of 8th graders, 23.9% of 10th graders, and 32.4% of 12th graders reporting past-year use. Heightening the concern over this stabilization in use is the finding that, compared to last year, the proportion of 8th graders who perceived smoking marijuana as harmful and the proportion who disapprove of the drug's use have decreased.

About This Chapter: Information in this chapter is excerpted from "NIDA InfoFacts: Marijuana," National Institute on Drug Abuse, a component of the United States Department of Health and Human Services, July 2009.

In the tables below, "Lifetime" refers to use at least once during a respondent's lifetime. "Past year" refers to use at least once during the year preceding an individual's response to the survey. "Past month" refers to use at least once during the 30 days preceding an individual's response to the survey.

Table 25.1. Percentage Of 8th Graders Who Have Used Marijuana (1995–2001)

	1995	1996	1997	1998	1999	2000	2001
Lifetime	19.9%	23.1%	22.6%	22.2%	22.0%	20.3%	20.4%
Past Year	15.8	18.3	17.7	16.9	16.5	15.6	15.4
Past Month	9.1	11.3	10.2	9.7	9.7	9.1	9.2
Daily	0.8	1.5	1.1	1.1	1.4	1.3	1.3

Table 25.2. Percentage Of 8th Graders Who Have Used Marijuana (2002–2008)

	2002	2003	2004	2005	2006	2007	2008
Lifetime	19.2%	17.5%	16.3%	16.5%	15.7%	14.2%	14.6%
Past Year	14.6	12.8	11.8	12.2	11.7	10.3	10.9
Past Month	8.3	7.5	6.4	6.6	6.5	5.7	5.8
Daily	1.2	1.0	0.8	1.0	1.0	0.8	0.9

Table 25.3. Percentage Of 10th Graders Who Have Used Marijuana (1995–2001)

	1995	1996	1997	1998	1999	2000	2001
Lifetime	34.1%	39.8%	42.3%	39.6%	40.9%	40.3%	40.1%
Past Year	28.7	33.6	34.8	31.1	32.1	32.2	32.7
Past Month	17.2	20.4	20.5	18.7	19.4	19.7	19.8
Daily	2.8	3.5	3.7	3.6	3.8	3.8	4.5

Table 25.4. Percentage Of 10th Graders Who Have Used Marijuana (2002–2008)

	2002	2003	2004	2005	2006	2007	2008
Lifetime	38.7%	36.4%	35.1%	34.1%	31.8%	31.0%	29.9%
Past Year	30.3	28.2	27.5	26.6	25.2	24.6	23.9
Past Month	17.8	17.0	15.9	15.2	14.2	14.2	13.8
Daily	3.9	3.6	3.2	3.1	2.8	2.8	2.7

Table 25.5. Percentage Of 12th Graders Who Have Used Marijuana (1995–2001)

	1995	1996	1997	1998	1999	2000	2001
Lifetime	41.7%	44.9%	49.6%	49.1%	49.7%	48.8%	49.0%
Past Year	34.7	35.8	38.5	37.5	37.8	36.5	37.0
Past Month	21.2	21.9	23.7	22.8	23.1	21.6	22.4
Daily	4.6	4.9	5.8	5.6	6.0	6.0	5.8

Table 25.6. Percentage Of 12th Graders Who Have Used Marijuana (2002–2008)

	2002	2003	2004	2005	2006	2007	2008
Lifetime	47.8%	46.1%	45.7%	44.8%	42.3%	41.8%	42.6%
Past Year	36.2	34.9	34.3	33.6	31.5	31.7	32.4
Past Month	21.5	21.2	19.9	19.8	18.3	18.8	19.4
Daily	6.0	6.0	5.6	5.0	5.0	5.1	5.4

Other Information Sources

For additional information on marijuana, please visit www.marijuana-info.org.

Chapter 26

Health Effects Of Marijuana

Marijuana is the most commonly abused illicit drug in the United States. It is a dry, shredded green and brown mix of flowers, stems, seeds, and leaves derived from the hemp plant Cannabis sativa. The main active chemical in marijuana is delta-9-tetrahydrocannabinol; THC for short.

How is marijuana abused?

Marijuana is usually smoked as a cigarette (joint) or in a pipe. It is also smoked in blunts, which are cigars that have been emptied of tobacco and refilled with marijuana. Since the blunt retains the tobacco leaf used to wrap the cigar, this mode of delivery combines marijuana's active ingredients with nicotine and other harmful chemicals. Marijuana can also be mixed in food or brewed as a tea. As a more concentrated, resinous form it is called hashish, and as a sticky black liquid, hash oil. Marijuana smoke has a pungent and distinctive, usually sweet-and-sour odor.

How does marijuana affect the brain?

Scientists have learned a great deal about how THC acts in the brain to produce its many effects. When someone smokes marijuana, THC rapidly passes from the lungs into the bloodstream, which carries the chemical to the brain and other organs throughout the body.

About This Chapter: Information in this chapter is excerpted from "NIDA InfoFacts: Marijuana," National Institute on Drug Abuse, a component of the United States Department of Health and Human Services, July 2009.

THC acts upon specific sites in the brain, called cannabinoid receptors, kicking off a series of cellular reactions that ultimately lead to the "high" that users experience when they smoke marijuana. Some brain areas have many cannabinoid receptors; others have few or none. The highest density of cannabinoid receptors are found in parts of the brain that influence pleasure, memory, thoughts, concentration, sensory and time perception, and coordinated movement.

Not surprisingly, marijuana intoxication can cause distorted perceptions, impaired coordination, difficulty in thinking and problem solving, and problems with learning and memory. Research has shown that marijuana's adverse impact on learning and memory can last for days or weeks after the acute effects of the drug wear off. As a result, someone who smokes marijuana every day may be functioning at a suboptimal intellectual level all of the time.

Research on the long-term effects of marijuana abuse indicates some changes in the brain similar to those seen after long-term abuse of other major drugs. For example, cannabinoid withdrawal in chronically exposed animals leads to an increase in the activation of the stress-response system and changes in the activity of nerve cells containing dopamine. Dopamine neurons are involved in the regulation of motivation and reward, and are directly or indirectly affected by all drugs of abuse.

Addictive Potential: Long-term marijuana abuse can lead to addiction; that is, compulsive drug seeking and abuse despite its known harmful effects upon social functioning in the context of family, school, work, and recreational activities. Long-term marijuana abusers trying to quit report irritability, sleeplessness, decreased appetite, anxiety, and drug craving, all of which make it difficult to quit. These withdrawal symptoms begin within about one day following abstinence, peak at two to three days, and subside within one or two weeks following drug cessation.

Marijuana And Mental Health: A number of studies have shown an association between chronic marijuana use and increased rates of anxiety, depression, suicidal ideation, and schizophrenia. Some of these studies have shown age at first use to be a factor, where early use is a marker of vulnerability to later problems. However, at this time, it is not clear whether marijuana use causes mental problems, exacerbates them, or is used in an attempt to self-medicate symptoms already in existence. Chronic marijuana use, especially in a very young person, may also be a marker of risk for mental illnesses, including addiction, stemming from genetic or environmental vulnerabilities, such as early exposure to stress or violence. At the present time, the strongest evidence links marijuana use and schizophrenia and/or related disorders. High doses of marijuana can produce an acute psychotic reaction; in addition, use of the drug may trigger the onset or relapse of schizophrenia in vulnerable individuals.

What other adverse effects does marijuana have on health?

Effects On The Heart: Marijuana increases heart rate by 20–100 percent shortly after smoking; this effect can last up to three hours. In one study, it was estimated that marijuana users have a 4.8-fold increase in the risk of heart attack in the first hour after smoking the drug. This may be due to the increased heart rate as well as effects of marijuana on heart rhythms, causing palpitations and arrhythmias. This risk may be greater in aging populations or those with cardiac vulnerabilities.

Effects On The Lungs: Numerous studies have shown marijuana smoke to contain carcinogens and to be an irritant to the lungs. In fact, marijuana smoke contains 50–70 percent more carcinogenic hydrocarbons than does tobacco smoke. Marijuana users usually inhale more deeply and hold their breath longer than tobacco smokers do, which further increase the lungs' exposure to carcinogenic smoke. Marijuana smokers show dysregulated growth of epithelial cells in their lung tissue, which could lead to cancer; however, a recent case-controlled study found no positive associations between marijuana use and lung, upper respiratory, or upper digestive tract cancers. Thus, the link between marijuana smoking and these cancers remains unsubstantiated at this time.

Nonetheless, marijuana smokers can have many of the same respiratory problems as tobacco smokers, such as daily cough and phlegm production, more frequent acute chest illness, and a heightened risk of lung infections. A study of 450 individuals found that people who smoke marijuana frequently but do not smoke tobacco have more health problems and miss more days of work than nonsmokers. Many of the extra sick days among the marijuana smokers in the study were for respiratory illnesses.

Effects On Daily Life: Research clearly demonstrates that marijuana has the potential to cause problems in daily life or make a person's existing problems worse. In one study, heavy marijuana abusers reported that the drug impaired several important measures of life achievement including physical and mental health, cognitive abilities, social life, and career status. Several studies associate workers' marijuana smoking with increased absences, tardiness, accidents, workers' compensation claims, and job turnover.

> **✣ It's A Fact!!**
> The latest treatment data indicate that in 2006 marijuana was the most common illicit drug of abuse and was responsible for about 16% (289,988) of all admissions to treatment facilities in the United States. Marijuana admissions were primarily male (73.8%), White (51.5%), and young (36.1% were in the 15–19 age range). Those in treatment for primary marijuana abuse had begun use at an early age: 56.2% had abused it by age 14 and 92.5% had abused it by age 18.

What treatment options exist?

Behavioral interventions, including cognitive behavioral therapy and motivational incentives (i.e., providing vouchers for goods or services to patients who remain abstinent) have shown efficacy in treating marijuana dependence. Although no medications are currently available, recent discoveries about the workings of the cannabinoid system offer promise for the development of medications to ease withdrawal, block the intoxicating effects of marijuana, and prevent relapse.

Chapter 27

Marijuana Smoking And Respiratory Disorders

A large new epidemiological study suggests that marijuana smoke can cause the same types of respiratory damage as tobacco smoke. Significant associations between marijuana smoking and a variety of respiratory diseases also have been confirmed by an extensive review of clinical literature.

Monitoring The Effects Of Tobacco And Marijuana

Dr. Brent Moore and colleagues at Yale University, the National Cancer Institute, and the University of Vermont evaluated data from a nationally representative sample of 6,728 adults. Their analysis indicated that a history of more than 100 lifetime episodes of smoking marijuana, with at least one episode in the past month, increased an individual's risk of chronic bronchitis, coughing on most days, wheezing, chest sounds without a cold, and increased phlegm.

"The most significant difference between tobacco smoke and marijuana smoke is their principal active ingredients—nicotine in tobacco and delta-9-tetrahydrocannabinol (THC) in marijuana. Beyond that, marijuana contains at least as much tar and half again as many carcinogens as smoke from conventional tobacco," says Dr. Moore. "Quitting marijuana smoking may benefit respiratory health as much as quitting cigarettes, in addition to the clear and considerable health, psychological, and social benefits of no longer abusing an illicit drug."

About This Chapter: Information in this chapter is from "Marijuana Smoking Is Associated with a Spectrum of Respiratory Disorders," by Patrick Zickler, in *NIDA Notes*, a publication of the National Institute on Drug Abuse, Vol. 21, No. 1, October 2006.

The information Dr. Moore and his colleagues analyzed was gathered through the third National Health and Nutrition Examination Survey (NHANES III), conducted between 1988 and 1994. Participants included 4,789 nonsmokers of either tobacco or marijuana; 1,525 smokers of tobacco but not marijuana; 320 smokers of both marijuana and tobacco; and 94 who smoked marijuana only. On average, marijuana abusers had smoked the drug on 10 of the preceding 30 days, with 16 percent reporting daily or almost daily smoking. Tobacco smokers consumed roughly the same number of cigarettes—averaging 19.2 per day—whether or not they also smoked marijuana. Survey participants answered questions about their experiences of a range of respiratory symptoms and were examined for signs of respiratory abnormalities.

The researchers concluded that tobacco smokers who also smoked marijuana had a higher prevalence of most respiratory symptoms than tobacco-only smokers. Compared with tobacco-only smokers, however, those who also smoked marijuana were less likely to have had pneumonia during the previous year or to show spirometric evidence of obstructive pulmonary disorder. Commenting on this finding, Dr. Moore says that it is important to note that the marijuana smokers in the sample were significantly younger (average age 31.2 years) than the tobacco smokers (average age 41.5 years). "The marijuana-related respiratory effects correspond to a relatively young population, and NHANES III did not ask participants older than age 59 about drug use," he adds. "It is likely that respiratory effects will be higher in older marijuana smokers, and, because of the high prevalence of tobacco use among marijuana smokers, there appears to be an increased risk for illness due to cumulative effects of smoking both drugs."

Marijuana's Long-Term Pulmonary Effects

Further evidence of marijuana's respiratory toxicity emerged from a study conducted by Dr. Donald Tashkin at the University of California, Los Angeles. Dr. Tashkin conducted an extensive review of clinical and epidemiological research to determine the extent to which chronic marijuana smoking might lead to long-term pulmonary effects and diseases similar to those caused by tobacco. Unlike the NHANES III data examined by Dr. Moore, the studies evaluated by Dr. Tashkin made it possible to assess a possible association between marijuana smoking and respiratory cancers.

✤ **It's A Fact!!**

Tobacco Versus Marijuana

Here's some of what science tells us:

- Marijuana smokers can develop phlegm and a daily cough.

- Marijuana smoke contains 50 to 70 percent more cancer-causing chemicals than tobacco smoke.

- Puff for puff, smoking marijuana may increase the risk of cancer more than smoking tobacco does.

- People who smoke marijuana are at greater risk for lung infections, like pneumonia.

- Chronic marijuana smokers are vulnerable to bronchitis, emphysema, and bronchial asthma.

- Scientists have found signs of lung tissue injured or destroyed due to marijuana use.

Source: From a Heads Up compilation by Scholastic and the National Institute on Drug Abuse, 2003. Despite the older date of this document, the facts about marijuana smoke are still pertinent for today's readers.

The results of animal and cell culture studies are mixed with respect to the carcinogenic effects of THC, some studies showing that THC promotes lung cancer growth and others showing an anti-tumoral effect on a variety of malignancies. Although the results of epidemiological studies are also mixed, a large, recently completed case-control study has failed to find a direct link between marijuana use (including heavy use) and lung, throat, or other head and neck cancers. "Nevertheless, there is evidence that suggests pre-carcinogenic effects in respiratory tissue," Dr. Tashkin says. "Biopsies of bronchial tissue provide evidence that regular marijuana smoking injures airway epithelial cells, leading to dysregulation of bronchial epithelial cell growth and eventually to possible malignant changes." Moreover, he adds, because marijuana smokers typically hold their breath four times as long as tobacco smokers after inhaling, marijuana smoking deposits significantly more tar and known carcinogens within the tar, such as polycyclic aromatic hydrocarbons, in the airways. In addition to precancerous changes, Dr. Tashkin found that marijuana smoking is associated with a range of damaging pulmonary effects, including inhibition of the tumor-killing and bactericidal activity of alveolar macrophages, the primary immune cells within the lung.

Taken together, Dr. Tashkin's survey of clinical and epidemiological studies and Dr. Moore's assessment of self-reported and clinically observed effects provide an extensive catalog of respiratory and pulmonary damage associated with marijuana smoking. Smokers are subject to these effects:

- Coughing and phlegm production on most days
- Wheezing and other chest sounds
- Acute and chronic bronchitis
- Injury to airway tissue, including edema (swelling), increased vascularity, and increased mucus secretion
- Impaired function of immune system components (alveolar macrophages) in the lungs

Chapter 28

Marijuana Abuse And Depression

Men and women who smoked marijuana before age 17 are 3.5 times as likely to attempt suicide as those who started later. Individuals who are dependent on marijuana have a higher risk than nondependent individuals of experiencing major depressive disorder and suicidal thoughts and behaviors. The researchers who discovered these relationships, in a recent National Institute on Drug Abuse (NIDA)-funded large-scale epidemiological study, say that although the causes are not clear, their findings demonstrate the importance of considering associated mental health issues in the treatment and prevention of marijuana abuse.

Dr. Michael Lynskey and colleagues at the Washington University School of Medicine in St. Louis, Missouri, gathered data from four groups of same-sex twin pairs (508 identical, 493 fraternal; 518 female, 483 male) enrolled in the Australian Twin Registry. The groups and findings were as follows:

- Among the 277 pairs who were discordant for marijuana dependence (that is, one twin but not the other met the criteria for a diagnosis of marijuana dependence), the dependent twins were 2.9 times as likely as their nondependent co-twins to think about suicide without attempting it, and 2.5 times as likely to make a suicide attempt

About This Chapter: Information in this chapter is from "Twin Study Links Marijuana Abuse, Suicide, and Depression," by Patrick Zickler, in *NIDA Notes*, a publication of the National Institute on Drug Abuse, Vol. 20, No. 2, August 2005.

- Among the 311 pairs discordant for early marijuana initiation (just one twin in each pair smoked marijuana before age 17), the early initiators were 3.5 times as likely as their twins to attempt suicide, but no more likely to suffer a Major Depressive Disorder (MDD)

- Among the 156 pairs discordant for diagnosis of MDD before age 17, fraternal but not identical twins with early diagnosis of MDD were 9.5 times as likely to develop marijuana dependence

- Among the 257 pairs discordant for having suicidal thoughts before age 17, fraternal but not identical twins with early suicidal thoughts were 5.5 times as likely as their twins to become dependent on marijuana.

"Overall, the associations between marijuana abuse and depressive disorders suggest a relationship that is contributory but not necessarily causal. Depressive disorders in and of themselves do not cause people to abuse marijuana, and marijuana abuse and dependence do not of themselves cause depression or suicidal behavior," Dr. Lynskey says. "Nevertheless, clinicians treating patients for one disorder should take the other into account at initial assessment and throughout treatment. In the context of treatment, both need to be addressed, because it is not necessarily the case that eliminating one disorder will get rid of the other." The fact that two of the relationships were observed in fraternal but not identical twins suggests that the experiences related in each—marijuana dependence and MDD, and marijuana dependence and suicidal thoughts—may share a common underlying genetic basis, notes Dr. Lynskey.

The associations identified in this study are complex, but point to a simple policy implication, observes Dr. Lynskey. "It is important to see that prevention efforts aimed at one disorder may well have the additional benefit of preventing or reducing the other," he says.

"Drug abuse and depression co-occur at rates much greater than chance and constitute a serious public health concern," says Dr. Naimah Weinberg of NIDA's Division of Epidemiology, Services and Prevention Research. "Understanding how each disorder may contribute to the development and course of the other, and what factors may underlie their co-occurrence, has important implications for prevention and treatment of these disabling conditions. Genetic epidemiologic approaches, such as those applied by Dr. Lynskey and his colleagues, are very powerful tools to help parse out the etiologic relationships between co-occurring disorders."

Chapter 29

Medical Marijuana And The Law

Attorney General Announces Formal Medical Marijuana Guidelines

Attorney General Eric Holder today announced formal guidelines for federal prosecutors in states that have enacted laws authorizing the use of marijuana for medical purposes. The guidelines make clear that the focus of federal resources should not be on individuals whose actions are in compliance with existing state laws, while underscoring that the Department will continue to prosecute people whose claims of compliance with state and local law conceal operations inconsistent with the terms, conditions, or purposes of those laws.

"It will not be a priority to use federal resources to prosecute patients with serious illnesses or their caregivers who are complying with state laws on medical marijuana, but we will not tolerate drug traffickers who hide behind claims of compliance with state law to mask activities that are clearly illegal," Holder said. "This balanced policy formalizes a sensible approach that the Department has been following since January: effectively focus our resources on serious drug traffickers while taking into account state and local laws."

About This Chapter: This chapter includes "Attorney General Announces Formal Medical Marijuana Guidelines" and "Investigations And Prosecutions In States Authorizing The Medical Use Of Marijuana," both publications of the U.S. Department of Justice, October 2009.

The guidelines set forth examples of conduct that would show when individuals are not in clear and unambiguous compliance with applicable state law and may indicate illegal drug trafficking activity of potential federal interest, including unlawful use of firearms, violence, sales to minors, money laundering, amounts of marijuana inconsistent with purported compliance with state or local law, marketing or excessive financial gains similarly inconsistent with

♣ It's A Fact!!
"Medical" Marijuana—The Facts

- Medical marijuana already exists. It's called Marinol.

- A pharmaceutical product, Marinol, is widely available through prescription. It comes in the form of a pill and is also being studied by researchers for suitability via other delivery methods, such as an inhaler or patch. The active ingredient of Marinol is synthetic THC, which has been found to relieve the nausea and vomiting associated with chemotherapy for cancer patients and to assist with loss of appetite with AIDS patients.

- Unlike smoked marijuana—which contains more than 400 different chemicals, including most of the hazardous chemicals found in tobacco smoke—Marinol has been studied and approved by the medical community and the Food and Drug Administration (FDA), the nation's watchdog over unsafe and harmful food and drug products. Since the passage of the 1906 Pure Food and Drug Act, any drug that is marketed in the United States must undergo rigorous scientific testing. The approval process mandated by this act ensures that claims of safety and therapeutic value are supported by clinical evidence and keeps unsafe, ineffective and dangerous drugs off the market.

- There are no FDA-approved medications that are smoked. For one thing, smoking is generally a poor way to deliver medicine. It is difficult to administer safe, regulated dosages of medicines in smoked form. Secondly, the harmful chemicals and carcinogens that are byproducts of smoking create entirely new health problems. There is four times the level of tar in a marijuana cigarette, for example, than in a tobacco cigarette.

- Morphine, for example, has proven to be a medically valuable drug, but the FDA does not endorse the smoking of opium or heroin. Instead, scientists have extracted active ingredients from opium, which are sold state or local law, illegal possession or sale of other controlled substances, and ties to criminal enterprises.

Fourteen states have enacted laws in some form addressing the use of marijuana for medical purposes. A copy of the guidelines, in a memo from Deputy Attorney General David W. Ogden to United states Attorneys, can be found here: http://blogs.usdoj.gov/blog/archives/192.

as pharmaceutical products like morphine, codeine, hydrocodone or oxycodone. In a similar vein, the FDA has not approved smoking marijuana for medicinal purposes, but has approved the active ingredient—THC—in the form of scientifically regulated Marinol.

- The DEA helped facilitate the research on Marinol. The National Cancer Institute approached the DEA in the early 1980s regarding their study of THC in relieving nausea and vomiting. As a result, the DEA facilitated the registration and provided regulatory support and guidance for the study.

- The DEA recognizes the importance of listening to science. That's why the DEA has registered seven research initiatives to continue researching the effects of smoked marijuana as medicine. For example, under one program established by the State of California, researchers are studying the potential use of marijuana and its ingredients on conditions such as multiple sclerosis and pain. At this time, however, neither the medical community nor the scientific community has found sufficient data to conclude that smoked marijuana is the best approach to dealing with these important medical issues.

- The most comprehensive, scientifically rigorous review of studies of smoked marijuana was conducted by the Institute of Medicine, an organization chartered by the National Academy of Sciences. In a report released in 1999, the Institute did not recommend the use of smoked marijuana, but did conclude that active ingredients in marijuana could be isolated and developed into a variety of pharmaceuticals, such as Marinol.

- In the meantime, the DEA is working with pain management groups, such as Last Acts, to make sure that those who need access to safe, effective pain medication can get the best medication available.

Source: From "'Medical' Marijuana—The Facts," an undated document produced by the U.S. Drug Enforcement Administration (www.justice.gov/dea), accessed August 29, 2010.

Investigations And Prosecutions In States Authorizing The Medical Use Of Marijuana

This information provides clarification and guidance to federal prosecutors in states that have enacted laws authorizing the medical use of marijuana. These laws vary in their substantive provisions and in the extent of state regulatory oversight, both among the enacting states and among local jurisdictions within those states. Rather than developing different guidelines for every possible variant of state and local law, this memorandum provides uniform guidance to focus federal investigations and prosecutions in these states on core federal enforcement priorities.

The Department of Justice is committed to the enforcement of the Controlled Substances Act in all states. Congress has determined that marijuana is a dangerous drug, and the illegal distribution and sale of marijuana is a serious crime and provides a significant source of revenue to large-scale criminal enterprises, gangs, and cartels. One timely example underscores the importance of our efforts to prosecute significant marijuana traffickers: marijuana distribution in the United States remains the single largest source of revenue for the Mexican cartels.

The Department is also committed to making efficient and rational use of its limited investigative and prosecutorial resources. In general, United States Attorneys are vested with "plenary authority with regard to federal criminal matters" within their districts. (USAM 9-2.001.) In exercising this authority, United States Attorneys are "invested by statute and delegation from the Attorney General with the broadest discretion in the exercise of such authority." This authority should, of course, be exercised consistent with Department priorities and guidance.

The prosecution of significant traffickers of illegal drugs, including marijuana, and the disruption of illegal drug manufacturing and trafficking networks continues to be a core priority in the Department's efforts against narcotics and dangerous drugs, and the Department's investigative and prosecutorial resources should be directed towards these objectives. As a general matter, pursuit of these priorities should not focus federal resources in your states on individuals whose actions are in clear and unambiguous compliance with existing state laws providing for the medical use of marijuana. For example, prosecution of individuals with cancer or other serious illnesses who use marijuana as part of a recommended treatment regimen consistent with applicable state law, or those caregivers in clear and unambiguous compliance with existing state law who provide such individuals with marijuana, is unlikely to be an efficient use of limited federal resources. On the other hand, prosecution of commercial enterprises that unlawfully market and sell marijuana for profit continues to be an enforcement priority of the Department. To be sure, claims of compliance with state or local law may mask operations inconsistent with the terms, conditions, or purposes of those laws, and federal law enforcement should not be deterred by such assertions when otherwise pursuing the Department's core enforcement priorities.

Typically, when any of the following characteristics is present, the conduct will not be in clear and unambiguous compliance with applicable state law and may indicate illegal drug trafficking activity of potential federal interest:

- Unlawful possession or unlawful use of firearms

- Violence

- Sales to minors

- Financial and marketing activities inconsistent with the terms, conditions, or purposes of state law, including evidence of money laundering activity and/or financial gains or excessive amounts of cash inconsistent with purported compliance with state or local law

- Amounts of marijuana inconsistent with purported compliance with state or local law

- Illegal possession or sale of other controlled substances

- Ties to other criminal enterprises

Of course, no state can authorize violations of federal law, and the list of factors above is not intended to describe exhaustively when a federal prosecution may be warranted. Accordingly, in prosecutions under the Controlled Substances Act, federal prosecutors are not expected to charge, prove, or otherwise establish any state law violations. Indeed, this memorandum does not alter in any way the Department's authority to enforce federal law, including laws prohibiting the manufacture, production, distribution, possession, or use of marijuana on federal property. This guidance regarding resource allocation does not "legalize" marijuana or provide a legal defense to a violation of federal law, nor is it intended to create any privileges, benefits, or rights, substantive or procedural, enforceable by any individual, party or witness in any administrative, civil, or criminal matter. Nor does clear and unambiguous compliance with state law or the absence of one or all of the above factors create a legal defense to a violation of the Controlled Substances Act. Rather, this memorandum is intended solely as a guide to the exercise of investigative and prosecutorial discretion.

Finally, nothing herein precludes investigation or prosecution where there is a reasonable basis to believe that compliance with state law is being invoked as a pretext for the production or distribution of marijuana for purposes not authorized by state law. Nor does this guidance preclude investigation or prosecution, even when there is clear and unambiguous compliance with existing state law, in particular circumstances where investigation or prosecution otherwise serves important federal interests.

Chapter 30

The U.S. Drug Enforcement Administration Position On Marijuana

The campaign to legitimize what is called "medical" marijuana is based on two propositions: that science views marijuana as medicine, and that the U.S. Drug Enforcement Administration (DEA) targets sick and dying people using the drug. Neither proposition is true. Smoked marijuana has not withstood the rigors of science—it is not medicine and it is not safe. DEA targets criminals engaged in cultivation and trafficking, not the sick and dying. No state has legalized the trafficking of marijuana, including the twelve states that have decriminalized certain marijuana use.

Smoked Marijuana Is Not Medicine

There is no consensus of medical evidence that smoking marijuana helps patients. Congress enacted laws against marijuana in 1970 based in part on its conclusion that marijuana has no scientifically proven medical value. The U.S. Food and Drug Administration (FDA) is the federal agency responsible for approving drugs as safe and effective medicine based on valid scientific data. FDA has not approved smoked marijuana for any condition or disease. The FDA noted that "there is currently sound evidence that smoked marijuana

About This Chapter: Information in this chapter is excerpted from "The DEA Position On Marijuana," U.S. Drug Enforcement Administration, U.S. Department of Justice, May 2006.

is harmful," and "that no sound scientific studies supported medical use of marijuana for treatment in the United States, and no animal or human data supported the safety or efficacy of marijuana for general medical use."

In 2001, the Supreme Court affirmed Congress's 1970 judgment about marijuana in United States v. Oakland Cannabis Buyers' Cooperative et al., 532 U.S. 438 (2001), which held that, given the absence of medical usefulness, medical necessity is not a defense to marijuana prosecution. Furthermore, in Gonzales v. Raich, 125 S.Ct. 2195 (2005), the Supreme Court reaffirmed that the authority of Congress to regulate the use of potentially harmful substances through the federal Controlled Substances Act includes the authority to regulate marijuana of a purely intrastate character, regardless of a state law purporting to authorize "medical" use of marijuana.

The DEA and the federal government are not alone in viewing smoked marijuana as having no documented medical value. Voices in the medical community likewise do not accept smoked marijuana as medicine:

- The American Cancer Society (ACS) "does not advocate inhaling smoke, nor the legalization of marijuana," although the organization does support carefully controlled clinical studies for alternative delivery methods, specifically a THC skin patch.

- The American Academy of Pediatrics (AAP) believes that "[a]ny change in the legal status of marijuana, even if limited to adults, could affect the prevalence of use among adolescents." While it supports scientific research on the possible medical use of cannabinoids as opposed to smoked marijuana, it opposes the legalization of marijuana.

- The National Multiple Sclerosis Society (NMSS) states that studies done to date "have not provided convincing evidence that marijuana benefits people with MS," and thus marijuana is not a recommended treatment. Furthermore, the NMSS warns that the "long-term use of marijuana may be associated with significant serious side effects."

- The British Medical Association (BMA) voiced extreme concern that down-grading the criminal status of marijuana would "mislead" the public into believing that the drug is safe. The BMA maintains that marijuana "has been linked to greater risk of heart disease, lung cancer, bronchitis and emphysema." The 2004 Deputy Chairman of the BMA's Board of Science said that "[t]he public must be made aware of the harmful effects we know result from smoking this drug."

- The American Academy of Pediatrics asserted that with regard to marijuana use, "from a public health perspective, even a small increase in use, whether attributable to increased availability or decreased perception of risk, would have significant ramifications."

In 1999, The Institute of Medicine (IOM) released a landmark study reviewing the supposed medical properties of marijuana. The study is frequently cited by "medical" marijuana advocates, but in fact severely undermines their arguments.

- After release of the IOM study, the principal investigators cautioned that the active compounds in marijuana may have medicinal potential and therefore should be researched further. However, the study concluded that "there is little future in smoked marijuana as a medically approved medication."

- For some ailments, the IOM found "...potential therapeutic value of cannabinoid drugs, primarily THC, for pain relief, control of nausea and vomiting, and appetite stimulation." However, it pointed out that "[t]he effects of cannabinoids on the symptoms studied are generally modest, and in most cases there are more effective medications [than smoked marijuana]."

- The study concluded that, at best, there is only anecdotal information on the medical benefits of smoked marijuana for some ailments, such as muscle spasticity. For other ailments, such as epilepsy and glaucoma, the study found no evidence of medical value and did not endorse further research.

- The IOM study explained that "smoked marijuana . . . is a crude THC delivery system that also delivers harmful substances." In addition, "plants contain a variable mixture of biologically active compounds and cannot be expected to provide a precisely defined drug effect." Therefore, the study concluded that "there is little future in smoked marijuana as a medically approved medication."

- The principal investigators explicitly stated that using smoked marijuana in clinical trials "should not be designed to develop it as a licensed drug, but should be a stepping stone to the development of new, safe delivery systems of cannabinoids."

Thus, even scientists and researchers who believe that certain active ingredients in marijuana may have potential medicinal value openly discount the notion that smoked marijuana is or can become "medicine."

DEA has approved and will continue to approve research into whether THC has any medicinal use. As of May 8, 2006, DEA had registered every one of the 163 researchers who requested to use marijuana in studies and who met Department of Health and Human Services standards. One of those researchers, The Center for Medicinal Cannabis Research (CMCR), conducts studies "to ascertain the general medical safety and efficacy of cannabis and cannabis products and examine alternative forms of cannabis administration." The CMCR currently has 11 on-going studies involving marijuana and the efficacy of cannabis and cannabis compounds as they relate to medical conditions such as HIV, cancer pain, MS, and nausea.

At present, however, the clear weight of the evidence is that smoked marijuana is harmful. No matter what medical condition has been studied, other drugs already approved by the FDA, such as Marinol—a pill form of synthetic THC—have been proven to be safer and more effective than smoked marijuana.

Marijuana Is Dangerous To The User And Others

Legalization of marijuana, no matter how it begins, will come at the expense of our children and public safety. It will create dependency and treatment issues, and open the door to use of other drugs, impaired health, delinquent behavior, and drugged drivers.

This is not the marijuana of the 1970s; today's marijuana is far more powerful. Average THC levels of seized marijuana rose from less than one percent in the mid-1970s to a national average of over eight percent in 2004. And the potency of "B.C. Bud" (British Columbia Bud) is roughly twice the national average—ranging from 15 percent to as high as 25 percent THC content.

Dependency And Treatment

- Adolescents are at highest risk for marijuana addiction, as they are "three times more likely than adults to develop dependency." This is borne out by the fact that treatment admission rates for adolescents reporting marijuana as the primary substance of abuse increased from 32% to 65% between 1993 and 2003. More young people ages 12–17 entered treatment in 2003 for marijuana dependency than for alcohol and all other illegal drugs combined.

✎ What's It Mean?

B.C. Bud: British Columbia bud; a potent form of marijuana grown in British Columbia, a Canadian province.

CB1 (Cannabinoid Receptor 1): One of two receptors in the brain's endo-cannabinoid (EC) system associated with the intake of food and tobacco dependency.

DEA: U.S. Drug Enforcement Administration; an agency of the U.S. Justice Department responsible for enforcing laws and regulations regarding controlled substances.

FDA: U.S. Food and Drug Administration; a government agency responsible for protecting public health by enforcing laws related to the safety of medicines, medical devices, and the nation's food supply.

HIV: Human immunodeficiency virus; the virus responsible for AIDS (acquired immunodeficiency syndrome).

IOP: Intraocular pressure; the pressure of fluid within the eyeball. Elevated IOP is a risk factor for glaucoma.

LSD: Diethylamide-lysergic acid; a hallucinogenic drug.

MS: Multiple sclerosis; a progressive disease that affects the central nervous system, thought to be related to an immune system dysfunction.

THC: Tetrahydrocannabinol; the substance in marijuana responsible for its psychoactive effects.

Source: U.S. Drug Enforcement Administration, May 2006, with explanations added by the editor.

- "[R]esearch shows that use of [marijuana] can lead to dependence. Some heavy users of marijuana develop withdrawal symptoms when they have not used the drug for a period of time. Marijuana use, in fact, is often associated with behavior that meets the criteria for substance dependence established by the American Psychiatric Association."

- Of the 19.1 million Americans aged 12 or older who used illicit drugs in the past 30 days in 2004, 14.6 million used marijuana, making it the most commonly used illicit drug in 2004.

- Among all ages, marijuana was the most common illicit drug responsible for treatment admissions in 2003, accounting for 15 percent of all admissions—outdistancing heroin, the next most prevalent cause.

- In 2003, 20% (185,239) of the 919,833 adults admitted to treatment for illegal drug abuse cited marijuana as their primary drug of abuse.

Marijuana As A Precursor To Abuse Of Other Drugs

- Marijuana is a frequent precursor to the use of more dangerous drugs, and signals a significantly enhanced likelihood of drug problems in adult life. The *Journal of the American Medical Association* (AMA) reported, based on a study of 300 sets of twins, "that marijuana-using twins were four times more likely than their siblings to use cocaine and crack cocaine, and five times more likely to use hallucinogens such as LSD."

- Long-term studies on patterns of drug usage among young people show that very few of them use other drugs without first starting with marijuana. For example, one study found that among adults (age 26 and older) who had used cocaine, 62% had initiated marijuana use before age 15. By contrast, less than one percent of adults who never tried marijuana went on to use cocaine.

- Columbia University's National Center on Addiction and Substance Abuse reports that teens who used marijuana at least once in the last month are 13 times likelier than other teens to use another drug like cocaine, heroin, or methamphetamine, and almost 26 times likelier than those teens who have never used marijuana to use another drug.

• In 2003, 3.1 million Americans aged 12 or older used marijuana daily or almost daily in the past year. Of those daily marijuana users, nearly two-thirds "used at least one other illicit drug in the past 12 months." More than half (53.3 percent) of daily marijuana users were also dependent on or abused alcohol or another illicit drug compared to those who were nonusers or used marijuana less than daily.

❖ It's A Fact!!

Marijuana use in early adolescence is particularly ominous. Adults who were early marijuana users were found to be five times more likely to become dependent on any drug, eight times more likely to use cocaine in the future, and fifteen times more likely to use heroin later in life.

• Healthcare workers, legal counsel, police and judges indicate that marijuana is a typical precursor to methamphetamine. For instance, Nancy Kneeland, a substance abuse counselor in Idaho, pointed out that "in almost all cases meth users began with alcohol and pot."

Mental And Physical Health Issues Related To Marijuana

• John Walters, Director of the Office of National Drug Control Policy, Charles G. Curie, Administrator of the Substance Abuse and Mental Health Services Administration, and experts and scientists from leading mental health organizations joined together in May 2005 to warn parents about the mental health dangers marijuana poses to teens. According to several recent studies, marijuana use has been linked with depression and suicidal thoughts, in addition to schizophrenia. These studies report that weekly marijuana use among teens doubles the risk of developing depression and triples the incidence of suicidal thoughts.

• Dr. Andrew Campbell, a member of the New South Wales (Australia) Mental Health Review Tribunal, published a study in 2005 which revealed that four out of five individuals with schizophrenia were regular cannabis users when they were teenagers. Between 75–80 percent of the patients involved in the study used cannabis habitually between the ages of 12 and 21. In addition, a laboratory-controlled study by Yale scientists, published in 2004, found that THC "transiently induced a range of schizophrenia-like effects in healthy people."

- Smoked marijuana has also been associated with an increased risk of the same respiratory symptoms as tobacco, including coughing, phlegm production, chronic bronchitis, shortness of breath and wheezing. Because cannabis plants are contaminated with a range of fungal spores, smoking marijuana may also increase the risk of respiratory exposure by infectious organisms (i.e., molds and fungi).

✤ **It's A Fact!!**
Marijuana takes the risks of tobacco and raises them: marijuana smoke contains more than 400 chemicals and increases the risk of serious health consequences, including lung damage.

- According to two studies, marijuana use narrows arteries in the brain, "similar to patients with high blood pressure and dementia," and may explain why memory tests are difficult for marijuana users. In addition, "chronic consumers of cannabis lose molecules called CB1 receptors in the brain's arteries," leading to blood flow problems in the brain which can cause memory loss, attention deficits, and impaired learning ability.

- Carleton University researchers published a study in 2005 showing that current marijuana users who smoke at least five "joints" per week did significantly worse than nonusers when tested on neurocognition tests such as processing speed, memory, and overall IQ.

Delinquent Behaviors And Drugged Driving

- In 2002, the percentage of young people engaging in delinquent behaviors "rose with [the] increasing frequency of marijuana use." For example, according to a National Survey on Drug Use and Health (NSDUH) report, 42.2% of youths who smoked marijuana 300 or more days per year and 37.1% of those who did so 50–99 days took part in serious fighting at school or work. Only 18.2% of those who did not use marijuana in the past year engaged in serious fighting.

- A large shock trauma unit conducting an ongoing study found that 17% (one in six) of crash victims tested positive for marijuana. The rates were slightly higher for crash victims under the age of eighteen, 19% of whom tested positive for marijuana.

• In a study of high school classes in 2000 and 2001, about 28,000 seniors each year admitted that they were in at least one accident after using marijuana.

• Approximately 15% of teens reported driving under the influence of marijuana. This is almost equal to the percentage of teens who reported driving under the influence of alcohol (16%).

• A study of motorists pulled over for reckless driving showed that, among those who were not impaired by alcohol, 45% tested positive for marijuana.

• The National Highway Traffic Safety Administration (NHTSA) has found that marijuana significantly impairs one's ability to safely operate a motor vehicle. According to its report, "[e]pidemiology data from road traffic arrests and fatalities indicate that after alcohol, marijuana is the most frequently detected psychoactive substance among driving populations." Problems reported include: decreased car handling performance, inability to maintain headway, impaired time and distance estimation, increased reaction times, sleepiness, lack of motor coordination, and impaired sustained vigilance.

The Foreign Experience

The Netherlands

• Due to international pressure on permissive Dutch cannabis policy and domestic complaints over the spread of marijuana "coffee shops," the government of the Netherlands has reconsidered its legalization measures. After marijuana became normalized, consumption nearly tripled—from 15% to 44%—among 18-to 20-year-old Dutch youth. As a result of stricter local government policies, the number of cannabis "coffeehouses" in the Netherlands was reduced—from 1,179 in 1997 to 737 in 2004, a 37 percent decrease in 7 years.

• About 70 percent of Dutch towns have a zero-tolerance policy toward cannabis cafes.

Switzerland

- Liberalization of marijuana laws in Switzerland has likewise produced damaging results. After liberalization, Switzerland became a magnet for drug users from many other countries. In 1987, Zurich permitted drug use and sales in a part of the city called Platzpitz, dubbed "Needle Park." By 1992, the number of regular drug users at the park reportedly swelled from a "few hundred at the outset in 1987 to about 20,000." The area around the park became crime-ridden, forcing closure of the park. The experiment has since been terminated.

Canada

- After a large decline in the 1980s, marijuana use among teens increased during the 1990s as young people became "confused about the state of federal pot law" in the wake of an aggressive decriminalization campaign, according to a special adviser to Health Canada's Director General of drug strategy. Several Canadian drug surveys show that marijuana use among Canadian youth has steadily climbed to surpass its 26-year peak, rising to 29.6% of youth in grades 7–12 in 2003.

United Kingdom

- In March 2005, British Home Secretary Charles Clarke took the unprecedented step of calling "for a rethink on Labour's legal down-grading of cannabis" from a Class B to a Class C substance. Mr. Clarke requested that the Advisory Council on the Misuse of Drugs complete a new report, taking into account recent studies showing a link between cannabis and psychosis and also considering the more potent cannabis referred to as "skunk."

The Legalization Lobby

The proposition that smoked marijuana is "medicine" is, in sum, false—trickery used by those promoting wholesale legalization. When a statute dramatically reducing penalties for "medical" marijuana took effect in Maryland in October 2003, a defense attorney noted that "[t]here are a whole bunch of people who like marijuana who can now try to use this defense." The attorney observed that lawyers would be "neglecting their clients if they did not try to find out what 'physical, emotional or psychological'" condition could be enlisted to develop a defense to justify a defendant's using the drug. "Sometimes people are self-medicating without even realizing it," he said.

- Ed Rosenthal, senior editor of *High Times*, a pro-drug magazine, once revealed the legalizer strategy behind the "medical" marijuana movement. While addressing an effort to seek public sympathy for glaucoma patients, he said, "I have to tell you that I also use marijuana medically. I have a latent glaucoma which has never been diagnosed. The reason why it's never been diagnosed is because I've been treating it." He continued, "I have to be honest, there is another reason why I do use marijuana . . . and that is because I like to get high. Marijuana is fun."

- A few billionaires—not broad grassroots support—started and sustain the "medical" marijuana and drug legalization movements in the United States. Without their money and influence, the drug legalization movement would shrivel. According to National Families in Action, four individuals—George Soros, Peter Lewis, George Zimmer, and John Sperling—contributed $1,510,000 to the effort to pass a "medical" marijuana law in California in 1996, a sum representing nearly 60 percent of the total contributions.

- In October 2005, Denver voters passed Initiative 100 decriminalizing marijuana based on incomplete and misleading campaign advertisements put forth by the Safer Alternative For Enjoyable Recreation (SAFER). A Denver City Councilman complained that the group used the slogan "Make Denver SAFER" on billboards and campaign signs to mislead the voters into thinking that the initiative supported increased police staffing. Indeed, the Denver voters were never informed of the initiative's true intent to decriminalize marijuana.

Chapter 31

An Opposing Point Of View: Against Marijuana Prohibition

Marijuana Prohibition Facts

- Very few Americans had even heard about marijuana when it was first federally prohibited in 1937. Today, between 95 and 100 million Americans admit to having tried it, and nearly 15 million say they have used it in the past month.[1] A study released in December 2006 found that marijuana is now the leading cash crop in the U.S., exceeding the value of corn and wheat combined.[2]

- According to government-funded researchers, high school seniors consistently report that marijuana is easily available, despite decades of a nationwide drug war. With little variation, every year about 85% consider marijuana "fairly easy" or "very easy" to obtain.[3]

- There have been almost 9.5 million marijuana arrests in the United States since 1995, including 872,720 arrests in 2007—more than for all violent crimes combined, and an all-time record. One person is arrested for marijuana every 36 seconds. About 89% of all marijuana arrests are for possession—not manufacture or distribution.

- Every comprehensive, objective government commission that has examined the marijuana phenomenon throughout the past 100 years has recommended that adults should not be criminalized for using marijuana.[5]

- Cultivation of even one marijuana plant is a federal felony.

- Lengthy mandatory minimum sentences apply to myriad offenses. For example, a person must serve a five-year mandatory minimum sentence if federally convicted of cultivating 100 marijuana plants—including seedlings or bug-infested, sickly plants. This is longer than the average sentences for auto theft and manslaughter![6]

- A one-year minimum prison sentence is mandated for "distributing" or "manufacturing" controlled substances within 1,000 feet of any school, university, or playground. Most areas in a city fall within these "drug-free zones." An adult who lives three blocks from a university is subject to a one-year mandatory minimum sentence for selling an ounce of marijuana to another adult—or even growing one marijuana plant in his or her basement.[7]

- Federal government figures indicate there are more than 41,000 Americans in state or federal prison on marijuana charges right now, not including those in county jails.[8] That's more than the number imprisoned on all charges combined in eight individual European Union countries.

- A recent study of prisons in four Midwestern states found that approximately one in ten male inmates reported that they had been raped while in prison.[9] Rates of rape and sexual assault against women prisoners, who are most likely to be abused by male staff members, have been reported to be as high as 27 percent in some institutions.[10]

- Civil forfeiture laws allow police to seize the money and property of suspected marijuana offenders—charges need not even be filed. The claim is against the property, not the defendant. The owner must then prove that the property is "innocent." Enforcement abuses stemming from forfeiture laws abound.[11]

- According to estimates by Harvard University economist Jeffrey Miron, replacing marijuana prohibition with a system of taxation and regulation would save between $10 billion and $14 billion per year in reduced government spending and increased tax revenues.[12]

- Another researcher recently estimated that the revenue lost from our failure to tax the marijuana industry could be as high as $31 billion![13]

- Many patients and their doctors find marijuana a useful medicine as part of the treatment for AIDS, cancer, glaucoma, multiple sclerosis, and other ailments. Yet the federal government allows only five patients in the United States to use marijuana as a medicine, through a program now closed to new applicants. Federal laws treat all other patients currently using medical marijuana as criminals. Doctors are presently allowed to prescribe cocaine and morphine—but not marijuana.[14, 15]

- Organizations that have endorsed medical access to marijuana include the American Public Health Association, AIDS Action Council, Leukemia & Lymphoma Society, American Academy of HIV Medicine, American Nurses Association, Lymphoma Foundation of America, National Association of People With AIDS, the state medical associations of New York, California, and Rhode Island, and many others.

- A few of the many editorial boards that have endorsed medical access to marijuana include: *Boston Globe, Chicago Tribune, Miami Herald, New York Times, Orange County Register, USA Today, Baltimore's Sun*, and *The Los Angeles Times*.

- Since 1996, a majority of voters in Alaska, Arizona, California, Colorado, the District of Columbia, Maine, Montana, Nevada, Oregon, and Washington state have voted in favor of ballot initiatives to remove criminal penalties for seriously ill people who grow or possess medical marijuana.

- Fifty-five percent of Americans believe possession of small amounts of marijuana should not be treated as a criminal offense. Seventy-eight percent support "making marijuana legally available for doctors to prescribe in order to reduce pain and suffering."[16]

- "Decriminalization" involves the removal of criminal penalties for possession of marijuana for personal use. Small fines may be issued (somewhat similarly to traffic tickets), but there is typically no arrest, incarceration, or criminal record. Marijuana is presently decriminalized in 11 states—California, Colorado, Maine, Minnesota, Mississippi,

Nebraska, Nevada, New York, North Carolina, Ohio, and Oregon. In these states, cultivation and distribution remain criminal offenses.

- Decriminalization saves a tremendous amount in enforcement costs. California saves $100 million per year.[17]

- A 2001 National Research Council study sponsored by the U.S. government found "little apparent relationship between the severity of sanctions prescribed for drug use and prevalence or frequency of use, and...perceived legal risk explains very little in the variance of individual drug use." The primary evidence cited came from comparisons between states that have and have not decriminalized marijuana.[18]

- In the Netherlands, where adult possession and purchase of small amounts of marijuana are allowed under a regulated system, the rate of marijuana use by teenagers is lower than in the U.S.[3,19] Under a regulated system, licensed merchants have an incentive to check ID and avoid selling to minors. Such a system also separates marijuana from the trade in hard drugs such as cocaine and heroin.

- "Zero tolerance" policies against "drugged driving" can result in "DUI" convictions of drivers who are not intoxicated at all. Trace amounts of THC metabolites—detected by commonly used tests—can linger in blood and urine for weeks after any psychoactive effects have worn off. This is equivalent to convicting someone of "drunk driving" weeks after he or she drank one beer.[20]

- The arbitrary criminalization of tens of millions of Americans who consume marijuana results in a large-scale lack of respect for the law and the entire criminal justice system.

- Marijuana prohibition subjects users to added health hazards:
  - Adulterants, contaminants, and impurities—Marijuana purchased through criminal markets is not subject to the same quality control standards as are legal consumer goods. Illicit marijuana may be adulterated with much more damaging substances; contaminated with pesticides, herbicides, or fertilizers; and/or infected with molds, fungi, or bacteria.

- Inhalation of hot smoke—One well-established hazard of marijuana consumption is the fact that smoke from burning plant material is bad for the respiratory system. Laws that prohibit the sale or possession of paraphernalia make it difficult to obtain and use devices such as vaporizers, which can reduce these risks.[21]

- Because vigorous enforcement of the marijuana laws forces the toughest, most dangerous criminals to take over marijuana trafficking, prohibition links marijuana sales to violence, predatory crime, and terrorism.

- Prohibition invites corruption within the criminal justice system by giving officials easy, tempting opportunities to accept bribes, steal and sell marijuana, and plant evidence on innocent people.

- Because marijuana is typically used in private, trampling the Bill of Rights is a routine part of marijuana law enforcement—e.g., use of drug dogs, urine tests, phone taps, government informants, curbside garbage searches, military helicopters, and infrared heat detectors.

- Because of marijuana prohibition, America's largest cash crop is grown exclusively by unregulated criminals, often in environmentally damaging locations such as national parks and wilderness areas. Such problems are virtually unknown with legal, regulated crops such as tobacco or wine grapes.

Notes

1. Substance Abuse and Mental Health Services Administration, U.S. Department of Health and Human Services, *National Survey on Drug Use and Health*, 2005, Table G.1 and G.5.

2. Gettman, Jon, "Marijuana Production in the United States", *The Bulletin of Cannabis Reform*, No. 2, December 2006.

3. Johnston, L. D., O'Malley, P. M., Bachman, J. G. & Schulenberg, J. E. (December 11, 2007). "Overall, illicit drug use by American teens continues gradual decline in 2007." University of Michigan News Service: Ann Arbor, MI.[Online]. Table 13. Available: www.monitoringthefuture.org; accessed December 17, 2007.

4. Federal Bureau of Investigation, Uniform Crime Reports, *Crime in the United States*, annually.

5. For example, *Report of the Indian Hemp Drugs Commission*, 1894; The Panama Canal Zone Military Investigations, 1925; *The Marihuana Problem in the City of New York* (LaGuardia Committee Report), 1944; *Marihuana: A Signal of Misunderstanding* (Nixon-Shafer Report), 1972; *An Analysis of Marijuana Policy* (National Academy of Sciences), 1982; *Cannabis, Our Position for a Canadian Public Policy* (Report of the Senate Special Committee on Illegal Drugs), 2002, and others.

6. 21USC841(b)(1)(B); 1996 *Sourcebook of Federal Sentencing Guidelines*, U.S. Sentencing Commission, 1997; p. 24.

7. 21USC860(a); report from Congressional Research Service, June 22, 1995.

8. Mumola, Christopher J. and Karberg, Jennifer C., Drug Use and Dependence, State and Federal Prisoners, 2004. Bureau of Justice Statistics, U.S. Department of Justice, October 2006.

9. Struckman-Johnson, Cindy, and Struckman-Johnson, David, Sexual Coercion Rates in Seven Midwestern Prisons for Men, *The Prison Journal*, December 2000, pp. 379-90.

10. Struckman-Johnson, Cindy, and Struckman-Johnson, David, "Summary of Sexual Coercion Data," for the conference "Not Part of the Penalty: Ending Prisoner Rape," Oct. 19, 2001.

11. U.S. Rep. Henry Hyde (R–IL), *Forfeiting Our Property Rights: Is Your Property Safe From Seizure?* Cato Institute, 1995.

12. Miron, Jeffrey L., *The Budgetary Implications of Marijuana Prohibition*, June 2005.

13. Gettman, Jon, "Lost Taxes and Other Costs of Marijuana Laws," *Bulletin of Cannabis Reform*, No. 4, October 2007.

14. Grinspoon, Lester, M.D., and Bakalar B., J.D., "Marijuana as Medicine: A Plea for Reconsideration," *Journal of the American Medical Association*, June 21, 1995.

15. Marijuana Policy Project, *Medical Marijuana Briefing Paper*, 2007.

16. National Gallup poll, Nov. 1, 2005.

17. Aldrich, Michael, Ph.D., and Mikuriya, Tod, M.D., "Savings in California Marijuana Law Enforcement Costs Attributable to the Moscone Act of 1976—A Summary," *Journal of Psychoactive Drugs*, Vol. 20(1), Jan.–March 1988; pp. 75-81.

18. National Research Council, *Informing America's Policy on Illegal Drugs: What We Don't Know Keeps Hurting Us*, National Academy Press, 2001; pp. 192-93.

19. Monshouwer, Karin et al., "First cannabis use: does onset shift to younger ages? Findings from the Dutch National School Survey on Substance Use," *Addiction*. 100, 963-970. 2005.

20. Swann, P., "The Real Risk of Being Killed When Driving Whilst Impaired by Cannabis," *Australian Studies of Cannabis and Accident Risk*, 2000.

21. Mirken, Bruce, "Vaporizers for Medical Marijuana," *AIDS Treatment News*, Issue #327, September 17, 1999.

Part Five

Abuse Of Legally Available Substances

Chapter 32

Facts About The Abuse Of Prescription And Over-The-Counter (OTC) Medications

Prescription medications such as pain relievers, central nervous system (CNS) depressants (tranquilizers and sedatives), and stimulants are highly beneficial treatments for a variety of health conditions. Pain relievers enable individuals with chronic pain to lead productive lives; tranquilizers can reduce anxiety and help patients with sleep disorders; and stimulants help people with attention deficit hyperactivity disorder (ADHD) focus their attention. Most people who take prescription medications use them responsibly. But when abused—that is, taken by someone other than the patient for whom the medication was prescribed, or taken in a manner or dosage other than what was prescribed—prescription medications can produce serious adverse health effects, including addiction.

Patients, health care professionals, and pharmacists all have roles in preventing the abuse of and addiction to prescription medications. For example, patients should follow the directions for use carefully; learn what effects and side effects the medication could have; and inform their doctor/pharmacist whether they are taking other medications [including over-the-counter (OTC)

About This Chapter: Information in this chapter is from "NIDA InfoFacts: Prescription and Over-the-Counter Medications," National Institute on Drug Abuse, a component of the United States Department of Health and Human Services, July 2009.

medications or health supplements], since these could potentially interact with the prescribed medication. The patient should read all information provided by the pharmacist. Physicians and other health care providers should screen for past or current substance abuse in the patient during routine examination, including asking questions about what other medications the patient is taking and why. Providers should note any rapid increases in the amount of a medication needed or frequent requests for refills before the quantity prescribed should have been finished, as these may be indicators of abuse.

Similarly, some OTC medications, such as cough and cold medicines containing dextromethorphan (DXM), have beneficial effects when taken as recommended, but they can also be abused and lead to serious adverse health consequences.

✔ Quick Tip

When a doctor prescribes medications to treat disease, he or she knows the patient's weight, warns of side effects, and prescribes a specific dose and form of the drug. When an abuser buys the medication on the street, he or she knows none of this, and problems—sometimes lethal—can occur. Emergency room doctors see many patients who have taken the wrong dose of a prescription drug or mixed OTC medications or prescription drugs with alcohol or other drugs.

Alcohol is especially dangerous when mixed with drugs. Alcohol slows the heart and respiratory system and changes the way messages travel in the brain. Alcohol can also intensify the effects of drugs in the body. Mixed with opioid painkillers or CNS depressants, alcohol can slow breathing, causing respiratory failure and death.

Source: From "A Dangerous Mix," an article in a Heads Up compilation from Scholastic and the National Institute on Drug Abuse, 2003. Despite the older date of this document, the cautions regarding drug interactions are still pertinent.

✤ It's A Fact!!

Here are some common myths about prescription medications—and the facts:

Myth: Prescription drugs come from a doctor and a pharmacy, so they must be safe.

Fact: If they are not taken responsibly and exactly as the doctor intended, prescription medicines can land you in the emergency room—or the morgue.

Myth: It's OK for me to use a prescription from the medicine cabinet that was prescribed for someone in my family.

Fact: Just because a medication has been prescribed doesn't mean it is appropriate and safe for everyone. Many prescribed medicines are custom fit to the patient's medical history, weight, allergies, etc. Bottom line: Never take anyone else's prescriptions. It's not only unsafe—it's illegal.

Source: From "Myths About Prescription Drugs—And the Facts," an article in a Heads Up compilation from Scholastic and the National Institute on Drug Abuse, 2006.

Commonly Abused Prescription Medications

Although many prescription medications can be abused, the following three classes are most commonly abused:

- **Opioids:** Usually prescribed to treat pain.
- **CNS Depressants:** Used to treat anxiety and sleep disorders.
- **Stimulants:** Prescribed to treat ADHD and narcolepsy.

Opioids

What are opioids?

Opioids are analgesic, or pain-relieving, medications. Studies have shown that properly managed medical use of opioid analgesics is safe, can manage pain effectively, and rarely causes addiction.

Among the compounds that fall within this class are hydrocodone (e.g., Vicodin), oxycodone (e.g., OxyContin—an oral, controlled-release form of the drug), morphine, fentanyl, codeine, and related medications. Morphine and fentanyl are often used to alleviate severe pain, while codeine is used for milder pain. Other examples of opioids prescribed to relieve pain include propoxyphene (Darvon); hydromorphone (Dilaudid®); and meperidine (Demerol®), which is used less often because of its side effects. In addition to their effective pain-relieving properties, some of these medications can be used to relieve severe diarrhea (for example, Lomotil®, also known as diphenoxylate) or severe coughs (codeine).

How are opioids abused?

Opioids can be taken orally, or the pills may be crushed and the powder snorted or injected. Snorting or injecting opioids results in the rapid release of the drug into the bloodstream, exposing the person to high doses and causing many of the reported overdose reactions.

How do opioids affect the brain?

Opioids act by attaching to specific proteins called opioid receptors, which are found in the brain, spinal cord, and gastrointestinal tract. When these compounds attach to certain opioid receptors in the brain and spinal cord, they can effectively change the way a person experiences pain.

In addition, opioid medications can affect regions of the brain that mediate perceived pleasure, resulting in the initial euphoria that many opioids produce. Repeated abuse of opioids can lead to addiction.

Are there treatments for opioid addiction?

Individuals who abuse or are addicted to prescription opioid medications can be treated. Initially, they may need to undergo medically supervised detoxification to help reduce withdrawal symptoms; however, that is just the first step. Options for effectively treating addiction to prescription opioids are drawn from research on treating heroin addiction. Behavioral treatments, usually combined with medications, have also been proven effective. Currently used medications are:

- **Methadone**, a synthetic opioid that eliminates withdrawal symptoms and relieves craving, has been used successfully for more than 30 years.

- **Buprenorphine**, another synthetic opioid, is a more recently approved medication for treating addiction to heroin and other opiates.

- **Naltrexone** is a long-acting opioid receptor blocker that can be employed to help prevent relapse. It is not widely used, however, because of poor compliance. This medication can only be used for someone who has already been detoxified, since it can produce severe withdrawal symptoms in a person continuing to abuse opioids.

- **Naloxone** is a short-acting opioid receptor blocker that counteracts the effects of opioids and can be used to treat overdoses.

CNS Depressants

What are CNS depressants?

CNS depressants (e.g., tranquilizers, sedatives) are medications that slow normal brain function. In higher doses, some CNS depressants can be used as general anesthetics or pre-anesthetics.

CNS depressants can be divided into three groups:

- **Barbiturates**, such as mephobarbital (Mebaral®) and sodium pentobarbital (Nembutal®), are used as pre-anesthetics, promoting sleep.

- **Benzodiazepines**, such as diazepam (Valium), alprazolam (Xanax), and estazolam (ProSom™), can be prescribed to treat anxiety, acute stress reactions, panic attacks, convulsions, and sleep disorders. Benzodiazepines are usually prescribed only for short-term relief of sleep problems because of the development of tolerance and risk of addiction.

- **Newer sleep medications**, such as zolpidem (Ambien®), zaleplon (Sonata®), and eszopiclone (Lunesta™), are now more commonly prescribed to treat sleep disorders. These medications are nonbenzodiazepines that act at a subset of the benzodiazepine receptors and appear to have a lower risk for abuse and addiction.

How are CNS depressants abused?

CNS depressants are usually taken orally, sometimes in combination with other drugs or to counteract the effects of other licit or illicit drugs (e.g., stimulants).

How do CNS depressants affect the brain?

Most of the CNS depressants have similar actions in the brain: they enhance the actions of the neurotransmitter gamma-aminobutyric acid (GABA). Neurotransmitters are brain chemicals that facilitate communication between brain cells. GABA works by decreasing brain activity. Although different classes of CNS depressants work in unique ways, it is ultimately their common ability to increase GABA activity that produces a drowsy or calming effect.

❖ **It's A Fact!!**

CNS Depressant Effects

Short-term use of CNS depressants can produce a "sleepy" and uncoordinated feeling during the first few days; as the body becomes accustomed (tolerant) to the effects, these feelings diminish. Long-term use creates the potential for physical dependence and addiction. Possible negative effects of use include seizures following a rebound in brain activity after reducing or discontinuing use.

Source: Excerpted from "Prescription Drugs: Abuse and Addiction," a research report from the National Institute on Drug Abuse, NIH Publication Number 05-4881, August 2005.

> ## ✔ Quick Tip
> ## Prescription Drugs And The Internet
>
> Drug dealers are using the Internet to sell their drugs. Some people believe that ordering drugs on the Internet—particularly prescription pills—is a safe, legal and easy way to get high. Nothing could be further from the truth.
>
> There are millions of websites offering drugs such as Vicodin and Xanax to Internet users. Spam messages to users' e-mails advertise that these drugs are available with the click of a mouse and a credit card number. Many sites claim you don't need a doctor's prescription to buy these powerful drugs. And some ask you to fill out a bogus questionnaire to make their drug dealing look more legitimate. What you don't know can really hurt you.
>
> Here's a few things to be aware of:
>
> - Selling or buying controlled substances without a legitimate doctor's prescription is a violation of law.
>
> - Many of the websites offering controlled substances are located overseas. Usually, there are no doctors involved in these enterprises. You have no idea where the drugs are made, what's actually in them, or who's behind the drug ring selling you controlled substances. This kind of a transaction is a felony (a violation of Sections 957 and 960 of Title 21, United States Code)—very serious stuff.
>
> - You might think that these pills come from a sterile factory overseas. Think twice: often these products are stored in trucks, cars, bathrooms, or homes with unsanitary conditions.
>
> Source: From "Drug Facts," Drug Enforcement Administration, U.S. Department of Justice, 2005.

Are there treatments for addiction to CNS depressants?

In addition to medical supervision during withdrawal, counseling can help people who are overcoming addiction to CNS depressants. For example, cognitive-behavioral therapy has been used successfully to help individuals in treatment for abuse of benzodiazepines. This type of therapy focuses on modifying a patient's thinking, expectations, and behaviors while simultaneously increasing his or her skills for coping with various life stressors.

Stimulants

What are stimulants?

Stimulants (amphetamines [Adderall®, Dexedrine®] and methylphenidate [Concerta®, Ritalin®]) increase alertness, attention, and energy. They also increase blood pressure and heart rate, constrict blood vessels, increase blood glucose, and open up the pathways of the respiratory system. Historically, stimulants were prescribed to treat asthma and other respiratory problems, obesity, neurological disorders, and a variety of other ailments. As their potential for abuse and addiction became apparent, the prescribing of stimulants by physicians began to wane. Now, stimulants are prescribed for treating only a few health conditions, most notably ADHD, narcolepsy, and, in some instances, depression that has not responded to other treatments.

How are stimulants abused?

Stimulants may be taken orally, but some abusers crush the tablets, dissolve them in water, and then inject the mixture; complications can arise from this because insoluble fillers in the tablets can block small blood vessels. Stimulants have been abused for both "performance enhancement" and to get high.

How do prescription stimulants affect the brain?

Stimulants have chemical structures that are similar to key brain neurotransmitters called monoamines, including dopamine and norepinephrine. Their therapeutic effect is achieved by slow and steady increases of dopamine that are similar to the natural production of this chemical by the brain. The doses prescribed by physicians start low and increase gradually until a therapeutic effect is reached.

Are there treatments for stimulant addiction?

Treatment of addiction to prescription stimulants is based on behavioral therapies proven effective for treating cocaine or methamphetamine addiction. At this time, there are no proven medications for the treatment of stimulant addiction.

Depending on the patient's situation, the first step in treating prescription stimulant addiction may be to decrease the drug's dose slowly and attempt to treat withdrawal symptoms. This process of detoxification could then be followed with one of many behavioral therapies: contingency management, for example, improves treatment outcomes by enabling patients to earn vouchers for drug-free urine tests; the vouchers can be exchanged for items that promote healthy living. Cognitive-behavioral therapies—which teach patients skills to recognize risky situations, avoid drug use, and cope more effectively with problems—are proving beneficial. Recovery support groups may also be effective in conjunction with a behavioral therapy.

Dextromethorphan (DXM)

What is DXM?

DXM is the active ingredient found in OTC cough and cold medications. When taken in recommended doses, these medications are safe and effective.

How is DXM abused?

DXM is taken orally. In order to experience the mind-altering effects of DXM, excessive amounts of liquid or Gelcaps must be consumed. The availability and accessibility of these products make them a serious concern, particularly for youth, who tend to be their primary abusers.

What are the consequences associated with the abuse of DXM?

In very large quantities, DXM can cause effects similar to those of ketamine and PCP because these drugs affect similar sites in the brain. These effects can include impaired motor function, numbness, nausea/vomiting, and increased heart rate and blood pressure. On rare occasions, hypoxic brain damage—caused by severe respiratory depression and a lack of oxygen to the brain—has occurred due to the combination of DXM with decongestants often found in the medication.

Chapter 33

Trends In The Abuse Of Prescription And OTC Medications Among U.S. Teens

What Are The Trends In The Abuse Of Prescription Drugs And OTC Medications?

Monitoring The Future (MTF) Survey

Each year, the Monitoring the Future (MTF) survey assesses the extent of drug use among 8th, 10th, and 12th graders nationwide. Nonmedical use of any prescription drug is reported only for 12th graders, and in 2008, 15.4% reported past-year use. Prescription and OTC medications were the most commonly abused drugs by high school students after marijuana. In addition, they represent six of the top 10 illicit drugs reported by 12th graders.

Prescription Painkillers: In 2002, MTF added questions to the survey about past-year nonmedical use of Vicodin and OxyContin. For Vicodin, past-year nonmedical use has remained stable at high levels for each grade since its inclusion in the survey.

CNS Depressants: Nonmedical use of tranquilizers (benzodiazepines and others) by 10th-grade students decreased between 2001 and 2008 for all prevalence periods (lifetime, past-year, and past-month use). Use of sedatives

About This Chapter: Information in this chapter is from "NIDA InfoFacts: Prescription and Over-the-Counter Medications," a publication of the National Institute on Drug Abuse, a component of the U.S. Department of Health and Human Services, July 2009.

(barbiturates), for which data are collected only from 12th graders, has remained steady.

Stimulants: Nonmedical use of stimulants is broken up by the type of stimulant used: amphetamines, methamphetamine, or Ritalin. For all three stimulants surveyed, rates have decreased significantly among 8th, 10th, and 12th graders in 2001–2008.

Cough Medicine: In 2006, a question about the use of cough and cold medicines to get high was asked for the first time.

Table 33.1. Prescription Painkillers: Rate Of Past-Year Use In 2008

Drug Name	8th Grade	10th Grade	12th Grade
Vicodin	2.9%	6.7%	9.7%
OxyContin	2.1%	3.6%	4.7%

Table 33.2. CNS Depressants: Rate Of Past Year Use In 2008

Drug Name	8th Grade	10th Grade	12th Grade
Tranquilizers	2.4%	4.6%	6.2%
Sedatives	—	—	5.8%

Table 33.3. Stimulants: Rate Of Past Year Use In 2008

Drug Name	8th Grade	10th Grade	12th Grade
Amphetamines	4.5%	6.4%	6.8%
Methamphetamine	1.2%	1.5%	1.2%
Ritalin	1.6%	2.9%	3.4%

Table 33.4. Cough Medicine: Rate Of Past Year Use In 2008

Drug Name	8th Grade	10th Grade	12th Grade
Cough Medicine	3.6%	5.3%	5.5%

National Survey On Drug Use And Health (NSDUH)

According to the 2007 NSDUH, an estimated 6.9 million persons, or 2.8 percent of the population, aged 12 or older had used prescription psychotherapeutic medications nonmedically in the month prior to being surveyed. This includes 5.2 million using pain relievers (an increase from 4.7 million in 2005), 1.8 million using tranquilizers, 1.1 million using stimulants, and 350,000 using sedatives.

Past-month nonmedical use of prescription drugs among young adults aged 18 to 25 increased from 5.5% in 2002 to 6% in 2007. This was primarily due to an increase in pain reliever use, which was 4.1% in 2002 and 4.6% in 2007. However, nonmedical use of tranquilizers remained the same over the six-year period.

Among persons aged 12 or older who used pain relievers nonmedically in the past 12 months, 56.5% reported that they got the drug most recently used from someone they knew and that they did not pay for it. Another 18.1% reported that they obtained the drug from one doctor. Only 4.1% purchased the pain reliever from a drug dealer or other stranger, and just 0.5% reported buying the drug on the Internet. Among those who reported getting the pain reliever from a friend or relative for free, 81% reported in a follow-up question that the friend or relative had obtained the drug from one doctor only.

Other Information Sources

For more information on addiction to prescription medications, visit http://www.drugabuse.gov/drugpages/prescription.html.

Chapter 34

Commonly Abused Pain Relievers

What Are Opioids?

Opioids are commonly prescribed because of their effective analgesic, or pain-relieving, properties. Medications that fall within this class—referred to as prescription narcotics—include morphine (Kadian, Avinza), codeine, oxycodone (OxyContin, Percodan, Percocet), and related drugs.

What Are The Possible Consequences Of Opioid Use And Abuse?

Taken as directed, opioids can be used to manage pain effectively. Many studies have shown that the properly managed, short-term medical use of opioid analgesic drugs is safe and rarely causes addiction or dependence, which occurs when the body adapts to the presence of a drug, and often results in withdrawal symptoms when that drug is reduced or stopped. Withdrawal symptoms include restlessness, muscle and bone pain, insomnia, diarrhea, vomiting, cold flashes with goose bumps ("cold turkey"), and involuntary leg movements. Long-term use of opioids can lead to physical dependence and addiction. Taking a large single dose of an opioid could cause severe respiratory depression that can lead to death.

About This Chapter: This chapter consists of excerpts from "Prescription Drugs: Abuse and Addiction," a publication of the National Institute on Drug Abuse, August 2005; "Hydrocodone" and "Oxycodone," articles from the Drug Enforcement Administration, October 2009; and "Fentanyl," a publication of the National Institute on Drug Abuse, July 2009.

Is It Safe To Use Opioid Drugs With Other Medications?

Only under a physician's supervision can opioids be used safely with other drugs. Typically, they should not be used with other substances that depress the central nervous system (CNS), such as alcohol, antihistamines, barbiturates, benzodiazepines, or general anesthetics, because these combinations increase the risk of life-threatening respiratory depression.

Hydrocodone

Trade Names: Vicodin, Lortab,
Lorcet, Hycodan®, Vicoprofen®

♣ It's A Fact!!
The Science Of Opioid Addiction

Opioids are medications often prescribed because of their pain-relieving properties. Used as prescribed by a doctor, these drugs can safely change the way a person experiences pain. Opioids work by attaching to specific proteins called opioid receptors that are found in the brain, spinal cord, and gastrointestinal tract. Opioids relieve pain by triggering excess flow of certain neurotransmitters such as dopamine. Yet, when opioids are abused, serious health risks, including overdose and death, can occur.

To understand opioid abuse, it's helpful to understand some fundamentals of how brain cells interact. First, the brain is made up of billions of nerve cells, also known as neurons (Figure 34.1). A neuron contains three important parts: a central cell body that directs all activities of the neuron; dendrites, short fibers that receive messages from other neurons and relay them to the cell body; and an axon, a fiber that transmits messages from the cell body to the dendrites of other neurons or to body tissues.

The communication of a message from the axon of one nerve cell to the dendrites of another is known as neurotransmission (Figure 34.1). Communication between nerve cells occurs mainly through the release of chemical messengers into the space between an axon and a dendrite (a synapse). Molecules called neurotransmitters are released from the axon of one neuron to molecules called receptors in the dendrites of another neuron.

Introduction

Hydrocodone diversion and abuse has been escalating in recent years. In 2008, hydrocodone was the most frequently encountered opioid pharmaceutical (37,804 items) in drug evidence submitted to state and local forensic laboratories as reported by the National Forensic Laboratory Information System (NFLIS). During the first six months of 2009, 20,128 hydrocodone items were reported by NFLIS. Drug Enforcement Administration (DEA) forensic laboratories identified 473 hydrocodone items/exhibits in 2008 and 294 items/exhibits from January to June 2009. The total number of drug items seized and reported to federal, state, and local laboratories has increased by 109 percent since 2004. The DEA is currently reviewing a petition to increase the regulatory controls on hydrocodone combination products from Schedule III to Schedule II of the Controlled Substances Act (CSA).

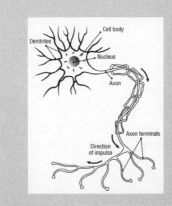

Figure 34.1. Neurons: Building Blocks Of The Brain. *The brain is made up of billions of nerve cells, also known as neurons. Neurons communicate with other neurons through a process known as neurotransmission.*

Figure 34.2. Neurotransmission: How Neurons Communicate With Each Other. *The communication of a message from one nerve cell to another is known as neurotransmission. Opioids relieve pain by triggering excess flow of certain neurotransmitters such as dopamine. When opioids are not used exactly as prescribed, serious health risks and even death can occur.*

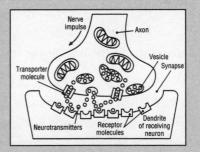

Source: This article originally appeared in a Heads Up compilation from Scholastic and the National Institute on Drug Abuse. NIH Publication No. HURN07-05SC, 2007.

Street Names

Vikes, Hydro, Norco

Licit Uses

Hydrocodone is an antitussive (cough suppressant) and analgesic agent for the treatment of moderate to moderately severe pain. Studies indicate that hydrocodone is as effective, or more effective, than codeine for cough suppression and nearly equipotent to morphine for pain relief.

Hydrocodone is the most frequently prescribed opiate in the United States with more than 136 million prescriptions for hydrocodone-containing products dispensed in 2008. There are several hundred brand name and generic hydrocodone products marketed. All are combination products and the most frequently prescribed combination is hydrocodone and acetaminophen (Vicodin®, Lortab®).

Illicit Uses

Hydrocodone is abused for its opioid effects. Widespread diversion via bogus call-in prescriptions, altered prescriptions, theft and illicit purchases from Internet sources are made easier by the present controls placed on hydrocodone products. Hydrocodone pills are the most frequently encountered dosage form in illicit traffic. Hydrocodone is generally abused orally, often in combination with alcohol.

Of particular concern is the prevalence of illicit use of hydrocodone among school-aged children. The 2008 Monitoring the Future Survey reports that 2.9%, 6.7% and 9.7% of 8th, 10th, and 12th graders, respectively, used Vicodin® nonmedically in the previous year.

The American Association of Poison Control Centers (AAPCC) reports that in 2007, there were 24,558 case mentions, 11,001 single exposures and 23 deaths associated with hydrocodone. According to the 2008 National Survey on Drug Use and Health (NSDUH), 22,838 people aged 12 and older used hydrocodone for nonmedical purposes in their lifetime.

As with most opiates, abuse of hydrocodone is associated with tolerance, dependence, and addiction. The co-formulation with acetaminophen carries an additional risk of liver toxicity when high, acute doses are consumed.

Some individuals who abuse very high doses of acetaminophen-containing hydrocodone products may be spared this liver toxicity if they have been chronically taking these products and have escalated their dose slowly over a long period of time.

User Population

Every age group has been affected by the relative ease of hydrocodone availability and the perceived safety of these products by medical prescribers. Sometimes viewed as a "white collar" addiction, hydrocodone abuse has increased among all ethnic and economic groups.

Illicit Distribution

Hydrocodone has been encountered in tablets, capsules, and liquid form in the illicit market. However, hydrocodone tablets with the co-ingredient, acetaminophen, are the most frequently encountered form. Hydrocodone is not typically found to be clandestinely produced; diverted pharmaceuticals are the primary source of the drug for abuse purposes. In 2006, the DEA has documented the diversion of millions of dosage units of hydrocodone from illicit Internet sources. Doctor shopping, altered or fraudulent prescriptions, bogus call-in prescriptions, diversion by unscrupulous physicians and pharmacists, and drug theft are also major sources of the diverted drug.

Oxycodone

Trade Names: Tylox®, Percodan, OxyContin

Introduction

Oxycodone is a Schedule II narcotic analgesic and is widely used in clinical medicine. It is marketed either alone as controlled release (OxyContin) and immediate release formulations (OxyIR®, OxyFAST®), or in combination with other nonnarcotic analgesics such as aspirin (Percodan®) or acetaminophen (Percocet). The introduction in 1996 of OxyContin, commonly known on the street as OC, OX, Oxy, Oxycotton, Hillbilly heroin, and kicker, led to a marked escalation of its abuse as reported by drug abuse treatment centers, law enforcement personnel, and health care professionals. Although the diversion and abuse of OxyContin® appeared initially in the eastern U.S., it has now spread to the western U.S. including Alaska and Hawaii. Oxycodone-related adverse health effects increased markedly in recent years. In 2004, Food and Drug Administration (FDA) approved generic forms of controlled release oxycodone products for marketing.

Street Names

Kicker, OC, Oxy, OX, Blue, Oxycotton, Hillybilly Heroin

Licit Uses

Products containing oxycodone in combination with aspirin or acetaminophen are used for the relief of moderate to moderately severe pain. Oxycodone controlled-release tablets are prescribed for the management of moderate to

---

♣ It's A Fact!!
Dangerous Liaisons:
Mixing Hydrocodone With Alcohol And Other Drugs

Hydrocodone, the active ingredient in pain relievers such as Vicodin, Anexsia®, Lorcet, and Norco®, is one of the most commonly abused prescription drugs among teens and is especially dangerous when mixed with other substances. Hydrocodone depresses the central nervous system and slows breathing. Mixing hydrocodone with other substances that also depress the central nervous system—such as alcohol, antihistamines, barbiturates, or benzodiazepines—could lead to life threatening respiratory problems.

Hydrocodone may make you drowsy, less alert, or unable to function well physically, so it's necessary to avoid using other medicines that also make you sleepy (such as cold medicines, other pain medications, muscle relaxants, and medicines for seizures, depression, or anxiety). The interaction between two medications could result in extreme drowsiness or coma, making it particularly dangerous to drive a car, operate machinery, or perform other activities.

Mixing hydrocodone with alcohol is extremely dangerous and can cause impairment of judgment, thinking, and psychomotor skills. Death has been reported due to overdose. Alcohol can be found in many over-the-counter medicines, such as cough syrup, so it is important to read all medicine labels to avoid the risk of taking medications that contain alcohol while using hydrocodone.

severe pain when a continuous, around-the-clock analgesic is needed for an extended period of time. Oxycodone is a widely prescribed in the U.S. In 2008, 50.1 million oxycodone prescriptions were dispensed (IMS Health™). The aggregate production quota for oxycodone in 2008 was 70,000 kilograms.

Illicit Uses

Oxycodone abuse has been a continuing problem in the U.S. since the early 1960s. Oxycodone is abused for its euphoric effects. It is equipotent to morphine in relieving abstinence symptoms from chronic opiate (heroin, morphine) administration.

For this reason, it is often used to alleviate or prevent the onset of opiate withdrawal by street users of heroin and methadone. The large amount of

Hydrocodone is usually formulated with acetaminophen, a drug commonly found in over the counter pain relievers like Tylenol. Acetaminophen can be toxic to the liver. Extended use of pain relievers such as Vicodin, or mixing them with over-the-counter medicines that also contain acetaminophen, may lead to an upset stomach, internal bleeding and ulcers, and serious long-term damage.

Get emergency medical help if you observe any of these signs of an allergic reaction: hives; difficulty breathing; swelling of the face, lips, tongue, or throat.

Call a doctor at once if you experience any of these other serious side effects:

- Slow heartbeat
- Seizures (convulsions)
- Cold, clammy skin
- Confusion
- Severe weakness or dizziness
- Feeling light-headed or faint

Source: This article originally appeared in a Heads Up compilation from Scholastic and the National Institute on Drug Abuse, August 2008.

oxycodone (10 to 80 mg) present in controlled release formulations (Oxy-Contin) renders these products highly attractive to opioid abusers and doctor-shoppers. They are abused either as intact tablets or by crushing or chewing the tablet and then swallowing, snorting, or injecting. Products containing oxycodone in combination with acetaminophen or aspirin are abused orally. Acetaminophen present in the combination products poses an additional risk of liver toxicity upon chronic abuse.

User Population

Every age group has been affected by the relative prevalence of oxycodone availability and the perceived safety of oxycodone products by professionals. Sometimes seen as a "white-collar" addiction, oxycodone abuse has increased among all ethnic and economic groups.

Illicit Distribution

Oxycodone-containing products are in tablet, capsule, and liquid forms. A variety of colors and markings are available. The main sources of oxycodone on the street are forged prescriptions, professional diversion through unscrupulous pharmacists, doctors, and dentists, "doctor-shopping," armed robberies, and night break-ins of pharmacies and nursing homes. The diversion and abuse of OxyContin has become a major public health problem in recent years. In 2008, 13.8 million people aged 12 or older used oxycodone (4.8 million used OxyContin) for nonmedical use at least once during their lifetime (National Survey on Drug Use and Health, 2008). The American Poison Control Centers reported 15,069 case mentions and 7,528 single exposures, involving 13 deaths, related to oxycodone in 2007.

Fentanyl

Fentanyl is a powerful synthetic opiate analgesic similar to but more potent than morphine. It is typically used to treat patients with severe pain, or to manage pain after surgery. It is also sometimes used to treat people with chronic pain who are physically tolerant to opiates. It is a Schedule II prescription drug.

In its prescription form, fentanyl is known as Actiq®, Duragesic, and Subli-maze®. Street names for the drug include Apache, China girl, China white, dance fever, friend, goodfella, jackpot, murder 8, TNT, as well as Tango and Cash.

Like heroin, morphine, and other opioid drugs, fentanyl works by binding to the body's opiate receptors, highly concentrated in areas of the brain that control pain and emotions. When opiate drugs bind to these receptors, they can drive up dopamine levels in the brain's reward areas, producing a state of euphoria and relaxation. Medications called opiate receptor antagonists act by blocking the effects of opiate drugs. Naloxone is one such antagonist. Overdoses of fentanyl should be treated immediately with an opiate antagonist.

When prescribed by a physician, fentanyl is often administered via injection, transdermal patch, or in lozenge form. However, the type of fentanyl associated with recent overdoses was produced in clandestine laboratories and mixed with (or substituted for) heroin in a powder form.

Mixing fentanyl with street-sold heroin or cocaine markedly amplifies the drugs' potency and potential dangers. Effects include: euphoria, drowsiness/respiratory depression and arrest, nausea, confusion, constipation, sedation, unconsciousness, coma, tolerance, and addiction.

Chapter 35

Commonly Abused Sedatives And Tranquilizers

CNS Depressants

What are CNS depressants?

Central nervous system (CNS) depressants, sometimes referred to as sedatives and tranquilizers, are substances that can slow normal brain function. Because of this property, some CNS depressants are useful in the treatment of anxiety and sleep disorders. Among the medications that are commonly prescribed for these purposes are the following:

- **Barbiturates**, such as mephobarbital (Mebaral) and pentobarbital sodium (Nembutal), are used to treat anxiety, tension, and sleep disorders.

- **Benzodiazepines**, such as diazepam (Valium), chlordiazepoxide HCl (Librium), and alprazolam (Xanax), are prescribed to treat anxiety, acute stress reactions, and panic attacks. The more sedating benzodiazepines, such as triazolam (Halcion) and estazolam (ProSom) are prescribed for short-term treatment of sleep disorders. Usually, benzodiazepines are not prescribed for long-term use.

About This Chapter: This chapter consists of excerpts from "Prescription Drugs: Abuse and Addiction," a publication of the National Institute on Drug Abuse, August 2005; and "Barbiturates" and "Benzodiazepines," undated articles from the Drug Enforcement Administration (www.justice.gov/dea), accessed August 29, 2010.

How do CNS depressants affect the brain and body?

There are numerous CNS depressants; most act on the brain by affecting the neurotransmitter gamma-aminobutyric acid (GABA). Neurotransmitters are brain chemicals that facilitate communication between brain cells. GABA works by decreasing brain activity. Although the different classes of CNS depressants work in unique ways, it is through their ability to increase GABA activity that they produce a drowsy or calming effect that is beneficial to those suffering from anxiety or sleep disorders.

What are the possible consequences of CNS depressant use and abuse?

Despite their many beneficial effects, barbiturates and benzodiazepines have the potential for abuse and should be used only as prescribed. During the first few days of taking a prescribed CNS depressant, a person usually feels sleepy and uncoordinated, but as the body becomes accustomed to the effects of the drug, these feelings begin to disappear. If one uses these drugs long term, the body will develop tolerance for the drugs, and larger doses will be needed to achieve the same initial effects. Continued use can lead to physical dependence and—when use is reduced or stopped—withdrawal. Because all CNS depressants work by slowing the brain's activity, when an individual stops taking them, the brain's activity can rebound and race out of control, potentially leading to seizures and other harmful consequences. Although withdrawal from benzodiazepines can be problematic, it is rarely life threatening, whereas withdrawal from prolonged use of other CNS depressants can have life-threatening complications. Therefore, someone who is thinking about discontinuing CNS depressant therapy or who is suffering withdrawal from a CNS depressant should speak with a physician or seek medical treatment.

Is it safe to use CNS depressants with other medications?

CNS depressants should be used in combination with other medications only under a physician's close supervision. Typically, they should not be combined with any other medication or substance that causes CNS depression, including prescription pain medicines, some OTC cold and allergy medications, and alcohol. Using CNS depressants with these other substances—particularly alcohol—can slow both the heart and respiration and may lead to death.

Barbiturates

Barbiturates were first introduced for medical use in the early 1900s. More than 2,500 barbiturates have been synthesized, and at the height of their popularity, about 50 were marketed for human use. Today, about a dozen are in medical use. Barbiturates produce a wide spectrum of central nervous system depression, from mild sedation to coma, and have been used as sedatives, hypnotics, anesthetics, and anticonvulsants. The primary differences among many of these products are how fast they produce an effect and how long those effects last. Barbiturates are classified as ultra short, short, intermediate, and long-acting.

The ultra short-acting barbiturates produce anesthesia within about one minute after intravenous administration. Those in current medical use are the Schedule IV drug methohexital (Brevital®), and the Schedule III drugs thiamylal (Surital®) and thiopental (Pentothal®). Barbiturate abusers prefer the Schedule II short-acting and intermediate-acting barbiturates that include amobarbital (Amytal®), pentobarbital (Nembutal), secobarbital (Seconal®), and Tuinal® (an amobarbital/secobarbital combination product). Other short and intermediate-acting barbiturates are in Schedule III and include butalbital (Fiorinal®), butabarbital (Butisol®), talbutal (Lotusate®), and aprobarbital (Alurate®). After oral administration, the onset of action is from 15 to 40 minutes, and the effects last up to six hours. These drugs are primarily used for insomnia and preoperative sedation. Veterinarians use pentobarbital for anesthesia and euthanasia.

Long-acting barbiturates include phenobarbital (Luminal®) and mephobarbital (Mebaral), both of which are in Schedule IV. Effects of these drugs are realized in about one hour and last for about 12 hours, and are used primarily for daytime sedation and the treatment of seizure disorders.

Benzodiazepines

The benzodiazepine family of depressants is used therapeutically to produce sedation, induce sleep, relieve anxiety and muscle spasms, and to prevent seizures. In general, benzodiazepines act as hypnotics in high doses, anxiolytics in moderate doses, and sedatives in low doses. Of the drugs marketed in the

United States that affect central nervous system function, benzodiazepines are among the most widely prescribed medications. Fifteen members of this group are presently marketed in the United States, and about 20 additional benzodiazepines are marketed in other countries. Benzodiazepines are controlled in Schedule IV of the Controlled Substances Act (CSA).

Short-acting benzodiazepines are generally used for patients with sleep-onset insomnia (difficulty falling asleep) without daytime anxiety. Shorter-acting benzodiazepines used to manage insomnia include estazolam (ProSom), flurazepam (Dalmane®), temazepam (Restoril®), and triazolam (Halcion). Midazolam (Versed®), a short-acting benzodiazepine, is utilized for sedation, anxiety, and amnesia in critical care settings and prior to anesthesia. It is available in the United States as an injectable preparation and as a syrup (primarily for pediatric patients).

Benzodiazepines with a longer duration of action are used to treat insomnia in patients with daytime anxiety. These benzodiazepines include alprazolam (Xanax), chlordiazepoxide (Librium), clorazepate (Tranxene®), diazepam (Valium), halazepam (Paxipam®), lorazepam (Ativan), oxazepam (Serax®), prazepam (Centrax®), and quazepam (Doral®). Clonazepam (Klonopin), diazepam, and clorazepate are also used as anticonvulsants.

Benzodiazepines are classified in the CSA as depressants. Repeated use of large doses or, in some cases, daily use of therapeutic doses of benzodiazepines is associated with amnesia, hostility, irritability, and vivid or disturbing dreams,

---

✤ It's A Fact!!
Newly Marked Drugs

Zolpidem (Ambien®) and zaleplon (Sonata®) are two relatively new, benzodiazepine-like CNS depressants that have been approved for the short-term treatment of insomnia. Both of these drugs share many of the same properties as the benzodiazepines and are in Schedule IV of the CSA.

Source: Drug Enforcement Administration (www.justice.gov/dea), undated; accessed August 29, 2010.

as well as tolerance and physical dependence. The withdrawal syndrome is similar to that of alcohol and may require hospitalization. Abrupt cessation of benzodiazepines is not recommended and tapering down the dose eliminates many of the unpleasant symptoms.

Given the millions of prescriptions written for benzodiazepines, relatively few individuals increase their dose on their own initiative or engage in drug-seeking behavior. Those individuals who do abuse benzodiazepines often maintain their drug supply by getting prescriptions from several doctors, forging prescriptions, or buying diverted pharmaceutical products on the illicit market. Abuse is frequently associated with adolescents and young adults who take benzodiazepines to obtain a "high." This intoxicated state results in reduced inhibition and impaired judgment. Concurrent use of alcohol or another depressant with benzodiazepines can be life threatening. Abuse of benzodiazepines is particularly high among heroin and cocaine abusers. A large percentage of people entering treatment for narcotic or cocaine addiction also report abusing benzodiazepines. Alprazolam and diazepam are the two most frequently encountered benzodiazepines on the illicit market.

Flunitrazepam (Rohypnol®) is a benzodiazepine that is not manufactured or legally marketed in the United States, but is smuggled in by traffickers. In the mid-1990s, flunitrazepam was extensively trafficked in Florida and Texas. Known as "rophies," "roofies," and "roach," flunitrazepam gained popularity among younger individuals as a "party" drug. It has also been used as a "date rape" drug. In this context, flunitrazepam is placed in the alcoholic drink of an unsuspecting victim to incapacitate him or her and prevent resistance from sexual assault. The victim is frequently unaware of what has happened to him or her and often does not report the incident to authorities. A number of actions by the manufacturer of this drug and by government agencies have resulted in reducing the availability and abuse of flunitrazepam in the United States.

Chapter 36

Commonly Abused Prescription Stimulants

Stimulants

What are stimulants?

As the name suggests, stimulants increase alertness, attention, and energy, as well as elevate blood pressure and increase heart rate and respiration. Stimulants historically were used to treat asthma and other respiratory problems, obesity, neurological disorders, and a variety of other ailments. But as their potential for abuse and addiction became apparent, the medical use of stimulants began to wane. Now, stimulants are prescribed for the treatment of only a few health conditions, including narcolepsy, attention deficit hyperactivity disorder (ADHD), and depression that has not responded to other treatments.

How do stimulants affect the brain and body?

Stimulants, such as dextroamphetamine (Dexedrine and Adderall) and methylphenidate (Ritalin and Concerta), have chemical structures similar to a family of key brain neurotransmitters called monoamines, which include norepinephrine and dopamine. Stimulants enhance the effects of these

About This Chapter: This chapter consists of excerpts from two publications of the National Institute on Drug Abuse: "Prescription Drugs: Abuse and Addiction," August 2005, and "InfoFacts: Stimulant ADHD Medications—Methylphenidate and Amphetamines," June 2009.

chemicals in the brain. Stimulants also increase blood pressure and heart rate, constrict blood vessels, increase blood glucose, and open up the pathways of the respiratory system. The increase in dopamine is associated with a sense of euphoria that can accompany the use of these drugs.

What are the possible consequences of stimulant use and abuse?

As with other drugs of abuse, it is possible for individuals to become dependent upon or addicted to many stimulants. Withdrawal symptoms associated with discontinuing stimulant use include fatigue, depression, and disturbance of sleep patterns. Repeated use of some stimulants over a short period can lead to feelings of hostility or paranoia. Further, taking high doses of a stimulant may result in dangerously high body temperature and an irregular heartbeat. There is also the potential for cardiovascular failure or lethal seizures.

Is it safe to use stimulants with other medications?

Stimulants should be used in combination with other medications only under a physician's supervision. Patients also should be aware of the dangers associated with mixing stimulants and OTC cold medicines that contain decongestants; combining these substances may cause blood pressure to become dangerously high or lead to irregular heart rhythms.

Stimulant ADHD Medications: Methylphenidate And Amphetamines

Stimulant medications (e.g., methylphenidate and amphetamines) are often prescribed to treat individuals diagnosed with ADHD. ADHD is characterized by a persistent pattern of inattention and/or hyperactivity and impulsivity that is more frequently displayed and more severe than is typically observed in individuals at a comparable level of development. This pattern of behavior usually becomes evident in the preschool or early elementary years, and the median age of onset of ADHD symptoms is seven years. For many individuals, ADHD symptoms improve during adolescence or as age increases, but the disorder can persist into adulthood. In the United States, ADHD is diagnosed in an estimated 8 percent of children ages 4–17 and in 2.9–4.4 percent of adults.

How do prescription stimulants affect the brain?

All stimulants work by increasing dopamine levels in the brain—dopamine is a brain chemical (or neurotransmitter) associated with pleasure, movement, and attention. The therapeutic effect of stimulants is achieved by slow and steady increases of dopamine, which are similar to the natural production of the chemical by the brain. The doses prescribed by physicians start low and increase gradually until a therapeutic effect is reached. However, when taken in doses and routes other than those prescribed, stimulants can increase brain dopamine in a rapid and highly amplified manner—as do most other drugs of abuse—disrupting normal communication between brain cells, producing euphoria, and increasing the risk of addiction.

What is the role of stimulants in the treatment of ADHD?

Treatment of ADHD with stimulants, often in conjunction with psycho-therapy, helps to improve the symptoms of ADHD, as well as the self-esteem, cognition, and social and family interactions of the patient. The most commonly prescribed medications include amphetamines (e.g., Adderall, a mix of amphetamine salts) and methylphenidate (e.g., Ritalin and Concerta—a formulation that releases medication in the body over a period of time). These medications have a paradoxically calming and "focusing" effect on individuals with ADHD. Researchers speculate that because methylphenidate amplifies the release of dopamine, it can improve attention and focus in individuals who have dopamine signals that are weak.

One of the most controversial issues in child psychiatry is whether the use of stimulant medications to treat ADHD increases the risk of substance abuse in adulthood. Research thus far suggests that individuals with ADHD do not become addicted to their stimulant medications when taken in the form and dosage prescribed by their doctors. Furthermore, several studies report that stimulant therapy in childhood does not increase the risk for subsequent drug and alcohol abuse disorders later in life. More research is needed, however, particularly in adolescents treated with stimulant medications.

Why and how are prescription stimulants abused?

Stimulants have been abused for both "performance enhancement" and recreational purposes (i.e., to get high). For the former, they suppress appetite (to facilitate weight loss), increase wakefulness, and increase focus and attention. The euphoric effects of stimulants usually occur when they are crushed and then snorted or injected. Some abusers dissolve the tablets in water and inject the mixture. Complications from this method of use can arise because insoluble fillers in the tablets can block small blood vessels.

What adverse effects does prescription stimulant abuse have on health?

Stimulants can increase blood pressure, heart rate, and body temperature and decrease sleep and appetite, which can lead to malnutrition and its consequences. Repeated use of stimulants can lead to feelings of hostility and paranoia. At high doses, they can lead to serious cardiovascular complications, including stroke.

✔ Quick Tip

Helpful When Needed

People with ADHD have lots of trouble concentrating. For them, the central nervous system (CNS) stimulant drugs Ritalin and Adderall have a calming effect, helping them focus. "When they are taken in the dosage and form prescribed by a physician, these are safe drugs that help a lot of kids," says Dr. Cindy Miner, deputy director of the Office of Science Policy and Communications at NIDA.

Research shows that people with ADHD don't get addicted when they take these drugs as prescribed. "The theory is that those kids have a brain chemistry imbalance that is stabilized by the medication," says Dr. Miner. But some teens steal or buy the drugs on the street. "If you're buying those drugs from other kids, you're playing with potent drugs. You're really putting yourself at risk," warns Dr. Miner. Effects of high doses can include paranoia, convulsions, muscle twitching, and addiction. Withdrawal symptoms include depression.

Source: From a Heads Up compilation from Scholastic and the National Institute on Drug Abuse, 2003. Despite the older date of this article, the cautions about risks associated with CNS stimulants is still pertinent.

Addiction to stimulants is also a very real consideration for anyone taking them without medical supervision. This most likely occurs because stimulants, when taken in doses and routes other than those prescribed by a doctor, can induce a rapid rise in dopamine in the brain. Furthermore, if stimulants are used chronically, withdrawal symptoms—including fatigue, depression, and disturbed sleep patterns—can emerge when the drugs are discontinued.

How widespread is prescription stimulant abuse?

Monitoring The Future Survey*: Each year, the Monitoring the Future (MTF) survey assesses the extent of drug use among 8th, 10th, and 12th graders nationwide. For amphetamines and methylphenidate, the survey measures only past-year use, which refers to use at least once during the year preceding an individual's response to the survey. Use outside of medical supervision was first measured in the study in 2001; nonmedical use of stimulants has been falling since then, with total declines between 25% and 42% at each grade level surveyed. MTF data for 2008 indicate past-year nonmedical use of Ritalin by 1.6% of 8th graders, 2.9% of 10th graders, and 3.4% of 12th graders.

Since its peak in the mid-1990s, annual prevalence of amphetamine use fell by one-half among 8th graders to 4.5% and by nearly one-half among 10th graders to 6.4% in 2008. Amphetamine use peaked somewhat later among 12th graders and has fallen by more than one-third to 6.8% by 2008. Although general nonmedical use of prescription stimulants is declining in this group, when asked, "What amphetamines have you taken during the last year without a doctor's orders?" 2.8% of all 12th graders surveyed in 2007 reported they had used Adderall. Amphetamines rank third among 12th graders for past-year illicit drug use.

*These data are from the 2008 Monitoring the Future survey, funded by the National Institute on Drug Abuse, National Institutes of Health, U.S. Department of Health and Human Services, and conducted annually by the University of Michigan's Institute for Social Research. The survey has tracked 12th graders' illicit drug use and related attitudes since 1975; in 1991, 8th and 10th graders were added to the study. The latest data are online at www .monitoringthefuture.org.

Chapter 37

What You Should Know About The Abuse Of Cold And Cough Medicines

The cough suppressant dextromethorphan (DXM) is found in more than 140 cough and cold medications that are available without a prescription (i.e., "over-the-counter," or OTC) in the United States and is generally safe when taken at the recommended doses. When taken in large amounts, however, DXM can produce hallucinations or dissociative, "out-of-body" experiences similar to those caused by the hallucinogens phencyclidine (PCP) and ketamine and can cause other adverse health effects. Abuse of DXM among American youths aged 12 to 17 and young adults aged 18 to 25 has become a matter of concern in a number of states and metropolitan areas due to increased poison control calls involving DXM.

The 2006 National Survey on Drug Use and Health (NSDUH) asks persons aged 12 or older questions related to their use of OTC cough or cold medications during their lifetime ("lifetime" or "ever used") and the past 12 months ("past year use") for the purpose of getting high ("misuse").

Persons who reported that they used OTC cough or cold medications to get high in the past year were asked to specify the names of up to five OTC medications that they had used for this purpose.

About This Chapter: Information in this chapter is from "The NSDUH Report: Misuse of Over-the-Counter Cough and Cold Medications among Persons Aged 12 to 25," Substance Abuse and Mental Health Services Administration, Office of Applied Studies, January 10, 2008.

This report examines the prevalence and patterns of the use of OTC cough and cold medications to get high among persons aged 12 to 25, the age group with the highest rates of such use. This report also examines the specific OTC cough and cold medications that were most commonly misused in the past year and the use of selected illicit drugs among persons who misused OTC cough and cold medications in their lifetime. Findings presented in this report are based on 2006 NSDUH data.

Lifetime Misuse Of OTC Cough And Cold Medications

About 3.1 million persons aged 12 to 25 (5.3%) had misused OTC cough and cold medications at least once in their lifetime (Table 37.1). Young adults aged 18 to 25 were more likely than youths aged 12 to 17 to have misused OTC cough and cold medications in their lifetime (6.5% vs. 3.7%).

What is DXM?

❖ It's A Fact!!

DXM, also known as dextromethorphan, is a safe and effective active ingredient found in many nonprescription cough syrups, tablets, and gel caps. When used accordingly to medicine label directions, the ingredient dextromethorphan produces few side effects and has a long history of safety. When abused in large amounts, it can produce a "high" feeling as well as a number of dangerous side effects.

What are slang terms for DXM?

Robo, Skittles, Triple C, Tussin, Dex

What does it look like?

Cough syrup and cough and cold tablets or gel caps that are available without a prescription. Also, dextromethorphan can be purchased in a powder form, often over the internet.

What is cough medicine abuse?

Cough medicine abuse is taking extremely large doses of cough medicine to get high. The "high" is caused by taking a large amount of dextromethorphan, which is often abbreviated DXM, a common active ingredient found in many cough medications. This sort of abuse—whether it's called cough medicine abuse, or dextromethorphan, or DXM abuse—can be dangerous.

Among persons aged 12 to 25 who had ever misused OTC cough and cold medications, 81.9 percent also were lifetime users of marijuana (Figure 37.1). Slightly less than half were lifetime users of the hallucinogens LSD, PCP, or Ecstasy (44.2%) or were lifetime users of inhalants (49.3%). Youths and young adults who had ever misused OTC cough and cold medications had comparable lifetime rates of inhalant use. However, young adults who had ever misused OTC cough and cold medications were more likely than the corresponding youths to have ever used marijuana or the hallucinogens LSD, PCP, or Ecstasy. Males aged 12 to 25 who had ever misused OTC cough and cold medications were more likely than their female counterparts to have used LSD, PCP, or Ecstasy. Males and females who had ever misused these medications had similar rates of lifetime use of marijuana and inhalants.

What are the short-term effects of DXM abuse?

The effects of DXM abuse vary with the amount taken. Common effects can include confusion, dizziness, double or blurred vision, slurred speech, impaired physical coordination, abdominal pain, nausea and vomiting, rapid heartbeat, drowsiness, numbness of fingers and toes, and disorientation. DXM abusers describe different "plateaus" ranging from mild distortions of color and sound to visual hallucinations and "out-of-body," feelings of detachment from the environment and self, sensations, and loss of motor control.

What are the long-term effects of DXM abuse?

Cough medications including DXM can contain other ingredients, such as acetaminophen, which can be very dangerous when taken in large quantities. At high enough doses, DXM alone can suppress the central nervous system. If this happens your brain can stop telling your lungs to breathe. Some drugs that people take to get the DXM high also include other ingredients which can interact in your body and have dangerous consequences. And remember, extremely high doses of DXM can induce a hallucinatory state which can lead to "accidents" that result in death.

Source: "DXM FAQ," © 2010 Partnership for a Drug-Free America (www.drug free.org). Reprinted with permission.

Table 37.1. Misuse Of Over-The-Counter (OTC) Cough Or Cold Medications In The Lifetime And The Past Year Among Persons Aged 12 To 25, By Demographic Characteristics: 2006

Demographic Characteristic	Lifetime		Past Year	
	Percent	Standard Error	Percent	Standard Error
Total Aged 12 to 25	5.3	0.15	1.7	0.08
Age Group				
12 to 17	3.7	0.16	1.9	0.12
18 to 25	6.5	0.24	1.6	0.12
Gender				
Male	5.6	0.22	1.7	0.12
Female	4.9	0.20	1.7	0.12
Age Group, by Gender				
12 to 17, Male	3.0	0.20	1.5	0.14
12 to 17, Female	4.3	0.24	2.3	0.18
18 to 25, Male	7.7	0.35	1.8	0.17
18 to 25, Female	5.4	0.29	1.3	0.16
*Race/Ethnicity**				
White	6.2	0.20	2.1	0.12
Black or African American	2.5	0.29	0.6	0.13
Hispanic or Latino	4.7	0.36	1.4	0.18

*Race/ethnicity categories are determined by combining the responses from two separate questions. For this report, respondents identifying themselves as Hispanic were assigned to the Hispanic group regardless of their racial identification. Respondents identifying themselves as non-Hispanic were grouped according to their racial identification. Thus, "white" refers to those identifying themselves as non-Hispanic and white. Estimates are presented only for white, black, and Hispanic because data for some other racial/ethnic groups are suppressed due to low precision.

Past Year Misuse Of OTC Cough And Cold Medications

Nearly 1 million persons aged 12 to 25 (1.7%) misused OTC cough and cold medications in the past year. Unlike the pattern for lifetime misuse, youths aged 12 to 17 were more likely than young adults aged 18 to 25 to have misused OTC cough and cold medications in the past year (1.9% vs. 1.6%). Males and females aged 12 to 25 had the same rate of past year misuse of these medications (1.7%). When examined separately for adolescents and young adults, however, the patterns varied by gender. Among youths aged 12 to 17, females were more likely than males to have misused OTC cough and cold medications in the past year (2.3% vs. 1.5%). Among young adults aged 18 to 25, however, males were more likely than females to have misused these medications (1.8% vs. 1.3%).

The rate of past year misuse of OTC cough and cold medications among whites aged 12 to 25 (2.1%) was about three times higher than the rate among blacks (0.6%) and was also higher than the rate among Hispanics (1.4%). In this age group, Hispanics also were more likely than blacks to be past year misusers. Rates of past year misuse among persons aged 12 to 25 did not differ significantly by county type or region.

Among persons aged 12 to 25 who had misused an OTC cough and cold medication in the past year, 30.5% misused a NyQuil® product, 18.1% misused a Coricidin® product, and 17.8% misused a Robitussin® product (Figure 37.2). More than 40 percent of the misusers in this age group misused any of a wide variety of other OTC medications.

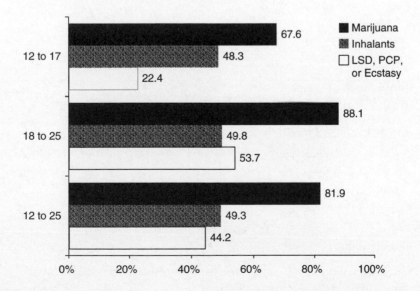

Figure 37.1. *Percentages Of Lifetime Illicit Drug Use Among Persons Aged 12 To 25 Who Had Ever Misused Over-The-Counter (OTC) Cough And Cold Medications, By Age Group: 2006*

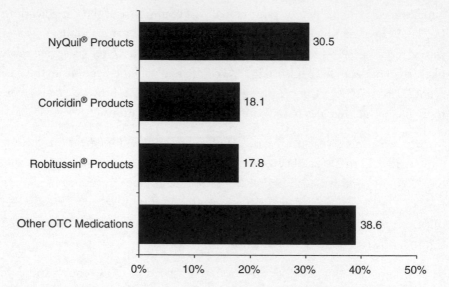

Figure 37.2. *Percentages Of Use Of Specific Over-The-Counter (OTC) Cough Or Cold Medications In The Past Year Among Past Year OTC Cough And Cold Medication Misusers Aged 12 To 25: 2006***

** Standard errors (SE) are as follows:

NyQuil product (SE = 2.30), Coricidin product (SE = 1.97), Robitussin product (SE = 1.83), and Other OTC Medication (SE = 2.23)

✤ It's A Fact!!

- In 2006, about 3.1 million persons aged 12 to 25 (5.3%) had ever used an OTC cough and cold medication to get high (i.e., "misused" the drug), and nearly 1 million (1.7%) had done so in the past year.

- Among youths aged 12 to 17, females were more likely than males to have misused OTC cough and cold medications in the past year, but among young adults aged 18 to 25, males were more likely than females to have misused these medications.

- Among persons aged 12 to 25 who had misused an OTC cough and cold medication in the past year, 30.5% misused a NyQuil® product, 18.1% misused a Coricidin® product, and 17.8% misused a Robitussin® product.

Chapter 38

Anabolic Steroids: Risks And Health Consequences

What are anabolic steroids?

Ever wondered how those bulky weight lifters got so big? While some may have gotten their muscles through a strict regimen of weightlifting and diet, others may have gotten that way through the illegal use of anabolic-androgenic steroids. "Anabolic" refers to a steroid's ability to help build muscle and "androgenic" refers to their role in promoting the development of male sexual characteristics. Other types of steroids, like cortisol, estrogen, and progesterone, do not build muscle, are not anabolic, and therefore do not have the same harmful effects.

Anabolic-androgenic steroids are usually synthetic substances similar to the male sex hormone testosterone. They do have legitimate medical uses. Sometimes doctors prescribe them to help people with certain kinds of anemia and men who don't produce enough testosterone on their own. But doctors never prescribe anabolic steroids to young, healthy people to help them build muscles. Without a prescription from a doctor, anabolic steroids are illegal.

About This Chapter: Information in this chapter is from "Anabolic Steroids," NIDA for Teens, National Institute on Drug Abuse, a component of the U.S. Department of Health and Human Services, 2009.

There are many different anabolic-androgenic steroids. Here's a list of some of the most common ones taken today: Andro, Oxandrin, Dianabol, Winstrol, Deca-Durabolin, and Equipoise.

What are the common street names?

Slang words for steroids are hard to find. Most people just say steroids. On the street, steroids may be called "roids" or "juice." The scientific name for this class of drugs is anabolic-androgenic steroids. But even scientists shorten it to anabolic steroids.

How are they used?

Some steroid users pop pills. Others use hypodermic needles to inject steroids directly into muscles. When users take drugs without regard for their legality or their adverse health effects they are called "abusers." Steroid abusers have been known to take doses 10 to 100 times higher than the amount prescribed by a doctor for medical reasons.

What is the scope of steroid abuse?

Most teens are smart and stay away from steroids. As part of a 2009 National Institute on Drug Abuse (NIDA)-funded study, teens were asked if they ever tried steroids—even once. Only 1.3% of 8th and 10th graders and 2.2% of 12th graders ever tried steroids. Abuse is also well known to occur in a number of professional sports, including fields such as bodybuilding and basebqall.

What are the effects?

A major health consequence from abusing anabolic steroids can include prematurely stunted growth through early skeletal maturation and accelerated puberty changes. This means that teens risk remaining short for the remainder of their lives if they take anabolic steroids before they stop growing. Other effects include jaundice (yellowish coloring of skin, tissues, and body fluids), fluid retention, high blood pressure, increases in LDL (bad cholesterol), decreases in HDL (good cholesterol), severe acne, trembling, and in very rare cases liver and kidney tumors. In addition, there are some gender-specific side effects:

- **For Guys:** Shrinking of the testicles, reduced sperm count, infertility, baldness, development of breasts, increased risk for prostate cancer.

- **For Girls:** Growth of facial hair, male-pattern baldness, changes in or cessation of the menstrual cycle, enlargement of the clitoris, and a permanently deepened voice.

Steroid abuse can also have an effect on behavior. Many users report feeling good about themselves while on anabolic steroids, but researchers report that extreme mood swings also can occur, including manic symptoms leading to violence. This is because anabolic steroids act in a part of the brain called the limbic system, which influences mood and is also involved in learning and memory.

Steroids can also lead to other changes in mood, such as feelings of depression or irritability. Depression, which can be life-threatening, often is seen when the drugs are stopped and may contribute to the continued use of anabolic steroids. Researchers also report that users may suffer from paranoia, jealousy, extreme irritability, delusions, and impaired judgment stemming from feelings of invincibility.

Can steroid abuse be fatal?

In some rare cases yes. When steroids enter the body, they go to different organs and muscles. Steroids are not friendly to the heart. In rare cases steroid abuse can create a situation where the body may be susceptible to heart attacks and strokes, which can be fatal. Here's how: Steroid use can lead to a condition called atherosclerosis, which causes fat deposits inside arteries to disrupt blood flow. When blood flow to the heart is blocked, a heart attack can occur. If blood flow to the brain is blocked, a stroke can result.

Bulking up the artificial way—by using steroids—puts teens at risk for more than cardiovascular disease. Steroids can weaken the immune system, which is what helps the body fight against germs and disease. That means that illnesses and diseases have an easy target in someone who is abusing steroids.

In addition, people who inject anabolic steroids may share non-sterile "works," or drug injection equipment, that can spread life-threatening viral infections such as HIV/AIDS or hepatitis, which causes serious damage to the liver.

♣ It's A Fact!!
More Than A Bad Hair Day

Ever had a bad hair day or a pimple and felt that you couldn't focus on anything else? Imagine if a small flaw (real or imagined) took over your life. That's what it's like for an estimated one to two percent of Americans with body dysmorphic disorder, or BDD.

Like anorexia nervosa, the eating disorder that causes people to see themselves as fat even as they starve their bodies into dangerous thinness, BDD involves a distortion in body image. In extreme cases, people with BDD can spend hours glued to a mirror or even become suicidal. When someone with BDD focuses on his or her muscles, the disorder can lead to steroid abuse.

We talked to Dr. Roberto Olivardia to find out more.

Q: What is BDD?

A: It's when you're very, very bothered by a part of your appearance. BDD can be a preoccupation with any body part—your hair, skin, nose.

Q: What causes BDD?

A: We live in a culture that praises a perfect appearance. But that's only part of the picture. There are also deeper psychological roots.

Q: How do I know if I have BDD?

A: Ask yourself: How much of my self-esteem is wrapped up in how I look? Does it prevent me from going to school? Am I still hanging out with friends?

Q: How can I get help for BDD?

A: The best treatment for the disorder is psychotherapy (counseling).

Source: From a Heads Up compilation from Scholastic and the National Institute on Drug Abuse, 2003. Despite the older date of this document, the information about BDD is still pertinent to today's readers.

Are anabolic steroids addictive?

It is possible that some steroid abusers may become addicted to the drugs, as evidenced by their continued use in spite of physical problems and negative effects on social relationships. Also, they spend large amounts of time and money obtaining the drugs and, when they stop using them, they experience withdrawal symptoms such as depression, mood swings, fatigue, restlessness, loss of appetite, insomnia, reduced sex drive, and the desire to take more steroids. The most dangerous of the withdrawal symptoms is depression, because it sometimes leads to suicide attempts. Untreated, some depressive symptoms associated with anabolic steroid withdrawal have been known to persist for a year or more after the abuser stops taking the drugs.

What can be done to prevent steroid abuse?

Research has shown that there is an effective program for preventing steroid abuse among players on high school sports teams. In the ATLAS (for guys) and ATHENA (for girls) programs, coaches and sports team leaders discuss the potential effects of anabolic steroids and other illicit drugs on immediate sports performance, and they teach how to refuse offers of drugs. They also discuss how strength training and proper nutrition can help adolescents build their bodies without the use of steroids. Later, special trainers teach the players proper weightlifting techniques. An ongoing series of studies has shown that this multi-component, team-centered approach reduces new steroid abuse by 50 percent and, at the same time, produces the kind of athletic performance that the teen desires.

What is the bottom line?

The bottom line is: Science proves that there are serious risks associated with the abuse of steroids and teens should never use anabolic steroids to help them bulk up.

Chapter 39

Sports Supplements

If you're a competitive athlete or a fitness buff, improving your sports performance is probably on your mind. Lots of people wonder if taking sports supplements could offer fast, effective results without so much hard work. But do sports supplements really work? And are they safe?

What Are Sports Supplements?

Sports supplements (also called ergogenic aids) are products used to enhance athletic performance that may include vitamins, minerals, amino acids, herbs, or botanicals (plants)—or any concentration, extract, or combination of these. These products are generally available over the counter without a prescription.

Sports supplement are considered a dietary supplement. Dietary supplements do not require U.S. Food and Drug Administration (FDA) approval before they come on the market. Supplement manufacturers do have to follow the FDA's current good manufacturing practices to ensure quality and safety of their product, though. And the FDA is responsible for taking action if a product is found to be unsafe after it has gone on the market.

Critics of the supplement industry point out cases where manufacturers haven't done a good job of following standards. They also mention instances where the FDA hasn't enforced regulations. Both of these can mean that supplements contain variable amounts of ingredients or even ingredients not listed on the label.

Some over-the-counter medicines and prescription medications, including anabolic steroids, are used to enhance performance but they are not considered supplements. Although medications are FDA approved, using medicines— even over-the-counter ones—in ways other than their intended purpose puts the user at risk of serious side effects. For example, teen athletes who use medications like human growth hormone (hGH) that haven't been prescribed for them may have problems with development and hormone levels.

Lots of sports organizations have developed policies on sports supplements. The National Football League (NFL), the National Collegiate Athletic Association (NCAA), and the International Olympic Committee (IOC) have banned the use of steroids, ephedra, and androstenedione by their athletes, and competitors who use them face fines, ineligibility, and suspension from their sports.

The National Federation of State High School Associations (NFHS) strongly recommends that student athletes consult with their doctor before taking any supplement.

Common Supplements And How They Affect The Body

Whether you hear about sports supplements from your teammates in the locker room or the sales clerk at your local vitamin store, chances are you're not getting the whole story about how supplements work, if they are really effective, and the risks you take by using them.

Androstenedione And DHEA

Androstenedione (also known as andro) and dehydroepiandrosterone (also known as DHEA) are prohormones or "natural steroids" that can be broken down into testosterone. When researchers studied these prohormones in adult athletes, DHEA and andro did not increase muscle size, improve strength or enhance performance.

The side effects of these "natural" steroid supplements like DHEA and andro aren't well known. But experts believe that, when taken in large doses, they cause effects similar to stronger anabolic steroids.

What is known is that andro and DHEA can cause hormone imbalances in people who use them. Both may have the same effects as taking anabolic steroids and may lead to dangerous side effects like testicular cancer, infertility, stroke, and an increased risk of heart disease. As with anabolic steroids, teens who use andro while they are still growing may not reach their full adult height. Natural steroid supplements can also cause breast development and shrinking of testicles in guys.

Creatine

Creatine is already manufactured by the body in the liver, kidneys, and pancreas. It also occurs naturally in foods such as meat and fish. Creatine supplements are available over the counter, and teens make up a large portion of the supplement's users.

People who take creatine usually take it to improve strength, but the long-term and short-term effects of creatine use haven't been studied in teens and kids. Research in adults found that creatine is most effective for athletes doing intermittent high-intensity exercise with short recovery intervals, such as sprinting and power lifting. However, researchers found no effect on athletic performance in nearly a third of athletes studied. Creatine has not been found to increase endurance or improve aerobic performance.

The most common side effects of creatine supplements include weight gain, diarrhea, abdominal pain, and muscle cramps. People with kidney problems should not use creatine because it may affect kidney function. The American College of Sports Medicine recommends that people younger than 18 years old do not use creatine. If you are considering using creatine, talk with your doctor about the risks and benefits, as well as appropriate dosing.

Fat Burners

Fat burners (sometimes known as thermogenics) were often made with an herb called ephedra, also known as ephedrine or ma huang, which acts as a stimulant and increases metabolism. Some athletes use fat burners to lose weight or to increase energy—but ephedra-based products can be one of the most dangerous supplements. Evidence has shown that it can cause heart problems, stroke, and occasionally even death.

Because athletes and others have died using this supplement, ephedra has been taken off the market. Since the ban, "ephedra-free" products have emerged, but they often contain ingredients with ephedra-like properties, including bitter orange or country mallow. Similar to ephedra, these supplements can cause high blood pressure, heart attack, stroke, and seizures.

Many of these products also contain caffeine, along with other caffeine sources (such as yerba mate and guarana). This combination may lead to restlessness, anxiety, racing heart, irregular heart beat, and increases the chance of having a life-threatening side effect.

Tips For Dealing With Athletic Pressure And Competition

Advertisements for sports supplements often use persuasive before and after pictures that make it look easy to get a muscular, toned body. But the goal of supplement advertisers is to make money by selling more supplements, and many claims may be misleading. Teens and kids may seem like an easy

♣ **It's A Fact!!**
Will supplements make me a better athlete?

Sports supplements haven't been tested on teens and kids. But studies on adults show that the claims of many supplements are weak at best. Most won't make you any stronger, and none will make you any faster or more skillful.

Many factors go into your abilities as an athlete—including your diet, how much sleep you get, genetics and heredity, and your training program. But the fact is that using sports supplements may put you at risk for serious health conditions. So instead of turning to supplements to improve your performance, concentrate on nutrition and follow a weight-training and aerobic-conditioning program.

sell on supplements because they may feel dissatisfied or uncomfortable with their still-developing bodies, and many supplement companies try to convince teens that supplements are an easy solution.

Don't waste your money on expensive and dangerous supplements. Instead, try these tips for getting better game:

- **Make downtime a priority.** Studies show that teens need more than eight hours of sleep a night, and sleep is important for athletes. Organize time for sleep into your schedule by doing as much homework as possible on the weekend or consider cutting back on after-school job hours during your sports season.

- **Try to relax.** Your school, work, and sports schedules may have you sprinting from one activity to the next, but taking a few minutes to relax can be helpful. Meditating or visualizing your success during the next game may improve your performance; sitting quietly and focusing on your breathing can give you a brief break and prepare you for your next activity.

- **Choose good eats.** Fried, fatty, or sugary foods will interfere with your performance. Instead, focus on eating foods such as lean meats, whole grains, vegetables, fruits, and low-fat dairy products. Celebrating with the team at the local pizza place after a big game is fine once in a while. But for most meals and snacks, choose healthy foods to keep your weight in a healthy range and your performance at its best.

- **Eat often.** Sometimes people skip breakfast or have an early lunch, then try to play a late afternoon game. Not getting enough food to fuel an activity can quickly wear you out—and even place you at risk for injury or muscle fatigue. Be sure to eat lunch on practice and game days. If you feel hungry before the game, pack easy-to-carry, healthy snacks in your bag, such as fruit, trail mix, or string cheese. It's important to eat well after a workout.

- **Avoid harmful substances.** Smoking will diminish your lung capacity and your ability to breathe, alcohol can make you sluggish and tired, and can impair your hand-eye coordination and reduce your alertness. And you can kiss your team good-bye if you get caught using drugs or alcohol— many schools have a no-tolerance policy for harmful substances.

- **Train harder and smarter.** If you get out of breath easily during your basketball game and you want to increase your endurance, work on improving your cardiovascular conditioning. If you think more leg strength will help you excel on the soccer field, consider weight training to increase your muscle strength. Before changing your program, though, get advice from your doctor.

- **Consult a professional.** If you're concerned about your weight or whether your diet is helping your performance, talk to your doctor or a registered dietitian who can evaluate your nutrition and steer you in the right direction. Coaches can help too. And if you're still convinced that supplements will help you, talk to your doctor or a sports medicine specialist. The doc will be able to offer alternatives to supplements based on your body and sport.

Chapter 40

Caffeine

It's 11:00 p.m. and Aaron has already had a full day of school, work, and after-school activities. He's tired and knows he could use some sleep. But Aaron still hasn't finished his homework. So he reaches for his headphones—and some caffeine.

What Is Caffeine?

Caffeine is a drug that is naturally produced in the leaves and seeds of many plants. It's also produced artificially and added to certain foods. Caffeine is defined as a drug because it stimulates the central nervous system, causing increased alertness. Caffeine gives most people a temporary energy boost and elevates mood.

Caffeine is in tea, coffee, chocolate, many soft drinks, and pain relievers and other over-the-counter medications. In its natural form, caffeine tastes very bitter. But most caffeinated drinks have gone through enough processing to camouflage the bitter taste.

Teens usually get most of their caffeine from soft drinks and energy drinks. (In addition to caffeine, these also can have added sugar and artificial flavors.) Caffeine is not stored in the body, but you may feel its effects for up to six hours.

About This Chapter: "Caffeine," January 2008, reprinted with permission from www.kids health.org. Copyright © 2008 The Nemours Foundation. This information was provided by KidsHealth, one of the largest resources online for medically reviewed health information written for parents, kids, and teens. For more articles like this one, visit www.KidsHealth .org, or www.TeensHealth.org.

Got The Jitters?

Many people feel that caffeine increases their mental alertness. Higher doses of caffeine can cause anxiety, dizziness, headaches, and the jitters. Caffeine can also interfere with normal sleep.

Caffeine sensitivity (the amount of caffeine that will produce an effect in someone) varies from person to person. On average, the smaller the person, the less caffeine needed to produce side effects. Caffeine sensitivity is most affected by the amount of caffeine a person has daily. People who regularly take in a lot of caffeine soon develop less sensitivity to it. This means they may need more caffeine to achieve the same effects.

Caffeine is a diuretic, meaning it causes a person to urinate (pee) more. It's not clear whether this causes dehydration or not. To be safe, it's probably a good idea to stay away from too much caffeine in hot weather, during long workouts, or in other situations where you might sweat a lot.

Caffeine may also cause the body to lose calcium, and that can lead to bone loss over time. Drinking caffeine-containing soft drinks and coffee instead of milk can have an even greater impact on bone density and the risk of developing osteoporosis.

Caffeine can aggravate certain heart problems. It may also interact with some medications or supplements. If you are stressed or anxious, caffeine can make these feelings worse. Although caffeine is sometimes used to treat migraine headaches, it can make headaches worse for some people.

♣ It's A Fact!!
Too Wired

People can now buy drinks with a whopping 500 mg of caffeine. This amount is risky for some people—even more so when these drinks are combined with other foods that contain caffeine (like a chocolate bar or soda) or medications.

Moderation Is The Key

Caffeine is usually thought to be safe in moderate amounts. Experts consider 200-300 mg of caffeine a day to be a moderate amount for adults. But consuming as little as 100 mg of caffeine a day can lead a person to become "dependent" on caffeine. This means that someone may develop withdrawal symptoms (like tiredness, irritability, and headaches) if he or she quits caffeine suddenly.

Teens should try to limit caffeine consumption to no more than 100 mg of caffeine daily, and kids should get even less. The following chart includes common caffeinated products and the amounts of caffeine they contain:

Table 40.1. Common Caffeinated Products

Drink/Food/Supplement	Amt. Of Drink/Food	Amt. Of Caffeine
SoBe No Fear	8 ounces	83 mg
Monster energy drink	16 ounces	160 mg
Rockstar energy drink	8 ounces	80 mg
Red Bull energy drink	8.3 ounces	80 mg
Jolt cola	12 ounces	72 mg
Mountain Dew	12 ounces	55 mg
Coca-Cola	12 ounces	34 mg
Diet Coke	12 ounces	45 mg
Pepsi	12 ounces	38 mg
7-Up	12 ounces	0 mg
Brewed coffee (drip method)	5 ounces	115 mg*
Iced tea	12 ounces	70 mg*
Cocoa beverage	5 ounces	4 mg*
Chocolate milk beverage	8 ounces	5 mg*
Dark chocolate	1 ounce	20 mg*
Milk chocolate	1 ounce	6 mg*
Jolt gum	1 stick	33 mg
Cold relief medication	1 tablet	30 mg*
Vivarin	1 tablet	200 mg
Excedrin extra strength	2 tablets	130 mg

*denotes average amount of caffeine

Source: U.S. Food and Drug Administration, National Soft Drink Association, Center for Science in the Public Interest.

Cutting Back

If you're taking in too much caffeine, you may want to cut back. The best way is to cut back slowly. Otherwise you could get headaches and feel tired, irritable, or just plain lousy.

Try cutting your intake by replacing caffeinated sodas and coffee with noncaffeinated drinks. Examples include water, caffeine-free sodas, and caffeine-free teas. Keep track of how many caffeinated drinks you have each day, and substitute one drink per week with a caffeine-free alternative until you've gotten below the 100-milligram mark.

As you cut back on the amount of caffeine you consume, you may find yourself feeling tired. Your best bet is to hit the sack, not the sodas: It's just your body's way of telling you it needs more rest. Your energy levels will return to normal in a few days.

Chapter 41

Inhalant Abuse

What Are Inhalants?

If you've ever come across a smelly marker, you've experienced an inhalant. They seem harmless, but they can actually be quite dangerous. Inhalants are chemical vapors that people inhale on purpose to get "high." The vapors produce mind-altering, and sometimes disastrous, effects. These vapors are in a variety of products common in almost any home or workplace. Examples are some paints, glues, gasoline, and cleaning fluids. Many people do not think of these products as drugs because they were never meant to be used to achieve an intoxicating effect. But when they are intentionally inhaled to produce a "high," they can cause serious harm.

Although inhalants differ in their effects, they generally fall into the following categories:

Volatile Solvents, liquids that vaporize at room temperature, present in:

- Certain industrial or household products, such as paint thinner, nail polish remover, degreaser, dry-cleaning fluid, gasoline, and contact cement

- Some art or office supplies, such as correction fluid, felt-tip marker fluid, and electronic contact cleaner

About This Chapter: Information in this chapter is from "Inhalants," NIDA for Teens, National Institute on Drug Abuse, a component of the U.S. Department of Health and Human Services, 2009.

Aerosols, sprays that contain propellants and solvents, include:

- Spray paint, hair spray, deodorant spray, vegetable oil sprays, and fabric protector spray

Gases that may be in household or commercial products, or used as medical anesthetics, such as in:

- Butane lighters, propane tanks, whipped cream dispensers, and refrigerant gases

- Anesthesia, including ether, chloroform, halothane, and nitrous oxide

Nitrites, a class of inhalants used primarily as sexual enhancers. Organic nitrites include amyl, butyl, and cyclohexyl nitrites and other related compounds. Amyl nitrite was used in the past by doctors to alleviate chest pain and is sometimes used today for diagnostic purposes in heart examinations. When marketed for illicit use these nitrites are often sold in small brown bottles and labeled as "video head cleaner," "room odorizer," "leather cleaner," or "liquid aroma."

What Are The Common Street Names?

Common slang for inhalants includes "laughing gas" (nitrous oxide), "snappers" (amyl nitrite), "poppers" (amyl nitrite and butyl nitrite), "whippets" (fluorinated hydrocarbons, found in whipped cream dispensers), "bold" (nitrites), and "rush" (nitrites).

Who Abuses Inhalants?

Inhalants are often among the first drugs that young adolescents use. In fact, they are one of the few classes of substances that are abused more by younger adolescents than older ones. Inhalant abuse can become chronic and continue into adulthood.

Data from national and state surveys suggest that inhalant abuse is most common among 7th through 9th graders. For example, in the Monitoring the Future Study, an annual National Institute on Drug Abuse (NIDA)-supported survey of the nation's secondary school students, 8th graders regularly report the highest rate of current, past-year, and lifetime inhalant abuse compared to 10th and 12th graders. One of the problems is that, according to the 2009 survey, 42% of 8th graders don't consider the regular use of inhalants to be harmful, and 66%

don't think trying inhalants once or twice is risky. It means that young teens may not understand the risks of inhalant use as well as they should.

How Are They Abused?

Inhalant abusers breathe in the vapors through their nose or mouth, usually in one of these ways:

- "Sniffing" or "snorting" fumes from containers

- Spraying aerosols directly into the nose or mouth

- Sniffing or inhaling fumes from substances sprayed or placed into a plastic or paper bag ("bagging")

- "Huffing" from an inhalant-soaked rag stuffed in the mouth

- Inhaling from balloons filled with nitrous oxide

Because the intoxication, or "high," lasts only a few minutes, abusers often try to make the feeling last longer by inhaling repeatedly over several hours.

What Are The Common Effects?

Initial Effects

The lungs absorb inhaled chemicals into the bloodstream very quickly, sending them throughout the brain and body. Within minutes of inhalation, users feel "high." The effects are similar to those produced by alcohol and may include slurred speech, lack of coordination, euphoria, and dizziness. Some inhalant users feel light-headed and have hallucinations and delusions. The high usually lasts only a few minutes.

With repeated inhalations, many users feel less inhibited and less in control. Some may feel drowsy for several hours and experience a lingering headache.

Effects On The Brain

Inhalants often contain more than one chemical. Some chemicals leave the body quickly, but others stay for a long time and get absorbed by fatty tissues in the brain and central nervous system.

One of these fatty tissues is myelin, a protective cover that surrounds many of the body's nerve fibers (neurons). Myelin helps nerve fibers carry their messages to and from the brain. Damage to myelin can slow down communication between nerve fibers.

Long-term inhalant use can break down myelin. When this happens, nerve cells are not able to transmit messages as efficiently, which can cause muscle spasms and tremors or even permanent difficulty with basic actions like walking, bending, and talking. These effects are similar to what happens to patients with multiple sclerosis—a disease that also affects myelin.

Inhalants also can damage brain cells by preventing them from receiving enough oxygen. The effects of this condition, also known as brain hypoxia, depend on the area of the brain affected. The hippocampus, for example, helps control memory, so someone who repeatedly uses inhalants may lose the ability to learn new things or may have a hard time carrying on simple conversations. If the cerebral cortex is affected, the ability to solve complex problems and plan ahead will be compromised. And, if the cerebellum is affected, it can cause a person to move slowly or clumsily.

Inhalants can be addictive. Long-term use can lead to compulsive drug seeking and use, and mild withdrawal symptoms.

✤ It's A Fact!!

Who Needs Myelin?

Inhalants can damage or destroy myelin. But who needs myelin? You do. Messages travel along the axons of your brain cells (or neurons) in the form of electricity. Think of myelin as the insulation around these electrical "wires." It's a fatty coating, or sheath, that protects the axons and helps conduct messages smoothly and speedily, ensuring that your muscles easily carry out your brain's orders.

When myelin deteriorates, this smooth flow of signals is disrupted. The result? Muscle spasms and tremors, or even permanent difficulty with basic actions like walking, bending, and talking.

Source: From a Heads Up compilation from Scholastic and the National Institute on Drug Abuse, 2003. Despite the older date of this document, the information about myelin is still pertinent to today's readers.

Other Health Effects

Regular abuse of inhalants can cause serious harm to vital organs besides the brain, like the heart, kidneys, and liver. Inhalants can cause heart damage, liver failure, and muscle weakness. Certain inhalants can also cause the body to produce fewer blood cells, which can lead to a condition known as aplastic anemia (in which the bone marrow is unable to produce blood cells). Frequent long-term use of certain inhalants can cause a permanent change or malfunction of peripheral nerves, called polyneuropathy.

Specific Effects By Type Of Inhalant

Depending on the type of inhalant abused, the harmful health effects will differ. The list below includes a few examples.

Toluene: Examples include spray paint, glue, dewaxer, and fingernail polish. Effects of use include hearing loss, damage to spinal cord or brain, and liver and kidney damage.

Trichloroethylene: Examples include cleaning fluid and correction fluid. Effects of use include hearing loss and liver and kidney damage.

Hexane: Examples include glue and gasoline. Effects of use include limb spasms and blackouts.

Nitrous Oxide: Examples include whipped cream dispensers and gas cylinders. Effects of use include limb spasms and blackouts.

Benzene: Gasoline contains benzene; bone marrow damage can result from use.

Butane gas, found in cigarette lighters and refills, makes the heart extra sensitive to a chemical naturally found in the body that carries messages from the central nervous system to the heart. This chemical, noradrenaline, tells the heart to beat faster when someone is in a stressful situation. If the heart becomes too sensitive to noradrenaline, it can affect the heart's rhythm, with potentially lethal consequences.

Nitrite abuse has other health risks. Unlike most other inhalants, which act directly on the brain, nitrites enlarge blood vessels, allowing more blood to flow through them. Inhaled nitrites make the heart beat faster and produce a sensation of heat and excitement that can last for several minutes. Nitrites can also cause dizziness and headaches. Nitrites are more often used by older adolescents and adults (primarily to enhance sexual pleasure and performance), and their abuse is associated with unsafe sexual practices that can increase the risk of contracting and spreading infectious diseases, such as HIV and hepatitis.

Lethal Effects

Prolonged sniffing of the highly concentrated chemicals in solvents or aerosol sprays can cause irregular or rapid heart rhythms and can lead to heart failure and death within minutes. This "sudden sniffing death" is particularly associated with the abuse of butane, propane, and chemicals in aerosols.

High concentrations of inhalants also can cause death from suffocation. This happens when the inhalant vapor takes the place of oxygen in the lungs and brain, causing breathing to stop. Deliberately inhaling from a paper or plastic bag or in a closed area, for example, greatly increases the chances of suffocation.

While high on inhalants, users also can die by choking on their own vomit or by fatal injury from accidents, including car crashes.

❖ It's A Fact!!

Inhalants Can Kill

You can die the first time you try inhalants. There are a number of ways huffing can kill. The most common is called sudden sniffing death syndrome. "The chemicals are acting neurologically to cause irregular heart rhythms that can lead to heart failure and then death," says Dr. David Shurtleff, the Acting Director of Neuroscience and Behavioral Research at the National Institute on Drug Abuse.

You can also die by asphyxiation (lack of oxygen). When you breathe in the fumes, you fill up the cells in your lungs with poisonous chemicals, leaving no room for the oxygen we all need to breathe and live. Lack of oxygen can lead to respiratory failure and death. In this country, approximately 100 teens die each year from inhalant abuse.

Source: From a Heads Up compilation from Scholastic and the National Institute on Drug Abuse, 2003. Despite the older date of this document, the information about inhalant risks is still pertinent to today's readers.

If Inhalants Are Harmful, Why Do Kids Use Them?

Many kids think inhalants are a harmless, cheap, and quick way to "catch a buzz." Because many inhalants can be found around the house, kids may not even think they are harmful. But the chemicals in the inhalant vapors can change the way the brain works and cause other complications in the body. What kids often don't know is that, in some cases, the harmful effects of inhalants can be irreversible.

Are Inhalants Addictive?

Some people, particularly those who abuse inhalants a lot and for a long time, report a strong need to continue using inhalants. Compulsive use and a mild withdrawal syndrome can occur. In fact, recent research in animal models has shown that toluene can affect the brain in a way that is like other drugs of abuse (i.e., amphetamines). Toluene increases dopamine activity in reward areas of the brain, and the long-term disruption of the dopamine system is one of the key factors leading to addiction.

How Can I Tell If Someone Is Abusing Inhalants?

Sometimes you can't tell. Other times you might see small signs that tell you a person is abusing inhalants. They might have chemical odors on their breath or clothing; paint or other stains on their face, hands, or clothing; nausea or loss of appetite; weight loss; muscle weakness; disorientation; or inattentiveness, uncoordinated movement, irritability, and depression.

Part Six

Abuse Of Illegal Substances

Chapter 42

Ecstasy, GHB, Rohypnol, And Ketamine

Club Drugs Facts And Figures

Club drugs are a pharmacologically heterogeneous group of psychoactive compounds that tend to be abused by teens and young adults at a nightclub, bar, rave, or trance scene. Gamma hydroxybutyrate (GHB), Rohypnol, ketamine, MDMA (ecstasy) and methamphetamine are some of the drugs in this group.

What are the health effects of club drugs?

In high doses, MDMA can interfere with the body's ability to regulate temperature, sometimes leading to a sharp increase in body temperature (hyperthermia), resulting in liver, kidney, and cardiovascular system failure, and death. MDMA users also risk increases in heart rate and blood pressure, and symptoms such as muscle tension, involuntary teeth clenching, nausea, blurred vision, faintness, and chills or sweating. Psychological effects of MDMA use

About This Chapter: Information in this chapter is from "Club Drugs Facts and Figures," Office of National Drug Control Policy, 2009; "MDMA (Ecstasy)," NIDA for Teens, the National Institute on Drug Abuse, a component of the United States Department of Health and Human Services, 2009; "GHB And Analogs Fast Facts," National Drug Intelligence Center, NDIC Product No. 2003-L0559-009, May 2003; "Rohypnol Fast Facts," National Drug Intelligence Center, NDIC Product No. 2003-L0559-020, August 2003; and "Ketamine Fast Facts," National Drug Intelligence Center, NDIC Product No. 2003-L0559-011, June 2003. Despite the older dates on some of these documents, the facts about the drugs discussed are still pertinent.

can include confusion, depression, sleep problems, drug craving, and severe anxiety. Additionally, these problems can occur during as well as sometimes days or weeks after using the drug.

Rohypnol, GHB, and ketamine are all central nervous system depressants. Lower doses of Rohypnol can cause muscle relaxation and can produce general sedative and hypnotic effects. In higher doses, Rohypnol causes a loss of muscle control, loss of consciousness, and partial amnesia. When combined with alcohol, the toxic effects of Rohypnol can be aggravated.

✣ It's A Fact!!

The Truth About Club Drugs

Club drugs affect your brain. The term "club drugs" refers to a wide variety of drugs often used at all-night dance parties ("raves"), nightclubs, and concerts. Club drugs can damage the neurons in your brain, impairing your senses, memory, judgment, and coordination.

Club drugs affect your body. Different club drugs have different effects on your body. Some common effects include loss of muscle and motor control, blurred vision, and seizures. Club drugs like ecstasy are stimulants that increase your heart rate and blood pressure and can lead to heart or kidney failure. Other club drugs, like GHB, are depressants that can cause drowsiness, unconsciousness, or breathing problems.

Club drugs affect your self-control. Club drugs like GHB and Rohypnol are used in "date rape" and other assaults because they are sedatives that can make you unconscious and immobilize you. Rohypnol can cause a kind of amnesia—users may not remember what they said or did while under the effects of the drug.

Club drugs are not always what they seem. Because club drugs are illegal and often produced in makeshift laboratories, it is impossible to know exactly what chemicals were used to produce them. How strong or dangerous any illegal drug is varies each time.

Club drugs can kill you. Higher doses of club drugs can cause severe breathing problems, coma, or even death.

Source: From "Tips for Teens: The Truth About Club Drugs," Substance Abuse and Mental Health Services Administration, 2004. Despite the older date of this document, the facts about club drugs are still pertinent.

✔ Quick Tip

Before You Risk It...

Know the law. It is illegal to buy or sell club drugs. It is also a federal crime to use any controlled substance to aid in a sexual assault.

Get the facts. Despite what you may have heard, club drugs can be addictive.

Stay informed. The club drug scene is constantly changing. New drugs and new variations of drugs appear all of the time.

Know the risks. Mixing club drugs together or with alcohol is extremely dangerous. The effects of one drug can magnify the effects and risks of another. In fact, mixing substances can be lethal.

Look around you. The vast majority of teens are not using club drugs. While ecstasy is considered to be the most frequently used club drug, less than two percent of 8th–12th graders use it on a regular basis. In fact, 94 percent of teens have never even tried ecstasy.

Source: From "Tips for Teens: The Truth About Club Drugs," Substance Abuse and Mental Health Services Administration, 2004. Despite the older date of this document, the facts about club drugs are still pertinent.

The sedative effects of GHB may result in sleep, coma, or death. Other effects of GHB use can include seizures, along with nausea and breathing difficulties when combined with alcohol. GHB has increasingly become involved in poisonings, overdoses, date rapes, and fatalities.

The use of ketamine produces effects similar to PCP and LSD, causing distorted perceptions of sight and sound and making the user feel disconnected and out of control. The overt hallucinatory effects of ketamine are relatively short-acting, lasting approximately one hour or less. However, the user's senses, judgment, and coordination may be affected for up to 24 hours after the initial use of the drug. Use of this drug can also bring about respiratory depression, heart rate abnormalities, and a withdrawal syndrome.

MDMA (Ecstasy)

What is Ecstasy?

"Ecstasy" is a slang term for MDMA, short for 3,4-methylene-dioxymethamphetamine, a name that's nearly as long as the all-night parties where MDMA is often used. That's why MDMA has been called a "club drug." It has effects similar to those of other stimulants, and it often makes the user feel like everyone is his or her friend, even when that's not the case.

MDMA is man-made—it doesn't come from a plant like marijuana does. Other chemicals or substances—such as caffeine, dextromethorphan (found in some cough syrups), amphetamines, PCP, or cocaine—are sometimes added to, or substituted for, MDMA in ecstasy tablets. Makers of MDMA can add anything they want to the drug, so its purity is always in question.

What are the common street names?

There are a lot of slang words for MDMA. "Ecstasy" is one of the most common. You might also hear "E," "XTC," "X," "Adam," "hug," "beans," "clarity," "lover's speed," and "love drug."

How is it used?

Most MDMA abusers take a pill, tablet, or capsule. These pills can be different colors, and sometimes have cartoon-like images on them. Some MDMA users take more than one pill at a time, called "bumping."

How many teens use it?

According to a 2009 National Institute on Drug Abuse (NIDA)-funded study, many smart young teens are turning their backs on MDMA. Since 2001, the percentage of 8th graders who have ever tried MDMA dropped from 5.2% in 2001 to 2.2% in 2009. The drop among 10th graders and 12th graders was similar. The percentage of 10th graders who had ever tried MDMA was 5.5% in 2009, down from an all-time high of 8.0% in 2001. In 2009, 6.5% of 12th graders had ever tried MDMA, down from 11.7% in 2001. Fewer 10th graders saw "great risk" in occasionally using MDMA, which means that they may not understand the health risks of using MDMA as well as they should.

Is MDMA addictive?

Like other drugs, MDMA can be addictive for some people. That is, people continue to take the drug despite experiencing unpleasant physical side effects and other social, behavioral, and health consequences.

What are the common effects?

For most abusers, a "hit" of MDMA lasts for three to six hours. Once the pill is swallowed, it takes only about 15 minutes for MDMA to enter the bloodstream and reach the brain. About 45 minutes later, a user experiences MDMA's "high." That's when the drug is at its peak level. MDMA users might feel very alert, or "hyper," at first. At clubs, they can keep on dancing for hours at a time. Some lose a sense of time and experience other changes in perception, such as an enhanced sense of touch. Others experience negative effects right away. They may become anxious and agitated. Sweating or chills may occur, and users may feel faint or dizzy.

MDMA can also cause muscle tension, nausea, and blurred vision, and increase heart rate and blood pressure. Forceful clenching of the teeth can occur, and individuals at clubs have been known to chew on pacifiers to relieve some of the tension.

What are the dangers?

In general, NIDA-supported research shows that abuse of any drug, including MDMA, can cause serious health problems and, in some instances, even death. Many drug abusers take combinations of drugs, including alcohol, which may further increase their risk.

MDMA users can also become dehydrated through vigorous activity in a hot environment. It may not seem like a big deal, but when MDMA interferes with the body's ability to regulate its temperature, it can cause dangerous overheating, called hyperthermia. This, in turn, can lead to serious heart and kidney problems— or, rarely, death. MDMA can be extremely dangerous in high doses or when multiple small doses are taken within a short time period to maintain the high. High levels of the drug in the blood stream can increase the risk of hyperthermia, seizures, and the ability of the heart to maintain its normal rhythms.

What are the risks to the brain?

Messages travel through our brains through nerve cells, or neurons. The neurons have thread-like fibers that release chemicals to send the messages to other neurons. Researchers that study the brain think that MDMA may affect neurons that use serotonin to communicate with other neurons. The serotonin system plays a direct role in controlling our mood, aggression, sexual activity, sleep, and sensitivity to pain. Another bit of bad news—researchers have seen memory loss among regular users of MDMA.

What are the long-term effects?

We still don't know whether MDMA causes long-term brain damage in humans, or whether the effects are reversible when someone stops using the drug. A study of animals showed that exposure to high doses of MDMA for four days produced brain damage that could still be seen six to seven years later. The good news is that the study researchers found that some of the nerve fibers grew back in the same places where the toxic reactions had occurred. But, we still don't know if these new neurons work like the old ones. It's like cutting off a branch of a fruit tree: The tree is still alive and can sprout a new limb near the site of the cut, but it may not bear as much fruit as the old one.

GHB And Its Analogs

What are GHB and its analogs?

GHB (gamma-hydroxybutyrate) is a powerful central nervous system depressant that the human body produces in small amounts. A synthetic (man-made) version of GHB was developed in the 1920s as an anesthetic. Individuals abuse synthetic GHB because of its euphoric and sedative effects. Because of its anesthetic properties, GHB also has been used by sexual predators to incapacitate their victims. GHB analogs, which include GBL, BD, GHV, and GVL, are drugs that possess chemical structures that closely resemble GHB. These analogs produce effects similar to those associated with GHB and are often used in its place.

What do they look like?

GHB and its analogs typically are sold either as a white powder or as a clear liquid. The drugs often have a salty taste.

How are they abused?

GHB and its analogs usually are taken orally. Because of the drugs' salty taste, they often are mixed with a flavored beverage. Sexual predators who administer GHB or an analog to their victims typically slip the drug into a drink, often at a bar or party.

Who uses GHB and its analogs?

Although information about the extent of GHB and analog use in the United States is limited, the data that are available indicate that these drugs primarily are used by young people. According to the Drug Abuse Warning Network, individuals aged 18 to 25 account for 58 percent of all GHB mentions in drug-related emergency department visits. GHB use among high school students is a particular concern. Nearly 2% of high school seniors in the United States used the drug at least once in the past year, according to the University of Michigan's Monitoring the Future Survey.

What are the risks?

Use of GHB and its analogs can cause nausea, vomiting, delusions, depression, dizziness, hallucinations, seizures, respiratory distress, loss of consciousness, slowed heart rate, lowered blood pressure, amnesia, coma, and death. Mixing GHB or its analogs with alcohol is particularly dangerous because alcohol enhances the drug's depressant effects.

Sustained use of GHB or its analogs can lead to addiction, and chronic users experience withdrawal symptoms when they stop using the drugs. These symptoms include anxiety, insomnia, tremors, tachycardia (abnormally fast heart rate), delirium, and agitation. Users may experience these symptoms within one to six hours of their last dose, and the symptoms may persist for months.

In addition to the risks associated with the drugs themselves, individuals who use GHB or its analogs may put themselves at risk of sexual assault.

What are they called?

The most common names for GHB are Georgia home boy, G, goop, grievous bodily harm, and liquid ecstasy.

Rohypnol

What is Rohypnol?

Rohypnol, a trade name for the drug flunitrazepam, is a central nervous system depressant. The drug is legally manufactured and available outside the United States but is neither manufactured nor approved for sale within the United States. Since the 1990s individuals in the United States have used Rohypnol illegally, often as a means of mitigating the depression that results from using stimulants such as cocaine and methamphetamine. Rohypnol also has been used in the commission of sexual assaults.

What does Rohypnol look like?

Rohypnol is manufactured as a caplet. In 1997 the manufacturer responded to concerns about the drug's role in sexual assaults by reformulating the white, 2-milligram (mg) tablets. (The original tablets dissolved clear in liquid, making it nearly impossible for a victim to detect their presence in a beverage.) The new smaller dosage (0.5 mg and 1.0 mg) caplets are dull green with a blue core that, when dissolved in light-colored drinks, will dye the liquid blue. However, the dye may be disguised in blue or dark-colored liquids, and generic versions of the drug may not contain the blue dye.

How is Rohypnol abused?

Individuals who abuse Rohypnol may swallow the caplets whole, crush and then snort the powdered caplets, or dissolve the caplets in liquid and then inject the solution. Sexual predators who administer Rohypnol to their victims typically slip the drug into a drink, often at a bar or party. The blue color that results from mixing Rohypnol with a beverage often is masked by serving blue tropical drinks or by serving the drink in dark or opaque containers. The effects of the drug typically are felt within 15 to 20 minutes of administration and may persist for more than 12 hours.

Who abuses Rohypnol?

Teenagers and young adults, primarily individuals aged 13 to 30, are the principal users of Rohypnol, and most users are male. The drug is popular on high school and college campuses and at raves and nightclubs. Rohypnol use among high school students is a particular problem. Nearly 2% of high school seniors in the United States used Rohypnol at least once in the past year, according to the University of Michigan's Monitoring the Future Survey.

What are the risks?

Individuals who abuse Rohypnol often experience drowsiness, headaches, memory impairment, dizziness, nightmares, confusion, and tremors. Although the drug is classified as a depressant, Rohypnol can induce aggression or excitability. In addition to the risks associated with the drug itself, individuals who use Rohypnol may put themselves at risk of sexual assault.

What is it called?

The most common names for Rohypnol are forget-me drug, roche, roofies, and ruffles.

Ketamine

What is ketamine?

Ketamine is an anesthetic that is abused for its hallucinogenic properties. Its predominant legitimate use is as a veterinary anesthetic; however, it has been approved for use with both animals and humans. Abuse of the drug gained popularity when users discovered that it produced effects similar to those associated with PCP. Because of its anesthetic properties, ketamine also reportedly has been used by sexual predators to incapacitate their intended victims.

What does ketamine look like?

Ketamine generally is sold as either a colorless, odorless liquid or as a white or off-white powder.

How is ketamine abused?

In either its powder or liquid forms, ketamine is mixed with beverages or added to smokable materials such as marijuana or tobacco. As a powder the drug is snorted or pressed into tablets—often in combination with other drugs such as 3,4-methylenedioxymethamphetamine (MDMA, also known as ecstasy). As a liquid, ketamine is injected; it often is injected intramuscularly.

Who uses ketamine?

Teenagers and young adults represent the majority of ketamine users. According to the Drug Abuse Warning Network, individuals aged 12 to 25 accounted for 74 percent of the ketamine emergency department mentions in the United States in 2000. Ketamine use among high school students is a particular concern. Nearly 3% of high school seniors in the United States used the drug at least once in the past year, according to the University of Michigan's Monitoring the Future Survey.

What are the risks?

Ketamine causes users to have distorted perceptions of sight and sound and to feel disconnected and out of control. Use of the drug can impair an individual's senses, judgment, and coordination for up to 24 hours after the drug is taken even though the drug's hallucinogenic effects usually last for only 45 to 90 minutes.

✔ Quick Tip

Know The Signs

How can you tell if a friend is using club drugs? Sometimes it's tough to tell. But there are signs you can look for. If your friend has one or more of the following warning signs, he or she may be using club drugs:

- Problems remembering things they recently said or did
- Loss of coordination, dizziness, fainting
- Depression
- Confusion
- Sleep problems
- Chills or sweating
- Slurred speech

What can you do to help someone who is using club drugs? Be a real friend. Save a life. Encourage your friend to stop or seek professional help.

Source: From "Tips for Teens: The Truth About Club Drugs," Substance Abuse and Mental Health Services Administration, 2004. Despite the older date of this document, the facts about club drugs are still pertinent.

Use of ketamine has been associated with serious problems—both mental and physical. Ketamine can cause depression, delirium, amnesia, impaired motor function, high blood pressure, and potentially fatal respiratory problems.

In addition to the risks associated with ketamine itself, individuals who use the drug may put themselves at risk of sexual assault. Sexual predators reportedly have used ketamine to incapacitate their intended victims—either by lacing unsuspecting victims' drinks with the drug or by offering ketamine to victims who consume the drug without understanding the effects it will produce.

What is it called?

The most common names for ketamine are K, special K, cat valium, and vitamin K.

Chapter 43

Club Drugs And Raves

Introduction

High energy, all-night dance parties and clubs known as "raves," which feature dance music with a fast, pounding beat and choreographed laser programs, have become increasingly popular over the last decade, particularly among teenagers and young adults. Beginning as an underground movement in Europe, raves have evolved into a highly organized, commercialized, worldwide party culture. Rave parties and clubs are now found throughout the United States and in countries around the world. Raves are held either in permanent dance clubs or at temporary venues set up for a single weekend event in abandoned warehouses, open fields, or empty buildings.

Attendance can range from 30 "ravers" in a small club to tens of thousands in a sports stadium or open field. While techno music and light shows are essential to raves, drugs such as MDMA (3,4-methylenedioxymethamphetamine), ketamine, GHB (gamma-hydroxybutyrate), Rohypnol, and LSD (lysergic acid diethylamide), have become an integral component of the rave culture.

About This Chapter: Information in this chapter is excerpted from "Information Bulletin: Raves," National Drug Intelligence Center, a component of the U.S. Department of Justice, Product ID: Product No. 2001-L0424-004, April 2001. Despite the older date of this document, the historical information about raves and their development may still be of interest to today's readers.

History

Raves evolved from 1980s dance parties, aided by the emergence of European techno music and American house music. European clubs that sponsored raves in the 1980s tried to limit the exposure of attendees to the public and to law enforcement. Raves were secretive, after-hours, private dance parties and were often held in gay clubs where attendance was restricted to invitees or friends of invitees. The site of the party was often kept confidential, and invitees usually were not told the location of the host club until the night of the party. Because of the restricted access and the secrecy surrounding the locations, the growing rave culture was often described as an "underground" movement.

As the movement continued to grow in the late 1980s, the first rave parties emerged in U.S. cities such as San Francisco and Los Angeles. Rave parties and clubs were present in most metropolitan areas of the United States by the early 1990s. Events became highly promoted, heavily commercialized, and less secretive. Many new U.S. rave promoters were career criminals who recognized the profitability of organizing events tailored to teens. Capitalizing on the growing popularity of raves, specialized industries were developed to market clothes, toys, drugs, and music. Private clubs and secret locations were replaced by stadium venues with off-duty police security.

By the late 1990s, raves in the United States had become so commercialized that events were little more than an exploitation of American youth. Today's raves are characterized by high entrance fees, extensive drug use, exorbitantly priced bottled water, very dark and often dangerously overcrowded dance floors, and "chill rooms," where teenage ravers go to cool down and often engage in open sexual activity.

Moreover, many club owners and promoters appear to promote the use of drugs—especially MDMA. They provide bottled water and sports drinks to manage hyperthermia and dehydration; pacifiers to prevent involuntary teeth clenching; and menthol nasal inhalers, chemical lights, and neon glow sticks to enhance the effects of MDMA. In addition, rave promoters often print flyers featuring prominent and repeated use of the letters "E" and "X" (E and X are MDMA monikers) or the word "rollin'" (refers to an MDMA high), surreptitiously promoting MDMA use along with the rave.

❖ It's A Fact!!

For more information about club drugs, including MDMA (ecstasy), ketamine, GHB (gamma-hydroxy-butyrate), and Rohypnol, see Chapter 42.

The increasing notoriety of raves has caused the rave culture to spread from major metropolitan areas to more rural or conservative locations. Rave parties are emerging in areas of Colorado, Iowa, Louisiana, Michigan, Minnesota, and Wisconsin that are not always prepared to manage unexpected crowds of teenagers.

Raves And Club Drugs

Drugs like MDMA, ketamine, GHB, Rohypnol, and LSD—known collectively as "club drugs"—are an integral part of the rave culture. Many ravers use club drugs and advocate their use, wrongly believing that they are not harmful if they are used "responsibly" and their effects are managed properly. Many of the commercially designed rave clothes display pro-drug messages, and rave posters and flyers often promote drug use.

Members of private drug education and drug testing organizations, called "harm reduction organizations," have appeared at raves. They attend rave events to test samples of illegal drugs so they can inform ravers of purity levels. Members of these organizations believe that they help reduce the number of overdoses by educating users on the physical effects of specific drugs. Conversely, many law enforcement agencies believe that the practices of harm reduction organizations encourage drug use, and they support their position with national statistics that show an increase in club drug overdoses as harm reduction organizations have become more active.

MDMA is unquestionably the most popular of the club drugs, and evidence of MDMA use by teenagers can be seen at most rave parties. Ketamine and GHB also are used at raves, as is Rohypnol, although to a lesser extent. A resurgence in the availability and use of some hallucinogens—LSD, PCP (phencyclidine), psilocybin, and peyote or mescaline—has also been noted at raves and dance clubs. Inhalants like nitrous oxide are sometimes found at rave events; nitrous oxide is sold in gas-filled balloons called "whippets."

Rampant use of club drugs at raves may be leading to the use of other, highly addictive drugs by youths. There have been reports of availability and use of Asian methamphetamine tablets (frequently referred to as "yaba") at California raves and nightclubs. Heroin is being encountered more frequently at raves and clubs in large metropolitan areas, especially in the eastern United States. A wider variety of visually appealing and easy-to-administer forms of MDMA, LSD, heroin, and combination tablets are also found at raves and on college campuses.

Conclusion

Raves developed from a small subculture to the highly commercialized and widespread exploitation of young people by large scale rave promoters. The growing awareness of the nature of rave activity and the effects of club drug use have moved many communities to action. In order to curtail rave activity, communities and law enforcement agencies are enforcing existing fire codes, health and safety ordinances, and liquor laws, and are establishing juvenile curfews and licensing requirements for large public gatherings. They are requiring rave promoters and club owners to pay for building or liquor licenses, medical services, and security for their events, all in an effort to force rave promoters to move or cease their operations.

Chapter 44

Hallucinogens: LSD, PCP, And Psilocybin

Hallucinogens Facts And Figures

Hallucinogenic substances are characterized by their ability to cause changes in a person's perception of reality. Persons using hallucinogenic drugs often report seeing images, hearing sounds, and feeling sensations that seem real, but do not exist. In the past, plants and fungi that contained hallucinogenic substances were abused. Currently, these hallucinogenic substances are produced synthetically to provide a higher potency.

LSD (lysergic acid diethylamide) is one of the major drugs making up the hallucinogen class of drugs. It was discovered in 1938 and is manufactured from lysergic acid, which is found in ergot, a fungus that grows on rye and other grains.

PCP (phencyclidine) was developed in the 1950s as an intravenous anesthetic, but its use in humans was discontinued in 1965, because patients often became agitated, delusional, and irrational while recovering from its anesthetic effects. PCP is now being illegally manufactured in laboratories. It is a white crystalline powder that is readily soluble in water or alcohol.

About This Chapter: Information in this chapter is from "Hallucinogens Facts and Figures," the Office of National Drug Control Policy, 2009; "LSD Fast Facts," National Drug Intelligence Center, NDIC Product No. 2003-L0559-007, May 2003; "PCP Fast Facts," National Drug Intelligence Center, NDIC Product No. 2003-L0559-008, May 2003; and "Psilocybin Fast Facts," National Drug Intelligence Center, NDIC Product No. 2003-L0559-018, August 2003. Despite the older dates on some of these documents, the facts about the drugs discussed are still pertinent.

Psilocybin is obtained from certain mushrooms found in South America, Mexico, and the U.S., although the substance can also be produced synthetically.

Mescaline is the active hallucinogenic ingredient in peyote. Peyote is a small, spineless cactus historically used by natives in Mexico and the southwestern U.S. as part of religious rites. Mescaline can also be produced synthetically.

DMT (dimethyltryptamine) is found in a number of plants and seeds, but can also be produced synthetically. DMT is usually ingested by snorting, smoking, or injecting the drug. DMT is not effective in producing hallucinogenic effects when ingested by itself and is therefore used in conjunction with another drug that inhibits its metabolism.

Foxy, also known as Foxy Methoxy, is available in powder, capsule, and tablet form and is usually ingested orally (although it can be snorted or smoked). Foxy capsules and tablets vary in color and logos sometimes appear on tablets. AMT (alpha-methyltryptamine), a chemically similar drug, is often found in tablet and capsule form.

Dextromethorphan (sometimes called "DXM" or "robo") is a cough-suppressing ingredient in a variety of over-the-counter cold and cough medications. At the doses recommended for treating coughs, the drug is safe and effective. At much higher doses, dextromethorphan produces dissociative effects similar to those of PCP and ketamine.

What is the extent of hallucinogen use?

According to the 2008 National Survey on Drug Use and Health (NS-DUH), approximately 36 million Americans aged 12 or older reported trying hallucinogens at least once during their lifetimes, representing 14.4% of the population in that age group. Approximately 3.7 million (1.5% of the population) reported past year hallucinogen use and approximately 1.1 million (0.4%) reported past month use of hallucinogens.

The 2008 NSDUH also provides specific survey results for LSD and PCP use. Regarding LSD use, 23.5 million Americans (9.4% of the population aged 12 or older) reported lifetime use, 802,000 (0.3%) reported past year use, and 154,000 (0.1%) reported past month use. Concerning PCP use, 6.6 million (2.7%) reported lifetime use, 99,000 (0.0%) reported past year use, and 24,000 (0.0%) reported past month use.

Results of the 2008 Monitoring the Future survey indicate that 3.3% of 8th graders, 5.5% of 10th graders, and 8.7% of 12th graders reported lifetime use of hallucinogens. In 2007, these percentages were 3.1%, 6.4%, and 8.4%, respectively.

Table 44.1. Percent Of Students Reporting Hallucinogen Use, 2007–2008

	8th Grade		10th Grade		12th Grade	
	2007	2008	2007	2008	2007	2008
Past month	1.0%	0.9%	1.7%	1.3%	1.7%	2.2%
Past year	1.9	2.1	4.4	3.9	5.4	5.9
Lifetime	3.1	3.3	6.4	5.5	8.4	8.7

Table 44.2. Percent Of Students Reporting LSD Use, 2007–2008

	8th Grade		10thGrade		12th Grade	
	2007	2008	2007	2008	2007	2008
Past month	0.5%	0.5%	0.7%	0.7%	0.6%	1.1%
Past year	1.1	1.3	1.9	1.8	2.1	2.7
Lifetime	1.6	1.9	3.0	2.6	3.4	4.0

Table 44.3. Percent Of Twelfth Graders Reporting PCP Use, 2007–2008

	2007	2008
Past month	0.5%	0.6%
Past year	0.9	1.1
Lifetime	2.1	1.8

Table 44.4. Percent Of Students Reporting Risk Of Using LSD, 2008

Say "great risk" to:	8th Grade	10th Grade	12th Grade
Take LSD once/twice	21.9%	34.6%	33.9%
Take LSD regularly	36.9	55.7	63.6

What are the health effects of hallucinogens?

Hallucinogens can produce physiological effects including elevated heart rate, increased blood pressure, and dilated pupils. These drugs are often unpredictable and a user may experience different effects compared to other users or past usage. Users often experience changes in perception, thought, and mood.

♣ It's A Fact!!
FAQs On LSD

Where does LSD come from? LSD (lysergic acid diethylamide) was invented by a chemist in 1938. Working in a lab in Switzerland, Albert Hofmann was trying to create medicine out of a fungus. He ended up with LSD. Five years after he created it, Hofmann accidentally ingested the drug and took the first bad trip: "A demon had invaded me," he said. "[It] had taken possession of my body, mind, and soul."

What are the short-term effects of LSD? LSD and other hallucinogens powerfully distort the functioning of the five senses, as well as one's sense of time and space. Some users even report a blending of the senses—seeing sounds and hearing colors—known as "synesthesia." An LSD trip may include terrifying experiences and inspire dangerous behavior on a user's part.

What are the long-term effects of LSD? Two long-term effects reported by former users are psychosis and hallucinogen persisting perception disorder (HPPD). Psychosis is a severe mental illness, in which a person loses contact with reality. HPPD (often but less accurately called "flashbacks") is a disorder that includes ongoing perception problems.

How does LSD work? LSD binds to and activates a specific receptor for serotonin, a brain chemical involved in emotions and the senses. It especially affects two brain regions: the cerebral cortex—involved in mood, cognition, and perception—and the locus ceruleus, which receives sensory signals.

If LSD isn't addictive, why is it dangerous? "The main reason LSD is dangerous is because it's unpredictable in its effects," says Dr. Jerry Frankenheim of the National Drug Institute (NIDA). "The most dangerous thing that can happen is that someone has a complete break with reality and thinks they can fly or stop traffic."

Source: From "FAQs on LSD," an article in a Heads Up compilation from Scholastic and the National Institute on Drug Abuse, 2003. Despite the older date of this document, facts about LSD are still pertinent.

The effects of LSD are unpredictable. They depend on the amount of the drug taken, the user's personality, mood, and expectations, and the surroundings in which the drug is used. Usually, the user feels the first effects of the drug within 30 to 90 minutes of ingestion. These experiences last for extended periods of time and typically begin to clear after about 12 hours. The physical effects include dilated pupils, higher body temperature, increased heart rate and blood pressure, sweating, loss of appetite, sleeplessness, dry mouth, and tremors. Sensations may seem to "cross over" for the user, giving the feeling of hearing colors and seeing sounds. If taken in a large enough dose, the drug produces delusions and visual hallucinations.

The effects of PCP use are unpredictable, can be felt within minutes of ingestion, and can last for many hours. Physical effects can include shallow, rapid breathing, increased blood pressure, elevated heart rate, and increased temperature. Nausea, blurred vision, dizziness, and decreased awareness can also occur. High doses of PCP can cause convulsions, coma, hyperthermia, and death. PCP is an addictive drug that can cause psychological dependence, cravings, and compulsive drug seeking behaviors.

Physical effects of psilocybin are usually experienced within 20 minutes of ingestion and can last for six hours. Negative physical symptoms of psilocybin use can include vomiting, muscle weakness, drowsiness, and panic reactions. Frequent use of this drug can result in the development of a tolerance.

AMT and Foxy share many chemical and pharmacological characteristics with other Schedule I hallucinogens and produce similar effects.

Dextromethorphan users describe a set of distinct dose-dependent "plateaus" ranging from a mild stimulant effect with distorted visual perceptions at low (approximately 2-ounce) doses to a sense of complete dissociation from one's body at doses of 10 ounces or more. The effects typically last for six hours.

Of an estimated 113 million emergency department (ED) visits in the U.S. during 2006, the Drug Abuse Warning Network (DAWN) estimates that 1,742,887 were drug-related. DAWN data indicate that LSD was involved in 4,002 ED visits; PCP was involved in 21,960 visits; and miscellaneous hallucinogens were involved in 3,898 visits.

LSD

What is LSD?

LSD (lysergic acid diethylamide) is a synthetic (man-made) drug that has been abused for its hallucinogenic properties since the 1960s. If consumed in a sufficiently large dose, LSD produces delusions and visual hallucinations that distort the user's sense of time and identity. The most common names for LSD are acid, boomers, and yellow sunshine.

What does it look like?

LSD typically is sold as a liquid (often packaged in small bottles designed to hold breath freshening drops) or applied to blotter paper, sugar cubes, gelatin squares, and tablets.

How is LSD abused?

LSD generally is taken by mouth. The drug is colorless and odorless but has a slightly bitter taste.

PCP

What is PCP?

PCP (phencyclidine) was developed in the 1950s as an intravenous anesthetic, but its use for humans was discontinued because it caused patients to become agitated, delusional, and irrational. Today individuals abuse PCP because of the mind-altering, hallucinogenic effects it produces.

What does PCP look like?

PCP is a bitter-tasting, white crystalline powder that is easy to dissolve in water or alcohol. PCP may be dyed various colors and often is sold as a tablet, capsule, liquid, or powder.

How is PCP abused?

Users snort PCP powder, swallow tablets and capsules, or smoke the drug by applying it (in powder form) to a leafy substance such as marijuana, mint, parsley, or oregano. In addition, users increasingly are dipping marijuana or tobacco cigarettes in liquid PCP and smoking them.

What are the risks?

PCP is an addictive drug; its use often results in psychological dependence, craving, and compulsive PCP-seeking behavior. PCP produces unpleasant psychological effects and users often become violent or suicidal.

PCP poses particular risks for young people. Even moderate use of the drug can negatively affect the hormones associated with normal growth and development. PCP use also can impede the learning process in teenagers.

High doses of PCP can cause seizures, coma, and even death (often as a consequence of accidental injury or suicide while under the drug's effects). At high doses, PCP's effects may resemble the symptoms associated with schizophrenia, including delusions and paranoia.

Long-term use of PCP can lead to memory loss, difficulty with speech or thought, depression, and weight loss. These problems can persist for up to a year after an individual has stopped using PCP.

What is it called?

The most common names for PCP are angel dust, animal tranquilizer, embalming fluid, ozone, rocket fuel, and wack. Marijuana or tobacco cigarettes that are dipped in PCP are called illy, wet, or fry.

Psilocybin

What is psilocybin?

Psilocybin is a hallucinogenic substance obtained from certain types of mushrooms that are indigenous to tropical and subtropical regions of South America, Mexico, and the United States. These mushrooms typically contain 0.2 to 0.4 percent psilocybin and a trace amount of psilocyn, another hallucinogenic substance. Both psilocybin and psilocin can be produced synthetically, but law enforcement reporting currently does not indicate that this is occurring.

What does psilocybin look like?

Mushrooms containing psilocybin are available fresh or dried and have long, slender stems topped by caps with dark gills on the underside. Fresh mushrooms have white or whitish-gray stems; the caps are dark brown around the edges and light brown or white in the center. Dried mushrooms are generally rusty brown with isolated areas of off-white.

How is it abused?

Psilocybin mushrooms are ingested orally. They may be brewed as a tea or added to other foods to mask their bitter flavor. Some users coat the mushrooms with chocolate—this both masks the flavor and disguises the mushrooms as candy. Once the mushrooms are ingested, the body breaks down the psilocybin to produce psilocyn.

What are the risks?

Use of psilocybin is associated with negative physical and psychological consequences. The physical effects, which appear within 20 minutes of ingestion and last approximately six hours, include nausea, vomiting, muscle weakness, drowsiness, and lack of coordination. While there is no evidence that users may become physically dependent on psilocybin, tolerance for the drug does develop when it is ingested continuously over a short period of time.

The psychological consequences of psilocybin use include hallucinations and an inability to discern fantasy from reality. Panic reactions and psychosis also may occur, particularly if a user ingests a large dose.

In addition to the risks associated with ingestion of psilocybin, individuals who seek to abuse psilocybin mushrooms also risk poisoning if one of the many varieties of poisonous mushrooms is incorrectly identified as a psilocybin mushroom.

What is psilocybin called?

The most common names for psilocybin are magic mushroom, mushroom, and shrooms.

Chapter 45

Stimulants: An Overview

What are stimulants?

Stimulants are a class of drugs that elevate mood, increase feelings of well-being, and increase energy and alertness. Examples include cocaine, methamphetamine, amphetamines, methylphenidate, nicotine, and MDMA (3,4-methylenedioxymethamphetamine), better known as "ecstasy."

Cocaine comes in two forms. Powder cocaine is a hydrochloride salt, made from the leaf of the coca plant. "Crack" is a smokable form of cocaine that is processed with ammonia or baking soda and water and heated to remove the hydrochloride.

Methamphetamine is a powerful stimulant, originally derived from amphetamine. It comes in clear crystals or powder and easily dissolves in water or alcohol. Although most of the methamphetamine used in the United States comes from "superlabs," it is also made in small laboratories using inexpensive over-the-counter and often toxic ingredients (such as drain cleaner, battery acid, and antifreeze).

Amphetamines, such as Adderall, are stimulants that often come in pill form and are sometimes prescribed by doctors for medical problems, most commonly attention deficit hyperactivity disorder (ADHD). Amphetamines

About This Chapter: Information in this chapter is from "Stimulants," NIDA for Teens, National Institute on Drug Abuse, a component of the U.S. Department of Health and Human Services, 2009.

✎ What's It Mean?

Stimulants: Stimulants are a class of drugs that "stimulate" the body's central nervous system, which includes the brain and spinal cord. They increase the levels of catecholamines—a family of brain chemicals that includes dopamine. These chemicals are used in the brain processes to signal reward and motivation. By increasing catecholamine levels, stimulants can temporarily increase a person's energy level and alertness. Stimulants may also cause other changes in the body. The effects vary according to the specific drug, the amount of the drug, and how the drug is taken. For instance, stimulants that are snorted or injected have more immediate effects than drugs that are swallowed.

Stimulants include the caffeine found in coffee, medications such as methylphenidate (Ritalin, Concerta), and abused drugs, such as methamphetamine and cocaine. Stimulants can have useful properties—under the right circumstances. For example, doctors use some stimulants to treat disorders such as ADHD. However, when abused, stimulants can pose serious health risks to your brain and your body.

Source: Excerpted from "Health Effects Of Stimulants," an article in a Heads Up compilation from Scholastic and the National Institute on Drug Abuse. Order No. HURN09-07SC, 2009.

can also be abused—that is, used in a way other than as prescribed (e.g., crushed and snorted) or used by someone without a prescription.

Methylphenidate, such as Concerta or Ritalin, is another medication prescribed for people with ADHD. As seen with amphetamines, including Adderall, numerous studies have shown its effectiveness when used as prescribed. When it is abused, however, methylphenidate can lead to many of the same problems seen with other stimulants. More information about prescription drug abuse can be found at http://www.nida.nih.gov/drugpages/prescription.html.

What are the common street names?

Cocaine is generally sold on the street as a fine, white, crystalline powder, known as "coke," "C," "snow," "flake," "blow," "bump," "candy," "Charlie," "rock," and "toot." "Crack," the street name for the smokable form of cocaine, got its name from the crackling sound made when it's smoked. A "speedball" is cocaine or crack combined with heroin, or crack and heroin smoked together.

Methamphetamine is commonly known as "speed," "meth," "chalk," and "tina." In its smokable form, it's often called "ice," "crystal," "crank," "glass," "fire," and "go fast."

Street names for amphetamines include "speed," "bennies," "black beauties," "crosses," "hearts," "LA turnaround," "truck drivers," and "uppers."

Street names for methylphenidate include "rits," "vitamin R," and "west coast."

How are they abused?

Stimulants are abused in several ways, depending on the drug. They can be:

- Swallowed in pill form.

- "Snorted" in powder form, through the nostrils, where the drug is absorbed into the bloodstream through the nasal tissues.

- Injected, using a needle and syringe, to release the drug directly into a vein.

- Heated in crystal form and smoked (inhaled into the lungs).

Injecting or smoking a stimulant produces a rapid high—or rush—because the drug is absorbed into the bloodstream quickly, intensifying its effects. Snorting or swallowing stimulants produces a high that is less intense but lasts longer.

Powder cocaine is usually snorted or injected (also called "mainlining"), or it can be rubbed onto mucous tissues, such as the gums. Street dealers generally dilute cocaine with other substances (such as cornstarch, talcum powder, or sugar), with active drugs (such as procaine, a chemical that produces local anesthesia), or with other stimulants (such as amphetamines). Crack cocaine is often smoked in a glass pipe.

❖ It's A Fact!!

Cocaine Risks

Cocaine, sometimes called "coke" or "blow," comes in powder or crystal form. It can be snorted, smoked, or injected. Cocaine blocks the dopamine transporter that is responsible for recycling dopamine at the end of a signal between brain cells (called neurons). When this happens, dopamine builds up in the gap between neurons (called the synapse) and overstimulates the neurons. That can cause a powerful but temporary sense of euphoria.

Prescribed Use: Cocaine is sometimes used during nose, mouth, or eye surgery, since it constricts blood vessels and helps to control blood flow during the surgery. Cocaine is also a local anesthetic—which means that it can help to numb an area of the body.

Health Risks

- Cocaine can speed up heart rate and cause the heart to lose its natural rhythm. In rare cases, this can lead to a heart attack.

- Cocaine constricts blood vessels, which forces the heart to work harder to pump blood.

- Cocaine can cause chest pain and difficulty breathing.

- Cocaine can cause a potentially dangerous increase in body temperature.

- Regularly snorting cocaine can lead to loss of sense of smell, nosebleeds, and problems with swallowing. The overall irritation can lead to a chronically inflamed, runny nose.

- Repeated use or high doses of cocaine can cause irritability, restlessness, panic attacks, and paranoia.

Source: Excerpted from "Health Effects Of Stimulants," an article in a Heads Up compilation from Scholastic and the National Institute on Drug Abuse. Order No. HURN09-07SC, 2009.

Methamphetamine is swallowed, snorted, injected, or smoked. "Ice," a smokable form of methamphetamine, is a large, usually clear crystal of high purity that is smoked, like crack, in a glass pipe.

Amphetamines and methylphenidate are usually swallowed in pill form.

How many teens use them?

A 2009 National Institute on Drug Abuse (NIDA)-funded study reported that the following percentages of 8th, 10th, and 12th graders had abused these drugs at least once in the past year:

- **Powder Cocaine:** 1.6% of 8th graders, 2.7% of 10th graders, and 3.4% of 12th graders

- **Crack Cocaine:** 1.1% of 8th graders, 1.2% of 10th graders, and 1.3% of 12th graders

- **Methamphetamine:** 1.0% of 8th graders, 1.6% of 10th graders, and 1.2% of 12th graders

- **Amphetamines:** 4.1% of 8th graders, 7.1 % of 10th graders, and 6.6% of 12th graders

- **Nonmedical Use Of Ritalin:** 1.8% of 8th graders, 3.6% of 10th graders, and 2.1% of 12th graders

- **Nonmedical Use Of Adderall:** 2.0% of 8th graders, 5.7% of 10th graders, and 5.4% of 12th graders

How do stimulants produce euphoria?

Stimulants change the way the brain works by changing the way nerve cells communicate. Nerve cells, called neurons, send messages to each other by releasing chemicals called neurotransmitters. Neurotransmitters work by attaching to key sites on neurons called receptors.

There are many neurotransmitters, but dopamine is one that is directly affected by most stimulants. Dopamine makes people feel good when they do something they enjoy, like eating a piece of chocolate cake or riding a roller coaster. Stimulants cause a buildup of dopamine in the brain, which can make people who abuse stimulants feel intense pleasure and increased energy. They can also make people feel anxious and paranoid. And with repeated use, stimulants can disrupt the functioning of the brain's dopamine system, dampening users' ability to feel any pleasure at all. Users may try to compensate by taking more and more of the drug to experience the same pleasure.

What are the short-term effects?

In the short term, stimulants can produce feelings of tremendous joy, increased wakefulness, and decreased appetite. Users can become more talkative, energetic, or anxious and irritable. Other short-term effects of stimulants can include increased body temperature, heart rate, and blood pressure; dilated pupils; nausea; blurred vision; muscle spasms; and confusion.

✤ It's A Fact!!
Prescription Stimulant Risks

Stimulant medications are often prescribed to treat individuals with ADHD. For example, Adderall is a brand-name amphetamine medication, and Ritalin and Concerta are brand names for methylphenidate. Like all stimulants, these medications increase dopamine levels in the brain. When used according to a doctor's orders, the drugs can help a person with ADHD to focus and reduce their ADHD symptoms. However, when taken in high doses, or in ways other than as prescribed (or by someone for whom the drug was not prescribed), stimulant medications can have harmful effects. The effects are similar to other drugs of abuse, and can lead to addiction.

Prescribed Use: Prescription stimulants can reduce ADHD symptoms and increase focus and attention in people who have ADHD.

Health Risks

- Abuse of prescription stimulants can increase heart rate, blood pressure, and body temperature.

- Stimulant medications can decrease sleep and appetite, and abuse can lead to malnutrition and its consequences.

Source: Excerpted from "Health Effects Of Stimulants," an article in a Heads Up compilation from Scholastic and the National Institute on Drug Abuse. Order No. HURN09-07SC, 2009.

Stimulants can also cause the body's blood vessels to narrow, constricting the flow of blood, which forces the heart to work harder to pump blood through the body. The heart may work so hard that it temporarily loses its natural rhythm. This is called fibrillation and can be very dangerous because it stops the flow of blood through the body.

What are the long-term effects?

As with many other drugs of abuse, repeated stimulant abuse can cause addiction. That means that someone repeatedly seeks out and uses the drug despite its harmful effects. Repeated drug use changes the brain in ways that contribute to the drug craving and continued drug seeking and use that characterizes addiction. Other effects of long-term stimulant abuse can include paranoia, aggressiveness, extreme anorexia, thinking problems, visual and auditory hallucinations, delusions, and severe dental problems.

Repeated use of cocaine can lead to tolerance of its euphoric effects, causing the user to take higher doses or to use the drug more frequently (e.g., binge use) to get the same effects. Such use can lead to bizarre, erratic behavior. Some cocaine users experience panic attacks or episodes of full-blown paranoid psychosis, in which the individual loses touch with reality and hears sounds that aren't there (auditory hallucinations). Different ways of using cocaine can produce different adverse effects. For example, regularly snorting cocaine can lead to hoarseness, loss of the sense of smell, nosebleeds, and a chronically runny nose. Cocaine taken orally can cause reduced blood flow, leading to bowel problems.

Repeated use of methamphetamine can cause violent behavior, mood disturbances, and psychosis, which can include paranoia, auditory hallucinations, and delusions (e.g., the sensation of insects creeping on the skin, called "formication"). The paranoia can result in homicidal and suicidal thoughts. Methamphetamine can increase a person's sex drive and is linked to risky sexual behaviors and the transmission of infectious diseases, such as HIV. However, research also indicates that long-term methamphetamine use may be associated with decreased sexual function, at least in men.

Can these drugs be lethal?

Yes, in rare instances, sudden death can occur on the first use of cocaine or unexpectedly thereafter. And, like most drugs, stimulants can be lethal when taken in large doses or mixed with other substances. Stimulant overdoses can lead to heart problems, strokes, hyperthermia (elevated body temperature), and convulsions, which if not treated immediately can result in death. Abuse of both cocaine and alcohol compounds the danger, increasing the risk of overdose.

✤ It's A Fact!!

Methamphetamine Risks

Methamphetamine, often called "meth," comes in a crystalline powder that can be smoked, snorted, or injected. Like other stimulants, meth increases dopamine levels and can increase energy and cause a temporary feeling of euphoria. However, methamphetamine stays in the body longer than some of the other stimulants, and therefore can have more harmful effects on the central nervous system.

Prescribed Use: A doctor may prescribe methamphetamine in low doses to treat ADHD or narcolepsy, a disorder in which a person experiences extreme sleepiness during the day and may fall asleep uncontrollably. However, due to the many serious harmful effects of methamphetamine, and the availability of other medications with lower risk, doctors rarely prescribe methamphetamine.

Health Risks

- Methamphetamine can cause rapid or irregular heartbeat and increased blood pressure. These effects can lead to a heart attack.

- Methamphetamine can increase body temperature. In rare cases, hyperthermia can lead to liver, kidney, and cardiovascular failure and death.

- Methamphetamine can cause the gums to decay and the teeth to rot, a condition known as "meth mouth."

- Long-term use of methamphetamine can cause changes to the structure of the brain in areas involved with memory and emotions. This can lead to memory problems and erratic behavior.

- Long-term use of methamphetamine can cause paranoia, hallucinations, and violent behavior.

Source: Excerpted from "Health Effects Of Stimulants," an article in a Heads Up compilation from Scholastic and the National Institute on Drug Abuse. Order No. HURN09-07SC, 2009.

❖ It's A Fact!!

MDMA Risks

MDMA, or "ecstasy," comes in the form of a pill. In addition to affecting dopamine levels in the brain, MDMA affects the nerve cells in the brain that use the chemical serotonin to communicate with other nerve cells. Like other stimulants, the effects of MDMA can include increased energy and feelings of well-being.

Prescribed Use: No medical uses.

Health Risks

- MDMA can increase heart rate and blood pressure.

- MDMA can increase body temperature. In rare cases, this can lead to liver, kidney, and cardiovascular failure and death.

- MDMA can cause muscle tension and involuntary teeth clenching.

- Repeated MDMA use can disrupt sleep, memory, and mood (at least temporarily).

Source: Excerpted from "Health Effects Of Stimulants," an article in a Heads Up compilation from Scholastic and the National Institute on Drug Abuse. Order No. HURN09-07SC, 2009.

What are the differences between cocaine and methamphetamine?

They act in different ways to increase dopamine in the brain. Cocaine works by blocking the dopamine transporter; that is, it doesn't allow dopamine to be recycled back into the neuron after it has done its work. Methamphetamine interferes with this recycling process as well, but it also causes too much dopamine to be released. Another difference is that cocaine disappears from the brain quickly, while methamphetamine has a much longer duration of action. The longer presence in the brain ultimately makes methamphetamine more harmful to brain cells.

✤ It's A Fact!!
Nicotine Risks

Nicotine is a highly addictive stimulant found in cigarettes and chewing tobacco. Like other stimulants, nicotine increases dopamine in the brain. It also stimulates the body's adrenal glands to release epinephrine (also called adrenaline). Epinephrine is normally released when a person experiences a stressful situation. Epinephrine stimulates the central nervous system, increasing heart rate, breathing rate, and blood pressure.

Prescribed Use: Medicinal nicotine in the form of a patch or gum is used to help people stop smoking and using other tobacco products. The nicotine in these products helps reduce the person's withdrawal symptoms.

Health Risks

- Nicotine increases heart rate and blood pressure.
- Nicotine increases blood sugar levels.
- Chewing or smoking tobacco discolors teeth and causes tooth decay.
- Chewing or smoking tobacco can cause cancer of the lungs, mouth, and throat.

Source: Excerpted from "Health Effects Of Stimulants," an article in a Heads Up compilation from Scholastic and the National Institute on Drug Abuse. Order No. HURN09-07SC, 2009.

If a pregnant woman uses stimulants, will the baby be hurt?

In the United States between 2006 and 2007, 22.6% (or 20,000) of teens ages 15 to 17 used an illicit drug during their pregnancy. Scientists have found that exposure to cocaine during fetal development may lead to subtle but significant deficits later in life, including problems with attention and information processing—abilities that are important for success in school. Research is also underway on the effects of methamphetamine use during pregnancy. So far, the data suggest that it may affect fetal growth and contribute to poor quality of movement in infants.

Research in this area is particularly difficult to interpret because it is often hard to single out a drug's specific effects among the multiple factors that can interact to affect maternal, fetal, and child outcomes. These factors include exposure to all drugs of abuse, including nicotine and alcohol; extent of prenatal care; possible neglect or abuse of the child; exposure to violence in the environment; socioeconomic conditions; maternal nutrition; other health conditions; and exposure to sexually transmitted diseases.

✔ Quick Tip

Getting Help For Stimulant Abuse

If you or someone you know is abusing or addicted to stimulants, there are many drug treatment programs and support groups that can help. Currently behavioral therapies are the most effective approach to treating stimulant addiction. Treatment programs seek to engage people in therapy, reward abstinence, and/or to help change the way a drug user thinks and behaves when faced with situations that may lead to drug use.

With the exception of nicotine (tobacco addiction), there are no medications approved to treat stimulant addiction. However, scientists are actively working in this area. They are studying different types of medications to help prevent cravings, reduce relapse, and address some of the mood and other problems that people addicted to stimulants often have. Scientists believe that a combination of medications (when they become available) and behavioral therapies will likely prove to be the most effective approach to treating stimulant addiction in the future.

For more facts about stimulants and other drugs, visit http://teens.drugabuse.gov/facts.

Source: Excerpted from "Health Effects Of Stimulants," an article in a Heads Up compilation from Scholastic and the National Institute on Drug Abuse. Order No. HURN09-07SC, 2009.

What treatments are available for stimulant abuse?

Several behavioral therapies are effective in treating addiction to stimulants. These approaches are designed to help the person think differently, change his or her expectations and behaviors, and increase his or her skills in coping with various stresses in life. One form that is showing positive results in people addicted to either cocaine or methamphetamine is called contingency management, or motivational incentives (MI). These programs reward patients who refrain from using drugs by offering vouchers or prizes. MI may be particularly useful for helping patients to initially stop taking the drug and for helping them to stay in treatment.

Currently, there are no medications approved by the U.S. Food and Drug Administration to treat people who are addicted to stimulants, although that is an active area of research for NIDA.

Chapter 46

Cocaine, Crack, And Khat

Cocaine

What is cocaine?

Cocaine is a powerfully addictive stimulant that directly affects the brain. Cocaine was labeled the drug of the 1980s and 1990s because of its extensive popularity and use during that period. However, cocaine is not a new drug. In fact, it is one of the oldest known psychoactive substances. Coca leaves, the source of cocaine, have been chewed and ingested for thousands of years, and the purified chemical, cocaine hydrochloride, has been an abused substance for more than 100 years. In the early 1900s, for example, purified cocaine was the main active ingredient in most of the tonics and elixirs that were developed to treat a wide variety of illnesses.

Cocaine is generally sold on the street as a fine, white, crystalline powder and is also known as "coke," "C," "snow," "flake," or "blow." Street dealers generally dilute it with inert substances such as cornstarch, talcum powder, or sugar, or with active drugs such as procaine (a chemically related local anesthetic) or amphetamine (another stimulant). Some users combine cocaine with heroin in what is termed a "speedball."

About This Chapter: Information in this chapter is from "Cocaine: Abuse and Addiction," a research report from the National Institute on Drug Abuse, a component of the U.S. Department of Health and Human Services, May 2009; "Crack Cocaine Fast Facts," National Drug Intelligence Center, NDIC Product No. 2003-L0559-005, April 2003 (despite the date of this document, it still provides an accurate description of crack cocaine and its effects); and "NIDA InfoFacts: Khat," National Institute on Drug Abuse, December 2007.

There are two chemical forms of cocaine that are abused: the water-soluble hydrochloride salt and the water-insoluble cocaine base (or freebase). When abused, the hydrochloride salt, or powdered form of cocaine, can be injected or snorted. The base form of cocaine has been processed with ammonia or sodium bicarbonate (baking soda) and water, and then heated to remove the hydrochloride to produce a smokable substance. The term "crack," which is the street name given to freebase cocaine, refers to the crackling sound heard when the mixture is smoked.

How is cocaine abused?

The principal routes of cocaine administration are oral, intranasal, intravenous, and inhalation. Snorting, or intranasal administration, is the process of inhaling cocaine powder through the nostrils, where it is absorbed into the bloodstream through the nasal tissues. The drug also can be rubbed onto mucous tissues. Injecting, or intravenous use, releases the drug directly into the bloodstream and heightens the intensity of its effects. Smoking involves inhaling cocaine vapor or smoke into the lungs, where absorption into the bloodstream is as rapid as by injection. This rather immediate and euphoric effect is one of the reasons that crack became enormously popular in the mid-1980s.

Cocaine use ranges from occasional to repeated or compulsive use, with a variety of patterns between these extremes. Other than medical uses, there is no safe way to use cocaine. Any route of administration can lead to absorption of toxic amounts of cocaine, possible acute cardiovascular or cerebrovascular emergencies, and seizures—all of which can result in sudden death.

What is the scope of cocaine use in the United States?

The National Survey on Drug Use and Health (NSDUH) estimates that in 2007 there were 2.1 million current (past-month) cocaine users, of which approximately 610,000 were current crack users. Adults aged 18 to 25 years have a higher rate of current cocaine use than any other age group, with 1.7% of young adults reporting past month cocaine use. Overall, men report higher rates of current cocaine use than women. Ethnic/racial differences also occur, with the highest rates in those reporting two or more races (1.1%), followed by Hispanics (1.0%), Whites (0.9%), and African-Americans (0.8%).

The 2008 Monitoring the Future survey, which annually surveys teen attitudes and drug use, reports that while there has been a significant decline in the 30-day prevalence of powder cocaine use among 8th, 10th, and 12th graders from its peak use in the late 1990s, there was no significant change in current cocaine use from 2001 to 2008; however, crack use declined significantly during this timeframe among 8th and 12th graders.

Repeated cocaine use can produce addiction and other adverse health consequences. In 2007, according to the NSDUH, nearly 1.6 million Americans met Diagnostic and Statistical Manual of Mental Disorders criteria for dependence or abuse of cocaine (in any form) in the past 12 months. Further, data from the 2005 Drug Abuse Warning Network (DAWN) report showed that cocaine was involved in 448,481 of the total 1,449,154 visits to emergency departments for drug misuse or abuse. This translates to almost one in three drug misuse or abuse emergency department visits (31 percent) that involved cocaine.

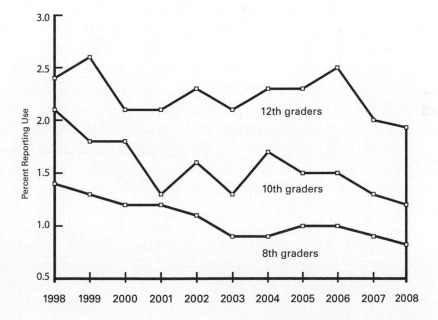

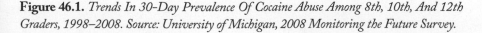

Figure 46.1. *Trends In 30-Day Prevalence Of Cocaine Abuse Among 8th, 10th, And 12th Graders, 1998–2008. Source: University of Michigan, 2008 Monitoring the Future Survey.*

What are the short-term effects of cocaine use?

Cocaine's effects appear almost immediately after a single dose and disappear within a few minutes or within an hour. Taken in small amounts, cocaine usually makes the user feel euphoric, energetic, talkative, and mentally alert, especially to the sensations of sight, sound, and touch. It can also temporarily decrease the need for food and sleep. Some users find that the drug helps them perform simple physical and intellectual tasks more quickly, although others experience the opposite effect.

The duration of cocaine's euphoric effect depends upon the route of administration. The faster the drug is absorbed, the more intense the resulting high, but also the shorter the duration. The high from snorting is relatively slow to arrive but may last 15 to 30 minutes; in contrast, the effects from smoking are more immediate but may last only 5 to 10 minutes.

The short term physiological effects of cocaine include constricted blood vessels, dilated pupils, and increased temperature, heart rate, and blood pressure. Large amounts of cocaine may intensify the user's high but can also lead to bizarre, erratic, and violent behavior. Some cocaine users report feelings of restlessness, irritability, and anxiousness. Users may also experience tremors, vertigo, muscle twitches, or paranoia. There can also be severe medical complications associated with cocaine abuse. Some of the most frequent are cardiovascular effects, including disturbances in heart rhythm and heart attacks; neurological effects, including strokes, seizures, headaches, and even coma; and gastrointestinal complications, including abdominal pain and nausea. In rare instances, sudden death can occur on the first use of cocaine or unexpectedly thereafter. Cocaine-related deaths are often a result of cardiac arrest or seizures followed by respiratory arrest.

Research has also revealed a potentially dangerous interaction between cocaine and alcohol. In fact, this mixture is the most common two-drug combination that results in drug-related death.

What are the long-term effects of cocaine use?

Cocaine is a powerfully addictive drug. Thus, it is unlikely that an individual will be able to reliably predict or control the extent to which he or she will continue to want or use the drug. And, if addiction takes hold, the risk for relapse is high even following long periods of abstinence. Recent studies have shown that during periods of abstinence, the memory of the cocaine experience or exposure to cues associated with drug use can trigger tremendous craving and relapse to drug use. With repeated exposure to cocaine, the brain starts to adapt, and the reward pathway becomes less sensitive to natural reinforcers and to the drug itself. Tolerance may develop, which means that higher doses and/or more frequent use of cocaine is needed to register the same level of pleasure experienced during initial use. At the same time, users can also become more sensitive (sensitization) to cocaine's anxiety-producing, convulsant, and other toxic effects.

Users take cocaine in "binges," during which the cocaine is used repeatedly and at increasingly higher doses. This can lead to increased irritability, restlessness, and paranoia—even a full-blown paranoid psychosis, in which the individual loses touch with reality and experiences auditory hallucinations. With increasing dosages or frequency of use, the risk of adverse psychological or physiological effects increases.

Different routes of cocaine administration can produce different adverse effects. Regularly snorting cocaine, for example, can lead to loss of sense of smell; nosebleeds; problems with swallowing; hoarseness; and an overall irritation of the nasal septum, which could result in a chronically inflamed, runny nose. Ingested cocaine can cause severe bowel gangrene, due to reduced blood flow. Persons who inject cocaine have puncture marks called "tracks," most commonly in their forearms, and may experience allergic reactions, either to the drug or to some additive in street cocaine, which in severe cases can result in death. Many chronic cocaine users lose their appetite and experience significant weight loss and malnourishment.

Are cocaine abusers at risk for contracting HIV/AIDS and hepatitis?

Yes, cocaine abusers are at increased risk for contracting such infectious diseases as human immunodeficiency virus/acquired immune deficiency syndrome (HIV/AIDS) and viral hepatitis. This risk stems not only from sharing contaminated needles and drug paraphernalia but also from engaging in risky behaviors as a result of intoxication. Research has shown that drug intoxication and addiction can compromise judgment and decision making, and potentially lead to risky sexual encounters, needle sharing, and trading sex for drugs—by both men and women. In fact, some studies are showing that among drug abusers, those who do not inject drugs are contracting HIV at rates equal to those who do inject drugs, further highlighting the role of sexual transmission of HIV in this population.

Additionally, hepatitis C (HCV) has spread rapidly among injecting drug users. Nearly 50 percent are exposed within two years of initiating injection drug use, and infection rates are between 40 and 98 percent in those injecting for more than two years. Although treatment for HCV is not effective for everyone and can have significant side effects, medical follow-up is essential for all those who are infected. There is no vaccine for the hepatitis C virus, and it is highly transmissible via injection; thus, HCV testing is recommended for any individual who has ever injected drugs.

What treatments are effective for cocaine abusers?

The widespread abuse of cocaine has stimulated extensive efforts to develop treatment programs for cocaine. As with any drug addiction, this is a complex disease that involves biological changes in the brain as well as myriad social, familial, and other environmental problems. Therefore, treatment of cocaine addiction must be comprehensive, and strategies need to assess the neurobiological, social, and medical aspects of the patient's drug abuse. Moreover, patients who have a variety of addictions often have other co-occurring mental disorders that require additional behavioral or pharmacological interventions.

Pharmacological Approaches: Presently, there are no Food and Drug Administration (FDA)-approved medications to treat cocaine addiction. Consequently, the National Institute on Drug Abuse (NIDA) is aggressively working to identify and test new medications to treat cocaine addiction safely and effectively.

Behavioral Interventions: Many behavioral treatments for cocaine addiction have proven to be effective in both residential and outpatient settings. These treatments include contingency management, or motivational incentives (MI), which use a voucher or prize-based system that rewards patients who abstain from cocaine and other drug use; cognitive-behavioral therapy (CBT), which is focused on helping cocaine-addicted individuals abstain and remain abstinent from cocaine and other substances; therapeutic communities (TCs), or residential programs, which usually require a 6- or 12-month stay and use the program's entire "community" as active components of treatment; and community-based recovery groups.

✎ What's It Mean?

Anesthetic: An agent that causes insensitivity to pain.

Coca: The plant, *Erythroxylon*, from which cocaine is derived. Also refers to the leaves of this plant.

Cocaethylene: A potent stimulant formed in the body when cocaine and alcohol are used together.

Crack: The slang term for a smokable form of cocaine.

Freebase: A solid, water-insoluble, and smokable form of cocaine that is produced when its hydrochloride salt form is processed with ammonia or sodium bicarbonate, and water, then heated to remove the hydrochloride. (Also, see "crack.")

Hydrochloride salt: A powdered, water-soluble form of cocaine that can be injected or snorted.

Polydrug user: An individual who uses more than one drug.

Rush: A surge of pleasure that rapidly follows administration of some drugs.

Stimulant: A class of drugs that increase or enhance the activity of monamines (such as dopamine) in the brain. Stimulants increase arousal, heart rate, blood pressure, and respiration, and decrease appetite. Includes some medications used to treat attention deficit hyperactivity disorder (e.g., methylphenidate and amphetamines), as well as cocaine and methamphetamine.

Tolerance: A condition in which higher doses of a drug are required to produce the same effect as during initial use.

Vertigo: The sensation of dizziness.

Source: National Institute on Drug Abuse, May 2009.

Crack Cocaine

What is crack cocaine?

Crack cocaine is a highly addictive and powerful stimulant that is derived from powdered cocaine using a simple conversion process. Crack emerged as a drug of abuse in the mid-1980s. It is abused because it produces an immediate high and because it is easy and inexpensive to produce, rendering it readily available and affordable.

How is it produced?

Crack is produced by dissolving powdered cocaine in a mixture of water and ammonia or sodium bicarbonate (baking soda). The mixture is boiled until a solid substance forms. The solid is removed from the liquid, dried, and then broken into the chunks (rocks) that are sold as crack cocaine.

What does it look like?

Crack typically is available as rocks. Crack rocks are white (or off-white) and vary in size and shape.

How is crack abused?

Crack is nearly always smoked. Smoking crack cocaine delivers large quantities of the drug to the lungs, producing an immediate and intense euphoric effect.

Who uses crack?

Individuals of all ages use crack cocaine—data reported in the National Household Survey on Drug Abuse indicate that an estimated 6,222,000 U.S. residents aged 12 and older used crack at least once in their lifetime. The survey also revealed that hundreds of thousands of teenagers and young adults use crack cocaine—150,000 individuals aged 12 to 17 and 1,003,000 individuals aged 18 to 25 used the drug at least once.

Crack cocaine use among high school students is a particular problem. Nearly 4% of high school seniors in the United States used the drug at least once in their lifetime, and more than 1% used the drug in the past month, according to the University of Michigan's Monitoring the Future Survey.

What are the risks?

Cocaine, in any form, is a powerfully addictive drug, and addiction seems to develop more quickly when the drug is smoked (as crack is) than snorted (as powdered cocaine typically is). In addition to the usual risks associated with cocaine use (constricted blood vessels; increased temperature, heart rate, and blood pressure; and risk of cardiac arrest and seizure), crack users may experience acute respiratory problems, including coughing, shortness of breath, and lung trauma and bleeding. Crack cocaine smoking also can cause aggressive and paranoid behavior.

What are street terms used for crack cocaine?

- 24-7
- Badrock
- Beat
- Candy
- Chemical
- Cloud
- Cookies
- Crumbs
- Crunch and munch
- Devil drug
- Dice
- Electric kool-aid

- Fat bags
- French fries
- Glo
- Gravel
- Grit
- Hail
- Hard ball
- Hard rock
- Hotcakes
- Ice cube
- Jelly beans
- Nuggets

- Paste
- Piece
- Prime time
- Product
- Raw
- Rock(s)
- Scrabble
- Sleet
- Snow coke
- Tornado
- Troop

Khat

Khat (pronounced "cot") is a stimulant drug derived from a shrub (*Catha edulis*) that is native to East Africa and southern Arabia. Although the khat plant itself is not scheduled under the Controlled Substances Act, one of its chemical constituents, cathinone, is a Schedule I drug. The Federal Government treats khat as equivalent to cathinone and therefore considers its use illegal.

What are the health/behavioral effects of khat?

The main psychoactive ingredients in khat are cathine and cathinone, chemicals that are structurally similar to, but less potent than, amphetamine, yet result in similar psychomotor stimulant effects. Chewing khat leaves induces a state of euphoria and elation as well as feelings of increased alertness and arousal. The user also experiences an increase in blood pressure and heart rate. The effects begin to subside after about 90 minutes to 3 hours, but can last 24 hours. At the end of a khat session, the user may experience a depressive mood, irritability, loss of appetite, and difficulty sleeping.

There are a number of adverse physical effects that have been associated with heavy or long-term use of khat, including tooth decay and periodontal disease; gastrointestinal disorders such as constipation, ulcers, inflammation of the stomach, and increased risk of upper gastrointestinal tumors; and cardiovascular disorders such as irregular heartbeat, decreased blood flow, and myocardial infarction. There is also consistent epidemiologic evidence for a weak association between chronic khat use and mental disorders. Although there is no evidence that khat use causes mental illness, chewing khat leaves may worsen symptoms in patients who have preexisting psychiatric conditions.

It is unclear whether khat causes tolerance, physical dependency, addiction, or withdrawal, but nightmares and slight trembling have been reported several days after ceasing to chew.

What is the extent of use?

It is estimated that 10 million people worldwide chew khat. It is commonly found in the southwestern part of the Arabian Peninsula and in East Africa, where it has been used for centuries as part of an established cultural tradition. In one large study in Yemen, 82% of men and 43% of women reported at least one lifetime (at least once during a respondent's lifetime) episode of khat use. Its current use among particular migrant communities in the United States and in Europe has caused alarm among policymakers and health care professionals. No reliable estimates of prevalence in the United States exist.

Chapter 47

Methamphetamine And Yaba

Methamphetamine

What is methamphetamine?

Methamphetamine is a highly addictive stimulant that affects the central nervous system. Although most of the methamphetamine used in this country comes from foreign or domestic superlabs, the drug is also easily made in small clandestine laboratories, with relatively inexpensive over-the-counter ingredients. These factors combine to make methamphetamine a drug with high potential for widespread abuse.

Methamphetamine is commonly known as "speed," "meth," and "chalk." In its smoked form, it is often referred to as "ice," "crystal," "crank," and "glass." It is a white, odorless, bitter-tasting crystalline powder that easily dissolves in water or alcohol. The drug was developed early last century from its parent drug, amphetamine, and was used originally in nasal decongestants and bronchial inhalers. Like amphetamine, methamphetamine causes increased activity and talkativeness, decreased appetite, and a general sense of well-being. However, methamphetamine differs from amphetamine in that at comparable

About This Chapter: Information in this chapter is from "Methamphetamine Abuse and Addiction," a research report from the National Institute on Drug Abuse, a component of the U.S. Department of Health and Human Services, September 2006; and "Yaba Fast Facts," National Drug Intelligence Center, NDIC Product No. 2003-L0559-015, June 2003. Despite the date of this document, the facts about yaba are still pertinent.

doses, much higher levels of methamphetamine get into the brain, making it a more potent stimulant drug. It also has longer lasting and more harmful effects on the central nervous system.

Methamphetamine is a Schedule II stimulant, which means it has a high potential for abuse and is available only through a prescription. It is indicated for the treatment of narcolepsy (a sleep disorder) and attention deficit hyperactivity disorder (ADHD), but these medical uses are limited, and the doses are much lower than those typically abused.

What is the scope of methamphetamine abuse in the United States?

According to the 2005 National Survey on Drug Use and Health (NSDUH), an estimated 10.4 million people aged 12 or older (4.3% of the population) have tried methamphetamine at some time in their lives. Approximately 1.3 million reported past-year methamphetamine use, and 512,000 reported current (past-month) use. Moreover, the 2005 Monitoring the Future (MTF) survey of student drug use and attitudes reported 4.5% of high school seniors had used methamphetamine within their lifetimes, while 8th graders and 10th graders reported lifetime use at 3.1% and 4.1%, respectively. However, neither of these surveys has documented an overall increase in the abuse of methamphetamine over the past few years. In fact, both surveys showed recent declines in methamphetamine abuse among the nation's youth.

In contrast, evidence from emergency departments and treatment programs attest to the growing impact of methamphetamine abuse in the country. The Drug Abuse Warning Network (DAWN), which collects information on drug-related episodes from hospital emergency departments (EDs) throughout the nation, has reported a greater than 50 percent increase in the number of ED visits related to methamphetamine abuse between 1995 and 2002, reaching approximately 73,000 ED visits, or four percent of all drug-related visits in 2004.

How is methamphetamine abused?

Methamphetamine comes in many forms and can be smoked, snorted, injected, or orally ingested. The preferred method of methamphetamine abuse varies by geographical region and has changed over time. Smoking methamphetamine, which leads to very fast uptake of the drug in the brain, has become more common in recent years, amplifying methamphetamine's addiction potential and adverse health consequences.

The drug also alters mood in different ways, depending on how it is taken. Immediately after smoking the drug or injecting it intravenously, the user experiences an intense rush or "flash" that lasts only a few minutes and is described as extremely pleasurable. Snorting or oral ingestion produces euphoria—a high but not an intense rush. Snorting produces effects within three to five minutes, and oral ingestion produces effects within 15 to 20 minutes.

As with similar stimulants, methamphetamine most often is used in a "binge and crash" pattern. Because the pleasurable effects of methamphetamine disappear even before the drug concentration in the blood falls significantly, users try to maintain the high by taking more of the drug. In some cases, abusers indulge in a form of binging known as a "run," foregoing food and sleep while continuing abuse for up to several days.

How is methamphetamine different from other stimulants, such as cocaine?

Methamphetamine is structurally similar to amphetamine and the neurotransmitter dopamine, but it is quite different from cocaine. Although these stimulants have similar behavioral and physiological effects, there are some major differences in the basic mechanisms of how they work. In contrast to cocaine, which is quickly removed and almost completely metabolized in the body, methamphetamine has a much longer duration of action and a larger percentage of the drug remains unchanged in the body. This results in methamphetamine being present in the brain longer, which ultimately leads to prolonged stimulant effects. And although both methamphetamine and cocaine increase levels of the brain chemical dopamine, animal studies reveal much higher levels of dopamine following administration of methamphetamine due to the different mechanisms of action within nerve cells in response to these drugs. Cocaine prolongs dopamine actions in the brain by blocking dopamine re-uptake. While at low doses, methamphetamine blocks dopamine re-uptake, methamphetamine also increases the release of dopamine, leading to much higher concentrations in the synapse, which can be toxic to nerve terminals.

✤ It's A Fact!!
One Pound Of Methamphetamine
Yields Five Pounds Of Toxic Waste

Manufacturing methamphetamine always produces toxic waste. Ingredients might include toluene, iodine, red phosphorus (used in road flares), sodium hydroxide, lithium/sodium metal, hydrochloric acid, anhydrous ammonia (a fertilizer), drain cleaner, battery acid, lye, pool acid, and antifreeze—many of which are severe eye, nose, and throat irritants or cause skin burns or breathing difficulty.

A "meth lab" is an illegal site where the drug is manufactured. Meth labs have been found in garages, kitchens, vehicles, hotel and motel rooms, storage lockers, campgrounds, abandoned dumps, restrooms, and mobile homes.

Toxic contamination remains behind from the manufacturing process on surfaces in the meth lab itself, including furniture, curtains, bedspreads, flooring, air vents, eating surfaces, and walls. Cleaning up a meth lab site requires hazardous waste protection and costs an average of $3,000—but can cost more than $100,000. In 2004 alone, there were more than 10,000 meth lab cleanups at a cost of $18.6 million.

Leftover chemicals and byproduct sludge from methamphetamine manufacture have been found along highways, in parks and forests, in the ground and groundwater, and in sewer systems. These solvents and other toxic byproducts pose long-term hazards to communities because they can persist in soil and groundwater for years. Of particular concern are labs in agricultural areas, because the hazardous wastes are often dumped where crops are grown and in the water sources used to nourish those crops.

Source: From a Heads Up compilation from Scholastic and the National Institute on Drug Abuse, 2006.

What are the immediate (short-term) effects of methamphetamine abuse?

As a powerful stimulant, methamphetamine, even in small doses, can increase wakefulness and physical activity and decrease appetite. Methamphetamine can also cause a variety of cardiovascular problems, including rapid heart rate, irregular heartbeat, and increased blood pressure. Hyperthermia (elevated body temperature) and convulsions may occur with methamphetamine overdose, and if not treated immediately, can result in death.

Table 47.1. Methamphetamine Vs. Cocaine

Methamphetamine	Cocaine
Stimulant	Stimulant and local anesthetic
Man-made	Plant-derived
Smoking produces a long-lasting high	Smoking produces a brief high
50% of the drug is removed from the body in 12 hours	50% of the drug is removed from the body in one hour
Increases dopamine release and blocks dopamine re-uptake	Blocks dopamine re-uptake
Limited medical use	Limited use as a local anesthetic in some surgical procedures

Most of the pleasurable effects of methamphetamine are believed to result from the release of very high levels of the neurotransmitter dopamine. Dopamine is involved in motivation, motor function, and the experience of pleasure, and is a common mechanism of action for most drugs of abuse. The elevated release of dopamine produced by methamphetamine is also thought to contribute to the drug's deleterious effects on nerve terminals in the brain.

What are the long-term effects of methamphetamine abuse?

Long-term methamphetamine abuse has many negative consequences, including addiction. Addiction is a chronic, relapsing disease, characterized by compulsive drug seeking and use, accompanied by functional and molecular changes in the brain. In addition to being addicted to methamphetamine, chronic abusers exhibit symptoms that can include anxiety, confusion, insomnia, mood disturbances, and violent behavior. They also can display a number of psychotic features, including paranoia, visual and auditory hallucinations, and delusions (for example, the sensation of insects creeping under the skin). Psychotic symptoms can sometimes last for months or years after methamphetamine abuse has ceased, and stress has been shown to precipitate spontaneous recurrence of methamphetamine psychosis in formerly psychotic methamphetamine abusers.

With chronic abuse, tolerance to methamphetamine's pleasurable effects can develop. In an effort to intensify the desired effects, abusers may take higher doses of the drug, take it more frequently, or change their method of drug intake. Withdrawal from methamphetamine occurs when a chronic abuser stops taking the drug; symptoms of withdrawal include depression, anxiety, fatigue, and an intense craving for the drug.

Chronic methamphetamine abuse also significantly changes the brain. Specifically, brain imaging studies have demonstrated alterations in the activity of the dopamine system that are associated with reduced motor speed and impaired verbal learning. Recent studies in chronic methamphetamine abusers have also revealed severe structural and functional changes in areas of the brain associated with emotion and memory, which may account for many of the emotional and cognitive problems observed in chronic methamphetamine abusers.

Are methamphetamine abusers at risk for contracting HIV/AIDS and hepatitis B and C?

Increased HIV and hepatitis B and C transmission are consequences of increased methamphetamine abuse, not only in individuals who inject the drug, but also in non-injecting methamphetamine abusers. Among injection drug

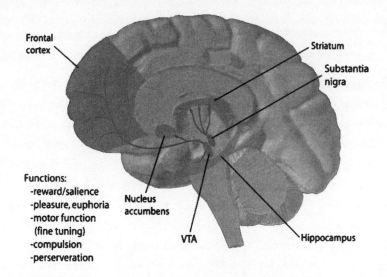

Figure 47.1. *In the brain, dopamine plays an important role in the regulation of reward and movement. As part of the reward pathway, dopamine is manufactured in nerve cell bodies located within the ventral tegmental area (VTA) and is released in the nucleus accumbens and the prefrontal cortex. Its motor functions are linked to a separate pathway, with cell bodies in the substantia nigra that manufacture and release dopamine into the striatum.*

users, infection with HIV and other infectious diseases is spread primarily through the re-use of contaminated syringes, needles, or other paraphernalia by more than one person. However, regardless of how it is taken, the intoxicating effects of methamphetamine can alter judgment and inhibition and lead people to engage in unsafe behaviors.

What treatments are effective for methamphetamine abusers?

At this time, the most effective treatments for methamphetamine addiction are behavioral therapies such as cognitive behavioral and contingency management interventions. For example, the Matrix Model, a comprehensive behavioral treatment approach that combines behavioral therapy, family education, individual counseling, 12-step support, drug testing, and encouragement for nondrug-related activities, has been shown to be effective in reducing methamphetamine abuse. Contingency management interventions, which provide tangible incentives in exchange for engaging in treatment and maintaining abstinence, have also been shown to be effective.

There are currently no specific medications that counteract the effects of methamphetamine or that prolong abstinence from and reduce the abuse of methamphetamine by an individual addicted to the drug. However, there are a number of medications that are Food and Drug Administration (FDA)-approved for other illnesses that might also be useful in treating methamphetamine addiction. Recent study findings reveal that bupropion, the anti-depressant marketed as Wellbutrin®, reduced the methamphetamine-induced "high" as well as drug cravings elicited by drug-related cues. This medication and others are currently in clinical trials, while new compounds are being developed and studied in preclinical models.

Yaba

What is yaba?

Yaba is a combination of methamphetamine (a powerful and addictive stimulant) and caffeine. Yaba, which means crazy medicine in Thai, is produced in Southeast and East Asia. The drug is popular in Asian communities in the United States and increasingly is available at raves and techno parties.

What does yaba look like?

Yaba is sold as tablets. These tablets are generally no larger than a pencil eraser. They are brightly colored, usually reddish-orange or green. Yaba tablets typically bear one of a variety of logos; R and WY are common logos.

How is yaba used?

Yaba tablets typically are consumed orally. The tablets sometimes are flavored like candy (grape, orange, or vanilla). Another common method is called chasing the dragon. Users place the yaba tablet on aluminum foil and heat it from below. As the tablet melts, vapors rise and are inhaled. The drug also may be administered by crushing the tablets into powder, which is then snorted or mixed with a solvent and injected.

✎ What's It Mean?

Attention Deficit Hyperactivity Disorder: A disorder that often presents in early childhood, characterized by inattention, hyperactivity, and impulsivity.

Central Nervous System (CNS): The brain and spinal cord.

Craving: A powerful, often uncontrollable desire for drugs.

Dopamine: A neurotransmitter present in regions of the brain that regulate movement, emotion, motivation, and feelings of pleasure.

Psychosis: A mental disorder characterized by symptoms such as delusions or hallucinations and disordered thinking.

Rush: A surge of euphoric pleasure that rapidly follows administration of a drug.

Tolerance: A condition in which higher doses of a drug are required to produce the same effect as experienced initially.

Toxic: Damage to an organ or group of organs.

Withdrawal: A variety of symptoms that occur after chronic abuse of an addictive drug is reduced or stopped.

Source: National Institute on Drug Abuse, September 2006.

What are the risks?

Individuals who use yaba face the same risks as users of other forms of methamphetamine: rapid heart rate, increased blood pressure, and damage to the small blood vessels in the brain that can lead to stroke. Chronic use of the drug can result in inflammation of the heart lining. Overdoses can cause hyperthermia (elevated body temperature), convulsions, and death. Individuals who use yaba also may have episodes of violent behavior, paranoia, anxiety, confusion, and insomnia.

Although most users administer yaba orally, those who inject the drug expose themselves to additional risks, including contracting HIV (human immunodeficiency virus), hepatitis B and C, and other blood-borne viruses.

What is it called?

The most common names for yaba are crazy medicine and Nazi speed.

Is yaba illegal?

Yes, yaba is illegal because it contains methamphetamine, a Schedule II substance under the Controlled Substances Act. Schedule II drugs, which include cocaine and PCP, have a high potential for abuse. Abuse of these drugs may lead to severe psychological or physical dependence.

Chapter 48

Opiates:
Heroin, Methadone, And Buprenorphine

Heroin

Heroin is an opiate drug that is synthesized from morphine, a naturally occurring substance extracted from the seed pod of the Asian opium poppy plant. Heroin usually appears as a white or brown powder or as a black sticky substance, known as "black tar heroin."

How is heroin abused?

Heroin can be injected, snorted/sniffed, or smoked—routes of administration that rapidly deliver the drug to the brain. Injecting is the use of a needle to administer the drug directly into the bloodstream. Snorting is the process of inhaling heroin powder through the nose, where it is absorbed into the bloodstream through the nasal tissues. Smoking involves inhaling heroin smoke into the lungs. All three methods of administering heroin can lead to addiction and other severe health problems.

About This Chapter: Information in this chapter is from "NIDA InfoFacts: Heroin," National Institute on Drug Abuse, a component of the U.S. Department of Health and Human Services, March 2010; "Introduction to Methadone," Substance Abuse and Mental Health Services Administration, 2006; and "Buprenorphine: Treatment for Opiate Addiction Right in the Doctor's Office," National Institute on Drug Abuse, August 2006.

How does heroin affect the brain?

Heroin enters the brain, where it is converted to morphine and binds to receptors known as opioid receptors. These receptors are located in many areas of the brain (and in the body), especially those involved in the perception of pain and in reward. Opioid receptors are also located in the brain stem—important for automatic processes critical for life, such as breathing (respiration), blood pressure, and arousal. Heroin overdoses frequently involve a suppression of respiration.

After an intravenous injection of heroin, users report feeling a surge of euphoria ("rush") accompanied by dry mouth, a warm flushing of the skin, heaviness of the extremities, and clouded mental functioning. Following this initial euphoria, the user goes "on the nod," an alternately wakeful and drowsy state. Users who do not inject the drug may not experience the initial rush, but other effects are the same.

With regular heroin use, tolerance develops, in which the user's physiological (and psychological) response to the drug decreases, and more heroin is needed to achieve the same intensity of effect. Heroin users are at high risk for addiction—it is estimated that about 23% of individuals who use heroin become dependent on it.

What other adverse effects does heroin have on health?

Heroin abuse is associated with serious health conditions, including fatal overdose, spontaneous abortion, and—particularly in users who inject the drug—infectious diseases, including HIV/AIDS and hepatitis. Chronic users may develop collapsed veins, infection of the heart lining and valves, abscesses, and liver or kidney disease. Pulmonary complications, including various types of pneumonia, may result from the poor health of the abuser as well as from heroin's depressing effects on respiration. In addition to the effects of the drug itself, street heroin often contains toxic contaminants or additives that can clog blood vessels leading to the lungs, liver, kidneys, or brain, causing permanent damage to vital organs.

Chronic use of heroin leads to physical dependence, a state in which the body has adapted to the presence of the drug. If a dependent user reduces or stops use of the drug abruptly, he or she may experience severe symptoms of withdrawal. These symptoms—which can begin as early as a few hours after the last drug administration—can include restlessness, muscle and bone pain, insomnia, diarrhea and vomiting, cold flashes with goose bumps ("cold turkey"), and kicking movements ("kicking the habit"). Users also experience severe craving for the drug during withdrawal, which can precipitate continued abuse and/or relapse. Major withdrawal symptoms peak between 48 and 72 hours after the last dose of the drug and typically subside after about one week. Some individuals, however, may show persistent withdrawal symptoms for months. Although heroin withdrawal is considered less dangerous than alcohol or barbiturate withdrawal, sudden withdrawal by heavily dependent users who are in poor health is occasionally fatal.

What treatment options exist?

A range of treatments exist for heroin addiction, including medications and behavioral therapies. Science has taught us that when medication treatment is combined with other supportive services, patients are often able to stop using heroin (or other opiates) and return to stable and productive lives.

Treatment usually begins with medically assisted detoxification to help patients withdraw from the drug safely. Medications such as clonidine and buprenorphine can be used to help minimize symptoms of withdrawal. However, detoxification alone is not treatment and has not been shown to be effective in preventing relapse—it is merely the first step.

Medications to help prevent relapse include the following:

- **Methadone** has been used for more than 30 years to treat heroin addiction. It is a synthetic opiate medication that binds to the same receptors as heroin; when taken orally, it has a gradual onset of action and sustained effects, reducing the desire for other opioid drugs while preventing withdrawal symptoms. Properly administered, methadone is not intoxicating or sedating, and its effects do not interfere with ordinary daily activities. Methadone maintenance treatment is usually conducted in specialized opiate treatment programs. The most effective methadone maintenance programs include individual and/or group counseling, as well as provision of or referral to other needed medical, psychological, and social services.

- **Buprenorphine** is a more recently approved treatment for heroin addiction (and other opiates). Compared with methadone, buprenorphine produces less risk for overdose and withdrawal effects and produces a lower level of physical dependence, so patients who discontinue the medication generally have fewer withdrawal symptoms than those who stop taking methadone. The development of buprenorphine and its authorized use in physicians' offices give opiate-addicted patients more medical options and extend the reach of addiction medication. Its accessibility may even prompt attempts to obtain treatment earlier. However, not all patients respond to buprenorphine—some continue to require treatment with methadone.

- **Naltrexone** is approved for treating heroin addiction but has not been widely used due to poor patient compliance. This medication blocks opioids from binding to their receptors and thus prevents an addicted individual from feeling the effects of the drug. Naltrexone as a treatment for opioid addiction is usually prescribed in outpatient medical settings, although initiation of the treatment often begins after medical detoxification in a residential setting. To prevent withdrawal symptoms, individuals must be medically detoxified and opioid-free for several days before taking naltrexone.

- **Naloxone** is a shorter-acting opioid receptor blocker, used to treat cases of overdose.

For pregnant heroin abusers, methadone maintenance combined with prenatal care and a comprehensive drug treatment program can improve many of the detrimental maternal and neonatal outcomes associated with untreated heroin abuse. Preliminary evidence suggests that buprenorphine may also be a safe and effective treatment during pregnancy, although infants exposed to either methadone or buprenorphine prenatally may still require treatment for withdrawal symptoms.

There are many effective behavioral treatments available for heroin addiction, usually in combination with medication. These treatments can be delivered in residential or outpatient settings.

How widespread is heroin abuse?

Monitoring The Future Survey*: According to the Monitoring the Future survey, there was little change between 2008 and 2009 in the proportion of 8th- and 12th-grade students reporting lifetime**, past-year, and past-month use of heroin. There also were no significant changes in past-year and past-month use among 10th graders; however, lifetime use increased significantly among this age group, from 1.2% to 1.5%. Survey measures indicate that injection use rose significantly among this population at the same time.

*These data are from the 2009 Monitoring the Future survey, funded by the National Institute on Drug Abuse, National Institutes of Health, Department of Health and Human Services, and conducted annually by the University of Michigan's Institute for Social Research. The survey has tracked 12th graders' illicit drug use and related attitudes since 1975; in 1991, 8th and 10th graders were added to the study. The latest data are online at www.drugabuse.gov.

**"Lifetime" refers to use at least once during a respondent's lifetime. "Past year" refers to use at least once during the year preceding an individual's response to the survey. "Past month" refers to use at least once during the 30 days preceding an individual's response to the survey.

National Survey On Drug Use And Health (NSDUH)***: According to the 2008 National Survey on Drug Use and Health, the number of current (past-month) heroin users aged 12 or older in the United States increased from 153,000 in 2007 to 213,000 in 2008. There were 114,000 first-time users of heroin aged 12 or older in 2008.

***NSDUH (formerly known as the National Household Survey on Drug Abuse) is an annual survey of Americans age 12 and older conducted by the Substance Abuse and Mental Health Services Administration.

Table 48.1. Heroin Use By Students, 2009: Monitoring The Future Survey

	8th Grade	10th Grade	12th Grade
Lifetime	1.3%	1.5%	1.2%
Past Year	0.7	0.9	0.7
Past Month	0.4	0.4	0.4

Methadone

Methadone is a long-acting opioid medication that is used as a pain reliever and, together with counseling and other psychosocial services, is used to treat individuals addicted to heroin and certain prescription drugs.

What is methadone maintenance treatment?

Methadone maintenance treatment (MMT) helps normalize your body's neurological and hormonal functions that have been impaired by the use of heroin or misuse of other short-acting opioids. Opioids are a group of drugs that act on the central nervous system. They include opiates such as codeine, morphine, and heroin as well as synthetic drugs such as oxycodone, OxyContin, hydrocodone, and methadone.

Appropriate MMT provides several benefits:

- Reduces or eliminates craving for opioid drugs
- Prevents the onset of withdrawal for 24 hours or more
- Blocks the effects of other opioids
- Promotes increased physical and emotional health
- Raises the overall quality of life of the patient

Is methadone maintenance treatment right for me?

Have you been through detoxification and found you couldn't feel normal? MMT can allow you to regain a sense of normalcy. Have you been using opioids such as heroin, codeine, or oxycodone but can't seem to stop? MMT can help you quit using those drugs and focus your life.

Are you pregnant and using heroin? Seek MMT right away to prevent miscarriage and protect your baby from life-threatening withdrawal.

Have you tested positive for HIV or hepatitis C? If you have tested positive, MMT can allow you to regain your quality of life and begin essential treatment of your viral infection. If you have not tested positive, MMT can help you stop using needles, which is the primary route of infection for drug users.

Beginning MMT can help stabilize and improve your health and can move you toward getting the care you need.

How do I start methadone maintenance treatment?

Depending on where you live, you may have a choice of methadone providers, or you may live in an area where methadone treatment is not available. If you have not already made contact with a doctor or clinic that treats opioid addiction, find out whether treatment is available nearby.

Treatment includes:

Assessment: Assessment includes determining your history with drug use as well as a physical examination by a doctor. You should be asked about medical problems that are commonly associated with opioid addictions, and you may be asked to consent to a blood test to check for HIV, hepatitis, and other infectious or sexually transmitted diseases.

Dosing: For safety, your first dose of methadone will be low or moderate. New patients usually start at a dose not to exceed 30 to 40 milligrams. A larger dose of 60 to 120 milligrams a day may be required for long-term maintenance. You and your physician should determine what dose works best for you.

Drug Testing: Routine tests of urine or oral fluids will show whether you have been using other illicit or inappropriate drugs and whether you have been taking your methadone. You may have to give supervised samples to ensure they are yours.

Confidentiality: Drug treatment patients are protected by special federal confidentiality regulations.

What is living with methadone like?

Take Home Doses: At the start of treatment, you will have to go to the clinic daily to take your dose under observation. This daily contact confirms to the staff that you are taking the dose ordered by the physician. It also helps the staff to see if your dose is enough or too much and whether you are experiencing side effects, in which case an adjustment may be necessary. After a few months, your provider may let you take home or "carry" doses for unsupervised use.

Safety And Storage: Your maintenance dose of methadone could seriously harm or kill someone who has no tolerance for the drug. Take precautions:

- Never transfer your medication to a container that might make it easier to mistake what's inside.

- Keep your doses in a locked box, such as one sold for fishing tackle or cash.

Hospital Stays: If you are admitted to the hospital, let the staff there know that you are a methadone patient. This is vital so that you can receive your dose and because other drugs can be dangerous if combined with methadone. Urge the hospital staff to talk with your MMT doctor about your medication and care.

Dealing With Side Effects: Methadone maintenance carries some side effects:

- **Constipation:** Eat foods that are high in fiber and drink plenty of water. You also should avoid foods that are high in fat; they are harder to digest and tend to make your system sluggish.

- **Excessive Sweating:** Adjusting the dose may stop the sweating, and there are other medications available to help control this.

- **Changes In Sex Drive:** Some people on methadone have little sex drive and are unable to have an orgasm. You may be taking a medication that affects your sex drive. Talk with your doctor about possible treatments that will improve this side effect.

Can I work when I'm on methadone?

Once you're on a stable dose of methadone, it shouldn't affect the work you do or how well you do your job. For most jobs, there's no need to mention that you take methadone. Your employer has no right to know.

Does methadone relieve pain?

Methadone can provide effective pain relief. Yet, once you are on a stable dose of methadone, you may be tolerant to its pain-relieving effects and may require additional pain medication. Some MMT patients need more pain medication than patients who are not a part of MMT.

Is it dangerous to mix methadone with other drugs?

Methadone interacts with many medications. This can change the safety of the methadone you are taking and potentially can cause withdrawal. It is important to tell your doctor about all of the drugs you take. Combining methadone with some drugs can result in withdrawal syndrome.

How long will I be on methadone?

The longer you've been dependent on opioids, the more likely it is that you would benefit from being on methadone. Those who withdraw from methadone after short-term treatment are more likely to return to drug use than those who stay in treatment until they have obtained the optimal benefits.

Recovery to a normal life is possible. You should stay in treatment as long as you are benefiting from it. The length of time you stay in MMT is an issue that should be decided solely by you and your physician. Some people are in MMT only for a few weeks, while others choose to stay in MMT indefinitely.

What is involved in ending treatment?

If you are thinking about ending MMT, talk with the doctor at the program. It can be a slow process to taper off of methadone. Though doses are tapered slowly to reduce withdrawal symptoms, you may experience some aching, insomnia, and lack of appetite for a few weeks. You also may feel a sense of loss, sadness, and sleeplessness for months. However, over time this should dissipate.

Long-term withdrawal can take from six months up to a year before you can completely taper off of methadone treatment. You should never set time

---

✦ It's A Fact!!
Patient Rights And Responsibilities

If you are unhappy with your treatment—for example, you feel your dose has not been adjusted correctly—talk it over with your doctor or counselor. If a treatment problem hasn't been fixed to your satisfaction by talking with your doctor or counselor, you may consider changing your provider.

You also can anonymously report problems with your treatment provider to his/her accrediting agency. To learn more about grievance procedures, you can visit the Patient Support and Community Education Project online at www.dpt .samhsa.gov/patient/index.htm.

As a patient in treatment, you are protected by a set of Medication-Assisted Treatment Patient Rights and Responsibilities. You can see the Substance Abuse and Mental Health Services Administration (SAMHSA) Guidelines for the Accreditation of Opioid Treatment Programs online at www.dpt.samhsa.gov/ guidelines.pdf.

Source: Substance Abuse and Mental Health Services Administration, 2006.

limitations on yourself—taper off at your own pace in cooperation with your treatment provider.

Buprenorphine

National Institute on Drug Abuse (NIDA)-supported basic and clinical research led to the development of buprenorphine, which culminated in a large NIDA-sponsored, multisite clinical trial demonstrating its effectiveness. The trial showed that, alone or in combination with naloxone, buprenorphine significantly reduced opiate drug abuse and cravings and was a safe and acceptable addiction treatment.

While these products were being developed in concert with industry partners, Congress passed the Drug Addiction Treatment Act (DATA 2000) permitting qualified physicians to prescribe narcotic medications (Schedules III to V) for the treatment of opioid addiction. This legislation created a major paradigm shift by allowing access to opiate treatment in a medical setting rather than limiting it to federally approved Opioid Treatment Programs.

The Food and Drug Administration (FDA) approved Subutex® (buprenorphine) and Suboxone® tablets (buprenorphine/naloxone) in October 2002, making them the first medications to be eligible for prescribing under the DATA 2000. To date, nearly 10,000 physicians have taken the training needed to prescribe these two medications, and nearly 7,000 have registered as potential providers.

What contributions has buprenorphine made to addiction treatment?

Buprenorphine's novel formulation with naloxone, an opioid antagonist, limits abuse and diversion potential. Scientific breakthroughs led to this formulation, which produces severe withdrawal symptoms in those who inject it to get "high" but no adverse effects when taken orally, as prescribed.

Buprenorphine represents a health services delivery innovation. The development of buprenorphine and its authorized use in physicians' offices gives opiate-addicted patients more medical options and extends the reach of addiction medication to remote populations. Its accessibility may even prompt earlier attempts to obtain treatment.

Part Seven

Other Drug-Related Health Concerns

Chapter 49

The Medical Consequences Of Drug Abuse

What are the medical consequences of drug addiction?

Individuals who suffer from addiction often have one or more accompanying medical issues, including lung and cardiovascular disease, stroke, cancer, and mental disorders. Imaging scans, chest x-rays, and blood tests show the damaging effects of drug abuse throughout the body. For example, tests show that tobacco smoke causes cancer of the mouth, throat, larynx, blood, lungs, stomach, pancreas, kidney, bladder, and cervix. In addition, some drugs of abuse, such as inhalants, are toxic to nerve cells and may damage or destroy them either in the brain or the peripheral nervous system.

Does drug abuse cause mental disorders, or vice versa?

Drug abuse and mental disorders often co-exist. In some cases, mental diseases may precede addiction; in other cases, drug abuse may trigger or exacerbate mental disorders, particularly in individuals with specific vulnerabilities.

What harmful consequences to others result from drug addiction?

Beyond the harmful consequences for the addicted individual, drug abuse can cause serious health problems for others. Three of the more devastating and troubling consequences of addiction are the following:

About This Chapter: Information in this chapter is excerpted from "Drugs, Brains, and Behavior—The Science of Addiction," National Institute on Drug Abuse, a component of the U.S. Department of Health and Human Services, February 2008.

- **Negative Effects Of Prenatal Drug Exposure On Infants And Children:** It is likely that some drug-exposed children will need educational support in the classroom to help them overcome what may be subtle deficits in developmental areas such as behavior, attention, and cognition. Ongoing work is investigating whether the effects of prenatal exposure on brain and behavior extend into adolescence to cause developmental problems during that time period.

- **Negative Effects Of Second-Hand Smoke:** Second-hand tobacco smoke, also referred to as environmental tobacco smoke (ETS), is a significant source of exposure to a large number of substances known to be hazardous to human health, particularly to children. According to the Surgeon General's 2006 Report, *The Health Consequences of Involuntary Exposure to Tobacco Smoke*, involuntary smoking increases the risk of heart disease and lung cancer in people who have never smoked by 25–30% and 20–30%, respectively.

> ✦ **It's A Fact!!**
> **The Impact Of Addiction Can Be Far Reaching**
>
> - Cardiovascular disease
> - Stroke
> - Cancer
> - HIV/AIDS
> - Hepatitis B and C
> - Lung disease
> - Obesity
> - Mental disorders
>
> Source: National Institute on Drug Abuse, February 2008.

- **Increased Spread Of Infectious Diseases:** Injection of drugs such as heroin, cocaine, and methamphetamine accounts for more than a third of new AIDS cases. Injection drug use is also a major factor in the spread of hepatitis C, a serious, potentially fatal liver disease and a rapidly growing public health problem. Injection drug use is not the only way that drug abuse contributes to the spread of infectious diseases. All drugs of abuse cause some form of intoxication, which interferes with judgment and increases the likelihood of risky sexual behaviors. This, in turn, contributes to the spread of HIV/AIDS, hepatitis B and C, and other sexually transmitted diseases.

What are some effects of specific abused substances?

- **Nicotine** is an addictive stimulant found in cigarettes and other forms of tobacco. Tobacco smoke increases a user's risk of cancer, emphysema, bronchial disorders, and cardiovascular disease. The mortality rate associated with tobacco addiction is staggering. Tobacco use killed approximately 100 million people during the 20th century and, if current smoking trends continue, the cumulative death toll for this century has been projected to reach 1 billion.

- **Alcohol** consumption can damage the brain and most body organs. Areas of the brain that are especially vulnerable to alcohol-related damage are the cerebral cortex (largely responsible for our higher brain functions, including problem solving and decision making), the hippocampus (important for memory and learning), and the cerebellum (important for movement coordination).

- **Marijuana** is the most commonly abused illicit substance. This drug impairs short-term memory and learning, the ability to focus attention, and coordination. It also increases heart rate, can harm the lungs, and can cause psychosis in those at risk.

- **Inhalants** are volatile substances found in many household products, such as oven cleaners, gasoline, spray paints, and other aerosols, that induce mind-altering effects. Inhalants are extremely toxic and can damage the heart, kidneys, lungs, and brain. Even a healthy person can suffer heart failure and death within minutes of a single session of prolonged sniffing of an inhalant.

- **Cocaine** is a short-acting stimulant, which can lead abusers to "binge" (to take the drug many times in a single session). Cocaine abuse can lead to severe medical consequences related to the heart, and the respiratory, nervous, and digestive systems.

- **Amphetamines**, including methamphetamine, are powerful stimulants that can produce feelings of euphoria and alertness. Methamphetamine's effects are particularly long lasting and harmful to the brain. Amphetamines can cause high body temperature and can lead to serious heart problems and seizures.

- **Ecstasy (MDMA)** produces both stimulant and mind-altering effects. It can increase body temperature, heart rate, blood pressure, and heart wall stress. Ecstasy may also be toxic to nerve cells.

- **LSD** is one of the most potent hallucinogenic, or perception-altering, drugs. Its effects are unpredictable, and abusers may see vivid colors and images, hear sounds, and feel sensations that seem real but do not exist. Abusers also may have traumatic experiences and emotions that can last for many hours. Some short-term effects can include increased body

♣ It's A Fact!!

Ask someone to name the harmful health effects of drug abuse and addiction, and you might get the following very scary list: overdose, cancer, heart disease, lung disease, liver dysfunction, mental disorders, infectious diseases such as HIV/AIDS, hepatitis, and tuberculosis.

All of these are correct. Research shows that drug abuse and addiction can cause or worsen a whole array of health problems. Some can occur when drugs are used in high doses or after prolonged use, and some after just one use.

But you're likely to be more aware of other effects, which may not seem as scary. Or are they? You probably know that drugs affect feelings, moods, judgment, learning, memory, and movement. What's harmful about these effects?

As it turns out, impairment from drug abuse can cause a lot of serious consequences. Impairment refers to diminished ability, such as when drug abuse interferes with thinking or muscle movements. When a person is impaired from drugs, he or she is open to a wide range of errors in judgment and perception, which can lead to making bad choices. Physical abilities also can be affected, so a person might not react as he or she normally would.

The consequences of impairment can be both short-term and long-term, and can impact the most important things to a person: family, friends, school, possessions, dreams, goals, even life itself.

Diminishing Returns

Drugs of abuse, such as marijuana, heroin, cocaine, inhalants, nicotine, and alcohol—even some medications when they are not taken according to dosage temperature, heart rate, and blood pressure; sweating; loss of appetite; sleeplessness; dry mouth; and tremors.

- **Heroin** is a powerful opiate drug that produces euphoria and feelings of relaxation. It slows respiration and can increase risk of serious infectious diseases, especially when taken intravenously. Other opioid drugs include morphine, OxyContin, Vicodin, and Percodan, which have legitimate medical uses; however, their nonmedical use or abuse can result in the same harmful consequences as abusing heroin.

and directions—can change the way a person's brain functions. This is important for teens to know because the teen brain's frontal cortical regions, which integrate all the various pieces of information that go into making good decisions, will still be developing until around age 25.

Since drugs act on the brain, they can affect a wide range of abilities. These include: perception (what someone understands or observes), cognition (knowledge gained, as through perception), judgment (the ability to make a decision), attention, balance, and coordination.

The consequences of impairment are almost infinite when you think about them. For example, after using drugs, someone might not score well on a test, thus affecting grades, college placement, or obtaining a particular job. Someone might misperceive a situation, respond inappropriately, and cause a regrettable argument. Someone could recklessly create serious physical risk by getting behind the wheel of a car. Or someone might become involved in a dangerous social situation that could lead to a sexually transmitted disease or an unwanted pregnancy.

As Nora D. Volkow, M.D., Director of NIDA, says: "The choices teens make can have profound effects, both immediate and long-term. It is important that teens understand the consequences associated with their decisions—particularly decisions that affect the brain and behavior."

Source: From "Out of It," an article in a Heads Up compilation from Scholastic and the National Institute on Drug Abuse, 2008.

- **Prescription Medications** are increasingly being abused or used for nonmedical purposes. This practice cannot only be addictive, but in some cases also lethal. Commonly abused classes of prescription drugs include painkillers, sedatives, and stimulants. Among the most disturbing aspects of this emerging trend is its prevalence among teenagers and young adults, and the common misperception that because these medications are prescribed by physicians, they are safe even when used illicitly.

- **Steroids**, which can also be prescribed for certain medical conditions, are abused to increase muscle mass and to improve athletic performance or physical appearance. Serious consequences of abuse can include severe acne, heart disease, liver problems, stroke, infectious diseases, depression, and suicide.

- **Drug Combinations**. A particularly dangerous and not uncommon practice is the combining of two or more drugs. The practice ranges from the co-administration of legal drugs, like alcohol and nicotine, to the dangerous random mixing of prescription drugs, to the deadly combination of heroin or cocaine with fentanyl (an opioid pain medication). Whatever the context, it is critical to realize that because of drug-drug interactions, such practices often pose significantly higher risks than the already harmful individual drugs.

For more information on the nature and extent of common drugs of abuse and their health consequences, go to the National Institute on Drug Abuse (NIDA)'s website (www.nida.nih.gov) to view the popular Research Reports, InfoFacts, and other publications.

Chapter 50

Substance Abuse And Stress

The Brain Connection

You are about to take a test. The coach is announcing who made the team. Your best friend is mad at you. Most people find such situations stressful. Stress can be defined as an emotional or physical demand or strain (a "stressor") that causes your body to release powerful neurochemicals and hormones.

These changes help your body gear up to respond to the stressor. Your blood-sugar levels and blood pressure rise; your heart beats faster; your muscles tense. There are different levels of stress: Short-term stress can cause uncomfortable physical reactions, but can also help you to focus. Long-term stress—such as stress caused by illness, divorce, or the death of a loved one—can lead to serious health problems. Traumatic events—such as natural disasters, violence, and terrorism—can cause post-traumatic stress disorder (PTSD), a serious illness.

Brain research now indicates that people exposed to stress are more likely to abuse alcohol or other drugs, or to relapse to drug addiction. Read on to get important facts about this connection.

About This Chapter: Information in this chapter is excerpted from "Stress and Drug Abuse," an article in a Heads Up compilation from Scholastic and the National Institute on Drug Abuse, 2007.

How Your Body Responds To Stress

Your body's central nervous, endocrine, immune, and cardiovascular systems are involved in responding to stress.

The physical responses can vary: Short-term responses can cause a racing heart, sweaty palms, and a pounding head. Long-term responses can cause back pain, high blood pressure, sleeplessness, and an inability to make decisions. Constant stress floods the body with stress hormones, which can increase the risk of serious health problems.

The hormone that initiates the body's response to stress, CRF, is found throughout the brain. Drugs of abuse also stimulate release of CRF.

Latest Research

National Institute on Drug Abuse (NIDA) researchers have found the following connections between stress and drug abuse:

- Stress can cause changes in the brain like those caused by addictive drugs. This suggests that some people who experience stress may be more vulnerable to drug addiction or drug relapse.
- Those who become addicted to drugs may already be hypersensitive to stress.
- Long-term potentiation (LTP) is a key brain mechanism involved in memory and learning. Researchers have shown that LTP is involved in how both drug exposure and stress affect the brain.
- Stress can put people at risk for substance abuse.
- Scientists have uncovered a rise in substance abuse among people in New York City neighborhoods affected by 9/11, which raises new questions about the public health effects of traumatic events such as disasters.

Myth Vs. Reality

Myth 1: Drug abuse is harmful, but it does relieve stress.

Reality: Some drugs of abuse affect your brain the same way stress does. Long-term abuse of drugs makes users more sensitive to everyday stress than nonusers.

✤ It's A Fact!!
Long-Term Potentiation

If you hit a fastball for a home run, chances are the next time you are at the plate and see a fastball coming, you'll be stoked. Why? Part of the reason is long-term potentiation (LTP). LTP is one of the brain's key mechanisms for registering experience and using it to shape future responses, as in learning and remembering. When an experience or some other stimulus induces LTP in a cell, the cell responds more strongly to future exposures to the same stimulus. For example, if you hit a fastball for a home run, LTP is part of the reason you might get excited the next time you are at the plate and see a fastball coming.

Scientists have made important discoveries in the role that LTP may play in drug addiction, as well as in the body's response to stress—which may help to explain a long-observed connection between the two. Researchers have shown that, in animal studies, a single exposure to some addictive drugs can establish LTP in dopamine-releasing cells in an area of the brain called the ventral tegmental area (VTA). LTP primes these brain cells to react more strongly—and release dopamine more abundantly—in response to future exposure to drugs. Dopamine is a chemical neurotransmitter that triggers feelings of pleasure and also plays a role in alerting people that something important is happening or about to happen.

Researchers have also found that stress alone can induce changes in dopamine-releasing VTA cells similar to those caused by drugs. This raises the possibility of a "priming mechanism" that could make someone who has experienced stress much more vulnerable to addiction, or to relapse during treatment for addiction.

Source: An article in a Heads Up compilation from Scholastic and the National Institute on Drug Abuse, 2007.

Myth 2: All stress is bad for you.

Reality: Stress can help you deal with tough situations. It can also be associated with positive changes, such as a new job. However, long-term stress can lead to physical and emotional health problems.

Myth 3: Everyone deals with stress in the same way.

Reality: People deal with stress in different ways. How you deal with stress determines how it affects your body.

For more information, visit: www.scholastic.com/headsup and http://teens.drugabuse.gov.

✔ Quick Tip
Managing Stress

Anyone can learn to manage stress, but it does take practice. Here are some practical tips:

- **Take care of yourself.** Healthy foods, exercise, and enough sleep really do make you feel better and better able to cope!

- **Focus.** To keep from feeling overwhelmed, concentrate on challenges one at a time.

- **Keep calm.** Step away from an argument or confrontation by taking a deep breath. Go for a walk or do some other physical activity.

- **Move on.** If you don't achieve something you were trying for, practice and prepare for the next time. Or check out some other activity.

- **Talk about it.** Talking to an understanding listener who remains calm can be very helpful.

Source: An article in a Heads Up compilation from Scholastic and the National Institute on Drug Abuse, 2007.

Chapter 51

Substance Abuse And Mental Illness

Comorbidity

When two disorders or illnesses occur in the same person, simultaneously or sequentially, they are called comorbid. Comorbidity also implies interactions between the illnesses that affect the course and prognosis of both.

Drug Addiction Is A Mental Illness

Drug addiction is considered a mental illness because addiction changes the brain in fundamental ways, disturbing a person's normal hierarchy of needs and desires and substituting new priorities connected with procuring and using the drug. The resulting compulsive behaviors that override the ability to control impulses despite the consequences are similar to hallmarks of other mental illnesses.

Co-Occurring Drug Use And Other Mental Disorders

Many people who regularly abuse drugs are also diagnosed with mental disorders and vice versa. The high prevalence of this comorbidity has been documented in multiple national population surveys since the 1980s. Data

About This Chapter: Information in this chapter is from "Comorbidity: Addiction and Other Mental Illnesses," a research report from the National Institute on Drug Abuse, a component of the U.S. Department of Health and Human Services, December 2008.

show that persons diagnosed with mood or anxiety disorders were about twice as likely to suffer also from a drug use disorder (abuse or dependence) compared with respondents in general. The same was true for those diagnosed with an antisocial syndrome, such as antisocial personality or conduct disorder. Similarly, persons diagnosed with drug disorders were roughly twice as likely to suffer also from mood and anxiety disorders.

Gender is also a factor in the specific patterns of observed comorbidities. For example, the overall rates of abuse and dependence for most drugs tend to be higher among males than females, and males are more likely to suffer also from antisocial personality disorder. In contrast, women have higher rates of amphetamine dependence and higher rates of mood and anxiety disorders.

Why Drug Use Disorders Often Co-Occur With Other Mental Illnesses

The high prevalence of comorbidity between drug use disorders and other mental illnesses does not mean that one caused the other, even if it appeared first. In fact, establishing causality is difficult for several reasons. Some symptoms of a mental disorder may not be recognized until the illness has substantially progressed, and imperfect recollections of when drug use/abuse started can also present timing issues. Still, three scenarios deserve consideration:

1. Drugs of abuse can cause abusers to experience one or more symptoms of another mental illness. The increased risk of psychosis in some marijuana abusers has been offered as evidence for this possibility.

2. Mental illnesses can lead to drug abuse. Individuals with overt, mild, or even subclinical mental disorders may abuse drugs as a form of self-medication.

3. Both drug use disorders and other mental illnesses are caused by overlapping factors such as underlying brain deficits, genetic vulnerabilities, and/or early exposure to stress or trauma.

All three scenarios probably contribute, in varying degrees, to how and whether specific comorbidities manifest.

✎ What's It Mean?

<u>Antisocial Personality Disorder:</u> A disorder characterized by antisocial behaviors that involve pervasive disregard for and violation of the rights, feelings, and safety of others, beginning in childhood or the early teenage years and continuing into adulthood.

<u>Anxiety Disorders:</u> Varied disorders that involve excessive or inappropriate feelings of anxiety or worry. Examples are panic disorder, post-traumatic stress disorder, social phobia, and others.

<u>Bipolar Disorder:</u> A mood disorder characterized by alternating episodes of depression and mania or hypo-mania.

<u>Comorbidity:</u> The occurrence of two disorders or illnesses in the same person, either at the same time (co-occurring comorbid conditions) or with a time difference between the initial occurrence of one and the initial occurrence of the other (sequentially comorbid conditions).

<u>Depression:</u> A disorder marked by sadness, inactivity, difficulty with thinking and concentration, significant increase or decrease in appetite and time spent sleeping, feelings of dejection and hopelessness, and sometimes, suicidal thoughts or an attempt to commit suicide.

<u>Mental Disorder:</u> A mental condition marked primarily by sufficient disorganization of personality, mind, and emotions to seriously impair the normal psychological or behavioral functioning of the individual. Addiction is a mental disorder.

<u>Psychosis:</u> A serious mental disorder (e.g., schizophrenia) characterized by defective or lost contact with reality. Symptoms often include hallucinations or delusions.

<u>Schizophrenia:</u> A psychotic disorder characterized by symptoms that fall into two categories: (1) positive symptoms, such as distortions in thoughts (delusions), perception (hallucinations), and language and thinking and (2) negative symptoms, such as flattened emotional responses and decreased goal-directed behavior.

<u>Self-Medication:</u> The use of a substance to lessen the negative effects of stress, anxiety, or other mental disorders (or side effects of their pharmacotherapy). Self-medication may lead to addiction and other drug- or alcohol-related problems.

✤ It's A Fact!!

Exposure To Traumatic Events Puts People At Higher Risk Of Substance Use Disorders

Emotionally traumatized people are at much higher risk of abusing licit, illicit, and prescription drugs. The strong association between post-traumatic stress disorder (PTSD) and substance abuse is particularly frequent and devastating among military veterans, among whom 38,000 PTSD cases have been documented in the past five years alone. Epidemiological studies suggest that as many as half of them may have a co-occurring substance use disorder (SUD). The growing incidence of PTSD among returning veterans poses an enormous challenge for a health care system in which PTSD programs don't accept individuals with active SUDs while traditional SUD clinics defer the treatment of trauma-related issues. There are treatment options for PTSD and SUD at different stages of clinical validation; however, more research is urgently needed to identify the best treatment strategies for addressing PTSD comorbidities.

Common Factors

Overlapping Genetic Vulnerabilities: It is estimated that 40–60 percent of an individual's vulnerability to addiction is attributable to genetics; most of this vulnerability arises from complex interactions among multiple genes and from genetic interactions with environmental influences.

Involvement Of Similar Brain Regions: Some areas of the brain are affected by both drug use disorders and other mental illnesses, which suggests that brain changes stemming from one may affect the other. For example, drug abuse that precedes the first symptoms of a mental illness may produce changes in brain structure and function that kindle an underlying propensity to develop that mental illness. If the mental disorder develops first, associated changes in brain activity may increase the vulnerability to abusing substances by enhancing their positive effects, reducing awareness of their negative effects, or alleviating the unpleasant effects associated with the mental disorder or the medication used to treat it.

The Influence Of Developmental Stage

Adolescence—A Vulnerable Time: Although drug abuse and addiction can happen at any time during a person's life, drug use typically starts in adolescence, a period when the first signs of mental illness commonly appear. It is therefore not surprising that comorbid disorders can already be seen among youth. Significant changes in the brain occur during adolescence, which may enhance vulnerability to drug use and the development of addiction and other mental disorders.

Early Occurrence Increases Later Risk: Strong evidence has emerged showing early drug use to be a risk factor for later substance abuse problems; additional findings suggest that it may also be a risk factor for the later occurrence of other mental illnesses. However, this link is not necessarily a simple one and may hinge upon genetic vulnerability, psychosocial experiences, and/or general environmental influences.

Diagnosing Comorbidity

The high rate of comorbidity between drug use disorders and other mental illnesses argues for a comprehensive approach to intervention that identifies, evaluates, and treats each disorder concurrently. The needed approach calls for broad assessment tools that are less likely to result in a missed diagnosis. Accordingly, patients entering treatment for psychiatric illnesses should also be screened for substance use disorders and vice versa. Accurate diagnosis is complicated, however, by the similarities between drug-related symptoms such as withdrawal and those of potentially comorbid mental disorders. Thus, when people who abuse drugs enter treatment, it may be necessary to observe them after a period of abstinence in order to distinguish the effects of substance intoxication or withdrawal from the symptoms of comorbid mental disorders—this would allow for a more accurate diagnosis.

Treating Comorbid Conditions

A fundamental principle emerging from scientific research is the need to treat comorbid conditions concurrently, which can be a difficult proposition. Patients who have both a drug use disorder and another mental illness often exhibit symptoms that are more persistent, severe, and resistant to treatment

> ## ✤ It's A Fact!!
> ## Smoking And Schizophrenia:
> ## Self-Medication Or Shared Brain Circuitry?
>
> Patients with schizophrenia have higher rates of alcohol, tobacco, and other drug abuse than the general population. Based on nationally representative survey data, 41% of respondents with past-month mental illnesses are current smokers, which is about double the rate of those with no mental illness. In clinical samples, the rate of smoking in patients with schizophrenia has ranged as high as 90%.
>
> Various self-medication hypotheses have been proposed to explain the strong association between schizophrenia and smoking, although none have yet been confirmed. Most of these relate to the nicotine contained in tobacco products: Nicotine may help compensate for some of the cognitive impairments produced by the disorder and may counteract psychotic symptoms or alleviate unpleasant side effects of antipsychotic medications. Nicotine or smoking behavior may also help people with schizophrenia deal with the anxiety and social stigma of their disease.
>
> Research on how both nicotine and schizophrenia affect the brain has generated other possible explanations for the high rate of smoking among people with schizophrenia. The presence of abnormalities in particular circuits of the brain may predispose individuals to schizophrenia, increase the rewarding effects of drugs like nicotine, or reduce an individual's ability to quit smoking. Understanding how and why patients with schizophrenia use nicotine is likely to help us develop new treatments for both schizophrenia and nicotine dependence.

compared with patients who have either disorder alone. Nevertheless, steady progress is being made through research on new and existing treatment options for comorbidity and through health services research on implementation of appropriate screening and treatment within a variety of settings.

Medications

Effective medications exist for treating opioid, alcohol, and nicotine addiction and for alleviating the symptoms of many other mental disorders. Most of these medications have not been studied in patients with comorbidities, although some may prove effective for treating comorbid conditions. More research is needed to fully understand and assess the actions of combined or dually effective medications.

Behavioral Therapies

Behavioral treatment (alone or in combination with medications) is the cornerstone to successful outcomes for many individuals with drug use disorders or other mental illnesses. And while behavior therapies continue to be evaluated for use in comorbid populations, several strategies have shown promise for treating specific comorbid conditions.

Most clinicians and researchers agree that broad spectrum diagnosis and concurrent therapy will lead to more positive outcomes for patients with comorbid conditions. Preliminary findings support this notion, but research is needed to identify the most effective therapies (especially studies focused on adolescents).

Examples Of Promising Behavioral Therapies For Adolescents With Comorbid Conditions

- **Multisystemic Therapy (MST):** MST targets key factors (attitudes, family, peer pressure, school and neighborhood culture) associated with serious antisocial behavior in children and adolescents who abuse drugs.

- **Brief Strategic Family Therapy (BSFT):** BSFT targets family interactions that are thought to maintain or exacerbate adolescent drug abuse and other co-occurring problem behaviors.

- **Cognitive-Behavioral Therapy (CBT):** CBT is designed to modify harmful beliefs and maladaptive behaviors. CBT is the most effective psychotherapy for children and adolescents with anxiety and mood disorders, and also shows strong efficacy for substance abusers.

Examples Of Promising Behavioral Therapies For Adults With Comorbid Conditions

- **Therapeutic Communities (TCs):** TCs focus on the "re-socialization" of the individual and use broad-based community programs as active components of treatment.

- **Assertive Community Treatment (ACT):** ACT programs integrate the behavioral treatment of other severe mental disorders, such as schizophrenia, and co-occurring substance use disorders.

- **Dialectical Behavior Therapy (DBT):** DBT is designed specifically to reduce self-harm behaviors (such as self-mutilation and suicidal attempts, thoughts, or urges) and drug abuse. It is one of the few treatments that are effective for individuals who meet the criteria for borderline personality disorder.

- **Exposure Therapy:** Exposure therapy is a behavioral treatment for some anxiety disorders that involves repeated exposure to or confrontation with a feared situation, object, traumatic event, or memory.

- **Integrated Group Therapy (IGT):** IGT is a new treatment developed specifically for patients with bipolar disorder and drug addiction, designed to address both problems simultaneously.

♣ It's A Fact!!
Childhood Attention Deficit Hyperactivity Disorder (ADHD) And Later Drug Problems

Numerous studies have documented an increased risk for drug use disorders in youth with untreated ADHD, although some suggest that only a subset of these individuals are vulnerable: those with comorbid conduct disorders. Given this linkage, it is important to determine whether effective treatment of ADHD could prevent subsequent drug abuse and associated behavioral problems. Treatment of childhood ADHD with stimulant medications such as methylphenidate or amphetamine reduces the impulsive behavior, fidgeting, and inability to concentrate that characterize ADHD. However, some physicians and parents have expressed concern that treating childhood ADHD with stimulants might increase a child's vulnerability to drug abuse later in life. Recent reviews of long-term studies of children with ADHD who received stimulant therapy found no evidence for this increase. However, most of these studies have methodological limitations, including small sample sizes and nonrandomized study designs, indicating that more research is needed, particularly in adolescents.

Chapter 52

Substance Abuse, Depression, And Suicide

Behaviors May Indicate Risk Of Adolescent Depression

New findings from a study supported by the National Institute on Drug Abuse (NIDA), National Institutes of Health, show that girls and boys who exhibit high levels of risky behaviors have similar chances of developing symptoms of depression. However, gender differences become apparent with low and moderate levels of risky behaviors, with girls being significantly more likely than boys to experience symptoms of depression. The study, which incorporates data from almost 19,000 teens, is published in the May 15, 2006 issue of the *Archives of Women's Mental Health*.

"The burden of illness associated with depression during adolescence is considerable, and psychosocial problems—including substance abuse—are associated with depressive disorders in teens," says NIDA Director Dr. Nora D. Volkow. "The findings from this study create a more complete picture of commonalities and differences of the risk of depression among boys and girls who engage in risky behaviors, and provide information for healthcare providers to consider as they screen, evaluate, and treat their young patients."

About This Chapter: Information in this chapter is from "Behaviors May Indicate Risk of Adolescent Depression," a news release from the National Institute on Drug Abuse, May 2006, and "Substance Use Associated with Low Response to Depression Treatment Among Teens," a science update from the National Institute on Drug Abuse, December 2009.

♣ It's A Fact!!
Depression Symptoms

Symptoms of depression include loss of appetite, feeling blue, loss of interest in things that used to be of interest, being bothered by things that previously were not bothersome, and not feeling hopeful about the future.

Source: National Institute on Drug Abuse, May 2006.

Dr. Martha Waller, of the Pacific Institute for Research and Evaluation, and her colleagues provided new findings from teen interviews conducted as part of the National Longitudinal Study of Adolescent Health in 1995. The researchers clustered the teens into 16 groups according to their behaviors and correlated these behaviors with symptoms of depression. Groups included abstainers, who refrained from engaging in sexual activity and from using alcohol, tobacco, or other drugs; teens who engaged in low and moderate risk behaviors, such as experimenting with substance abuse or sex; and teens who engaged in high-risk behaviors, such as exchanging sex for drugs or money or abuse of intravenous drugs.

"Differences in symptoms of depression between girls and boys were guided by risk behaviors," says Dr. Waller. "Among abstainers, there were no differences between girls and boys in their likelihood of having symptoms of depression."

When abstaining girls were compared with risk-taking girls, the researchers observed that any risk activity, no matter how modest in degree, was associated with an increased risk of symptoms of depression. For example, girls who experimented with drugs and girls who experimented with tobacco and alcohol were more than twice as likely to have symptoms of depression as girls who abstained completely. Girls who experimented with sex were almost four times as likely to have such symptoms, while girls who used intravenous drugs were almost 18 times as likely to have symptoms of depression as girls who abstained completely.

Among boys, most, but not all risk profiles were associated with a greater likelihood of such symptoms, compared to abstainers. Boys who drank alcohol and boys who were binge drinkers were about two-and-one-half times as likely to experience symptoms of depression, while those who abused intravenous drugs were about six times as likely to have symptoms of depression as boys who abstained completely.

For most of the high-risk behaviors profiled there were also no significant gender differences in symptoms of depression. However, for one—exchanging sex for money or drugs—girls were seven times more likely than boys to report such symptoms. Among teens who engaged in low and moderate risk behaviors, girls were significantly more likely than boys to report symptoms of depression.

"Although it has not been shown that these behaviors trigger depression, it may be that screening for substance abuse and other behaviors in teens may provide enough information to the healthcare provider to also warrant screening for depression, particularly for girls," says Dr. Waller. "Both substance abuse and sexual activity may alter a girl's social context, which could induce stress and/or change self-perceptions, both of which could contribute to depression. In addition, there may be differences in how girls and boys physically respond to substance abuse that help explain the gender differences."

Because girls who exhibited low and moderate risk behaviors were observed to be at greater risk for depression than boys, the scientists suggest that future research should examine the characteristics of these groups to determine the mechanisms underlying this difference.

"There are significant changes in the brain during adolescence and there is growing interest in understanding how substance abuse may change brain structure and chemistry, and in turn, cognition and emotion," says Dr. Volkow. "Future research will investigate more closely the roles of risky behaviors and the influence of gender in the development of adolescent depression."

Substance Use Associated With Low Response To Depression Treatment Among Teens

Depressed teens who report low levels of impairment related to drug or alcohol use tended to respond better to depression treatment than depressed teens with higher levels of substance-related impairment, according to an analysis of data from the National Institute of Mental Health (NIMH)-funded Treatment of SSRI-Resistant Depression in Adolescents (TORDIA) study. However, it is unclear whether less substance-related impairment allowed for better response to depression treatment, or if better treatment response led to less substance-related impairment. The study was published in the December 2009 issue of the *Journal of the American Academy of Child and Adolescent Psychiatry*.

Background

Substance use is more common among teens with depression than among those without depression. Researchers have also found that depression can inhibit teens' response to treatment of substance abuse, and substance abuse is associated with a poorer response to treatment of depression. Still, few trials have examined how coexisting depression and substance use among teens may affect treatment outcomes for both.

In the TORDIA study, 334 teens who did not respond to a type of antidepressant called a selective serotonin reuptake inhibitor (SSRI) before the trial were randomly assigned to one of four treatments for 12 weeks:

- Switch to another SSRI
- Switch to venlafaxine (Effexor®), a different type of antidepressant
- Switch to another SSRI and add cognitive behavioral therapy (CBT), a type of psychotherapy
- Switch to venlafaxine and add CBT

Results of the trial were previously reported in February 2008. They showed that teens who received combination therapy, with either type of antidepressant, were more likely to improve than those on medication alone.

In this new analysis, Benjamin Goldstein, M.D., of the University of Toronto, and colleagues examined TORDIA data to determine the relationship, if any, between substance use, major depression, and response to depression treatment. Substance use was defined as using alcohol or drugs without meeting criteria for having a full-blown substance abuse disorder. Teens that were diagnosed with a substance abuse disorder were excluded from the TORDIA study.

Results Of The Study

Substance use was fairly common among TORDIA participants. At baseline, about 28 percent reported experimenting with drugs or alcohol. Those who showed more substance-related impairment were older, felt more hopeless, had greater family conflict, developed depression at an earlier age, were more likely to have a history of physical or sexual abuse, and were more likely to have coexisting oppositional defiant disorder (ODD) or conduct disorder (CD). Substance-related impairment included certain attitudes and behaviors such as craving the substance, feeling hooked on it, accidentally hurting oneself or others while using it, and other similar effects.

Participants with low levels of substance use and substance-related impairment throughout the study tended to respond better to depression treatment than those who showed persistently high or increasing levels of substance-related impairment. There were no significant differences in rates of substance use and impairment among the treatment groups.

Significance

This study is one of the first to examine the association between substance use and depression treatment among depressed teens. The findings are consistent with other studies that found depression severity to be associated with a history of physical or sexual abuse, coexisting ODD or CD, and substance-related impairment. However, the direction of the association is uncertain. The data could not determine whether low substance-related impairment facilitates improvement in depression symptoms, or whether improvement in depressed mood leads to a decrease in substance-related impairment.

What's Next

The authors caution that the study does not provide definitive conclusions about depression treatment and substance use. However, they do suggest that clinicians treating teens for depression screen for signs of substance use and address those issues as well, even if the teen does not meet criteria for a full-blown substance abuse disorder.

Chapter 53

Drug Use And Infectious Diseases

HIV And AIDS

What are HIV and AIDS?

HIV (human immunodeficiency virus) is the virus that causes AIDS (acquired immune deficiency syndrome). AIDS is a disease of the immune system that has treatment options, but no cure, at the present time. Most people just say "HIV/AIDS" when they are talking about either the virus (HIV) or the disease it causes (AIDS).

HIV is a blood-borne virus. That means it can spread when the blood or bodily fluids of someone who's infected comes in contact with the blood, broken skin, or mucous membranes of an uninfected person. Sharing needles or other equipment used for injection drug use and engaging in other risky behaviors are the two main ways that HIV is spread. Infected pregnant women also can pass HIV to their babies during pregnancy, delivery, and breastfeeding.

About This Chapter: Information in this chapter is from "HIV/AIDS—The Link," NIDA for Teens, the National Institute on Drug Abuse, a component of the U.S. Department of Health and Human Services, August 2008, and "NIDA Community Drug Alert Bulletin—Hepatitis," National Institute on Drug Abuse, May 2000. Despite the older date of this document, the information about hepatitis is still pertinent.

How many people have HIV/AIDS?

HIV/AIDS has been a global epidemic for more than 25 years; today's youth have never known a world without it. In the United States, the estimates indicate that more than 1 million people are living with HIV or AIDS.

In 2007, 37,041 new AIDS disease cases were reported. Recently, the Centers for Disease Control and Prevention (CDC) published HIV incidence estimates using new methods. They found that in 2006, an estimated 56,300 new HIV infections occurred—a number that is much higher than the previous estimate of 40,000 new infections annually. This means that more people are infected with HIV than we originally thought.

CDC estimates that close to one-quarter of the people in the United States who are infected with HIV do not know they are infected.

How are drug abuse and HIV related?

Drug abuse and addiction have been closely linked with HIV/AIDS since the beginning of the epidemic. Although injection drug use is well known in this regard, the role that non-injection drug abuse plays more generally in the spread of HIV is less recognized.

Injection Drug Use: People typically associate drug abuse and HIV/AIDS with injection drug use and needle sharing. Injection drug use refers to when a drug is injected into a tissue or vein with a needle. When injection drug users share "equipment"—such as needles, syringes, and other drug injection paraphernalia—HIV can be transmitted between users. Other infections—such as hepatitis C—can also be spread this way. Hepatitis C can cause liver disease and permanent liver damage.

Poor Judgment And Risky Behavior: Drug abuse by any method (not just injection) can put a person at risk for contracting HIV. Drug and alcohol intoxication affect the way a person makes decisions and can lead to unsafe sexual practices, which puts him or her at risk for getting HIV or transmitting it to someone else.

Biological Effects Of Drugs: Drug abuse and addiction can affect a person's overall health, making him or her more susceptible to HIV or, in someone with HIV, worsen the progression of HIV and its consequences, especially in the brain. For example, research has shown that HIV causes more harm to nerve cells in the brain and greater cognitive damage among methamphetamine abusers than among people with HIV who do not abuse drugs. In animal studies, methamphetamine has been shown to increase the amount of HIV in brain cells.

Drug Abuse Treatment: Since the late 1980s, researchers found that if you treat drug abuse you can prevent the spread of HIV. Drug abusers in treatment stop or reduce their drug use and related risk behaviors, including drug injection and unsafe sexual practices. Drug treatment programs also serve an important role in getting out good information on HIV/AIDS and related diseases, providing counseling and testing services, and offering referrals for medical and social services.

How are teens affected?

Young people are at risk for contracting HIV and developing AIDS. According to CDC, about 45,433 young people aged 13 to 24 in the United States had been diagnosed with AIDS by the end of 2007. In the past, most of those cases were in adolescent males. That ratio is changing as more females become infected.

In youth, as in adults, some populations are disproportionately affected. That means that some populations are more affected than others. For example, Blacks/African Americans aged 13 to 19 represent only 17 percent of the U.S. teenage population, but accounted for 72 percent of new AIDS cases in 2007. The reasons for this gap aren't completely understood; in fact, Black/African American youth have lower rates of drug abuse than Whites and Hispanics. This remains a strong research priority for the National Institute on Drug Abuse (NIDA).

In general, middle and late adolescence is a time when young people engage in risk-taking and sensation-seeking behaviors that may put them in jeopardy of contracting HIV. Regardless of whether a young person takes drugs, unsafe sexual practices increase a person's risk of contracting HIV. But drugs and alcohol can increase the chances of unsafe behavior by altering judgment and decision making.

❖ It's A Fact!!

The good news is that HIV isn't the death sentence it was when the epidemic began. This is thanks in large part to a treatment called HAART (highly active antiretroviral therapy). HAART is a combination of three or more antiretroviral medications that can hold back the virus and prevent or decrease symptoms of illness.

Source: National Institute on Drug Abuse, August 2008.

How can teens protect themselves?

The best way to protect yourself is to stay healthy and think clearly. Choose not to use drugs. Know that drug use can change the brain and affect the way people make decisions and weigh risks.

Hepatitis C

What is hepatitis C?

- Hepatitis C infection is caused by the hepatitis C virus, also known as HCV, a virus that infects cells in the liver.

- Chronic infection with HCV can result in cirrhosis (liver scarring) or primary liver cancer (hepatocellular carcinoma).

- Hepatitis C is the most common chronic blood-borne infection in the United States, infecting an estimated 4 million Americans.

- Hepatitis C is transmitted primarily through direct exposure to infected blood.

- Hepatitis C is linked to injection drug use, which accounts for most HCV transmission in the United States.

- The highest rates of new hepatitis C infection are among persons 20 to 39 years old and the highest rates of chronic infection are among persons 30 to 49 years old.

What are facts about hepatitis C transmission?

- Sharing contaminated needles is the most common route of infection. Injection drug use is responsible for at least 60 percent of HCV infection in the United States.

- The risk of sexual transmission of HCV is much lower than the risk associated with contaminated needles, but still present. Sexual transmission is estimated to account for less than 20 percent of HCV transmission.

- Prior to the discovery of the virus and the development of a screening test for blood, many people were infected through contaminated blood transfusions. Since 1992, infection from blood transfusions is rare in the United States.

- The average rate of transmission from an infected pregnant mother to her infant is 5% to 6% (range 0% to 25%). This risk increases if the mother is infected with both HCV and HIV, with reported transmission rates of 5% to 36%.

- Other potential risks for transmission include sharing contaminated straws during intranasal use of cocaine, and sharing items such as razors and toothbrushes, which may be contaminated with infected blood. Data on exposure risks from tattooing or piercing in the United States are sparse.

♣ It's A Fact!!
What other infectious diseases
are associated with HIV/AIDS?

Besides increasing their risk of HIV infection, individuals who take drugs or engage in high-risk behaviors associated with drug use also put themselves and others at risk for contracting or transmitting hepatitis C (HCV), hepatitis B (HBV), tuberculosis (TB), and a number of sexually transmitted diseases, including syphilis, chlamydia, trichomoniasis, gonorrhea, and genital herpes. Injecting drug users (IDUs) are also commonly susceptible to skin infections at the site of injection and to bacterial and viral infections, such as bacterial pneumonia and endocarditis, which, if left untreated, can lead to serious health problems.

Source: Excerpted from "NIDA InfoFacts: Drug Abuse and the Link to HIV/AIDS and Other Infectious Diseases," National Institute on Drug Abuse, August 2008.

How is hepatitis C treated?

While some antiviral treatment is available for HCV, it has not been found to be highly effective. It also has been shown to have toxic effects, and is often poorly tolerated. Research efforts to develop more effective treatment approaches that are appropriate for broader patient populations are ongoing. At present, the antiviral drug interferon, used alone or in combination with ribavirin, is approved for treatment of HCV. When interferon is combined with ribavirin, the effectiveness of treatment is improved. Studies indicate that the combination is effective in 30 to 40 percent of those treated, but that many patients relapse when therapy is stopped. Currently, treatment is recommended only for patients at greatest risk for progression to cirrhosis. Individuals found to be infected with HCV need to be assessed and monitored by a specialist for the presence and severity of chronic liver disease and for treatment eligibility. Infected persons should be advised to reduce alcohol intake and to abstain from using illicit drugs. Those using illicit drugs should be referred to drug treatment programs.

✤ It's A Fact!!
Injection Drug Use And Hepatitis C Infection

Although new infections among injection drug users in the United States have declined since 1989, both the incidence and prevalence of infection remain high. Studies have shown that infection is widespread in populations of experienced injectors, with rates in many areas of the United States exceeding 80 percent. Acquisition of hepatitis C infection is very rapid among new injectors following initiation of injection, with 50 to 80 percent infected within 6 to 12 months.

Risks for infection include needle sharing, frequent daily injection, cocaine injection, and sharing needles with a long-term injector. Because of the efficiency of blood-to-blood transmission and the high prevalence of infection among injectors, anyone who has ever injected drugs, even if he or she may have experimented only once in the past, is at risk for infection. Due to common modes of transmission, a large proportion of injection drug users infected with HCV are also infected with hepatitis B virus and/or HIV.

Source: National Institute on Drug Abuse, May 2000.

Are there screening and prevention programs for hepatitis C?

Unlike hepatitis A and hepatitis B, there is no vaccine to prevent hepatitis C infection. Thus, prevention efforts must rely on behavioral techniques.

Persons who have injected illicit drugs, including those who injected only once or occasionally many years ago and who may not consider themselves to be drug users, should be tested for hepatitis C infection. Because of similar risk factors for infection, drug users should also be tested for HIV and hepatitis B. Those at risk should receive immunization for hepatitis A and B. Persons with known HIV infection should be screened for HCV as well.

Chapter 54

Substance Abuse And Sexual Health

Sexual activity and substance use are not uncommon among youth today. According to the Centers for Disease Control and Prevention, 79 percent of high-school students report having experimented with alcohol at least once, and a quarter report frequent drug use. Half of all 9th–12th graders have had sexual intercourse, and 65 percent will by the time they graduate. While it has been difficult to show a direct causal relationship, there is some evidence that alcohol and drug use by young people is associated with risky sexual activity.

Risky Sexual Behaviors And Substance Use

Sexual Initiation

- Current data suggest that those who engage in any "risk behaviors" tend to take part in more than one, and that many health risk behaviors occur in combination with other risky activities.

About This Chapter: This chapter begins with "Sexual Activity and Substance Use Among Youth," (#3213), The Henry J. Kaiser Family Foundation, February 2002. The complete text of this document, including references, is available at http://www.kff.org. This information was reprinted with permission from the Henry J. Kaiser Family Foundation. The Kaiser Family Foundation is a non-profit private operating foundation, based in Menlo Park, California, dedicated to producing and communicating the best possible analysis and information on health issues. Additional text, "Frequently Asked Questions: Date Rape Drugs," is from a fact sheet produced by the National Women's Health Information Center, U.S. Department of Health and Human Services, December 2008.

- Prior substance use increases the probability that an adolescent will initiate sexual activity, and sexually experienced adolescents are more likely to initiate substance use—including alcohol and cigarettes.

- Teens who use alcohol or drugs are more likely to have sex than those who do not: Adolescents who drink are seven times more likely, while those who use illicit substances are five times more likely—even after adjusting for age, race, gender, and parental educational level.

- Up to 18% of young people aged 13 to 19 report that they were drinking at the time of first intercourse. Among teens aged 14 to 18 who reported having used alcohol before age fourteen, 20% said they had sex at age fourteen or earlier, compared with 7% of other teens.

- One-quarter of sexually active 9–12th grade students report using alcohol or drugs during their last sexual encounter, with males more likely than females to have done so (31% vs. 19%).

- For a significant proportion of adults aged 18 to 30, having sex and heavy drinking occur together in a single episode. Among men, 35% said they had sex when consuming five to eight drinks, compared with 17% of those who had one or two drinks. Among women aged 18 to 30, 39% had sex while consuming five to eight drinks, compared with 14% of women who had one or two drinks.

Unprotected Sex

- 38% of sexually active teenage women and 26% of women aged 20 to 24 rely on the condom as their contraceptive method, making it second only to the pill (used by 44% of teens and 52% of young adults).

- Research on the association between condom use and substance use is mixed. According to one analysis of a large national sample of high school students, sexually active adolescents who use alcohol and/or drugs are somewhat less likely than other students to have used a condom the last time they had sex. However, the differences were not statistically significant after controlling for other factors.

- The more substances that sexually active teens and young adults have ever tried, the less likely they are to have used a condom the last time they had sex: Among those aged 14 to 22, 78% of boys and 67% of girls who reported never using a substance said that they used a condom, compared with only 35% of boys and 23% of girls who reported ever having used five substances.

- Teen girls and young women aged 14 to 22 who have recently used multiple substances are less likely to have used a condom the last time they had sex: 26% of young women with four recent alcohol or drug use behaviors reported using a condom at last intercourse, compared with 44% of those who reported no recent alcohol or drug use.

Multiple Partners

- For teenagers as well as adults aged 18 to 30, having multiple sexual partners has been associated with both every using and currently using alcohol or other substances.

- 39% of sexually active students in 9th–12th grades who report ever using alcohol have had sex with four or more partners, compared with 29% of students who never drink.

- 44% of sexually active students in 9th–12th grades who report ever using drugs have had sex with four or more partners, compared with 24% of students who use drugs.

- Among sexually active young people aged 14 to 22 who used a substance the last time they had intercourse, 61% of men and 44% of women had had multiple partners during the three months prior to being surveyed, compared with 32% of men and 14% of women who did not use drugs or alcohol the last time they had sex.

- Sexually active women aged 14 to 22 who recently used alcohol or drugs four times are more likely than those who do not drink or take drugs to have had more than one sex partner in the last three months (48% compared with 8%). The number of different substances women aged 14 to 22 use in their lifetimes significantly increases their likelihood of having multiple sex partners. Among 18- to 22-year-old men and women, an earlier age at initiation of alcohol use is associated with the later likelihood of having multiple sex partners. For example, among those who reported having initiated alcohol use at age 10 or younger, 44% of men and 31% of women said they had had more than one sex partner in the three months prior to the survey, compared with 37% of men and 12% of women who said that they first drank alcohol at age 17 or older.

Unintended Consequences

Sexually Transmitted Diseases (STDs)

- There are approximately fifteen million new cases of sexually transmitted diseases (STDs) annually in the United States. About two-thirds of new cases occur among adolescents and young adults under 25, a group that is also more likely to engage in both risky sexual activity and alcohol and drug use.

♣ **It's A Fact!!**
Sexual Risk Behaviors

Vaginal, anal, and oral intercourse place young people at risk for HIV infection and other sexually transmitted diseases (STDs). Vaginal intercourse carries the additional risk of pregnancy. In the United States:

- In 2009, 46% of high school students had ever had sexual intercourse, and 14% of high school students had had four or more sex partners during their life.

- In 2009, 34% of currently sexually active high school students did not use a condom during last sexual intercourse.

- In 2002, 11% of males and females aged 15–19 had engaged in anal sex with someone of the opposite sex; 3% of males aged 15–19 had had anal sex with a male.

- In 2002, 55% of males and 54% of females aged 15–19 had engaged in oral sex with someone of the opposite sex.

- In 2006, an estimated 5,259 young people aged 13–24 in the 33 states reporting to CDC were diagnosed with HIV/AIDS, representing about 14% of the persons diagnosed that year.

- Each year, there are approximately 19 million new STD infections, and almost half of them are among youth aged 15 to 24.

- Young women may be biologically more susceptible to chlamydia, gonorrhea, and HIV than older women.

- In a single act of unprotected sex with an infected partner, a teenage woman has a one percent risk of acquiring HIV, a 30 percent risk of getting genital herpes, and a 50 percent chance of contracting gonorrhea.

Unintended Pregnancy

- Substance use and unintended pregnancies often occur among the same populations.

- Fifty-five percent of teenagers say that having sex while drinking or on drugs is often a reason for unplanned teen pregnancies.

- Almost one million adolescents—or 19 percent of those who have had sexual intercourse—become pregnant each year. Among women aged 15

- In 2002, 12% of all pregnancies, or 757,000, occurred among adolescents aged 15–19.

In addition, young people in the United States use alcohol and other drugs at high rates. Adolescents are more likely to engage in high-risk behaviors, such as unprotected sex, when they are under the influence of drugs or alcohol. In 2009, 22% of high school students who had sexual intercourse during the past three months drank alcohol or used drugs before last sexual intercourse.

Abstinence from vaginal, anal, and oral intercourse is the only 100 percent effective way to prevent HIV, other STDs, and pregnancy. The correct and consistent use of a male latex condom can reduce the risk of STD transmission, including HIV infection. However, no protective method is 100 percent effective, and condom use cannot guarantee absolute protection against any STD or pregnancy.

HIV/STD prevention education should be developed with the active involvement of parents, be locally determined, and be consistent with community values. It should address the needs of youth who are not engaging in sexual intercourse as well as youth who are currently sexually active, while ensuring that all youth are provided with effective education to protect themselves and others from HIV infection and STDs now and lifelong.

Source: Excerpted from "Healthy Youth: Sexual Risk Behaviors," the Centers for Disease Control and Prevention, July 2009.

to 19, 78 percent of pregnancies are believed to be unintended, accounting for about one-quarter of all accidental pregnancies each year.

• The pregnancy rate among women aged 20 to 24 is 183.3 per 1,000
women; it is thought that 59 percent of pregnancies in this age group
are unintended.

Sexual Assault And Violence

• Estimates of substance use during instances of sexual violence and rape
in the general population range from 30% to 90% for alcohol use, and
from 13% to 42% for the use of illicit substances.

• Alcohol use by the victim, perpetrator, or both has been implicated in
46% to 75% of date rapes among college students.

✔ **Quick Tip**

Preventing Pregnancy

• Thinking "it won't happen to me" is stupid—if you don't protect yourself,
it probably will.

• Sex is serious. Make a plan.

• Just because you think "everybody's doing it," doesn't mean they are. Some
are, some aren't—and some are lying.

• There are a lot of good reasons to say "no, not yet." Protecting your feelings
is one of them.

• You're in charge of your life. Don't let anyone pressure you into a relationship until you are absolutely sure you're ready. And never, ever let anyone
pressure you into having sex. Remember, you are the decider.

• Are you with Mr./Ms. Right? If you answer yes to any of the following
questions, he/she is probably not right for you. Does he or she: Act jeal-
ous or possessive? Ignore boundaries of any sort? Insult you privately or
in front of others? Not let you have your own identify? Text or IM you
constantly? Refuse to consider your point of view? Keep you from spending time with close friends?

• You can always say "no"—even if you've said "yes" before.

- One survey of college students found that 78% of women had experienced sexual aggression (any type of sexual activity, including kissing, unwanted by the woman). Dates on which sexual aggression occurred were more likely to include heavy drinking or drug use than those dates that were not marked by sexually aggressive activity.

- While 93% of teenage women report that their first intercourse was voluntary, one-quarter of these young women report that it was unwanted.

- Seven out of ten women who first had intercourse before age 13 say it was unwanted or involuntary.

- Compared with women in other age groups, women aged 19 to 29 report more violent incidents with intimate partners, for a rate of 21.3 violent victimizations per 1,000 women.

- Using protection is just being smart—it doesn't mean you're pushy or easy.

- If you think carrying a condom ruins the mood, consider what a pregnancy will do to it.

- If you're drunk or high you can't make good decisions about anything—especially sex.

- Don't do something you might not remember or might really regret. Sex won't make him yours, and a baby won't make him stay.

- Not ready to be a parent? It's simple: don't have sex or use protection every time.

- Think sending nude pictures or explicit text messages is fun and flirty? Keep in mind that there's no changing your mind in cyberspace—once it's out there, it's out of your control and out there forever.

- Help your parents out—be patient if they want to talk to you about relationships, sex, or contraception. These conversations can be awkward for them, too.

Source: "iPlan: Tips from Teens for Teens about Life, Love, and Not Getting Pregnant," © 2009 National Campaign to Prevent Teen Pregnancy (www.thenationalcampaign.org). Reprinted with permission.

Frequently Asked Questions: Date Rape Drugs

What are date rape drugs?

These are drugs that are sometimes used to assist a sexual assault. Sexual assault is any type of sexual activity that a person does not agree to. It can include touching that is not okay, putting something into the vagina, sexual intercourse, rape, and attempted rape.

These drugs are powerful and dangerous. They can be slipped into your drink when you are not looking. The drugs often have no color, smell, or taste, so you can't tell if you are being drugged. The drugs can make you become weak and confused—or even pass out—so that you are unable to refuse sex or defend yourself. If you are drugged, you might not remember what happened while you were drugged. Date rape drugs are used on both females and males.

The three most common date rape drugs are Rohypnol, GHB, and ketamine. For more information about these drugs, see Chapter 42.

Is alcohol a date rape drug? What about other drugs?

Any drug that can affect judgment and behavior can put a person at risk for unwanted or risky sexual activity. Alcohol is one such drug. In fact, alcohol is the drug most commonly used to help commit sexual assault. When a person drinks too much alcohol:

- It's harder to think clearly.
- It's harder to set limits and make good choices.
- It's harder to tell when a situation could be dangerous.
- It's harder to say "no" to sexual advances.
- It's harder to fight back if a sexual assault occurs.
- It's possible to blackout and to have memory loss.

The club drug "ecstasy" (MDMA) has been used to commit sexual assault. It can be slipped into someone's drink without the person's knowledge. Also, a person who willingly takes ecstasy is at greater risk of sexual assault. Ecstasy can make a person feel "lovey-dovey" towards others. It also can lower a person's ability to give reasoned consent. Once under the drug's influence, a person is less able to sense danger or to resist a sexual assault.

Even if a victim of sexual assault drank alcohol or willingly took drugs, the victim is NOT at fault for being assaulted. You cannot "ask for it" or cause it to happen.

How can I protect myself from being a victim?

- Don't accept drinks from other people.

- Open containers yourself.

- Keep your drink with you at all times, even when you go to the bathroom.

- Don't share drinks.

- Don't drink from punch bowls or other common, open containers. They may already have drugs in them.

- If someone offers to get you a drink from a bar or at a party, go with the person to order your drink. Watch the drink being poured and carry it yourself.

- Don't drink anything that tastes or smells strange. Sometimes, GHB tastes salty.

- Have a nondrinking friend with you to make sure nothing happens.

- If you realize you left your drink unattended, pour it out.

- If you feel drunk and haven't drunk any alcohol—or, if you feel like the effects of drinking alcohol are stronger than usual—get help right away.

Are there ways to tell if I might have been drugged and raped?

It is often hard to tell. Most victims don't remember being drugged or assaulted. The victim might not be aware of the attack until eight or 12 hours after it occurred. These drugs also leave the body very quickly. Once a victim gets help, there might be no proof that drugs were involved in the attack. But there are some signs that you might have been drugged:

- You feel drunk and haven't drunk any alcohol—or, you feel like the effects of drinking alcohol are stronger than usual.

- You wake up feeling very hung over and disoriented or having no memory of a period of time.

- You remember having a drink, but cannot recall anything after that.

- You find that your clothes are torn or not on right.

- You feel like you had sex, but you cannot remember it.

✔ Quick Tip

If You Think You Have Been Drugged And Raped

- **Get medical care right away.** Call 911 or have a trusted friend take you to a hospital emergency room. Don't urinate, douche, bathe, brush your teeth, wash your hands, change clothes, or eat or drink before you go. These things may give evidence of the rape. The hospital will use a "rape kit" to collect evidence.

- **Call the police from the hospital.** Tell the police exactly what you remember. Be honest about all your activities. Remember, nothing you did—including drinking alcohol or doing drugs—can justify rape.

- **Ask the hospital to take a urine (pee) sample that can be used to test for date rape drugs.** The drugs leave your system quickly. Rohypnol stays in the body for several hours, and can be detected in the urine up to 72 hours after taking it. GHB leaves the body in 12 hours. Don't urinate before going to the hospital.

- **Don't pick up or clean up where you think the assault might have occurred.** There could be evidence left behind—such as on a drinking glass or bed sheets.

- **Get counseling and treatment.** Feelings of shame, guilt, fear, and shock are normal. A counselor can help you work through these emotions and begin the healing process. Calling a crisis center or a hotline is a good place to start. One national hotline is the National Sexual Assault Hotline at 1-800-656-HOPE.

Source: National Women's Health Information Center, December 2008.

Chapter 55

Substance Abuse And Pregnancy

Nearly 4% of pregnant women in the United States use illicit drugs such as marijuana, cocaine, ecstasy and other amphetamines, and heroin.[1] These and other illicit drugs may pose various risks for pregnant women and their babies. Some of these drugs can cause a baby to be born too small or too soon, or to have withdrawal symptoms, birth defects, or learning and behavioral problems.

Because many pregnant women who use illicit drugs also use alcohol and tobacco, which also pose risks to unborn babies, it often is difficult to determine which health problems are caused by a specific illicit drug. Additionally, illicit drugs may be prepared with impurities that may be harmful to a pregnancy.

Finally, pregnant women who use illicit drugs may engage in other unhealthy behaviors that place their pregnancy at risk, such as having extremely poor nutrition or developing sexually transmitted infections. All of these factors make it difficult to know exactly what the effects of illicit drugs are on pregnancy.

What are the risks with use of marijuana during pregnancy?

Marijuana is the most frequently used illicit drug among women of child-bearing age in the United States.[1] Some studies suggest that use of marijuana

About This Chapter: Information in this chapter is from "Illicit Drug Use During Pregnancy," © 2008 March of Dimes Birth Defects Foundation. All rights reserved. For additional information, contact the March of Dimes at their website www.marchofdimes.com.

✤ It's A Fact!!
Drug Abuse Among Pregnant Women In The U.S.

Exposure to substances of abuse can affect individuals across the lifespan, starting in utero. While most pregnant women do not abuse illicit drugs, combined 2006 and 2007 data from the National Survey on Drug Use and Health found that among pregnant women ages 15 to 44, the youngest ones reported the greatest substance use. In fact, pregnant women aged 15 to 17 had a higher rate of use (22.6% or 20,000 women) than women of the same age who were not pregnant (13.3% or 832,000 women).

The Effects Of Prenatal Drug Exposure

Tobacco: Smoking during pregnancy is associated with several adverse outcomes for fetuses, including increased risk for stillbirth, infant mortality, sudden infant death syndrome, preterm birth, and respiratory problems. Carbon monoxide and nicotine from tobacco smoke may interfere with fetal oxygen supply—and because nicotine readily crosses the placenta, it can reach concentrations in the fetus that are much higher than maternal levels. Nicotine concentrates in fetal blood, amniotic fluid, and breast milk, exposing both fetuses and infants to toxic effects.

Cocaine, Marijuana, And Other Illicit Drugs: Illicit drug use during pregnancy has been associated with a variety of adverse effects, though more research is needed to draw causal connections. While some effects may be subtle, they generally range from low birth weight to behavioral and cognitive deficits developmentally.

Promising Treatment Approaches For Pregnant Women

Medications: Research shows that some medications shown to be effective in drug-abusing populations can be safe and effective for pregnant women (and their babies) as well.

Behavioral Treatments: National Institute on Drug Abuse (NIDA)-supported research has established that the positive results of evidence-based treatments to change drug abuse and addiction behaviors in the general population now extend to pregnant women.

Source: Excerpted from "Prenatal Exposure to Drugs of Abuse," a research update from the National Institute on Drug Abuse, May 2009.

during pregnancy may slow fetal growth and slightly decrease the length of pregnancy (possibly increasing the risk of premature birth). These effects are seen mainly in women who use marijuana regularly (six or more times a week).[2]

After delivery, some babies who were regularly exposed to marijuana before birth appear to undergo withdrawal-like symptoms, including excessive crying and trembling.[2,3] These babies have difficulty with state regulation (the ability to easily adjust to touch and changes in their environment), are more sensitive to stimulation, and have poor sleep patterns.

Couples who are planning pregnancy should keep in mind that marijuana can reduce fertility in both men and women, making it more difficult to conceive.[2]

What is the long-term outlook for babies exposed to marijuana before birth?

There have been a limited number of studies following marijuana-exposed babies through childhood. Some did not find any increased risk of learning or behavioral problems. However, others found that children who were exposed to marijuana before birth are more likely to have subtle problems that affect their ability to pay attention.[2,3] Exposed children do not appear to have a decrease in IQ.

What are the risks with use of ecstasy, methamphetamine, and other amphetamines during pregnancy?

The use of ecstasy, methamphetamine, and other amphetamines has increased dramatically in recent years. There have been few studies on how ecstasy may affect pregnancy. One small study did find a possible increase in congenital heart defects and, in females only, of a skeletal defect called club-foot.[4] Babies exposed to ecstasy before birth also may face some of the same risks as babies exposed to other types of amphetamines.

Another commonly abused amphetamine is methamphetamine, also known as speed, ice, crank, and crystal meth. A 2006 study found that babies of women who used this drug were more than three times as likely than un-exposed babies to grow poorly before birth.[5] Even when born at term, affected babies tend to be born with low birth weight (less than 5½ pounds) and have a smaller-than-normal head circumference.

Use of methamphetamine during pregnancy also increases the risk of pregnancy complications, such as premature birth and placental problems.[5] There also have been cases of birth defects, including heart defects and cleft lip/palate, in exposed babies, but researchers do not yet know whether the drug contributed to these defects.[5]

After delivery, some babies who were exposed to amphetamines before birth appear to undergo withdrawal-like symptoms, including jitteriness, drowsiness, and breathing problems.

What is the long-term outlook for babies exposed to ecstasy, methamphetamine, and other amphetamines before birth?

The long-term outlook for these children is not known. Children who are born with low birth weight are at increased risk of learning and other problems. Children with reduced head circumference are more likely to have learning problems than those with low birth weight and normal head size.[5] More studies are needed to determine the long-term outlook for children exposed to amphetamines before birth.

What are the risks with use of heroin during pregnancy?

Women who use heroin during pregnancy greatly increase their risk of serious pregnancy complications. These risks include poor fetal growth, premature rupture of the membranes (the bag of waters that holds the fetus breaks too soon), premature birth, and stillbirth.

As many as half of all babies of heroin users are born with low birth weight.[6] Many of these babies are premature and often suffer from serious health problems during the newborn period, including breathing problems. They also are at increased risk of lifelong disabilities.

Use of heroin in pregnancy may increase the risk of a variety of birth defects.[6] What is not entirely clear is whether these effects are caused by the drug itself or related to the poor health behaviors that women who take heroin often have. The substances that the heroin often is mixed with when it is made also may play a role.

Most babies of heroin users show withdrawal symptoms during the three days after birth, including fever, sneezing, trembling, irritability, diarrhea, vomiting, continual crying, and seizures. These symptoms usually subside by one week of age. The severity of a baby's symptoms is related to how long the mother has been using heroin or other narcotics and how high a dose she has taken. The longer the baby's exposure in the womb and the greater the dose, the more severe the withdrawal. Babies exposed to heroin before birth also face an increased risk of sudden infant death syndrome (SIDS).

While heroin can be sniffed, snorted or smoked, most users inject the drug into a muscle or vein. Pregnant women who share needles are at risk of contracting HIV (the virus that causes AIDS) and the hepatitis C virus. These infections can be passed on to the infant during pregnancy or at birth.

A pregnant woman who uses heroin should not attempt to suddenly stop taking the drug. This can put her baby at increased risk of death. She should consult a health care provider or drug-treatment center about treatment with a drug called methadone.

Infants born to mothers taking methadone have withdrawal symptoms that can be safely treated. Methadone-exposed babies have higher birth weights than babies born to women who continue to use heroin. It is important for families to be aware that infants who are withdrawing from narcotics, including methadone, may continue to have symptoms of withdrawal for weeks after discharge from the nursery. There are effective ways to reduce the baby's discomfort using pacifiers, swaddling, and cuddling. Parents and caregivers benefit from support from family and friends and should seek out assistance if they are feeling stressed or overwhelmed.

What is the long-term outlook for babies exposed to heroin before birth?

The outlook for these children depends on a number of factors, including whether they suffered serious prematurity-related or other complications. Some studies suggest that children exposed to heroin before birth are at increased risk of learning and behavioral problems.[6]

What are the risks of use of "T's and Blues" and opioid painkillers during pregnancy?

"T's and Blues" is the street name for a mixture of a prescription opioid (related to morphine) painkiller called pentazocine and an over-the-counter allergy medicine. Individuals who abuse the mixture inject it into a vein. Babies of women who use T's and Blues during pregnancy are at increased risk of slow growth and may suffer withdrawal symptoms.[7]

Babies of women who abuse prescription oral (taken by mouth) opioid painkillers, such as oxycodone (OxyContin), also may undergo withdrawal.

What are the risks with use of cocaine during pregnancy?

Cocaine use during pregnancy can affect a pregnant woman and her baby in many ways. During the early months of pregnancy, cocaine may increase the risk of miscarriage. Later in pregnancy, it may trigger preterm labor (labor that occurs before 37 completed weeks of pregnancy) or cause the baby to grow poorly. As a result, cocaine-exposed babies are more likely than unexposed babies to be born prematurely and with low birth weight. Premature and low-birth weight babies are at increased risk of health problems during the newborn period, lasting disabilities such as mental retardation and cerebral palsy, and even death. Cocaine-exposed babies also tend to have smaller heads, which generally reflect smaller brains and an increased risk of learning problems.[8]

Some studies suggest that cocaine-exposed babies are at increased risk of birth defects involving the urinary tract and, possibly, other birth defects.[9, 10] Cocaine may cause an unborn baby to have a stroke, which can result in irreversible brain damage and sometimes death.

Cocaine use during pregnancy can cause placental problems, including placental abruption. In this condition, the placenta pulls away from the wall of the uterus before labor begins. This can lead to heavy bleeding that can be life threatening for both mother and baby. The baby may be deprived of oxygen and adequate blood flow when an abruption occurs. Prompt cesarean delivery, however, can prevent most deaths but may not prevent serious complications for the baby caused by lack of oxygen.

After birth, some babies who were regularly exposed to cocaine before birth may have mild behavioral disturbances. As newborns, some are jittery and irritable, and they may startle and cry at the gentlest touch or sound.[11] These babies may be difficult to comfort and may be withdrawn or unresponsive. Other cocaine-exposed babies "turn off" surrounding stimuli by going into a deep sleep for most of the day. Generally, these behavioral disturbances are temporary and resolve over the first few months of life.[11]

Cocaine-exposed babies may be more likely than unexposed babies to die of SIDS. However, studies suggest that poor health practices that often accompany maternal cocaine use (such as use of other drugs and smoking) may play a major role in these deaths.[12]

What is the long-term outlook for babies who were exposed to cocaine before birth?

Most children who were exposed to cocaine before birth have normal intelligence.[13] This is encouraging, in light of earlier predictions that many of these children would be severely brain damaged. A 2004 study at Case Western Reserve University found that four-year-old children who were exposed to cocaine before birth scored just as well on intelligence tests as unexposed children.[13]

However, the Case Western study and other studies suggest that cocaine may sometimes contribute to subtle learning and behavioral problems, including language delays and attention problems.[13,14,15,16] A good home environment appears to help reduce these effects.[13,15,16] A recent study also suggests that cocaine-exposed children grow at a slower rate through age 10 than unexposed children, suggesting some lasting effect on development.[17]

What are the risks of "club drugs," such as PCP (angel dust), ketamine (Special K), and LSD (acid)?

There are few studies on the risks of these drugs during pregnancy. Babies of mothers who used PCP in pregnancy may have withdrawal symptoms.[7,18] Babies exposed before birth to PCP or ketamine may be at increased risk of learning and behavioral problems.[7,18] There have been occasional reports of birth defects in babies of women who used LSD during pregnancy, but it is not known whether or not the drug contributed to the defects.[7]

✤ It's A Fact!!

When You Are Pregnant Drinking Can Hurt Your Baby

If you drink alcohol, it can hurt your baby's growth. Your baby may have physical and behavioral problems that can last for the rest of his or her life. Children born with the most serious problems caused by alcohol have fetal alcohol syndrome.

Children with fetal alcohol syndrome may:

- Be born small.

- Have problems eating and sleeping.

- Have problems seeing and hearing.

- Have trouble following directions and learning how to do simple things.

- Have trouble paying attention and learning in school.

- Need special teachers and schools.

- Have trouble getting along with others and controlling their behavior.

- Need medical care all their lives.

Here are some questions you may have about alcohol and drinking while you are pregnant.

Can I drink alcohol if I am pregnant? No. Do not drink alcohol when you are pregnant. Why? Because when you drink alcohol, so does your baby.

Is any kind of alcohol safe to drink during pregnancy? No. Drinking any kind of alcohol when you are pregnant can hurt your baby. Alcoholic drinks are beer, wine, wine coolers, liquor, or mixed drinks. A glass of wine, a can of beer, and a mixed drink all have about the same amount of alcohol.

Will these problems go away? No. These problems will last for a child's whole life. People with severe problems may not be able to take care of themselves as adults. They may never be able to work.

How can I stop drinking? If you cannot stop drinking, GET HELP. You may have a disease called alcoholism. Your doctor or nurse can find a program to help you.

Source: Excerpted from "Drinking and Your Pregnancy," National Institute on Alcohol Abuse and Alcoholism, 2005.

What are the risks of inhaling glues and solvents during pregnancy?

Individuals, pregnant or not, who inhale these substances risk liver, kidney, and brain damage and even death. Abusing these substances during pregnancy can contribute to miscarriage, slow fetal growth, preterm birth and birth defects.[7] They also may cause withdrawal symptoms in the newborn.

How can a woman protect her baby from the dangers of illicit drugs?

Birth defects and other problems caused by illicit drugs are completely preventable. The March of Dimes advises women who use illicit drugs to stop before they become pregnant or to delay pregnancy until they believe they can avoid the drug completely throughout pregnancy. The March of Dimes also encourages pregnant women who use illicit drugs (with the exception of heroin) to stop using the drug immediately, because of the harm continued drug use may cause. Women who use heroin should consult their health care provider or a drug treatment center about methadone treatment.

Does the March of Dimes support research on illicit drug use during pregnancy?

The March of Dimes has supported a number of research grants on drug use during pregnancy. For example, a recent grantee was studying physical and behavioral reasons that motivate pregnant women to abuse drugs such as cocaine, in order to improve drug treatment programs for pregnant women and reduce the risks to their babies. The March of Dimes also produces a variety of information and educational materials that inform pregnant women and others of the dangers of using drugs during pregnancy.

References

1. Substance Abuse and Mental Health Administration. Results from the 2006 National Survey on Drug Use and Health: National Findings. Office of Applied Studies, NS-DUH Series H-32, DHHS, Publication No. SMA 07-4293, Rockville, MD, 2007.

2. Reproductive Toxicology Center. *Cannabis*. Updated 12/1/05.

3. National Institute on Drug Abuse. Research Report Series–Marijuana Abuse. Updated 11/2/06.

4. Reproductive Toxicology Center. MDMA. Updated 3/1/07.

5. Smith, L.M., et al. The Infant Development, Environment, and Lifestyle Study: Effects of Prenatal Methamphetamine Exposure, Polydrug Exposure, and Poverty on Intrauterine Growth. *Pediatrics*, volume 118, number 3, September 2006, pages 1149-1156.

6. Briggs, G.G., et al. *Drugs in Pregnancy and Lactation 7th edition*. Philadelphia, PA, Lippincott Williams and Wilkins, 2005.

7. American College of Obstetricians and Gynecologists (ACOG). *Your Pregnancy and Birth 4th edition*. ACOG, Washington, DC, 2005.

8. Bateman, D.A., Chiriboga, C.A. Dose-Response Effect of Cocaine on Newborn Head Circumference. *Pediatrics*, volume 106, number 3, September 2000, p.e33.

9. Vidaeff. A.C., Mastrobattista, J.M. In Utero Cocaine Exposure: A Thorny Mix of Science and Mythology. *American Journal of Perinatology*, volume 20, number 4, 2003, pages 165-172.

10. Reproductive Toxicology Center. Cocaine. Last updated 12/1/05.

11. Bauer, C.R., et al. Acute Neonatal Effects of Cocaine Exposure During Pregnancy. *Archives of Pediatric and Adolescent Medicine*, volume 159, September 2005, pages 824-834.

12. Fares, I., et al. Intrauterine Cocaine Exposure and the Risk for Sudden Infant Death Syndrome: A Meta-Analysis. *Journal of Perinatology*, volume 17, number 3, May-June 1997, pages 179-182.

13. Singer, L.T., et al. Cognitive Outcomes of Preschool Children with Prenatal Cocaine Exposure. *Journal of the American Medical Association*, volume 291, number 20, May 26, 2004, pages 2448-2456.

14. Linares, T.J., et al. Mental Health Outcomes of Cocaine-Exposed Children at 6 Years of Age. *Journal of Pediatric Psychology*, volume 31, number 1, January-February 2006, pages 85-97.

15. Lewis, B.A., et al. Prenatal Cocaine and Tobacco Effects on Children's Language Trajectories. *Pediatrics*, volume 120, number 1, July 2007, pages e78-e85.

16. Bada, H.S., et al. Impact of Prenatal Cocaine Exposure on Child Behavior Problems through School Age. *Pediatrics*, volume 119, number 2, February 2007, pages e348-e359.

17. Richardson, G.A., et al. Effects of Prenatal Cocaine Exposure on Growth: A Longitudinal Analysis. *Pediatrics*, volume 120, number 4, October 2007, pages e1017-e1027.

18. Reproductive Toxicology Center. Phencyclidine. Updated 12/1/05.

Chapter 56

Substance Abuse And Military Families

Army Cracks Down As Drug, Alcohol Cases Rise

Drug and alcohol abuse in the ranks is on the rise, and Army officials say commanders are largely to blame for failing to take control of the situation.

Vice Chief of Staff Gen. Peter Chiarelli issued commanders across the service a message directing them to do a better job of getting offenders into treatment or separated from the Army.

Chiarelli is leading an Army-wide crackdown on violations and placed renewed emphasis on reporting requirements. That could mean increased inspections of barracks rooms and more visits by leaders to soldiers' off-post homes to make cursory evaluations of their living conditions.

Soldiers can expect stricter disciplinary action for positive urine analysis results and a possible wave of separations for soldiers who have a pattern of substance abuse after receiving help, Army leaders said. The requirement to randomly test 16 percent of a company's soldiers each month and as directed by commanders will remain unchanged.

About This Chapter: Information in this chapter is from "Army cracks down as drugs, alcohol cases rise," by Gina Cavallaro, *Army Times*, June 10, 2009. © 2009 Army Times Publishing Company. Reprinted with permission.

The substance abuse problem and lack of compliance by leaders came to light May 8 in an internal message from Chiarelli. His message is part of a larger campaign plan launched in April to uncover the reasons behind a record number of suicides among soldiers. In the plan, he said that until leaders become more fully engaged with their soldiers and their well-being, the Army's burgeoning suicide rate will not be fully understood or stemmed.

"There is a growing population of soldiers with substance abuse problems, as indicated by multiple positive urinalysis results and alcohol-related actions that have not been referred to the [Army Substance Abuse Program, or ASAP] by their commanders," Chiarelli said.

✤ It's A Fact!!

With wartime injuries and post traumatic stress disorder on the rise, it's easier than ever for soldiers to get hooked on pain relievers, tranquilizers, sedatives and stimulants.

"We often run into patients who have developed injuries while deployed, and they are often given pain killers. Patients with emotional disorders are often given sedatives to calm them. So, there's clear overlap with our military community with the physical injuries and the anxiety and distress," said Dr. David Dodd, a psychologist with Community Mental Health. "Those medicines they are prescribed, when the symptoms are acute, they are given in higher doses. That gives the patient the opportunity, very quickly, to abuse them. And then if you combine both, and we know a lot of people who have been injured physically also have psychological distress and disorders, they are so concerned about alleviating their pain and distress, that they're willing to do anything or take anything they can to feel better."

Dodd described drug abuse as the overuse of a drug to the point where it's causing social or occupational dysfunction. People who are abusing a drug, whether it's a prescription drug or a street drug, develop a tolerance to the drug, Dodd said. Tolerance is where the user must take more and more of the drug to get the same effect. For some drugs, it does not take very long for a tolerance to develop.

Abuse also includes using prescription drugs for recreational purposes, not taking them as prescribed, and sharing medication.

Source: From "Prescription drug abuse on rise in DoD" a news release from the U.S. Army, by Robyn Baer, Fort Sill Cannoneer, April 2009.

Only 70 percent of the soldiers who tested positive for illegal drug use have been referred to ASAP for treatment in the past three years, according to ASAP officials.

That rate should be 100 percent, ASAP director Les McFarling, said, "and that's the point of Gen. Chiarelli's message. ... He's not about crushing soldiers and getting them out. He's about getting them the help they need."

Chiarelli's assessment of drug use is validated by data from ASAP, which provides prevention and drug test coordination assistance to commanders.

Over the past five years, positive test results have risen steadily.

The percentage has gone from 1.72% for the active component in fiscal 2004 to 2.38 percent in fiscal 2008, said McFarling, who said the 2008 data was based on the Army's end strength of about 540,000.

That would mean about 8,600 soldiers in fiscal 2004, and about 12,800 in fiscal 2008, tested positive.

Alcohol abuse also remains a problem with about 25 percent of soldiers found to be heavy drinkers in a 2005 Defense Department study, the most recent data available.

The incidence of alcohol abuse is detected differently than that for drugs, usually by military police or local police outside post, for driving under the influence or in observations by peers.

Alcohol is a factor in many soldier suicides, which are also tied to failed relationships, financial problems, or pending legal actions.

"Alcohol use is greater than anything else. We are most concerned about alcohol use and abuse," said Maj. Gen. Anthony Cucolo, commanding general of the 3rd Infantry Division's 26,500 soldiers, who said he and his command sergeant major take twice as long now to review all substance abuse cases for extenuating circumstances, rejecting a "standard punishment" for everyone because of the war.

Col. Tom James, 3rd ID chief of staff, cited the case of a master sergeant who had an incident involving alcohol. A look into his record revealed he had no previous offenses, but had deployed three times and gone through nine roadside bomb incidents. They said they got him the help he needed.

"I would rather deploy under strength with good soldiers than keep marginal soldiers in the formation," Cucolo said. "When we have drug- and alcohol-related offenses, we look at each soldier individually, but there is no blind eye to aberrant behavior."

Chiarelli, who was named the Army's point man on suicide prevention in February, kicked off a massive house-cleaning plan with orders to renew neglected health and welfare programs and to sweep up an accumulation of bad habits after seven years of war with a return to discipline in the garrison.

The Army Campaign Plan for Health Promotion, Risk Reduction and Suicide Prevention was launched in April and seeks to address almost 250 issues for updating or fixing in the areas of policy, training, organization, doctrine, leadership, facilities, resources and personnel, most before the end of the fiscal year.

His message, ordering commanders to comply with a requirement to refer soldiers to the ASAP for treatment, called substance abuse "one of the largest challenges in maintaining health" among soldiers.

"Substance abuse affects the health and morale of our force. I saw that when I visited a number of installations in March," Chiarelli said in an e-mail to *Army Times*, explaining that while substance abuse is a problem, it's not the only focus of his campaign to address suicides.

"My intent for sending out my message was to remind everyone of the resources available and regulatory requirements for dealing with substance abuse so that it doesn't have a negative impact on the force."

The predominant illegal substance found regularly in positive urine analysis tests, McFarling said, is marijuana, and the primary users are white male soldiers younger than 25, a demographic that has remained steady for years, he said. Cocaine is the second most common drug found in tests, but other substances such as LSD, methamphetamines, heroin and illegally used prescription drugs have also been found, said Brig. Gen. Colleen McGuire, director of the Suicide Prevention Task Force.

She and her team accompanied Chiarelli for an eight-day tour of six posts in mid-March, in which they learned, for example, that 1,000 soldiers at one unnamed post had "popped hot" on urine analyses in a one-year period. Of those, 372 were repeat abusers. None had been referred for treatment.

"I don't think there was any blatant attempt to disregard regulations," McGuire said, but rather it could be a combination of factors, including the inexperience of junior leaders, officers and noncommissioned officers, who haven't known anything but the combat zone and are unfamiliar with leadership in garrison.

She pointed to "the old adage that people only do what the boss checks, or possibly some concern that they have to manage closely who they chapter and who they retain to make sure they've got the requisite unit fill."

A unit may be reluctant to get rid of its only communications repairman if he "pops hot," she said, because there may not be a replacement.

If soldiers are found to be using drugs, the Army may keep them in rather than separating them from service.

"Chaptering is at the discretion of the commander. On every hot UA, commanders are to initiate a chapter, that is by regulation, but you don't have to follow through on that. It starts a process and depending on their treatment and how well they do, it will determine whether or not they stay in the military," McGuire explained.

The soldiers most likely to feel the impact of Chiarelli's global assessment of order and discipline are those living in the Army's 167,000 barracks rooms, because that is where the youngest, newest population lives.

McGuire and other leaders acknowledged that the Army's continuing effort to give soldiers more freedom and a greater degree of privacy, by building barracks that are more like apartments, has had the unintended consequence of allowing prohibited activities to flourish.

Senior NCOs interviewed by *Army Times* said they saw the handwriting on the wall when the 1989 initiative to give soldiers more autonomy, known as Better Opportunities for Single Soldiers, changed the barracks configuration and did away with the shared environment—and discipline.

✣ It's A Fact!!

To address the social problems both caused by and contributing to drug use, the Department of Defense and partners are developing and testing novel treatment approaches with veterans. For example, Rosen's Money Management Intervention trains those in drug treatment to better manage their money by linking access to funds to treatment goal completion. For relapse prevention, McKay's telephone treatment approach delivers counseling at home for several months once a veteran has completed an initial face-to-face treatment episode.

While the National Institute on Drug Abuse (NIDA) is striving to expand its portfolio of research related to trauma, stress, and substance use and abuse among veterans and their families, a number of promising projects are already being funded. These include studies on: smoking cessation and PTSD, behavioral interventions for the dually diagnosed, substance use and HIV progression, and virtual reality treatment of PTSD and substance abuse. Additionally, NIDA's National Drug Abuse Treatment Clinical Trials Network (CTN) is developing, in conjunction with researchers from the Veterans Administration, a protocol concept on the treatment of PTSD/SUD in veteran populations.

Further, efforts are underway to make it easier for veterans to access treatments. Research on drug courts, for example, is now being applied to developing courts for veterans, the former having demonstrated their effectiveness in addressing nonviolent crimes by drug abusers and ushering them into needed treatment instead of prison. Because the criminal justice system is a frequent treatment referral source for veterans, such specialized courts may give them the opportunity to access the services and support they may not otherwise receive. While New York has the only court that exclusively handles nonviolent crimes committed by veterans, other states are considering establishing such courts.

Source: From "Substance Abuse among the Military, Veterans, and their Families," a research update from the National Institute on Drug Abuse, July 2009.

"In the old days, your rooms were subject to inspections all the time, so it was all about the wall locker display, the shoe display, the hospital corners on the beds. When you walked in it looked like the Army," said an NCO who declined to be identified because he was not authorized to speak to the media.

The NCO also noted that when soldiers worked and lived together, it fostered a tighter unit environment and "cliques didn't form because we all hung out together."

The absence of that shared environment, regular room inspections and main entries in today's barracks also means that troubled soldiers can hide their problems from the rest of the population and from the unit chain of command.

By reinstituting regular inspections at some posts and promoting a return to a true buddy system, those troubled soldiers might be found sooner and illicit activity forced out, McGuire predicted.

During the tour of the six posts, she said, feedback indicated an "overwhelming anti-drug sentiment," and an outcry from soldiers to send in drug-sniffing dogs to clean up the barracks.

Improper behavior in the barracks "has an effect on morale, too. We've got systems that address this, but again, the systems are not disciplined. This is tied to risk reduction and how [it may be] linked to suicide," McGuire said.

"The garrison environment needs to be the hometown; it's the bedrock, it's the foundation, it's where the family resides, it's where your friends are," she said.

Chapter 57

Substance Abuse And Violence

Youth Violence And Illicit Drug Use

Research suggests a strong relationship between the use of drugs and youth violence. The National Survey on Drug Use and Health (NSDUH) asks youths aged 12 to 17 to report on their involvement in violent behaviors during the 12 months before the survey. In this report, a past year violent behavior is defined as getting into a serious fight at school or work, participating in a group-against-group fight, or attacking others with the intent of seriously hurting them. NSDUH also includes questions about respondents' use of illicit drugs during the past year. Any illicit drug refers to marijuana/hashish, cocaine (including crack), inhalants, hallucinogens, heroin, and prescription drugs used nonmedically.

This report presents the estimated number and percentage of youths aged 12 to 17 who engaged in violent behavior in the past year. It further compares rates of violent behavior for those who used and those who did not use illicit drugs in the past year. All findings presented in this report are annual averages based on combined 2002, 2003, and 2004 NSDUH data.

About This Chapter: Information in this chapter is from "Youth Violence and Illicit Drug Use," a report from the National Survey on Drug Use and Health, an annual survey sponsored by the Substance Abuse and Mental Health Services Administration (SAMHSA), 2006; and excerpted from "Violent Behaviors among Adolescent Females," a report from the National Survey on Drug Use and Health, an annual survey sponsored by the Substance Abuse and Mental Health Services Administration (SAMHSA). December 2009.

Violent Behavior Among Youths

Based on data from 2002 through 2004, an estimated 31.6% of youths aged 12 to 17 (approximately 7.9 million adolescents) engaged in violent behavior in the past year. Rates of past year violent behavior were higher among youths aged 13, 14, and 15 (33.2%, 33.3%, and 33.1%, respectively) than those younger (aged 12, 30.2%) or older (ages 16 and 17, 30.7% and 28.7%, respectively).

Males aged 12 to 17 were more likely than females in this age group to have engaged in violent behavior in the past year (35.6% vs. 27.4%). Additionally, adolescents who were not attending or enrolled in school at the time of the interview were more likely to have engaged in violent behavior than those who were attending or enrolled in school (39.9% vs. 31.4%). The rate of past year violent behavior was higher among adolescents in families with incomes less than 125 percent of the federal poverty threshold than those in income categories further above the poverty threshold.

Adolescents in the west were less likely to have engaged in past year violent behavior (30.0%) than those in the south (31.5%), the midwest (31.9%), and the northeast (33.4%). However, rates of violent behavior were similar among youths in large metropolitan areas, small metropolitan areas, and non-metropolitan areas.

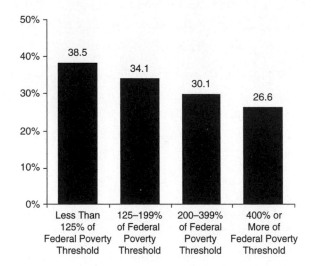

Figure 57.1. *Percentages Of Youths Aged 12 To 17 Engaging In Past Year Violent Behavior, By Family Income Relative To Federal Poverty Threshold: 2002, 2003, And 2004*

Violent Behavior And Illicit Drug Use

Youths aged 12 to 17 who used any illicit drug in the past year were almost twice as likely to have engaged in violent behavior as those who did not use any illicit drug (49.8% vs. 26.6%). This finding was consistent across age and gender, as well as other demographic and geographic variables. For example, among adolescents who lived in the northeast, 52.3% of those who used an illicit drug reported violent behavior compared to 28.1% of those who did not use an illicit drug.

An estimated 49.7% of the adolescents who used marijuana in the past year engaged in past year violent behavior, as did 55.4% of those who used inhalants. About two-thirds (69.3%) of the adolescents who used methamphetamine in the past year engaged in past year violent behavior.

The likelihood of having engaged in violent behavior increased with the number of drugs used in the past year. Approximately 26.6% of adolescents who did not use any illicit drugs reported past year violent behavior compared to 45.6% of those who used one illicit drug, 54.9% of those who used two illicit drugs, and 61.9% of those who used three or more illicit drugs.

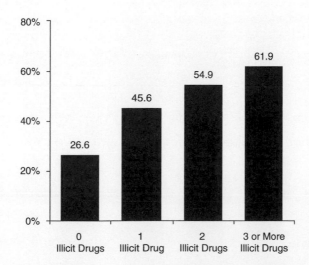

Figure 57.2. *Percentages Of Youths Aged 12 To 17 Engaging In Past Year Violent Behavior, By Number Of Illicit Drugs Used In The Past Year: 2002, 2003, And 2004*

Table 57.1. Percentages Of Youths Aged 12 To 17 Engaging In Past Year Violent Behavior, By Past Year Illicit Drug Use And Sociodemographic Characteristics: 2002, 2003, And 2004

	Past Year Illicit Drug Use (Percent)	No Past Year Illicit Drug Use (Percent)
School Status		
Currently enrolled/attending	49.6	26.5
Not currently enrolled/attending	54.0	27.4
Poverty Threshold		
Less than 125% of Federal Poverty Threshold	57.3	33.4
125–199% of Federal Poverty Threshold	51.9	29.3
200–399% of Federal Poverty Threshold	48.0	25.1
400% or More of Federal Poverty Threshold	45.0	21.4
Region		
Northeast	52.3	28.1
Midwest	49.9	26.9
South	48.6	27.0
West	49.3	24.4
County Type		
Large Metropolitan	50.3	26.7
Small Metropolitan	49.1	26.6
Non-metropolitan	49.5	25.9

Table 57.2. Percentages Of Youths Aged 12 To 17 Engaging In Past Year Violent Behavior, By Type Of Illicit Drug Used In Past Year: 2002, 2003, And 2004

Type of Illicit Drug	Past Year Violent Behavior (Percent)
Marijuana	49.7
Cocaine	61.8
Hallucinogens	61.4
Inhalants	55.4
Nonmedical Use of Prescription Pain Relievers	53.6
Methamphetamine	69.3

Violence, Adolescent Females, And Drug Use

According to a 2009 report from the National Survey on Drug Use and Health, adolescent females who engaged in a violent behavior were more likely than those who did not to have reported binge drinking and illicit drug use. For example, 15.1% of the females who engaged in a violent behavior in the past year indicated past month binge alcohol use compared with 6.9% of those who did not engage in any violent behavior. In addition, the rate of substance use increased steadily as the number of types of violent behaviors increased. For example, 6.9% of girls with no violent behavior indicated past month binge alcohol use compared with 12.6% of those with one type of violent behavior, 17.3% of those with two types, and 27.2% of those with three types.

Table 57.3. Past Month Substance Use Among Females Aged 12 To 17, By Past Year Violent Behaviors: 2006 To 2008

Past Year Violent Behavior	Binge Alcohol Use* (%)	Marijuana Use (%)	Illicit Drugs Other Than Marijuana** (%)
Violent Behavior***			
Yes	15.1%	11.4%	9.2%
No	6.9%	4.1%	3.2%
Serious Fight at School or Work			
Yes	16.6%	12.1%	10.5%
No	7.4%	4.7%	3.5%
Group Against Group Fight			
Yes	15.6%	12.1%	10.1%
No	8.0%	5.1%	4.0%
Attacked Others with Intent to Seriously Hurt Them			
Yes	20.9%	18.8%	14.6%
No	8.4%	5.3%	4.2%

* Binge alcohol use is defined as drinking five or more drinks on the same occasion (i.e., at the same time or within a couple of hours of each other) on at least one day in the past 30 days.

** Includes cocaine (including crack), inhalants, hallucinogens, heroin, or prescription drugs used nonmedically.

*** Violent behavior is defined as getting into a serious fight at school or work, participating in a group-against-group fight, or attacking others with the intent to seriously hurt them.

Source: 2006 to 2008 SAMHSA National Surveys on Drug Use and Health (NSDUHs).

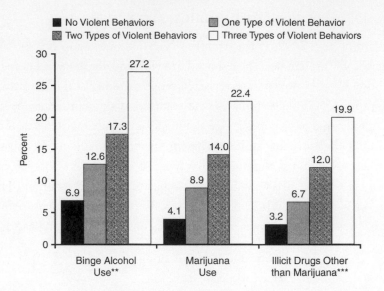

Figure 57.3. *Past Month Substance Use Among Females Aged 12 To 17, By Number Of Types Of Violent Behaviors*: 2006 To 2008.*

Table 57.4. Past Month Substance Use Among Females Aged 12 To 17, By Number Of Types Of Violent Behaviors*: 2006 To 2008

Substance Use	No Violent Behaviors	One Type of Violent Behavior	Two Types of Violent Behaviors	Three Types of Violent Behaviors
Binge Alcohol Use**	6.9%	12.6%	17.3%	27.2%
Marijuana Use	4.1%	8.9%	14.0%	22.4%
Illicit Drugs Other than Marijuana***	3.2%	6.7%	12.0%	19.9%

* Violent behavior is defined as getting into a serious fight at school or work, participating in a group-against-group fight, or attacking others with the intent to seriously hurt them.

** Binge alcohol use is defined as drinking five or more drinks on the same occasion (i.e., at the same time or within a couple of hours of each other) on at least one day in the past 30 days.

*** Includes cocaine (including crack), inhalants, hallucinogens, heroin, or prescription drugs used nonmedically.

Source for table: 2006 to 2008 SAMHSA National Surveys on Drug Use and Health (NSDUHs).

Chapter 58

Drugged Or Drunk Driving

What is drugged driving?

"Have one [drink] for the road" was once a commonly used phrase in American culture. It has only been within the past 25 years that as a nation, we have begun to recognize the dangers associated with drunk driving. Through a multipronged and concerted effort involving many stakeholders, including educators, media, legislators, law enforcement, and community organizations such as Mothers Against Drunk Driving, the nation has seen a decline in the numbers of people killed or injured as a result of drunk driving. It is now time that we recognize and address the similar dangers that can occur with drugged driving.

The principal concern regarding drugged driving is that driving under the influence of any drug that acts on the brain could impair one's motor skills, reaction time, and judgment. Drugged driving is a public health concern because it puts not only the driver at risk, but also passengers and others who share the road.

Despite these acknowledged concerns, drugged driving laws have lagged behind alcohol legislation, in part because of limitations in the current technology

About This Chapter: Information in this chapter is from "NIDA InfoFacts: Drugged Driving," from the National Institute on Drug Abuse, a component of the U.S. Department of Health and Human Services, October 2009.

for determining drug levels and resulting impairment. For alcohol, detection of its blood concentration (BAC) is relatively simple and concentrations greater than .08% have been shown to impair driving performance. Thus, .08% is the legal limit in this country. For illicit drugs, there is no agreed upon limit for which impairment has been reliably demonstrated. And determining current drug levels can be difficult, since some drugs linger in the body for a period of days or weeks after initial ingestion.

Some states (Arizona, Georgia, Indiana, Illinois, Iowa, Michigan, Minnesota, Nevada, North Carolina, Ohio, Pennsylvania, Rhode Island, Utah, Virginia, and Wisconsin), have passed "per se" laws—in which it is illegal to operate a motor vehicle if there is any detectable level of a prohibited drug, or its metabolites, in the driver's blood. Other state laws define "drugged driving" as driving when a drug "renders the driver incapable of driving safely" or "causes the driver to be impaired."

In addition, 44 states and the District of Columbia have implemented Drug Evaluation and Classification Programs, designed to train police officers as Drug Recognition Experts. Officers learn to detect characteristics in a person's behavior and appearance that may be associated with drug intoxication. If the officer suspects drug intoxication a blood or urine sample is submitted to a laboratory for confirmation.

How many people take drugs and drive?

According to the National Highway and Safety Administration's (NHTSA) 2007 National Roadside Survey, more than 16% of weekend, nighttime drivers tested positive for illegal, prescription, or over-the-counter medication. More than 11% tested positive for illicit drugs—a sign that continued substance abuse education, prevention, and law enforcement efforts are critical to public health and safety.

According to the 2008 National Survey on Drug Use and Health, an estimated 10 million people aged 12 and older reported driving under the influence of illicit drugs during the year prior to being surveyed. This corresponds to 4% of the population aged 12 and older, similar to the rate in 2007 (4.2%), but lower than the rate in 2002 (4.7%). In 2008, the rate was highest among young adults aged 18 to 25 (12.3%). In addition:

- In 2008, an estimated 12.4% of persons aged 12 and older drove under the influence of alcohol at least once in the past year. This percentage has dropped since 2002, when it was 14.2%. The 2008 estimate corresponds to 30.9 million persons.

- Driving under the influence of an illicit drug or alcohol was associated with age. In 2008, an estimated 7.2% of youth aged 16 or 17 drove under the influence. This percentage steadily increased with age to reach a peak of 26.1% among young adults aged 21 to 25. Beyond the age of 25, these rates showed a general decline with increasing age.

- Also in 2008, among persons aged 12 and older, males were nearly twice as likely as females (16.0% versus 9.0%) to drive under the influence of an illicit drug or alcohol in the past year.

In recent years, more attention has been given to drugs other than alcohol that have increasingly been recognized as hazards to road traffic safety. Some of this research has been done in other countries or in specific regions within the United States, and the prevalence rates for different drugs used varies accordingly. Overall, marijuana is the most prevalent illegal drug detected in impaired drivers, fatally injured drivers, and motor vehicle crash victims. Other drugs also implicated include benzodiazepines, cocaine, opiates, and amphetamines.

A number of studies have examined illicit drug use in drivers involved in motor vehicle crashes, reckless driving, or fatal accidents. For example:

- One study found that about 34% of motor vehicle crash victims admitted to a Maryland trauma center tested positive for "drugs only"; about 16% tested positive for "alcohol only." Approximately 9.9% (or 1 in 10) tested positive for alcohol and drugs, and within this group, 50% were younger than age 18. Although it is interesting that more people in this study tested positive for "drugs only" compared with "alcohol only," it should be noted that this represents one geographic location, so findings cannot be generalized. In fact, the majority of studies among similar populations have found higher prevalence rates of alcohol compared with drug use.

- Studies conducted in several localities have found that approximately 4% to 14% of drivers who sustained injury or died in traffic accidents tested positive for delta-9-tetrahydrocannabinol (THC), the active ingredient in marijuana.

• In a large study of almost 3,400 fatally injured drivers from three Australian states (Victoria, New South Wales, and Western Australia) between 1990 and 1999, drugs other than alcohol were present in 26.7% of the cases. These included cannabis (13.5%), opioids (4.9%), stimulants (4.1%), benzodiazepines (4.1%), and other psychotropic drugs (2.7%). Almost 10 percent of the cases involved both alcohol and drugs.

✤ It's A Fact!!
Teens And Drugged Driving

• According to the Centers for Disease Control and Prevention, vehicle accidents are the leading cause of death among young people aged 16 to 19. It is generally accepted that because teens are the least experienced drivers as a group, they have a higher risk of being involved in an accident compared with more experienced drivers. When this lack of experience is combined with the use of marijuana or other substances that impact cognitive and motor abilities, the results can be tragic.

• Results from the National Institute on Drug Abuse (NIDA)'s Monitoring the Future survey indicate that, in 2008, more than 12 percent of high school seniors admitted to driving under the influence of marijuana in the two weeks prior to the survey.

• The 2007 State of Maryland Adolescent Survey indicates that 11.1% of the state's licensed adolescent drivers reported driving under the influence of marijuana on three or more occasions and 10% reported driving while using a drug other than marijuana (not including alcohol).

Why is drugged driving hazardous?

Drugs acting on the brain can alter perception, cognition, attention, balance, coordination, reaction time, and other faculties required for safe driving. The effects of specific drugs of abuse differ depending on their mechanisms of action, the amount consumed, the history of the user, and other factors.

Marijuana: THC affects areas of the brain that control the body's movements, balance, coordination, memory, and judgment, as well as sensations. Because these effects are multifaceted, more research is required to understand marijuana's impact on the ability of drivers to react to complex and unpredictable situations. However, we do know that:

- A meta-analysis of approximately 60 experimental studies, including laboratory, driving simulator, and on-road experiments, found that behavioral and cognitive skills related to driving performance were impaired in a dose-dependent fashion with increasing THC blood levels.

- Evidence from both real and simulated driving studies indicates that marijuana can negatively affect a driver's attentiveness, perception of time and speed, and the ability to draw on information obtained from past experiences.

- A study of over 3,000 fatally injured drivers in Australia showed that when marijuana was present in the blood of the driver he or she was much more likely to be at fault for the accident. And the higher the THC concentration, the more likely the driver was to be culpable.

- Research shows that impairment increases significantly when marijuana use is combined with alcohol. Studies have found that many drivers who test positive for alcohol also test positive for THC, making it clear that drinking and drugged driving are often linked behaviors.

Prescription Drugs: Many medications (e.g., benzodiazepines and opiate analgesics) act on systems in the brain that could impair driving ability. In fact, many prescription drugs come with warnings against the operation of machinery—including motor vehicles—for a specified period of time after use. When prescription drugs are taken without medical supervision (i.e., when abused), impaired driving and other harmful reactions can also result.

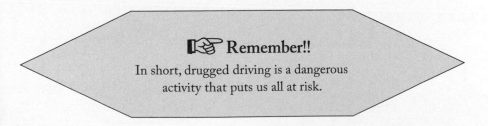

☞ Remember!!
In short, drugged driving is a dangerous
activity that puts us all at risk.

Part Eight

Treatment For Addiction

Chapter 59

Dealing With Addiction

Jason's life is beginning to unravel. His grades have slipped, he's moody, he doesn't talk to his friends, and he has stopped showing up for practice. Jason's friends know he has been experimenting with drugs and now they're worried he has become addicted.

Defining an addiction is tricky, and knowing how to handle one is even harder.

What Are Substance Abuse And Addiction?

The difference between substance abuse and addiction is very slight. Substance abuse means using an illegal substance or using a legal substance in the wrong way. Addiction begins as abuse, or using a substance like marijuana or cocaine. You can abuse a drug (or alcohol) without having an addiction. For example, just because Sara smoked weed a few times doesn't mean that she has an addiction, but it does mean that she's abusing a drug—and that could lead to an addiction.

About This Chapter: Information in this chapter is from "Dealing with Addiction," November 2007, reprinted with permission from www.kidshealth.org. Copyright © 2007 The Nemours Foundation. This information was provided by KidsHealth, one of the largest resources online for medically reviewed health information written for parents, kids, and teens. For more articles like this one, visit www.KidsHealth.org, or www.TeensHealth.org.

People can get addicted to all sorts of substances. When we think of addiction, we usually think of alcohol or illegal drugs. But people become addicted to medications, cigarettes, even glue! And some substances are more addictive than others: Drugs like crack or heroin are so addictive that they might only be used once or twice before the user loses control.

Addiction means a person has no control over whether he or she uses a drug or drinks. Someone who's addicted to cocaine has grown so used to the drug that he or she has to have it. Addiction can be physical, psychological, or both.

Physical Addiction

Being physically addicted means a person's body actually becomes dependent on a particular substance (even smoking is physically addictive). It also means building tolerance to that substance, so that a person needs a larger dose than ever before to get the same effects. Someone who is physically addicted and stops using a substance like drugs, alcohol, or cigarettes may experience withdrawal symptoms. Common symptoms of withdrawal are diarrhea, shaking, and generally feeling awful.

Psychological Addiction

Psychological addiction happens when the cravings for a drug are psychological or emotional. People who are psychologically addicted feel overcome by the desire to have a drug. They may lie or steal to get it.

A person crosses the line between abuse and addiction when he or she is no longer trying the drug to have fun or get high, but has come to depend on it. His or her whole life centers around the need for the drug. An addicted person—whether it's a physical or psychological addiction or both—no longer feels like there is a choice in taking a substance.

Signs Of Addiction

The most obvious sign of an addiction is the need to have a particular drug or substance. However, many other signs can suggest a possible addiction, such as changes in mood or weight loss or gain. (These also are signs of other conditions, too, though, such as depression or eating disorders.)

Signs that you or someone you know may have a drug or alcohol addiction include:

Psychological Signals

- Use of drugs or alcohol as a way to forget problems or to relax
- Withdrawal or keeping secrets from family and friends
- Loss of interest in activities that used to be important
- Problems with schoolwork, such as slipping grades or absences
- Changes in friendships, such as hanging out only with friends who use drugs
- Spending a lot of time figuring out how to get drugs
- Stealing or selling belongings to be able to afford drugs
- Failed attempts to stop taking drugs or drinking
- Anxiety, anger, or depression
- Mood swings

Physical Signals

- Changes in sleeping habits
- Feeling shaky or sick when trying to stop
- Needing to take more of the substance to get the same effect
- Changes in eating habits, including weight loss or gain

Getting Help

If you think you're addicted to drugs or alcohol, recognizing that you have a problem is the first step in getting help.

A lot of people think they can kick the problem on their own, but that doesn't work for most people. Find someone you trust to talk to. It may help to talk to a friend or someone your own age at first, but a supportive and understanding adult is your best option for getting help. If you can't talk to your parents, you might want to approach a school counselor, relative, doctor, favorite teacher, or religious leader.

Unfortunately, overcoming addiction is not easy. Quitting drugs or drinking is probably going to be one of the hardest things you've ever done. It's not a sign of weakness if you need professional help from a trained drug counselor or therapist. Most people who try to kick a drug or alcohol problem need professional assistance or a treatment program to do so.

Tips For Recovery

Once you start a treatment program, try these tips to make the road to recovery less bumpy:

- **Tell your friends about your decision to stop using drugs.** Your true friends will respect your decision. This might mean that you need to find a new group of friends who will be 100% supportive. Unless everyone decides to kick their drug habit at once, you probably won't be able to hang out with the friends you did drugs with before.

- **Ask your friends or family to be available when you need them.** You may need to call someone in the middle of the night just to talk. If you're going through a tough time, don't try to handle things on your own—accept the help your family and friends offer.

- **Accept invitations only to events that you know won't involve drugs or alcohol.** Going to the movies is probably safe, but you may want to skip a Friday night party until you're feeling more secure. Plan activities that don't involve drugs. Go to the movies, try bowling, or take an art class with a friend.

- **Have a plan about what you'll do if you find yourself in a place with drugs or alcohol.** The temptation will be there sometimes, but if you know how you're going to handle it, you'll be OK. Establish a plan with your parents or siblings so that if you call home using a code, they'll know that your call is a signal you need a ride out of there.

- **Remind yourself that having an addiction doesn't make you bad or weak.** If you fall back into old patterns (backslide) a bit, talk to an adult as soon as possible. There's nothing to be ashamed about, but it's important to get help soon so that all of the hard work you put into your recovery is not lost.

If you're worried about a friend who has an addiction, use these tips to help him or her, too. For example, let your friend know that you are available to talk or offer your support. If you notice a friend backsliding, talk about it openly and ask what you can do to help. If your friend is going back to drugs or drinking and won't accept your help, don't be afraid to talk to a nonthreatening, understanding adult, like your parent or school counselor. It may seem like you're ratting your friend out, but it's the best support you can offer.

Above all, offer a friend who's battling an addiction lots of encouragement and praise. It may seem corny, but hearing that you care is just the kind of motivation your friend needs.

Staying Clean

Recovering from a drug or alcohol addiction doesn't end with a 6-week treatment program. It's a lifelong process. Many people find that joining a support group can help them stay clean. There are support groups specifically for teens and younger people. You'll meet people who have gone through the same experiences you have, and you'll be able to participate in real-life discussions about drugs that you won't hear in your school's health class.

Many people find that helping others is also the best way to help themselves. Your understanding of how difficult the recovery process can be will help you to support others—both teens and adults—who are battling an addiction.

☞ Remember!!

If you do have a relapse, recognizing the problem as soon as possible is critical. Get help right away so that you don't undo all the hard work you put into your initial recovery. And, if you do have a relapse, don't ever be afraid to ask for help!

Chapter 60

Substance Abuse Treatment

Drug addiction is a complex illness characterized by intense and, at times, uncontrollable drug craving, along with compulsive drug seeking and use that persist even in the face of devastating consequences. While the path to drug addiction begins with the voluntary act of taking drugs, over time a person's ability to choose not to do so becomes compromised, and seeking and consuming the drug becomes compulsive. This behavior results largely from the effects of prolonged drug exposure on brain functioning. Addiction is a brain disease that affects multiple brain circuits, including those involved in reward and motivation, learning and memory, and inhibitory control over behavior.

Because drug abuse and addiction have so many dimensions and disrupt so many aspects of an individual's life, treatment is not simple. Effective treatment programs typically incorporate many components, each directed to a particular aspect of the illness and its consequences. Addiction treatment must help the individual stop using drugs, maintain a drug-free lifestyle, and achieve productive functioning in the family, at work, and in society. Because addiction is typically a chronic disease, people cannot simply stop using drugs for a few days and be cured. Most patients require long-term or repeated episodes of care to achieve the ultimate goal of sustained abstinence and recovery of their lives.

About This Chapter: Information in this chapter is from "NIDA InfoFacts: Treatment Approaches for Drug Addiction," National Institute on Drug Abuse, a component of the U.S. Department of Health and Human Services, September 2009.

Too often, addiction goes untreated: According to the National Survey on Drug Use and Health (NSDUH), which is conducted by the Substance Abuse and Mental Health Services Administration (SAMHSA), 23.2 million persons (9.4% of the U.S. population) aged 12 or older needed treatment for an illicit drug or alcohol use problem in 2007. Of these individuals, 2.4 million (10.4% of those who needed treatment) received treatment at a specialty facility (i.e., hospital, drug or alcohol rehabilitation or mental health center). Thus, 20.8 million persons (8.4% of the population aged 12 or older) needed treatment for an illicit drug or alcohol use problem but did not receive it. These estimates are similar to those in previous years.

Principles Of Effective Treatment

Scientific research since the mid-1970s shows that treatment can help patients addicted to drugs stop using, avoid relapse, and successfully recover their lives. Based on this research, key principles have emerged that should form the basis of any effective treatment programs:

- Addiction is a complex but treatable disease that affects brain function and behavior.

- No single treatment is appropriate for everyone.

- Treatment needs to be readily available.

- Effective treatment attends to multiple needs of the individual, not just his or her drug abuse.

- Remaining in treatment for an adequate period of time is critical.

- Counseling—individual and/or group—and other behavioral therapies are the most commonly used forms of drug abuse treatment.

- Medications are an important element of treatment for many patients, especially when combined with counseling and other behavioral therapies.

- An individual's treatment and services plan must be assessed continually and modified as necessary to ensure that it meets his or her changing needs.

- Many drug-addicted individuals also have other mental disorders.

- Medically assisted detoxification is only the first stage of addiction treatment and by itself does little to change long-term drug abuse.

- Treatment does not need to be voluntary to be effective.

- Drug use during treatment must be monitored continuously, as lapses during treatment do occur.

- Treatment programs should assess patients for the presence of HIV/ AIDS, hepatitis B and C, tuberculosis, and other infectious diseases as well as provide targeted risk-reduction counseling to help patients modify or change behaviors that place them at risk of contracting or spreading infectious diseases.

Effective Treatment Approaches

Medication and behavioral therapy, especially when combined, are important elements of an overall therapeutic process that often begins with detoxification, followed by treatment and relapse prevention. Easing withdrawal symptoms can be important in the initiation of treatment; preventing relapse is necessary for maintaining its effects. And sometimes, as with other chronic conditions, episodes of relapse may require a return to prior treatment components. A continuum of care that includes a customized treatment regimen—addressing all aspects of an individual's life, including medical and mental health services—and follow-up options (e.g., community- or family-based recovery support systems) can be crucial to a person's success in achieving and maintaining a drug-free lifestyle.

Medications

Medications can be used to help with different aspects of the treatment process.

Withdrawal: Medications offer help in suppressing withdrawal symptoms during detoxification. However, medically assisted detoxification is not in itself "treatment"—it is only the first step in the treatment process. Patients who go through medically assisted withdrawal but do not receive any further treatment show drug abuse patterns similar to those who were never treated.

Treatment: Medications can be used to help reestablish normal brain function and to prevent relapse and diminish cravings. Currently, we have medications for opioids (heroin, morphine), tobacco (nicotine), and alcohol addiction and are developing others for treating stimulant (cocaine, meth-amphetamine) and cannabis (marijuana) addiction. Most people with severe addiction problems, however, are polydrug users (users of more than one drug) and will require treatment for all of the substances that they abuse.

- **Opioids:** Methadone, buprenorphine and, for some individuals, nal-trexone are effective medications for the treatment of opiate addiction. Acting on the same targets in the brain as heroin and morphine, metha-done and buprenorphine suppress withdrawal symptoms and relieve cravings. Naltrexone works by blocking the effects of heroin or other opioids at their receptor sites and should only be used in patients who have already been detoxified. Because of compliance issues, naltrexone

✔ Quick Tip

A Quick Guide To Finding
Effective Alcohol And Drug Addiction Treatment

If you or someone you care for is dependent on alcohol or drugs and needs treatment, it is important to know that no single treatment approach is appro-priate for all individuals. Finding the right treatment program involves careful consideration of such things as the setting, length of care, philosophical approach and your or your loved one's needs.

Here are 12 questions to consider when selecting a treatment program:

1. Does the program accept your insurance? If not, will they work with you on a payment plan or find other means of support for you?

2. Is the program run by state-accredited, licensed and/or trained professionals?

3. Is the facility clean, organized and well-run?

4. Does the program encompass the full range of needs of the individual (medical, including infectious diseases; psychological, including co-occurring mental illness; social; vocational; legal; etc.)?

5. Does the treatment program also address sexual orientation and physical disabili-ties as well as provide age, gender and culturally appropriate treatment services?

is not as widely used as the other medications. All medications help patients disengage from drug seeking and related criminal behavior and become more receptive to behavioral treatments.

• **Tobacco:** A variety of formulations of nicotine replacement therapies now exist—including the patch, spray, gum, and lozenges—that are available over the counter. In addition, two prescription medications have been Food and Drug Administration (FDA)-approved for tobacco addiction: bupropion and varenicline. They have different mechanisms of action in the brain, but both help prevent relapse in people trying to quit. Each of the above medications is recommended for use in combination with behavioral treatments, including group and individual therapies, as well as telephone quitlines.

6. Is long-term aftercare support and/or guidance encouraged, provided and maintained?

7. Is there ongoing assessment of an individual's treatment plan to ensure it meets changing needs?

8. Does the program employ strategies to engage and keep individuals in longer-term treatment, increasing the likelihood of success?

9. Does the program offer counseling (individual or group) and other behavioral therapies to enhance the individual's ability to function in the family/community?

10. Does the program offer medication as part of the treatment regimen, if appropriate?

11. Is there ongoing monitoring of possible relapse to help guide patients back to abstinence?

12. Are services or referrals offered to family members to ensure they understand addiction and the recovery process to help them support the recovering individual?

Source: From "A Quick Guide to Finding Effective Alcohol and Drug Addiction Treatment," Substance Abuse and Mental Health Services Administration, NCADI Publication No. PHD877, 2001. Despite the older date of this document, the suggestions are still helpful to today's readers.

- **Alcohol:** Three medications have been FDA-approved for treating alcohol dependence: naltrexone, acamprosate, and disulfiram. A fourth, topiramate, is showing encouraging results in clinical trials. Naltrexone blocks opioid receptors that are involved in the rewarding effects of drinking and in the craving for alcohol. It reduces relapse to heavy drinking and is highly effective in some but not all patients—this is probably related to genetic differences. Acamprosate is thought to reduce symptoms of protracted withdrawal, such as insomnia, anxiety, restlessness, and dysphoria (an unpleasant or uncomfortable emotional state, such as depression, anxiety, or irritability). It may be more effective in patients with severe dependence. Disulfiram interferes with the degradation of alcohol, resulting in the accumulation of acetaldehyde, which, in turn, produces a very unpleasant reaction that includes flushing, nausea, and palpitations if the patient drinks alcohol. Compliance can be a problem, but among patients who are highly motivated, disulfiram can be very effective.

Behavioral Treatments

Behavioral treatments help patients engage in the treatment process, modify their attitudes and behaviors related to drug abuse, and increase healthy life skills. These treatments can also enhance the effectiveness of medications and help people stay in treatment longer. Treatment for drug abuse and addiction can be delivered in many different settings using a variety of behavioral approaches.

Outpatient Behavioral Treatment encompasses a wide variety of programs for patients who visit a clinic at regular intervals. Most of the programs involve individual or group drug counseling. Some programs also offer other forms of behavioral treatment such as:

- **Cognitive-behavioral therapy**, which seeks to help patients recognize, avoid, and cope with the situations in which they are most likely to abuse drugs.

- **Multidimensional family therapy**, which was developed for adolescents with drug abuse problems—as well as their families—addresses a range of influences on their drug abuse patterns and is designed to improve overall family functioning.

- **Motivational interviewing**, which capitalizes on the readiness of individuals to change their behavior and enter treatment.

- **Motivational incentives** (contingency management), which uses positive reinforcement to encourage abstinence from drugs.

Residential treatment programs can also be very effective, especially for those with more severe problems. For example, therapeutic communities (TCs) are highly structured programs in which patients remain at a residence, typically for six to 12 months. TCs differ from other treatment approaches principally in their use of the community—treatment staff and those in recovery—as a key agent of change to influence patient attitudes, perceptions, and behaviors associated with drug use. Patients in TCs may include those with relatively long histories of drug addiction, involvement in serious criminal activities, and seriously impaired social functioning. TCs are now also being designed to accommodate the needs of women who are pregnant or have children. The focus of the TC is on the re-socialization of the patient to a drug-free, crime-free lifestyle.

Treatment Within The Criminal Justice System

Treatment in a criminal justice setting can succeed in preventing an offender's return to criminal behavior, particularly when treatment continues as the person transitions back into the community. Studies show that treatment does not need to be voluntary to be effective.

Chapter 61

When A Family Member Is Dealing With Substance Abuse

Facts About Substance Abuse

Alcoholism and drug dependence and addiction, known as substance use disorders, are complex problems. People with these disorders once were thought to have a character defect or moral weakness; some people mistakenly still believe that. However, most scientists and medical researchers now consider dependence on alcohol or drugs to be a long-term illness, like asthma, hypertension (high blood pressure), or diabetes. Most people who drink alcohol drink very little, and many people can stop taking drugs without a struggle. However, some people develop a substance use disorder—use of alcohol or drugs that is compulsive or dangerous (or both).

Why do some people develop a problem but others don't?

Substance use disorder is an illness that can affect anyone: rich or poor, male or female, employed or unemployed, young or old, and any race or ethnicity. Nobody knows for sure exactly what causes it, but the chance of developing a substance use disorder depends partly on genetics—biological traits

About This Chapter: Information in this chapter is excerpted from "What Is Substance Abuse Treatment? A Booklet for Families." Center for Substance Abuse Treatment, Substance Abuse and Mental Health Services Administration, DHHS Publication No. (SMA) 04-3955, 2004; reviewed by David A. Cooke, MD, FACP, September 2010.

passed down through families. A person's environment, psychological traits, and stress level also play major roles by contributing to the use of alcohol or drugs. Researchers have found that using drugs for a long time changes the brain in important, long-lasting ways. It is as if a switch in the brain turned on at some point. This point is different for every person, but when this switch turns on, the person crosses an invisible line and becomes dependent on the substance. People who start using drugs or alcohol early in life run a greater risk of crossing this line and becoming dependent. These changes in the brain remain long after a person stops using drugs or drinking alcohol.

Who provides substance abuse treatment?

Many different kinds of professionals provide treatment for substance use disorders. In most treatment programs, the main caregivers are specially trained individuals certified or licensed as substance abuse treatment counselors. About half these counselors are people who are in recovery themselves. Many programs have staff from several different ethnic or cultural groups. Most treatment programs assign patients to a treatment team of professionals. Depending on the type of treatment, teams can be made up of social workers, counselors, doctors, nurses, psychologists, psychiatrists, or other professionals.

What will happen first?

Everyone entering treatment receives a clinical assessment. A complete assessment of an individual is needed to help treatment professionals offer the type of treatment that best suits him or her. The assessment also helps

☞ Remember!!

Even though your family member has an illness, it does not excuse the bad behavior that often accompanies it. Your loved one is not at fault for having a disease, but he or she is responsible for getting treatment.

Source: Substance Abuse and Mental Health Services Administration, 2004; reviewed September 2010.

program counselors work with the person to design an effective treatment plan. Although clinical assessment continues throughout a person's treatment, it starts at or just before a person's admission to a treatment program. The counselor will begin by gathering information about the person, asking many questions.

The counselor may invite you, as a family member, to answer questions and express your own concerns as well. Be honest—this is not the time to cover up your loved one's behavior. The counselor needs to get a full picture of the problem to plan and help implement the most effective treatment. It is particularly important for the counselor to know whether your family member has any serious medical problems or whether you suspect that he or she may have an emotional problem. You may feel embarrassed answering some of these questions or have difficulty completing the interview, but remember: the counselor is there to help you and your loved one. The treatment team uses the information gathered to recommend the best type of treatment. No one type of treatment is right for everyone; to work, the treatment needs to meet your family member's individual needs.

After the assessment, a counselor or case manager is assigned to your family member. The counselor works with the person (and possibly his or her family) to develop a treatment plan. This plan lists problems, treatment goals, and ways to meet those goals.

Based on the assessment, the counselor may refer your family member to a physician to decide whether he or she needs medical supervision to stop alcohol or drug use safely.

What actually happens in treatment programs?

Although treatment programs differ, the basic ingredients of treatment are similar. Most programs include many or all elements presented below.

Assessment: As we discussed earlier, all treatment programs begin with a clinical assessment of a person's individual treatment needs. This assessment helps in the development of an effective treatment plan.

Medical Care: Programs in hospitals can provide this care on site. Other outpatient or residential programs may have doctors and nurses come to the program site for a few days each week, or a person may be referred to other places for medical care. Medical care typically includes screening and treatment for HIV/AIDS, hepatitis, tuberculosis, and women's health issues.

A Treatment Plan: The treatment team, along with the person in treatment, develops a treatment plan based on the assessment. A treatment plan is a written guide to treatment that includes the person's goals, treatment activities designed to help him or her meet those goals, ways to tell whether a goal has been met, and a timeframe for meeting goals. The treatment plan helps both the person in treatment and treatment program staff stay focused and on track. The treatment plan is adjusted over time to meet changing needs and ensure that it stays relevant.

> ✣ **It's A Fact!!**
> **What types of treatment programs are available?**
>
> Several types of treatment programs are available:
>
> - Inpatient treatment
> - Residential programs
> - Partial hospitalization or day treatment
> - Outpatient and intensive outpatient programs
> - Methadone clinics (also called opioid treatment programs)
>
> Source: Substance Abuse and Mental Health Services Administration, 2004; reviewed September 2010.

Group And Individual Counseling: At first, individual counseling generally focuses on motivating the person to stop using drugs or alcohol. Treatment then shifts to helping the person stay drug and alcohol free. Group counseling is different in each program, but group members usually support and try to help one another cope with life without using drugs or alcohol.

Individual Assignments: People in treatment may be asked to read certain things (or listen to audiotapes), to complete written assignments (or record them on audiotapes), or to try new behaviors.

Education About Substance Use Disorders: People learn about the symptoms and the effects of alcohol and drug use on their brains and bodies. Education groups use videotapes or audiotapes, lectures, or activities to help people learn about their illness and how to manage it.

Life Skills Training: This training can include learning and practicing employment skills, leisure activities, social skills, communication skills, anger management, stress management, goal setting, and money and time management.

Testing For Alcohol Or Drug Use: Program staff members regularly take urine samples from people for drug testing. Some programs are starting to test saliva instead of urine. They also may use a Breathalyzer™ to test people for alcohol use.

Relapse Prevention Training: Relapse prevention training teaches people how to identify their relapse triggers, how to cope with cravings, how to develop plans for handling stressful situations, and what to do if they relapse. A trigger is anything that makes a person crave a drug. Triggers often are connected to the person's past use, such as a person he or she used drugs with, a time or place, drug use paraphernalia (such as syringes, a pipe, or a bong), or a particular situation or emotion.

Orientation To Self-Help Groups: Participants in self-help groups support and encourage one another to become or stay drug and alcohol free. Twelve-Step programs are perhaps the best known of the self-help groups. These programs include Alcoholics Anonymous (AA), Narcotics Anonymous (NA), Cocaine Anonymous, and Marijuana Anonymous. Many treatment programs recommend or require attendance at self-help groups.

Treatment For Mental Disorders: Many people with a substance use disorder also have emotional problems such as depression, anxiety, or posttraumatic stress disorder. Adolescents in treatment also may have behavior problems, conduct disorder, or attention deficit/hyperactivity (ADHD) disorder. Treating both the substance use and mental disorders increases the chances that the person will recover. Some counselors think people should be alcohol and drug free for at least three to four weeks before a treatment professional can identify emotional illness correctly. The program may provide mental health care, or it may refer a person to other sites for this care. Mental health care often includes the use of medications, such as antidepressants.

Family Education And Counseling Services: This education can help you understand the disease and its causes, effects, and treatment. Programs provide this education in many ways: lectures, discussions, activities, and group meetings. Some programs provide counseling for families or couples.

Family counseling is especially critical in treatment for adolescents. Parents need to be involved in treatment planning and follow-up care decisions for the adolescent. Family members also need to participate as fully as possible in the family counseling the program offers.

Medication: Many programs use medications to help in the treatment process. Although no medications cure dependence on drugs or alcohol, some do help people stay abstinent and can be lifesaving.

Follow-Up Care (Also Called Continuing Care): Even when a person has successfully completed a treatment program, the danger of returning to alcohol or drug use (called a "slip" or relapse) remains. The longer a person stays in treatment, including follow-up, the more likely he or she is to stay in recovery. Once a person has completed basic treatment, a program will offer a follow-up care program at the treatment facility or will refer him or her to another site. Most programs recommend that a person stay in follow-up care for at least one year. Adolescents often need follow-up care for a longer period.

✔ Quick Tip
Does your mom or dad drink too much?

Lots of teens live in families with alcohol abuse or alcoholism—one in four. Many also live with parental drug abuse. You are not alone.

Addiction to alcohol or drugs affects all members of the family, even if only one person has this disease. This is why it is called a "family disease."

Nothing you have done has ever caused anyone else to drink too much or use drugs. It's not your fault. You need and deserve help for yourself.

- You didn't cause it.

- You can't cure it.

- You can't control it.

If you feel bad because your mom or dad is drinking too much or using drugs, there are steps you can take to make things better for yourself even though you cannot stop your parent from drinking or using.

Just For You

Now that your family member is in treatment, things are starting to change. Some of the tension and turmoil that probably were part of your life may be starting to ease. But the first weeks of treatment are stressful. Each family member is adjusting to changes, starting to deal with past conflicts, and establishing new routines. Amid all these changes, it is important that you take good care of yourself—get enough sleep, eat right, rest, exercise, and talk to supportive friends and relatives. Your church, mosque, synagogue, temple, or other spiritual organization also may be a good source of support.

Recovery is not just an adjustment for the person in treatment—it also is an adjustment for you. For the past few years, you may have assumed roles or taken care of tasks that were your loved one's responsibilities. Now, as time passes, you and he or she may need to learn new ways of relating to each other and learn different ways of sharing activities and chores. If you are the parent of an adolescent in treatment, you will need to be closely involved in treatment

---

- **Talk to a caring adult.** There are many adults who will listen and help you deal with problems at home, even when it seems no one has noticed. Sometimes they are not sure if you want or need support and are waiting for you to say something first. Often a teacher, a counselor at school, a youth minister, a coach, doctor, nurse, friend's parent, grandparent, aunt or uncle is knowledgeable and anxious to help.

- **Families with alcohol or drug problems often try to keep it a secret.** It is important to find caring adults who can help you. Talking to them really helps, and it is not being disloyal to your family if you seek help for yourself. If you don't get the help you need from the first person you approach, it is important to reach out to another adult you can trust.

- **Get involved in youth programs.** Join in activities offered through your church or synagogue, your school's extracurricular programs, or your community recreational departments. Here you can hang out with other young people, use your special talents and strengths and learn new skills while making friends and having fun.

Source: From "It Feels So Bad," a publication by the Substance Abuse and Mental Health Services Administration, 2005.

planning and treatment activities. You may need to adjust your life and family relationships to allow for the extra time this involvement will take.

You may have many questions about how your family member will behave in these early stages of recovery. Everyone acts differently. Some people are very happy to be getting treatment at last; others suffer a great deal while they adjust to a new life and attempt to live it without alcohol and drugs. They may be sad, angry, or confused. It is important for you to realize that these are normal reactions and to get support for yourself.

Al-Anon is the best-known and most available resource for family members and friends of alcoholics. Al-Anon was founded 50 years ago to provide support for those living with someone with alcoholism. Alateen, for older children and adolescents, was founded somewhat later on. Today, many family members of people who use drugs also participate in Al-Anon or Alateen. These meetings are free and available in most communities. Your community also may have Nar-Anon meetings. This group was founded for families and friends of those using drugs. Other groups also may be helpful, such as Co-Dependents Anonymous and Adult Children of Alcoholics. The treatment program should be able to give you schedules of local meetings of all these groups, or you can find contact information at the end of this chapter.

Many treatment professionals consider substance use disorders family diseases. To help the whole family recover and cope with the many changes going on, you may be asked to take part in treatment. This approach may involve going to a family education program or to counseling for families or couples.

It is important to remember the following points as you and your family member recover:

- You are participating in treatment for yourself, not just for the sake of the person who used substances.

- Your loved one's recovery, sobriety, or abstinence does not depend on you.

- Your family's recovery does not depend on the recovery of the person who used substances.

- You did not cause your family member's substance use disorder. It is not your fault.

You still may have hurt feelings and anger from the past that need to be resolved. You need support to understand and deal with these feelings, and you need to support your loved one's efforts to get well. Remember: Help is always there for you, too. Ask the counselor for some suggestions or see the resource chapters at the end of this book.

What if I need help with basic living issues?

You may need very practical help while your family member is in treatment. If your family member is the sole financial provider and unable to work because he or she is in treatment, how will the bills get paid? If your family member is the primary caregiver for children or an elderly adult, how will these needs be met? The treatment program may be able to help you arrange disability leave or insurance through your loved one's employer. Ask the counselor about different types of assistance that may be available to help you meet various needs. Most treatment programs work with other community programs. These programs may include food pantries, clothing programs, transportation assistance, child care, adult day care, legal assistance, financial counseling, and health care services. Your family may be eligible for help from programs that help those in recovery.

What if I'm afraid it won't work?

Treatment is just the first step to recovery. During this process family members sometimes have mixed feelings. You may feel exhausted, angry, relieved, worried, and afraid that, if this doesn't work, nothing will. You may feel as if you are walking on eggshells and that, if you do something wrong, you may cause your loved one to relapse. It is important for you to remember that you cannot cause a relapse—only the person who takes a drug or picks up a drink is responsible for that.

No one can predict whether your family member will recover, or for how long, but many people who receive treatment do get better. The longer people stay in treatment the more likely they will remain drug and alcohol free. About half the people who complete treatment for the first time continue to recover.

Of course, this means that about half will return to drinking alcohol and using drugs (called relapse) before they finally give them up for good. Adolescents are even more likely to use drugs or alcohol or both again. It is not uncommon for a person to need to go through treatment more than one time. Often the person needs to return to treatment quickly to prevent a slip or relapse from leading to a chronic problem. It is important for you to understand that relapse is often a part of the recovery process. Do not be discouraged if your family member uses alcohol or drugs again. Many times relapses are short and the person continues to recover.

A treatment program may involve you in relapse prevention planning and may help you learn what to do if your family member relapses. Your family member will benefit if you do not drink or use drugs around him or her, especially in the first months after his or her treatment begins. When you choose not to use drugs or alcohol, you help your loved one avoid triggers. As you both begin to understand and accept the illness, the risk of relapse decreases. The changes in attitudes, behaviors, and values that you both are learning and practicing will become part of your new recovering lifestyle.

Chapter 62

Helping A Friend With A Substance Abuse Problem

It's never easy to tell a friend that he or she has a problem, but isn't that what a friend would do? No one ever thinks that "trying" drugs is going to lead to a life-threatening addiction. Yet, millions of people have to deal with this tough issue every year. In this chapter, you will find information on how to recognize a problem and some suggestions on how to have a talk with your friend.

Does My Friend Have A Drug Problem?

Does your friend seem like a different person when she drinks or gets high? Maybe he/she has been letting you down lately and you think it's connected to drug use. Or maybe some of the things he/she does when he/she is drunk or high are just scary. This can be a difficult situation to deal with, and sometimes the situation gets worse before it gets better. Don't make excuses. Talk to your friend.

About This Chapter: Information in this chapter is from "Helping A Friend With A Substance Abuse Problem," National Youth Anti-Drug Media Campaign (a program of the Office of National Drug Control Policy), 2010. Information under the heading "Detailed Signs And Symptoms Of Drug Abuse" is from The National Youth Anti-Drug Media Campaign, 2010.

♣ It's A Fact!!
Symptoms Of A Drug Overdose:
Why You Must Act Immediately

If you suspect a friend may be suffering from an overdose or a toxic reaction to a drug, you must act. Call 911 or get to a hospital. You or your friend might get in trouble when an adult finds out that you've been around drugs, but that's far better than your friend being dead or in a coma. It's not possible for someone to sleep off an overdose. Taking a cold shower or drinking coffee will not help either. Drug and alcohol overdoses can stop the heart from beating or the lungs from breathing. Drug overdose symptoms vary widely depending on the specific drug(s) used, but may include:

- Abnormal pupil size (either too small or too large)

- Sweating

- Agitation (restlessness, increased tension, irritability)

- Tremors (involuntary shaking movements)

- Seizures

- Problems with walking

- Difficulty breathing

- Drowsiness

- Unconsciousness

- Hallucinations

- Delusional or paranoid behavior

- Violent or aggressive behavior

Remember, if you suspect a friend may be suffering from a drug overdose, get help immediately.

Source: From a Heads Up compilation from Scholastic and the National Institute on Drug Abuse, 2005-2006.

Signs Of Drug Use

If your friend does one or more of the following, you should talk to him/her:

- Gets drunk or high on a regular basis.

- Drinks or uses drugs when he/she is alone.

- Shows up at school drunk or high or has skipped class to use.

- Needs drugs or alcohol to have a good time or cope with everyday life.

- Plans for drug use in advance.

- Starts hanging out with new friends who will do drugs with him/her or can score for him/her.

- Lies about drug use.

- Pressures others to use drugs.

- Has broken plans with you, or showed up late, because he/she was getting drunk or high.

- Shows little interest in or quits sports or activities he/she once enjoyed.

- Has driven a car while drunk or high.

- Borrows or steals money to buy drugs or alcohol.

Also, even if your friend doesn't exactly fit any of these, but you feel like he/she is headed in the wrong direction, you can say something. You don't have to wait for it to get worse.

Detailed Signs And Symptoms Of Drug Abuse

Alcohol: Odor on the breath. Intoxication/drunkenness. Difficulty focusing: glazed appearance of the eyes. Uncharacteristically passive behavior or combative and argumentative behavior. Gradual decline in personal appearance and hygiene. Gradual development of difficulties, especially in school work or job performance. Absenteeism (particularly on Monday). Unexplained bruises and accidents. Irritability. Flushed skin. Loss of memory (blackouts). Availability and consumption of alcohol becomes the focus of social activities.

Changes in peer-group associations and friendships. Impaired interpersonal relationships (unexplainable termination of relationships, and separation from close family members).

Cocaine/Crack/Methamphetamines/Stimulants: Extremely dilated pupils. Dry mouth and nose, bad breath, frequent lip licking. Excessive activity, difficulty sitting still, lack of interest in food or sleep. Irritable, argumentative, nervous. Talkative, but conversation often lacks continuity; changes subjects rapidly. Runny nose, cold or chronic sinus/nasal problems, nose bleeds. Use or possession of paraphernalia including small spoons, razor blades, mirror, little bottles of white powder and plastic, glass or metal straws.

Depressants: Symptoms of alcohol intoxication with no alcohol odor on breath. (Remember that depressants are frequently used with alcohol.) Lack of facial expression or animation. Flat affect. Limp appearance. Slurred speech. Note: There are few readily apparent symptoms. Abuse may be indicated by activities such as frequent visits to different physicians for prescriptions to treat "nervousness," "anxiety," "stress," etc.

Ecstasy: Confusion, blurred vision, rapid eye movement, chills or sweating, high body temperature, sweating profusely, dehydrated, confusion, faintness, paranoia or severe anxiety, panic attacks, trance-like state, transfixed on sights and sounds, unconscious clenching of the jaw, grinding teeth, muscle tension, very affectionate. Depression, headaches, dizziness (from hangover/ after effects), possession of pacifiers (used to stop jaw clenching), lollipops, candy necklaces, mentholated vapor rub, vomiting or nausea (from hangover/ after effects).

Hallucinogens/LSD/Acid: Extremely dilated pupils. Warm skin, excessive perspiration, and body odor. Distorted sense of sight, hearing, touch; distorted image of self and time perception. Mood and behavior changes, the extent depending on emotional state of the user and environmental conditions Unpredictable flashback episodes even long after withdrawal (although these are rare). Hallucinogenic drugs, which occur both naturally and in synthetic form, distort or disturb sensory input, sometimes to a great degree. Hallucinogens occur naturally in primarily two forms, (peyote) cactus and psilocybin mushrooms.

Several chemical varieties have been synthesized, most notably LSD, MDMA, STP, and PCP. Hallucinogen usage reached a peak in the United States in the late 1960s, but declined shortly thereafter due to a broader awareness of the detrimental effects of use. However, a disturbing trend indicating resurgence in hallucinogen use by high school and college age persons nationwide has been acknowledged by law enforcement. With the exception of PCP, all hallucinogens seem to share common effects of use. Any portion of sensory perceptions may be altered to varying degrees. Synesthesia, or the "seeing" of sounds, and the "hearing" of colors, is a common side effect of hallucinogen use. Depersonalization, acute anxiety, and acute depression resulting in suicide have also been noted as a result of hallucinogen use.

Inhalants: Substance odor on breath and clothes. Runny nose. Watering eyes. Drowsiness or unconsciousness. Poor muscle control. Prefers group activity to being alone. Presence of bags or rags containing dry plastic cement or other solvent at home, in locker at school or at work. Discarded whipped cream, spray paint or similar chargers (users of nitrous oxide). Small bottles labeled "incense" (users of butyl nitrite).

Marijuana/Pot: Rapid, loud talking and bursts of laughter in early stages of intoxication. Sleepy or dazed in the later stages. Forgetfulness in conversation. Inflammation in whites of eyes; pupils unlikely to be dilated. Odor similar to burnt rope on clothing or breath. Brown residue on fingers. Tendency to drive slowly (below the speed limit).

Distorted sense of time passage; tendency to overestimate time intervals. Use or possession of paraphernalia including roach clip, packs of rolling papers, pipes or bongs. Marijuana users are difficult to recognize unless they are under the influence of the drug at the time of observation. Casual users may show none of the general symptoms. Marijuana does have a distinct odor and may be the same color or a bit greener than tobacco.

Narcotics/Prescription Drugs/Heroin/Opium/Codeine/OxyContin: Lethargy, drowsiness. Constricted pupils fail to respond to light. Redness and raw nostrils from inhaling heroin in power form. Scars (tracks) on inner arms or other parts of body, from needle injections. Use or possession of paraphernalia, including syringes, bent spoons, bottle caps, eye droppers, rubber tubing, cotton, and needles. Slurred speech. While there may be no readily apparent symptoms of analgesic abuse, it may be indicated by frequent visits to different physicians or dentists for prescriptions to treat pain of non-specific origin. In cases where the patient has chronic pain and abuse of medication is suspected, it may be indicated by amounts and frequency taken.

PCP: Unpredictable behavior; mood may swing from passiveness to violence for no apparent reason. Symptoms of intoxication. Disorientation; agitation and violence if exposed to excessive sensory stimulation. Fear, terror. Rigid muscles. Strange gait. Deadened sensory perception (may experience severe injuries while appearing not to notice). Pupils may appear dilated. Mask-like facial appearance. Floating pupils, which appear to follow a moving object. Comatose (unresponsive) if large amount consumed. Eyes may be open or closed.

Solvents, Aerosols, Glue, Petrol: Slurred speech, impaired coordination, nausea, vomiting, slowed breathing. Brain damage, pains in the chest, muscles, joints, heart trouble, severe depression, fatigue, loss of appetite, bronchial spasm, sores on nose or mouth, nosebleeds, diarrhea, bizarre or reckless behavior, sudden death, suffocation.

♣ It's A Fact!!
What can happen if my friend keeps using drugs?

If your friend continues using, he or she could face some pretty serious consequences like getting caught or arrested, losing his or her driver's license, getting thrown off the team or suspended, being involved in a car crash, or worse.

Source: National Youth Anti-Drug Media Campaign, 2010.

Prepare For The Talk

Discussing a friend's drug or alcohol use isn't an easy thing to do. People with drug problems usually defend their use or make excuses. It can be hard for people to admit to themselves that they have a problem.

This means that when you talk, your friends will listen—even if you've tried drugs or alcohol yourself. You may be worried that your friend will be mad at you—but if you really think that he or she needs help, you need to say something.

Here are a few things to keep in mind if you have to have that talk with your friend.

- **Be Safe:** Never confront your friend when he/she is drunk or high. And you should talk to your friend in a place where you feel safe. If your friend becomes angry or violent, leave and bring up the subject later when he/she is calm.

- **It's Not Your Fault:** Remember that your friend's use is not your fault and you should never blame yourself.

- **The Tone:** Remember, how you say something is as important as what to say. A supportive, caring tone usually works best. Be assertive, not aggressive.

- **Be Discreet:** No one likes to be called out in front of others. Wait until the right time and place to have this talk. It's best not to start the conversation if they're high, angry or upset. And afterwards, keep the details of your conversation private.

- **Plan What To Say:** You may want to reference some specifics like if your friend skips class, takes stupid risks or is frequently hung over. Tell him or her that you're concerned and that's why you want to talk. If you are nervous about talking with him, ask another friend who knows the situation if you can practice with him or her, to help work out ahead of time what you are going to say. You may want to have a hotline number or some facts on hand. That way, your friend can call for confidential help or check out the facts.

- **Balance:** Your friend may think you're just being "critical," so try to give examples of how you feel when you see him or her use drugs. For example, "You are my best friend. But I feel like you're a different person when you're high and that's really disappointing." Or you can write an email or note if you feel uncomfortable talking face-to-face.

- **Listen:** After you finish talking, ask your friend what he or she thinks—and listen. It's critical that you hear what your friend's saying so you can offer to help. But you shouldn't feel like you have to personally solve your friend's problem—there are counselors who can help at times like this.

- **Keep At It:** Talking to your friend about drugs may be a continuous process—not a one-time event—so you may want to check in with him or her from time to time. You may want to recommend that your friend talk to a counselor—and have a hotline number ready.

What To Say

You've already learned the things to keep in mind when talking with a friend who is using drugs or alcohol. But approaching a friend and finding the right words can still be tough and scary sometimes. Remember that 50 percent of all current marijuana users report feeling they should reduce or stop their marijuana use. So your friend likely wants to stop and may need your help. Here are some short sample conversations. You can personalize them or add some facts, but this gives you a good start. Remember that you can always get some confidential help from a trusted adult (teacher, coach, nurse, or counselor) or from a hotline with trained teens and adult experts.

Before you think about having the conversation with your friend, it's important to think about where and when you'll have "the talk." You should pick a time and place that feels private for you and your friend—maybe when you're walking or driving home from school or an activity together. The bottom line is that you should have this conversation at a time and place that feels familiar and kind of "safe" for you and your friend.

I'm Worried About You

We're going to be friends no matter what, so don't worry about that. We've had some great adventures together and it's been fun. But I'm getting worried about your drug/alcohol use. I've seen you stoned/high a few times now and it's not healthy—I'm afraid that you are hurting yourself. I'm also afraid that you are going to get into trouble if you keep going the way you're going. Plus, when you're using, you can get me in trouble, too. I just really hope we can talk about what's going on with you. There are also people you can talk to confidentially who can help. It's not too late for you to change things in your life.

You're Using Drugs/Alcohol To Deal With Your Other Problems

I'm concerned you are using drugs/alcohol because you are unhappy or depressed—or maybe some other things are bothering you at home or at school. I know it's hard, but drugs/alcohol are not the way to deal with your problems. Actually, you might not know this, but drug use can actually increase a person's likelihood of experiencing mental health problems like depression and anxiety. I feel like you will be making your problems worse by using drugs and alcohol.

I want to help you work through this, and if we can't fix it, there are people you can confidentially talk with who can help.

Your Drug/Alcohol Use Is Giving You A Bad Reputation

I'm afraid that people are starting to talk about you and your drug/alcohol use. It's not healthy, and I think you need to stop. You're getting a bad reputation. Sooner or later, other people are going to find out (like school or your parents) and that will cause even more problems for you.

I'm also concerned about the messages online you are posting about using drugs. Did you know that school can suspend you for what you do/say online, and college admissions officers and potential employers check your online profiles when you apply for colleges or jobs? You don't want to ruin your reputation or future for something stupid like this.

☞ Remember!!

If your friend insists that his or her drug use isn't a big deal, don't be too surprised—this is a pretty common response. But don't let this stop you from talking to your friend. Chances are that he or she will see that you're concerned.

Source: National Youth Anti-Drug
Media Campaign, 2010.

I'm Here To Help

I don't like having to talk about this, but I am worried about your drug/alcohol use. I'm here to help you and so are the rest of your friends. We can do fun things that don't include drugs/alcohol use. There are confidential hotlines that can help and you can call them without getting into trouble. If you think you need to talk with an adult like a counselor, your parents, or a health care professional, I can go with you. I can even start the conversation. Just let me know.

> ✔ **Quick Tip**
>
> ### What if my friend doesn't stop using?
>
> Helping a friend with a drug problem can be stressful and difficult. You may feel a lot of pressure to get your friend to stop, or you may get totally discouraged if your friend doesn't listen to you. But remember, your friend's drug or alcohol use is not your fault. It's up to him or her to stop using. Remember to never put yourself in a dangerous situation while trying to help and don't get yourself in trouble. If you think that your friend is in immediate danger (for example, if he/she is having suicidal thoughts, driving while under the influence of drugs or alcohol, or passes out or becomes unresponsive from an overdose), you should definitely call 911 and also talk with a trusted adult or call a help hotline.
>
> Source: National Youth Anti-Drug Media Campaign, 2010.

Part Nine

If You Need More Information

Chapter 63

National Organizations For Drug Information

Action on Smoking and Health (ASH)
2013 H Street NW
Washington, DC 20006
Phone: 202-659-4310
Fax: 202-833-2314
Website: http://www.ash.org

Alcoholics Anonymous (AA)
AA World Services, Inc.
P.O. Box 459
New York, NY 10163
Phone: 212-870-3400
Website: http://www.aa.org

Al-Anon
1600 Corporate Landing Pkwy.
Virginia Beach, VA 23454
Phone: 757-563-1600
Fax: 757-563-1655
E-mail: wso@al-anon.org
Website: http://www.al-anon
.alateen.org

American Council for Drug Education (at Phoenix House)
50 Jay Street
Brooklyn, NY 11201
Phone: 718-222-6641
E-mail: acde@phoenixhouse.org
Website: http://www.acde.org

Resources in this chapter were compiled from several sources deemed reliable; all contact information was verified and updated in August 2010.

Campaign for Tobacco-Free Kids

1400 Eye Street, NW, Suite 1200
Washington, DC 20005
Phone: 202-296-5469
Website: http://
www.tobaccofreekids.org

Center of Alcohol Studies

Rutgers, the State
University of New Jersey
607 Allison Rd.
Piscataway, NJ 08854
Phone: 732-445-2190
Fax: 732-445-5300
Website: http://www.alcoholstudies
.rutgers.edu

Center for Substance Abuse Prevention (CSAP)

Substance Abuse and Mental
Health Services Administration
1 Choke Cherry Rd.
Rockville, MD 20857
Phone: 240-276-2420
Fax: 301-443-5447
Website: http://www.csap.samhsa.gov

Center for Substance Abuse Treatment (SAMHSA)

Toll-Free: 800-662-HELP (4357)
Toll-Free TDD: 800-487-4889
Phone: 240-276-2750
Website: http://csat.samhsa.gov
Substance Abuse Treatment Facility
Locator: http://www.findtreatment
.samhsa.gov

Centers for Disease Control and Prevention (CDC)

1600 Clifton Rd.
Atlanta, GA 30333
Toll-Free: 800-CDC-INFO
(232-4636)
Toll-Free TTY: 888-232-6348
E-mail: cdcinfo@cdc.gov
Website: http://www.cdc.gov

Co-Anon Family Groups World Services

P.O. Box 12722
Tucson, AZ 85732
Toll-Free: 800-898-9985
Phone: 520-513-5028
E-mail: info@co-anon.org
Website: http://www.co-anon.org

Cocaine Anonymous World Services

21720 S. Wilmington Ave., Suite 204
Long Beach, CA 90810
Phone: 310-559-5833
Fax: 310-559-2554
E-mail: cawso@ca.org
Website: http://www.ca.org

Do It Now Foundation (Drug Information)

P.O. Box 27568
Tempe, AZ 85285
Phone: 480-736-0599
Fax: 480-736-0771
E-mail: email@doitnow.org
Website: http://www.doitnow.org

Drug Enforcement Administration (DEA)
Office of Diversion Control
8701 Morrissette Dr.
Mailstop: AES
Springfield, VA 22152
Toll-Free: 800-882-9539
Phone: 202-307-1000
E-mail: ODE@usdoj.gov
Website: http://www.justice.gov/dea

Drug Policy Information Clearinghouse
Office of National Drug Control Policy
P.O. Box 6000
Rockville, MD 20849
Toll-Free: 800-666-3332
Fax: 301-519-5212
Website: http://www.whitehouse
drugpolicy.gov/about/clearingh.html

Families Anonymous, Inc.
P.O. Box 3475
Culver City, CA 90231-3475
Phone: 800-736-9805
Fax: 310-815-9682
E-mail:
famanon@FamiliesAnonymous.org
Website: www.FamiliesAnonymous.org

Hazelden Foundation
P.O. Box 11
Center City, MN 55012-0011
Toll-Free: 800-257-7810
Phone: 651-213-4200
E-mail: info@hazelden.org
Website: http://www.hazelden.org

Health Information Network (SAMHSA)
P.O. Box 2345
Rockville, MD 20847
Toll-Free: 877-726-4727
Toll-Free TTY: 800-487-4889
Fax: 240-221-4292
E-mail: SHIN@samhsa.hhs.gov
Website: http://www.samhsa.gov/
shin

Higher Education Center for Alcohol and Other Drug Abuse and Violence Prevention
Education Development Center, Inc.
55 Chapel St.
Newton, MA 02458
Toll-Free: 800-676-1730 (TDD Relay Friendly, Dial 711)
Fax: 617-928-1537
E-mail: HigherEdCtr@edc.org
Website: http://www.highered
center.org

Institute on Black Chemical Abuse
African American
Family Services
2616 Nicollet Avenue
Minneapolis, MN 55408
Phone: 612-871-7878
Fax: 612-871-2567
E-mail: contact@aafs.net
Website: http://www.aafs.net

Join Together

580 Harrison Avenue, 3rd Floor
Boston, MA 02118
Phone: 617-437-1500
Fax: 617-437-9394
E-mail: info@jointogether.org
Website: http://www.jointogether
.org

Nar-Anon Family Group Headquarters, Inc.

22527 Crenshaw Blvd. #200B
Torrance, CA 90505
Toll-Free: 800-477-6291
Phone: 310-534-8188
Fax: 310-534-8688
E-mail: naranonWSO@hotmail
.com
Website: http://www.nar-anon.org

Narcotics Anonymous

P.O. Box 9999
Van Nuys, CA 91409
Phone: 818-773-9999
Fax: 818-700-0700
Website: http://www.na.org

National Asian Pacific American Families Against Drug Abuse

340 East 2nd Street, Suite 409
Los Angeles, CA 90012
Phone: 213-625-5795
Fax: 213-625-5796
E-mail: napafasa@napafasa.org
Website: http://www.napafasa.org

National Association for Children of Alcoholics

11426 Rockville Pike, Suite 301
Rockville, MD 20852
Toll-Free: 888-55-4COAS (2627)
Phone: 301-468-0985
Fax: 301-468-0987
E-mail: nacoa@nacoa.org
Website: http://www.nacoa.net

National Black Alcoholism and Addictions Council (NBAC)

1500 Golden Valley Rd.
Minneapolis, MN 55411
Toll-Free: 877-NBAC-ORG or
877-622-2674
Fax: 407-532-2815
E-mail: infomation@nbacinc.org
Website: www.nbacinc.org

National Center on Addiction and Substance Abuse at Columbia University (CASA)

633 Third Ave., 19th Fl.
New York, NY 10017
Phone: 212-841-5200
Fax: 212-956-8020
Website: http://www.casacolumbia
.org

National Council on Alcoholism and Drug Dependence
244 East 58th St., 4th Fl.
New York, NY 10022
Toll-Free Hopeline: 800-NCA-CALL (622-2255)
Phone: 212-269-7797
Fax: 212-269-7510
E-mail: national@ncadd.org
Website: http://www.ncadd.org

National Criminal Justice Reference Service (NCJRS)
P.O. Box 6000
Rockville, MD 20849
Toll-Free: 800-851-3420
Toll-Free TTY: 877-712-9279
Phone: 301-519-5500 (international callers)
Fax: 301-519-5212
Website: http://www.ncjrs.gov

National Drug Intelligence Center
U.S. Department of Justice
Robert F. Kennedy Bldg., Rm. 3341
950 Pennsylvania Ave., NW
Washington, DC 20530
Phone: 202-532-4040
E-mail: NDIC.Contacts@usdoj.gov
Website: http://www.justice.gov/ndic

National Institute on Alcohol Abuse and Alcoholism (NIAAA)
5635 Fishers Ln., MSC 9304
Bethesda, MD 20892
Phone: 301-443-3860
E-mail: niaaaweb-r@exchange.nih.gov
Website: http://www.niaaa.nih.gov

National Institute on Drug Abuse (NIDA)
6001 Executive Blvd., Rm. 5213
Bethesda, MD 20892
Phone: 301-443-1124 (Public information and liaison in science and communications)
Fax: 301-443-7397
E-mail: information@nida.nih.gov
Websites: http://www.nida.nih.gov; and http://www.drugabuse.gov

NIDA-Sponsored Websites
http://www.backtoschool.drugabuse.gov
http://www.clubdrugs.gov
http://www.hiv.drugabuse.gov
http://www.inhalants.drugabuse.gov
http://www.marijuana-info.org
http://www.researchstudies.drugabuse.gov
http://www.smoking.drugabuse.gov
http://www.steroidabuse.gov
http://www.teens.drugabuse.gov

National Institute of Justice

810 7th Street NW, 7th Floor
Washington, DC 20531
Toll-Free: 800-851-3420 (National
Criminal Justice Reference Service)
Phone: 202-307-2942
Fax: 202-307-6394
Website: http://www.ojp.usdoj.gov/nij

National Parents Resource Institute for Drug Education (PRIDE)

PRIDE Youth Programs
4 W. Oak St.
Fremont, MI 49412
Toll-Free: 800-668-9277
Phone: 231-924-1662
Fax: 231-924-5663
E-mail: info@pridyouthprograms.org
Website: http://www.prideyouth
programs.org

Nemours Foundation

1600 Rockland Rd.
Wilmington, DE 19803
Phone: 302-651-4000
E-mail: info@kidshealth.org
Website: http://www.kidshealth.org

Office of Applied Studies (OAS) (SAMHSA)

Phone: 240-276-1212
E-mail: oaspubs@samhsa.hhs.gov
Website: http://www.oas.samhsa.gov

Office of National Drug Control Policy (ONDCP)

Drug Policy Information Clearinghouse
P.O. Box 6000
Rockville, MD 20849
Toll-Free: 800-666-3332
Fax: 301-519-5212
E-mail: ondcp@ncjrs.gov
Website: http://www.whitehouse
drugpolicy.gov

ONDCP Sponsored Websites

Above the Influence: http://www
.abovetheinfluence.com
MethResources.gov: http://www
.methresources.gov
National Youth Anti-Drug Media
Campaign: http://www.whitehouse
drugpolicy.gov/mediacampaign
Pushing Back: http://pushingback
.com

Partnership for a Drug-Free America

352 Park Ave. South, 9th Floor
New York, NY 10174
Phone: 212-922-1560
Fax: 212-922-1570
Website: http://www.drugfree
america.org

Phoenix House

164 W. 74th Street
New York, NY 10023
Toll-Free: 800-DRUG HELP
Phone: 212-595-5810
Fax: 212-4966035
Website: http://www.phoenixhouse
.org

Safe and Drug-Free Schools

400 Maryland Ave. SW
Washington, DC 20202
Toll-Free: 800-872-5327 (Information Resource Center at U.S.
Department of Education)
Toll-Free TTY: 800-437-0833
E-mail: safeschl@ed.gov
Website: http://www.ed.gov/offices/
OESE/SDFS

Students Against Destructive Decisions (SADD)

255 Main Street
Marlborough, MA 01752
Toll-Free: 877-SADD-INC
(7233-462)
Fax: 508-481-5759
E-mail: info@sadd.org
Website: http://www.sadd.org

Substance Abuse and Mental Health Services Administration (SAMHSA)

1 Choke Cherry Rd.
Rockville, MD 20857
Phone: 240-276-2130
Website: http://www.samhsa.gov

U.S. Bureau of Alcohol, Tobacco, Firearms, and Explosives

Office of Public and
Governmental Affairs
99 New York Avenue, NE
Room 5S 144
Washington, DC 20226 USA
Toll Free: 800-800-3855
Website: http://www.atf.gov

U.S. Food and Drug Administration (FDA)

10903 New Hampshire Ave.
Silver Spring, MD 20993
Toll-Free: 888-INFO-FDA
(463-6332)
Website: http://www.fda.gov

Chapter 64

Substance Abuse Hotlines And Helplines

Al-Anon/Alateen Information Line
800-344-2666
Monday–Friday, 8:00 a.m.–6:00 p.m. ET

Alcohol and Drug Help Line
WellPlace
800-821-4357

Alcohol Hotline
Adcare Hospital
800-ALCOHOL (800-252-6465)
7 days a week, 24 hours a day

American Council on Alcoholism
800-527-5344
10:00–6:00 p.m. MT

Center for Substance Abuse Treatment
800-662-HELP (800-662-4357) (English)
877-767-8432 (Spanish)
800-487-4889 (TDD)

Ecstasy Addiction
800-468-6933

Emergency Shelter for Battered Women (and Their Children)
888-291-6228

Girls and Boys Town National Hotline
800-448-3000

Marijuana Anonymous
800-766-6779
7 days a week, 24 hours a day

About This Chapter: Information in this chapter was compiled from many sources deemed reliable. Inclusion does not constitute endorsement, and there is no implication associated with omission. All contact information was verified in August 2010.

NAMI Information Helpline
Nation's Voice on Mental Illness
800-950-NAMI (6264)
Monday–Friday, 10:00 a.m.–6:00
p.m. ET

Narconon International Help Line
800-893-7060

National Child Abuse Hot Line
Childhelp USA
800-4-A-CHILD (800-422-4453)

National Clearinghouse for Alcohol and Drug Information
800-729-6686
Monday–Friday, 9:00 a.m.–7:00
p.m. ET

National Council on Alcoholism and Drug Dependence
800-622-2255
7 days a week, 24 hours a day

National Domestic Violence Hot Line
800-799-7233
800-787-3224 (TTY)

National Drug and Alcohol Treatment Referral Service
800-662-HELP (4357)
Monday–Friday, 9:00 a.m.–3:00 a.m.

National Organization for Victim Assistance
800-TRY-NOVA (800-879-6682)
Monday–Friday, 9:00 a.m.–5:00
p.m. ET

National Runaway Switchboard
800-RUNAWAY (800-786-2929)
TDD: 800-621-0394

National Sexual Assault Hotline
Rape, Abuse, and Incest National
Network (RAINN)
800-656-HOPE (800-656-4673)

National Suicide Hopeline
800-SUICIDE (800-784-2433)
7 days a week, 24 hours a day

National Suicide Prevention Lifeline
800-273-TALK (800-273-8255)

Stop It Now!
888-PREVENT (888-773-8368)
Limited phone hours; also online at
www.stopitnow.org

Victims of Crime Help Line
800-FYI-CALL (800-394-2255)
Monday–Friday, 8:30a.m.–8:30 p.m.
ET

Chapter 65

State-By-State List Of Alcohol And Drug Referral Phone Numbers

Alabama
Substance Abuse Services Div.
Toll-Free: 800-367-0955
Phone: 334-242-3454
Fax: 334-242-0725
Website: http://www.mh.alabama.gov

Alaska
Div. of Behavioral Health
Dept. of Health and Social Services
Phone: 907-465-3370
Fax: 907-465-2668
Website: http://www.hss.state.ak.us

American Samoa
American Samoa Government
Dept. of Human and Social Services
Phone: 684-633-2609
Fax: 684-633-7449

Arizona
Div. of Behavioral Health Services
Dept. of Health Services
Toll-Free: 800-867-5808
Phone: 602-542-1025
Fax: 602-364-4558
Website: http://www.azdhs.gov

Arkansas
Office of Alcohol and Drug Abuse
Prevention
Div. of Behavioral Health Services
Phone: 501-686-9866
Website: http://www.arkansas
.gov/dhs/dmhs/alco_drug_abuse_
prevention.htm

Excerpted from "Facility Locator," Substance Abuse and Mental Health Services Administration (SAMHSA). All contact information was verified as current in May 2010.

California

Dept. of Alcohol and Drug Programs
Toll-Free: 800-879-2772
Website: http://www.adp.ca.gov/
default.asp
E-mail: ResourceCenter@adp
.ca.gov

Colorado

Div. of Behavioral Health
Dept. of Human Services
Phone: 303-866-7400
Fax: 303-866-7481
Website: http://www.cdhs.state
.co.us/adad

Connecticut

Toll-Free: 800-446-7348
Phone: 860-418-7000
TTY: 860-418-6707
Website: http://www.ct.gov/dmhas

Delaware

Alcohol and Drug Services
Div. of Substance Abuse and MH
Phone: 302-255-9399
Fax: 302-255-4427
Website: http://www.dhss.delaware
.gov/dsamh/index.html

District of Columbia

Addiction, Prevention, and Recovery Administration
Phone: 202-727-8857
Fax: 202-777-0092
Website: http://www.dchealth
.dc.gov/doh

Florida

Substance Abuse Program Office
Dept. of Children and Families
Phone: 850-487-1111
Fax: 850-922-4996
Website: http://www.dcf.state.fl.us/
mentalhealth/sa

Georgia

Addictive Diseases Services
Toll-Free: 800-715-4225
Phone: 404-657-2331
Fax: 404-657-2256
Website: http://mhddad.dhr
.georgia.gov

Guam

Drug and Alcohol Treatment Services
Dept. of Mental Health and Substance Abuse
Phone: 671-647-5330
Fax: 671-649-6948

Hawaii

Alcohol and Drug Abuse Division
Dept. of Health
Phone: 808-692-7506
Fax: 808-692-7521
Website: http://hawaii.gov/health/
substance-abuse

Idaho

Div. of Behavioral Health
Dept. of Health and Welfare
Toll-Free: 800-926-2588
Phone: 208-334-5935
Fax: 208-332-7305
Website: http://healthandwelfare
.idaho.gov

Illinois

Div. of Alcoholism and Substance
Abuse
Dept. of Human Services
Toll-Free: 800-843-6154
Toll-Free TTY: 800-447-6404
Website: http://www.dhs.state.il.us/
page.aspx?item=29725

Indiana

Div. of Mental Health
and Addiction
Family and Social Services
Administration
Toll-Free: 800-457-8283
Phone: 317-232-7895
Fax: 317-233-3472
Website: http://www.in.gov/fssa/
dmha/index.htm

Iowa

Div. of Behavioral Health
Dept. of Public Health
Toll-Free: 866-227-9878
Phone: 515-281-7689
Website: http://www.idph.state
.ia.us/bh/substance_abuse.asp

Kansas

Addiction and Prevention Services
Dept. of Social and Rehab Services
Phone: 785-296-6807
Website: http://www.srskansas.org/
hcp/AAPSHome.htm

Kentucky

Div. of Mental Health and Sub-
stance Abuse
Dept. for MH/MR Services
Phone: 502-564-4456
Fax: 502-564-9010
Website: http://mhmr.ky.gov/mhsas

Louisiana

Office for Addictive Disorders
Toll-Free: 877-664-2248
Phone: 225-342-6717
Fax: 225-342-3875
Website: http://www.dhh.louisiana
.gov/offices/?ID=23

Maine

Maine Office of Substance Abuse
Toll-Free (ME only): 800-499-0027
Toll-Free TTY: 800-606-0215
Phone: 207-287-2595
Fax: 207-287-8910
Website: http://www.maine.gov/
dhhs/osa
E-mail: osa.ircosa@maine.gov

Maryland
Alcohol and Drug Abuse Administration
Dept. of Health and Mental Hygiene
Phone: 410-402-8600
Website: http://dhmh.maryland.gov/adaa
E-mail: adaainfo@dhmh.state.md.us

Massachusetts
Bureau of Substance Abuse Services
Dept. of Public Health
Toll-Free: 800-327-5050
Toll-Free TTY: 888-448-8321
Website: http://www.mass.gov/dph/bsas

Michigan
Bureau of Substance Abuse and Addiction Services
Phone: 517-373-4700
TTY: 571-373-3573
Fax: 517-335-2121
Website: http://www.michigan.gov/mdch-bsaas
E-mail: MDCH-BSAAS@michigan.gov

Minnesota
Alcohol and Drug Abuse Division
Dept. of Human Services
Toll-Free Disability Linkage Line: 866-333-2466
Phone: 651-431-2460
Fax: 651-431-7449
Website: http://www.minnesota help.info/public (online access to state resources)
Website: http://www.dhs.state.mn.us (click Disabilities, then Alcohol and Drug Abuse)
E-mail: dhs.adad@state.mn.us

Mississippi
Bureau of Alcohol and Drug Abuse
Dept. of Mental Health
Toll-Free: 877-210-8513
Phone: 601-359-1288
Fax: 601-359-6295
TDD: 601-359-6230
Website: http://www.dmh.state.ms.us/substance_abuse.htm

Missouri
Div. of Alcohol and Drug Abuse
Missouri Dept. of Mental Health
Toll-Free: 800-364-9687
Phone: 573-751-4122
TTY: 573-526-1201
Fax: 573-751-8224
Website: http://www.dmh.missouri.gov/ada/adaindex.htm
E-mail: dmhmail@dmh.mo.gov

Montana
Addictive and Mental Disorders
Division
Dept. of PH and HS
Phone: 406-444-3964
Fax: 406-444-4435
Website: http://www.dphhs.mt.gov/
amdd

Nebraska
DHHS Division of Behavioral
Health
Substance Abuse Hotline:
402-473-3818
Phone: 402-471-7818
Fax: 402-471-7859
Website: http://www.dhhs.ne.gov/
sua/suaindex.htm
E-mail: BHDivision@dhhs.ne.gov

Nevada
DHHS Mental Health and
Developmental Services
Phone: 775-684-5943
Fax: 775-684-5964
Website: http://mhds.state.nv.us

New Hampshire
DHHS Bureau of Drug and
Alcohol Services
Phone: 603-271-6110
Website: http://www.dhhs.state
.nh.us/dhhs/atod/a1-treatment

New Jersey
Div. of Addiction Services
NJ Addictions Hotline: 800-238-2333
Website: http://www.njdrughotline
.org
E-mail: contact@addictionshot
lineofnj.org

New Mexico
Behavioral Health Services Div.
Dept. of Health
Toll-Free Consumer Hotline:
866-660-7185
Toll-Free TTY Hotline: 800-855-2881
Website: http://www.bhc.state.nm.us
Website for Consumer Assistance:
http://www.optumhealthnew
mexico.com

New York
Office of Alcoholism and Substance
Abuse Services
Phone: 518-473-3460
Website: http://www.oasas.state
.ny.us/index.cfm
E-mail: communications@oasas
.state.ny.us

North Carolina
Community Policy Management
Div. of MH/DD/SA Services
Toll-Free: 800-662-7030
Phone: 919-733-4670
Fax: 919-733-4556
Website: http://www.dhhs.state
.nc.us/mhddsas
E-mail: contactdmh@ncmail.net

North Dakota

Div. of MH and SA Services
Dept. of Human Services
Toll-Free (ND only): 800-472-2622
Phone: 701-328-2310
Fax: 701-328-2359
Website: http://www.nd.gov/dhs/
services/mentalhealth
E-mail: dhseo@nd.gov

Ohio

Dept. of Alcohol and
Drug Addiction Services
Toll-Free: 800-788-7254
Phone: 614-466-3445
Fax: 614-752-8645
Website: http://www.ada.ohio.gov/
public
E-mail: info@ada.ohio.gov

Oklahoma

ODMHSAS
Toll-Free: 800-522-9054
Phone: 405-522-3908
TDD: 405-522-3851
Fax: 405-522-3650
Website: http://www.odmhsas.org

Oregon

Addictions and Mental Health Div.
Dept. of Human Services
Toll-Free: 800-544-7078
Toll-Free TTY: 800-375-2863
Phone: 503-945-5763
Fax: 503-378-8467
Website: http://www.oregon.gov/
DHS/addiction/index.shtml
E-mail: omhas.web@state.or.us

Pennsylvania

Bureau of Drug and Alcohol Programs
Pennsylvania Dept. of Health
Toll-Free: 877-724-3258
Phone: 717-783-8200
Fax: 717-787-6285
Website: http://www.portal.state
.pa.us/portal/server.pt/community/
drug_alcohol/14221

Puerto Rico

Mental Health and Anti-Addiction
Services Administration
Toll-Free 800-981-0023
Phone: 787-763-7575
Fax: 787-765-5888
Website: http://www.gobierno.pr/
assmca/inicio

Rhode Island

Div. of Behavioral Health
Phone: 401-462-4680
Fax: 401-462-6078
Website: http://www.mhrh.ri.gov/SA

South Carolina
SC Dept. of Alcohol and Other
Drug Abuse Services
Phone: 803-896-5555
Fax: 803-896-5557
Website: http://www.daodas.state
.sc.us

South Dakota
DHS Div. of Alcohol and Drug
Abuse
Toll-Free: 800-265-9684
Phone: 605-773-3123
Fax: 605-773-7076
Website: http://dhs.sd.gov
E-mail: infodada@dhs.state.sd.us

Tennessee
Dept. of Mental Health and DD
TN Dept. of Health
Toll-Free Crisis: 800-809-9957
Phone: 615-741-3111
Website: http://health.state.tn.us/
index.htm
E-mail: tn.health@tn.gov

Texas
DSHS Substance Abuse Services
Toll-Free: 866-378-8440
Toll-Free Hotline: 877-966-3784
Phone: 512-206-5000
Fax: 512-206-5714
Website: http://www.dshs.state
.tx.us/sa/default.shtm
E-mail: contact@dshs.state.tx.us

Utah
Div. of Substance Abuse and
Mental Health
Utah Dept. of Human Services
Phone: 801-538-3939
Fax: 801-538-9892
Website: http://www.dsamh.utah.gov
E-mail: dsamhwebmaster@utah.gov

Vermont
Alcohol and Drug Abuse Programs
Dept. of Health
Toll-Free (VT only): 800-464-4343
Phone: 802-863-7200
Fax: 802-865-7754
Website: http://healthvermont.gov/
adap/adap.aspx
E-mail: vtadap@vdh.state.vt.us

Virginia
Office of Substance Abuse Services
Dept. of MH, MR, and SAS
Phone: 804-786-3921
TTY: 804-786-1587
Fax: 804-371-6638
Website: http://www.dbhds.virginia
.gov/OSAS-default.htm

Virgin Islands
Div. of MH, Alcoholism, and Drug
Dependency Services
Dept. of Health
Phone: 340-774-4888
Fax: 340-774-4701

Washington
Div. of Alcohol and Substance Abuse
Dept. of Social and Health Services
Toll-Free (WA only):
800-737-0617
Phone: 877-301-4557
Website: http://www.dshs.wa.gov/DASA
E-mail: DASAInformation@dshs.wa.gov

West Virginia
Bureau for Behavioral Health and Health Facilities
Phone: 304-558-0627
Fax: 304-558-1008
Website: http://www.wvdhhr.org/bhhf/ada.asp

E-mail: obhs@wvdhhr.org

Wisconsin
Bureau of Prevention, Treatment, and Recovery
Phone: 608-266-1865
Toll-Free TTY: 888-701-1251
Fax: 608-266-1533
Website: http://dhs.wisconsin.gov/substabuse/INDEX.HTM

Wyoming
Mental Health and Substance Abuse Services Division
Toll-Free: 800-535-4006
Phone: 307-777-6494
Fax: 307-777-5849
Website: http://wdh.state.wy.us/mhsa/index.html

Chapter 66

Additional Reading About Substance Abuse

Books

Abusing Prescription Drugs
Philip Wolny; Rosen Central/Rosen Pub.; New York; 2008
ISBN: 9781404219557

Addictions and Risky Behaviors: Cutting, Bingeing, Snorting, and Other Dangers
Renée C. Rebman; Enslow Publishers; Berkeley Heights, NJ; 2006
ISBN: 0766021653

Addictive Personality
Richard Juzwiak; Rosen Pub. Group; New York; 2009
ISBN: 9781404218024

Alcoholism
Jacqueline Langwith; Gale/Cengage Learning; Detroit; 2010
ISBN: 9780737745504

Caffeine and Nicotine: A Dependent Society
Heather Hasan; Rosen Pub.; New York; 2009; ISBN: 9781435850156

Inhalants And Solvents: Sniffing Disaster
Noa Flynn; Mason Crest Publishers; Philadelphia; 2008
ISBN: 9781422201572

I've Got This Friend Who—: Advice for Teens and Their Friends on Alcohol, Drugs, Eating Disorders, Risky Behaviors, and More
Anna Radev, ed., KidsPeace Corporation; Hazelden, Center City, MN; 2007
ISBN: 9781592854585

Marijuana
Joseph C. Tardiff; Greenhaven Press; Detroit; 2008; ISBN: 9780737727753

On the Rocks: Teens and Alcohol
David Aretha; Franklin Watts; New York; 2007; ISBN: 0531167925

The Facts About Drugs And Society
Joan Axelrod-Contrada; Marshall Cavendish Benchmark; New York; 2007
ISBN: 9780761426745

The Facts About Over-the-Counter Drugs
Lorrie Klosterman; Marshall Cavendish Benchmark; New York; 2007
ISBN: 9780761422464

Articles

"A Review of Alcoholics Anonymous/Narcotics Anonymous Programs for Teens," by Steve Sussman, *Evaluation & the Health Professions*, 2010, 33, no. 1, pp. 26–55.

"Alcohol and Tobacco Use During Adolescence: The Importance of the Family Mealtime Environment," *Journal of Health Psychology*, May 2010, 15(4), pp. 526–32.

"Alcohol Use by Youth and Adolescents: a Pediatric Concern," *Pediatrics*, May 2010, 125(5), pp. 1078–87.

"Comment—Nora Volkow Discusses Why Effective Policy on Drug Abuse Should Be Guided by Science, Not Stigma," *Science News*, 2008, 174, no. 10, p. 40.

"Does the Adolescent Brain Make Risk Taking Inevitable?" by Michael Males, *Journal of Adolescent Research*, 2009, 24, no. 1, pp. 3–20.

"Early Course of Nicotine Dependence in Adolescent Smokers," by CA Doubeni, G Reed, and JR Difranza, *Pediatrics*, June 2010, 125(6), pp. 1127–33.

"Impulsivity and Its Relationship to Risky Sexual Behaviors and Drug Abuse," by Ken Winters, Andria Botzet, Tamara Fahnhorst, Lindsey Baumel, and Susanne Lee, *Journal of Child & Adolescent Substance Abuse*, 2009, 18, no. 1, pp. 43–56.

"Mass Media for Smoking Cessation in Adolescents," by Laura Solomon, Janice Bunn, Brian Flynn, Phyllis Pirie, John Worden, and Takamaru Ashikaga, *Health Education & Behavior*, 2009, 36, no. 4, pp. 642–659.

"Prescription Drug Abuse—We report on the scary trend," *Seventeen*, June 2008, p. 68.

"Prescription Drug Deaths Increase Dramatically," by Katherine Harmon, *Scientific American*, April 6, 2010.

"Special Report—Drug Abuse as a Disease," *U.S. News and World Report*, 2007, 142, no. 11, p. 59.

"Sports Participation and Problem Alcohol Use: a Multi-Wave National Sample of Adolescents," by D Mays, L Depadilla, NJ Thompson, HI Kushner, and M Windle, *American Journal of Preventative Medicine*, May 2010, 38(5), pp. 491–8.

"Teens and Prescription Drugs: a Potentially Dangerous Combination," by S Simmons, *Nursing*, May 2010, 40(5), pp. 42–6.

"Update on Marijuana," by TM McGuinness, *Journal of Psychosocial Nursing and Mental Health Services*, Oct. 2009, 47(10), pp.19–22.

Web Page Documents

Alcoholism
The Mayo Clinic
http://www.mayoclinic.com/print/alcoholism/DS00340/
METHOD=print&DSECTION=all

Drug Prevention 4 Teens
Learning for Life
http://www.learning-forlife.org/lfl/resources/99-349.pdf

Drugs + HIV: Learn the Link
National Institute on Drug Abuse
http://hiv.drugabuse.gov

Glaucoma and Marijuana Use
National Eye Institute
http://www.nei.nih.gov/news/statements/marij.asp

HIV Testing Resources
The Nemours Foundation
http://kidshealth.org/teen/drug_alcohol/getting_help/hiv_tests.html

Marijuana: Facts for Teens
National Institute on Drug Abuse
http://www.nida.nih.gov/MarijBroch/Marijteens.html

National Prescription Drug Threat Assessment 2009
National Drug Intelligence Center
http://www.justice.gov/ndic/pubs33/33775/index.htm

PEERx: Rx Abuse is Drug Abuse
National Institute on Drug Abuse
http://teens.drugabuse.gov/peerx/

Prescription Drug Abuse
The Nemours Foundation
http://kidshealth.org/teen/drug_alcohol/drugs/prescription_drug_abuse.html

Smoking and Asthma
The Nemours Foundation
http://kidshealth.org/teen/drug_alcohol/tobacco/smoking_asthma.html

Two Teen Health Dangers: Obesity and Drug Addiction
Scholastic and the National Institute on Drug Abuse
http://teacher.scholastic.com/scholasticnews/indepth/headsup/support/
NIDA4-Article.pdf

Women, Girls, and Drugs: Facts and Figures
Office of National Drug Control Policy
http://www.whitehousedrugpolicy.gov/drugfact/women/women_ff.html

Index

Index

Page numbers that appear in *Italics* refer to tables or illustrations. Page numbers that have a small 'n' after the page number refer to information shown as Notes at the beginning of each chapter. Page numbers that appear in **Bold** refer to information contained in boxes on that page (except Notes information at the beginning of each chapter).